Political Violence
and Terror

Political Violence and Terror

Motifs and Motivations

EDITED BY
PETER H. MERKL

Berkeley

Los Angeles

London

UNIVERSITY OF CALIFORNIA PRESS

University of California Press
Berkeley and Los Angeles, California
University of California Press, Ltd.
London, England
Copyright © 1986 by
The Regents of the University of California

Library of Congress Cataloging in Publication Data

Main entry under title:

Political violence and terror.

Includes index.
1. Terrorism—Addresses, essays, lectures.
2. Radicalism—Addresses, essays, lectures.
I. Merkl, Peter H.
HV6431.P63   1986   303.6'25   85-24505
ISBN 0-520-05605-1 (alk. paper)
OCLC#: 12722803
Printed in the United States of America

1 2 3 4 5 6 7 8 9

CONTENTS

Prologue   1

PART I
Aspects of Political Violence   17

PETER H. MERKL
1. Approaches to the Study of
   Political Violence   19

RICHARD H. DRAKE
2. Julius Evola and the Ideological
   Origins of the Radical Right in
   Contemporary Italy   61

ADRIAN GUELKE
3. Loyalist and Republican Perceptions
   of the Northern Ireland Conflict:
   The UDA and Provisional IRA   91

ROBERT P. CLARK
4. Patterns of ETA Violence, 1968–1980   123

PART II
Individual Motifs and Motivations   143

LEONARD WEINBERG
5. The Violent Life: Left- and Right-Wing
   Terrorism in Italy   145

GIANFRANCO PASQUINO AND
DONATELLA DELLA PORTA
6. Interpretations of Italian Left-Wing
   Terrorism   169

KLAUS WASMUND
7. The Political Socialization of
   West German Terrorists   191

PETER H. MERKL
8. Rollerball or Neo-Nazi Violence?   229

PETER WALDMANN
9. Guerrilla Movements in Argentina,
   Guatemala, Nicaragua, and Uruguay   257

ROBERT P. CLARK
10. Patterns in the Lives of ETA Members   283

ABRAHAM ASHKENASI
11. Social-Ethnic Conflict and Paramilitary
    Organization in the Near East   311

PETER H. MERKL
12. Conclusion: Collective Purposes
    and Individual Motives   335

Contributors   375
Index   377

PROLOGUE

"Write me a prologue," Bottom, the weaver, says in A Midsummer Night's Dream, "and let the prologue seem to say, we will do no harm with our swords." He worries that the drawing of theatrical swords for his tragicomedy might alarm the ladies of King Theseus's court and would like to be doubly sure that his playful intent not be misunderstood. The baring of weapons in the presence of the king, he could have added, might in itself be even more alarming if they were not immediately recognized as mere theater props. Any hint of violence directed at political authority, it seems, causes understandable apprehension and possible misunderstandings. A collection of essays on certain aspects of political violence such as this also requires a prologue to tell the reader of its intent lest there be misapprehensions.

THE ORIGINS AND PLAN FOR THIS BOOK

The ideas for this book grew out of discussions among scholars interested in the study of political violence at meetings of the International Society of Political Psychology at Mannheim (1981) and Oxford (1983), the Council of European Studies in Washington, D.C., and the International Political Science Association (1982) in Rio de Janeiro. Although there already exists a large literature on political violence and terror, it was felt that there were significant gaps both in the general methodology of research on political violence, and in the understanding of the individual motivations of members of violent political organizations in particular.

Political violence is a subject that everybody in a way "understands" and which is written about in newspapers nearly every week, even if this is done mostly in an impressionistic and journalistic way. Social scientists and historians also have examined incidents of political violence or whole revolutions and learned that there is a wide range of possible social-scientific approaches to these phenomena which have been employed or could be employed. Writers and their readers, in fact, have often used some of these methods interchangeably, in many instances almost unaware that they were doing so. To them, particular cases of political violence seem to have been so shrouded in moral judgments pro or con, and in strong, emotional reactions to the violence itself, that one kind of account seemed to be as good as any other. Social scientists, however, must be self-conscious about the methods they employ in studying a subject and quite aware that the choice of method may determine the character of what they find. If we look for high ideals and high-minded idealists in a revolution, we shall find some, and if we look for brutal coercion and cold executioners, they will be found as well.

Perhaps, every conceivable complementary approach should be used for a more complete understanding of a particular case of political violence. But given the limits of scholarly patience, of funds, and frequently of exhaustive data—not to mention the limited patience of the readers—case studies will probably always remain limited to only a few systematic approaches and, hence, will be somewhat incomplete. In any case, questions of social science methodology are an object of interest in themselves and it is the purpose of this book to bring out the various methods used to study political violence as clearly as possible. To this end, the book has been divided into two parts, one dealing with various methods already widely in use, and the other concentrating on one of the newer methods; namely, the psychological or social-psychological approach that focuses on individual motivations and the factors that may account for them. This division is not meant to make light of the methods illustrated in the first part. On the contrary, the "ideological origins," or roots, of Italian right-wing terror (chapter 2), the escalation of violence as a result of conflicting perceptions of the ethnic-cultural confrontation in Northern Ireland (chapter 3), and the "events data" approach to Basque terror in Spain (chapter 4) are all important and legitimate approaches to the phenomenon of political violence which cannot simply be replaced by the social-psychological approach. The latter in turn opens up new perspectives that complement the existing ones and contributes significant insights to an extraordinarily complex and diverse subject.

In the first chapter, I undertake to define political violence in an operational sense and to look at a random sampling of reported incidents in a systematic way. I propose to distinguish these and the other studies of political violence presented in Part One by the units of analysis used in them: ideologies, individual acts of violence, collective perceptions, process variables, individual motivations of violent persons, or whole revolutions. There is also a discussion of how political ideologies, right, left, and ethnic, have related to violent action, with particular emphasis on how the seemingly less political ultraright has spawned violent neofascist movements during the twentieth century. Since there is already a large literature on the "ideological origins" of the left, and almost nothing on neofascist ideology, I decided not to match the chapter on Julius Evola (chapter 2) with one on his left-wing equivalents. Like the latter, Evola's traditionalist "revolt against the modern world" with its mixture of spiritual mysticism, pseudoanthropology, and calls for a biologically based caste society gives little clue to why he has such appeal for the radical right except that he advocates the use of force. So, for that matter, does the French apostle of neofascism, Alain de Benoist, whose "subjective heroism" and Nietzschean will-to-power also call for the establishment of a hierarchic society after the violent destruction of the present order. Richard Drake's essay on Evola, in any case, puts this enigmatic right-wing guru—whose life (1898–1974) spans the history of Italian fascism as well as that of postwar neofascism—in the proper perspective with some comparisons to the Italian radical left.[1]

Adrian Guelke's essay on the Provisional IRA and the Ulster Defense Association of Northern Ireland since 1968 (chapter 3) was selected because of his imaginative use of mutual perceptions to rationalize involvement in violence. Political violence, as he reminds us, generates a constant and pressing need to justify itself by pointing to a concrete menace, or at least to a continuing siege by an even more violent enemy. For the purposes of this book, this aspect is far more important than a blow-by-blow account of the Irish troubles for which the reader can go elsewhere. The mutual perceptions can also actually steer the violent encounters to greater or lower levels of political violence. We shall come back to the need for justification of political violence below.

Robert P. Clark, in his discussion of the patterns of Basque political violence (chapter 4), offers a good example of the use of violent event data to describe the patterns between 1968 and 1980. His skillful use of quantitative approaches admirably demonstrates the usefulness of event analysis to determine and compare levels of violence and to relate them to other variables. In the Basque case, examining such empirical findings together with the chronology of events may also raise an intriguing question: If it is true that the ETA has such impressive control over its instrumental use of violence, why then has the violence escalated dramatically with the granting of Basque autonomy (1978/1979) and the establishment of a Basque regional government? To what end have the ETA policymakers been stepping up the level of violence? Was this really the original plan of the ETA leaders or are the members of terrorist organizations, once assembled, like the sorcerer's apprentice who, unwilling to be dismissed when the job is done, continues the violence?

The second part of the book is concentrated broadly on the motivations, political or prepolitical, of politically violent individuals. These motives of members of violent groups, of course, can be approached in several ways: there are sociological interpretations (for example, in terms of the social background of terrorists); conspiracy theories (including those linking violence to foreign machinations); explanations inherent in the ideologies of the movements; approaches based on processes of political socialization, or on the life cycle; social-psychological and individual-psychological, not necessarily "psycho-pathological," theories, and many others. Their plausibility generally rests on our commonsense understanding of the individual case. The essays on individual motivation begin with Leonard Weinberg's exploration of the mentalities behind the violent life of left- and right-wing terrorists in Italy (chapter 5). Italy is a particularly fruitful area for studying terrorism today, because the dust of a decade and a half of (mostly left-wing) terrorist battles has settled somewhat and the owl of Minerva, the goddess of wisdom, can take flight to survey the battlefield. Weinberg stresses particularly the vivid spirit of the memory of the antifascist Resistance on the one hand and of the painful defeat of the fascists on the other as inspirations of the "violent life," picking up rifles that fell from the antagonists' hands thirty, forty years ago. He also emphasizes the generational motive of the young terrorists against both the background of the waning faith of Catholic and Marxist subcultures and of the political parties spawned by them. Weinberg also stresses the historical and political circumstances of the 1970s when the Italian Communist party, at least in the eyes of the young dissidents, was on the verge of shameful compromises of principle in order to be accepted by the political establishment.

In the second essay on motivation, Gianfranco Pasquino and Donatella della Porta (chapter 6) systematically evaluate various rival interpretations of Italian left-wing terrorism, some "nonsociological"—terror as the product of international conspiracy or of psychopathic personalities—and three theories the authors regard as "major": One is the *social marginalization* thesis favored by prominent Italian sociologists, that is, terrorism caused by the society's inability to integrate its uprooted peasants into the spreading urban-industrial society. The second attributes it to the failure of the Communist party to pursue its mandate of fundamental change against the "stalemate" political system. The third explanation pictures the "red" terrorist phalanx as having started in reaction to a perceived fascist threat and then to have turned into an armed assault on the democratic order in general, making the Red Brigades unwitting comrades in arms with the neo-fascist militants. The authors' preferred method is a complex analysis based on the nature and decomposition of social movements and the relations between individuals and the fringe movements on the left. I have picked up this thesis as the "fire-sale" theory of burned-out revolutionary movements in chapter 8 and the concluding chapter.

In the third essay on motivation (chapter 7) political psychologist Klaus Wasmund focuses on the small-group dynamics and the process of political socialization of West German terrorists. The author describes the evolution of West German terrorism from the background of the disintegrating student movement, sectarian left-wing groups, and the counterculture of West Berlin, and then proceeds to analyze the social background and presumable motivations of the Red Army Faction (RAF) membership of record: high educational level and social origin, disturbed relations with parents, and frequently failed careers. Professor Wasmund then sketches, with the help of autobiographical accounts, the likely path of West German terrorists from counterculture communes to ever-deeper involvement with the RAF, with appropriate emphasis on key experiences, identification with personal leaders, and the surrender to the intense small-group dynamics of the RAF cells.

Wasmund's essay is followed by my second essay (chapter 8) in which I attempt to fill in some of the missing information on the extreme right of the West German spectrum, between the neofascist, but rather tame, National Democratic party (NPD), and the right-wing terrorists about whom very little is known beyond their foul deeds. In particular, I describe the seemingly unpolitical, but extremely violent, subculture of the soccer fan rowdies, many of whom belong to the NPD—in Britain to the National Front—and exhibit swastikas and aggressive attitudes toward foreigners, especially the so-called guest workers. In the account, I go on to evaluate other forms of right-wing violence in the Federal Republic and among the storm troopers of the Weimar Republic, and end with comparative reflections on certain aspects of German and Italian political violence.

The ninth, tenth, and eleventh chapters deal predominantly with Third World or irredentist movements of political violence that, with the exception of Uruguay's Tupámaros, developed under repressive governments rather than in open, democratic systems such as Italy's and West Germany's. Chapter 9 is a comparative essay on guerrilla movements in Argentina, Guatemala, Nicaragua, and Uruguay by Peter Waldmann who supplies a thumbnail sketch of the history and circumstances for each of the movements. Waldmann first disposes of some dubious interpretations, such as the Cuban conspiracy theory, or the stress on ideological, strategic, or organizational prerequisites for success in overthrowing a government. Then he compares the social composition of the various movements, their origins and motivations, and the popular support they have received as well as the reasons for their success or failure.

The tenth essay, by Robert P. Clark, comes back to the ETA but this time for the purpose of comparing patterns in the backgrounds and lives of its members, based in part on prison and court records, just as was some of the information on Italian and West German terrorists. Youth, masculinity, social class background as far as it could be gathered, ethnic background—half of the *etarras*, it turns out, have only one or no Basque parents and a similar share comes from towns where less than 20 percent speak Euskera—and their paths of recruitment into ETA are all dealt with. Being an etarra is obviously very different from being a member of an urban guerrilla movement like the Red Brigades, RAF, or Tupámaros, but is also different from being a member of the rural guerrilla armies of Guatemala or Nicaragua in years past.

In the last essay, by Abraham Ashkenasi, the motivation of ethnic movements is again examined, but this time by approaching it from theories of ethnic conflict and of nationalism as a social movement aiming at the creation of a nation-state for a geographically concentrated (more than the Basques) minority.[2] Professor Ashkenasi applies this perspective to various national movements of the Middle East without, however, going once more over the familiar ground of early Zionist and later Palestinian terror activity for which the curious reader will need to turn elsewhere. The author's interest, instead, lies in relating the various movements to the social structure of their societies—traditional family- and clan-orientated Kurdish and Palestinian society as compared with the petit-bourgeois Irgun and the farmer-worker-intellectual Hagana—and in the rise and fall of paramilitary organizations rather than in particular violent deeds or clashes. The failure of Kurdish and, by implication, Palestinian nationalist movements to reach their goals of a nation-state of their own has structural reasons, the author believes, leaving their sanguinary violence and terrorist attacks to look like Pyrrhic victories at best. This too, of course, is a comment on our propensity to take the measure of violent movements by a confused standard, mixing their avowed goals with the degree of violence they wreak on others.

I begin my conclusion by stating that this book was never meant to provide exhaustive geographic coverage or a systematic catalog of all the violent movements proliferating in the world today. Instead, its emphasis has been on approaches to the study of violence—in particular as surveyed in Part One and discussed in the first chapter—and, specifically, the social-psychological approach exemplified in the contributions to Part Two. In the concluding essay I discuss and summarize only these papers on the social-psychological motivation of violent political movements and attempt to separate analytically the motives of the individual member from the announced collective purposes of violent movements. My interpretation of violent motives naturally focuses on the groups about which we have the most information, especially on the violent left and right of Italy and West Germany: How do the collective purposes of these movements and the individual motivations of members relate to one another? How do violent individuals reconcile what may be an unbridgeable gap between their individual lives and their collective ideologies? How do these better-known cases fit in with the systematic comparison of the process variables in our sampling of contemporary cases of political violence presented in chapter 1?

Inevitably, the discussion of left-wing terrorists in Italy and West Germany also brings us back to the question of exactly how political violence seems to be related to ideology, and in this case to the antiauthoritarian, anarchistic subcultures of Berlin and Frankfurt, or their Italian equivalents. The differences between the rather nonviolent advocates of anarchism and "critical theory" and the extremely violent terrorists are very revealing inasmuch as they show the crucial importance of personality and situation as compared with substantial agreement on ideology among both sets of groups. Why do some anarchists throw bombs while others are more likely to write or sign brave manifestos or, even more typically, to withdraw from political participation into oases of escapism? The relationship between the two is somewhat analogous to that between the alienated ultraright of the interwar years and the violent assassins and fascists discussed in chapter 1. Aside from the age and social position of an individual, a telling clue to violent proclivities is the "idea-emotions" described in the concluding chapter, such as the "myth of the rifle," the allegedly "fascist character" of democratic Italy or Germany, or what the German sociologist Helmut Schelsky once called the "borrowed misery" of the Third World or the proletariat as a motivation for violent deeds.

INDIVIDUAL MOTIVATION AND COLLECTIVE PURPOSES

One key formula of the second part of this book is the attempt to separate the individual motives of the membership from the collective purposes of violent movements. The collective purpose, say of ETA or the Red Brigades, is usually spelled out in manifestos, authoritative statements by leaders or members, and in the ideological literature with which they identify. To be sure, there will be disagreements among leaders or factions; some statements or manifestos may be deliberately misleading; and the direction or goals of a movement, including its designated enemies, may change over time. It ought to make a difference, for example, whether the ETA is fighting against Franco's nationalist dictatorship, which suppressed all striving for Basque autonomy, or against a democratic government that has granted Basque home rule and, by implication then, against the moderate Basque nationalists who have accepted regional devolution. But, by and large, the collective purpose of a violent movement is likely to be a logically rather cohesive and consistent system of ideas that direct the movement's political action and against which we can measure individual conduct. Its rationale can easily be stretched to cover such ancillary activities as bank robberies and kidnappings to bankroll the movement, or spectacular actions to spring imprisoned members from confinement, although there may be limits to justification in the individual case.[3]

Ideology plays a particularly prominent role among the expressions of the collective purposes of violent movements and for that reason it has been accorded a prominent place throughout this book. We have to remember, however, that most ideologies relevant to violent movements touch only in small part and often rather vaguely on specific political actions. Though Marxism is obviously relevant to many violent left-wing groups, Marx never suggested anything like kidnapping bank executives, assassinating local officials or party leaders, or "knee-capping" judges or police chiefs. Neither did Lenin nor even the patron saint of Italian left-wing terror, Antonio Gramsci. The Red Brigades had to come up with their own choice of relevant enemies and, even more important, think up cruel and inhumane things to do to them. In much of the currently fashionable literature on terrorism and guerrilla warfare there is no mention at all of this considerable gap between ideology and the concrete actions that cannot be attributed to the authors of the ideologies but had to be filled in by these militants as suited their preferences or, as Wasmund argues below, as dictated by group dynamics. Still, their violent ways of interpreting their professed ideology may also be part of the umbrella of well-understood collective purposes rather than a matter of individual preference.

The ethnic or right-wing equivalents of left-wing ideology may be even less specific as a guide to action. In ethnic terrorist or guerrilla movements, at least, the "enemy" seems well identified, namely, a member of the rival or dominant nationality, but exactly who and what is to be done to him is, again, strictly up to the organization. Is it to be just any Turk who can be brought into the gunsight of an Armenian terrorist rifle? Why does ETA mark a particular, lowly Guardia Civil, a cabdriver, or the retired female mayor of Bilbao for assassination, rather than the highest commanders or officeholders of an allegedly still oppressive state? And, if the object is to show the powerlessness of the established authorities, why kill rather than, say, ridicule or humiliate them, or why not blow up bridges and power stations instead? Once we insist on inquiring about the objective of violent collective action, moreover, we are bound to ask also whether the collective purpose really has any chance of succeeding. Wouldn't it make more logical sense as a collective purpose if it were likely to succeed?

All these perspectives and questions apply to neofascist violent groups with redoubled force. The ideologies are generally even vaguer, and not even Adolf Hitler ever advocated publicly the street violence or anything like the mass killings that were in fact carried out in his name. Julius Evola, the *maestro segreto* of the Italian far right, is quoted in Richard Drake's essay, below, as calling on young neofascists to "extirpate the communist cancer" with "iron and fire" which to them, at least, suggested bombs and physical attacks. But who exactly is to be blown up or attacked by these "spiritual warriors with souls of steel"?—all the "communists" of Italy and the world, plus all the representatives of the Christian Democratic "hegemony," and of bourgeois capitalism in Europe and America? The actual targets chosen by Italian right-wing terrorists, such as the general public present at the Piazza Fontana (Milan) explosion, the people in Brescia, those on the train between Florence and Bologna, or at the Bologna railroad station (see Weinberg, below) suggest that they too are rather confused about just how to go about establishing the spiritual new order. Evola's ideology, though it may have generally inspired them, simply did not tell them.

The interface between a collective purpose of some logical cohesion and individual conduct is a critical juncture in any voluntary organization, whether we are dealing with a business firm, a trade union, a political party, or a terrorist group. The degree of conformity of the individual to the collective purpose—especially when the latter is vague—will depend on many factors such as the backgrounds and motivations of the recruits, the process by which they are socialized and trained, the length of their service, or the extent to which their daily lives are spent in and dependent on the organization. The organization leaders, of course, wish for total conformity to the collective purpose but even an official army's military commanders know that, depending on recruitment, training, morale, and the situation, this is more likely to be a dream than a reality. A terrorist organization, which lacks the military's coercive frame and its control over the daily lives of its recruits, has to rely almost exclusively on its members' self-propelled motivation, given the intermittent, clandestine opportunities for training and indoctrination. This is a good reason for focusing research on any clue to these individual motivations: social background, age, sex, previous political involvement, reasons for joining and fighting, education and, of course, any manifestations of their opinions on their violent pursuit and other relevant subjects.

RATIONALITY VERSUS IRRATIONALITY

It is important at this point to clean out a frequent error in approaching the subject of political violence and terror, namely, the unscientific attribution of "rationality" or "irrationality" to the individual motivations of members of politically violent groups. With a subject like violence and terror, which excites the emotion and has attracted a great deal of journalistic and sensationalistic writing, it is natural that the dichotomy rational-irrational would come to serve as a shorthand emotional simplification for highly subjective judgments: people shocked by the violence of the acts will denounce individual terrorists as "irrational"—really meaning crazy or insane—while those secretly admiring the terrorist posture, or sympathizing with the cause, will usually point to the collective purpose of the movement in question and pronounce it "rational." Many people do sympathize, if not openly or admittedly, with certain guerrilla or terrorist movements without necessarily knowing much about them. Few Palestinians are objective about the PLO, nor do many Irish Catholics view the Provisional IRA with detachment. There is also a secret admiration for the *macho* pose of the terrorist, which used to be reserved for Western heroes or notorious bank robbers and outlaws in our culture.

The dichotomy rational-irrational, of course, is of little help in analyzing the complex subject of individual motivation in a terrorist, or in anyone else for that matter, however much the mind may strain for rational consistency. Rational, in the sense of purposive, is a term difficult to apply to an individual life, as any biographer or life histories researcher has found out. Individuals are free to pursue several purposes at once or in succession, change their minds, or float for years in purposeless confusion or bliss. There are, moreover, various kinds of rationality that particularly need to be considered with regard to an individual life: There is the biological rationality of being born and living a natural life span which is negated by risking or sacrificing one's own life for any cause but to save the lives of offspring. There is also a social rationality that binds a normal individual into a network of social relationships with his or her parents, siblings, friends, fellow workers and, with maturity, with mates and perhaps even children. In a classic article more than twenty years ago, Egon Bittner pointed up as a key question of analyzing the sociology of extremist movements how individual members "face down the common sense rhetoric" against their "bizarre" behavior.[4] How indeed does a terrorist face his or her mother, old friends, or neighbors when they become aware of curious goings-on or of the terrorist's profound hatreds? Very likely terrorists contend with this by a certain withdrawal from their closest social relationships, which may reduce the likelihood of embarrassment or confrontation, not to mention discovery (which is not the point of focus here). Changes in the "social rationality," or social relatedness, of the individual are very interesting to those of us who emphasize individual motivation—and so are loners and loneliness among members of violent groups—and will draw editoral comment throughout this volume.[5] By the same token, the intense interpersonal relations within West German terrorist groups, described by Wasmund below, are revealing and fascinating. The other contributors did not address themselves to the internal group dynamics of their terrorist groups, and yet it is likely that most of them would find similar interpersonal relationships there if they seriously tried.

There is also a cultural rationality about individual lives that is relevant to our subject because it is here that the collective purpose, or ideology, of the violent movement demands its due from the individual member. There are further problems that militate against the single-minded rationality of a collective purpose: Not only will its rationality contradict the biological and social rationality of an individual but most terrorists, like most ordinary people, are torn between two or more mutually contradictory sets of cultural rationality. Many *brigatisti*, like their leader Renato Curcio, for example, come from a rather devout Catholic background, which must have taught them such things as not to kill, and that the injustices of this world are less important than salvation in the next. Some Baader-Meinhof terrorists came from ministers' families. All terrorists as small children are likely to have been socialized in attitudes rather different from those acquired during their "resocialization" as murderous terrorists. The interest of the analyst, of course, is not in chronicling their moral downfall, but in examining as far as possible just how they have combined these differing cultural rationalities and how, in many cases, they actually manage to embrace glaring contradictions, such as using blackmail and coercion for the advancement of democracy or liberty.

With all these rationalities in conflict, are we not saying in effect that violent individuals, of course, like all other people, are *irrational?* In the sense that their lives are difficult to reduce to any one rational purpose, we must answer yes. It is, of course, possible that some members of certain groups are so monomaniacal that they subordinate all their sets of rationality to one, sacrificing their biological, social, and any other cultural purposes to that of the movement, but this will have to be demonstrated and would in itself be psychologically so abnormal as to call for comment. Most likely, I would venture to guess, politically violent persons vary over a scale from monomania— usually rather limited to a brief moment in the time spans of their adult lives—to degrees of rather marginal commitment to the cause as one of several preoccupations. By saying that, for the most part (that is, most politically violent persons during most of their lives), violent people are irrational, or not uni-rational, I am of course *not* calling them insane or crazy either, whatever those words may denote to the lay reader. Was Dominic "Mad Dog" McGlinchey, the recently captured leader of a Marxist offshoot of the IRA who boasted of having killed at least thirty people over a decade of life as an outlaw, really "mad"? Certainly not in a clinical sense or he could not have been as effective as he was for such a long time, but he was hardly an average or normal Irishman with the preoccupations of millions of others. The point at issue is to determine just how much and in what ways a McGlinchey may differ from the norm and whether some of the difference may explain his violent involvements.

It is unfortunate that such crude and emotional dichotomies as rational-irrational or rational-crazy should preoccupy anyone seriously studying political violence even for a moment. It has been decades since, for example, the study of international politics abandoned such simplistic juxtapositions as "rational man vs. irrational international politics." Criminology has always been careful to leave the determination of "insanity" in violent criminals to psychiatric experts without abandoning its lively interest in criminal psychology. Is it not about time for the study of political violence and terror to move beyond the simplistic approaches of its infancy?

THE COMPARATIVE APPROACH

Since this symposium consists of chapters dealing with, among other things, various countries, it seems appropriate to mention what may not be obvious to all but old hands in the study of comparative politics. This book was not meant to be a travelogue of political violence. The systematic comparison of political phenomena is by no means limited to setting entire political systems or their violent movements side by side and comparing them, so to speak, piece by piece, nor is it practical to expect anything like a representative sample of all relevant countries and movements. Like other social science topics, political violence and terror have far too many variables and too few similar cases to lend themselves to sampling in this sense. Questions of cost and of the training required to understand even just a few countries and movements well, moreover, tend to reduce most viable comparative research projects mainly to targets of opportunity related to one another by a body of comparative politics theory.

In this case, the theoretical ground was prepared well before the recruitment began for the conferences mentioned at the outset of this prologue. In particular, I had been working for a decade and a half on an ambitious study of the individual motivations and collective purpose of the pre-1933 Nazi movement,[6] which was based on auto-biographical statements of several hundred rank-and-file Nazi members and storm troopers and involved quantitative processing and elaborate methodological explorations and social-psychological speculations against an extremely complex historical background. The other contributors too have each been working on their respective movements for years and, in most cases, have already published some of their findings elsewhere.

Since there is such a welter of facts and relationships to discover about each movement—enough to fill whole volumes rather than the brief articles in this book—the approaches and interpretations are not identical. They are, nevertheless, complementary to one another and, taken together, form a meaningful set of interpretations, even though at times they may be in disagreement. It is too much to expect simple causal explanations to fit such a broad range of phenomena the way a passkey opens all the doors of a building. The complementarity instead consists in a critical, comparative assessment of common interpretations by the contributors, with differing examples of right-wing and left-wing activities, and examples from various countries and social settings. The cultural roots of violent movements alone—and we have not tried to fathom them here—would defy any attempt to give them all one common causal denominator.

In the end, it is not popular simplifications of left-wing terrorism or romantic myths of each ethnic movement which can stand up to critical scrutiny but only psychological constructs of attitudes and violent behavior that appear to fit all the various movements, such as weapons fetishes, process or generational and life cycle models, and the cycle of violent repression and reaction. The thought that political violence can be explained in terms of "social causation," by the way, also falls short of explaining the human motivations behind it in a satisfactory way, and this not only because causality is a crude, deterministic simplification of complex social-psychological processes but it is also inadequate because no observer, not even the authors of this volume, is truly able to penetrate the complex reality before him in more than a tentative and speculative way. We are reminded of the playwright, Harold Pinter, who responded to his critics by saying:

> I do so hate the becauses of drama. Who are we to say that this happens because that happened, that one thing is the consequence of another? How do we know? What reason have we to suppose that life is so neat and tidy? The most we know for sure is that the things which have happened have happened in a certain order: any connections we think we see, or choose to make, are pure guesswork. Life is much more mysterious than plays make it out to be.[7]

The contributors to this book make no claim to an all-knowing and ultimate penetration of the mysterious processes that produced the IRA, the Red Brigades, or the Kurdish nationalist movement, and we would view anyone pretending to possess such complete and ultimate knowledge with skepticism even if he or she had been a participant. Readers will need to remind themselves of the incomplete and speculative nature of all social knowledge as they judge the plausibility or implausibility of the interpretations presented here.

Finally, this prologue would not be complete without acknowledgment of the cross-fertilizing influence of various other scholarly enterprises and individuals during the earlier phases of this project. One of these was a 1974 conference on comparative fascism in the interwar years at Bergen, Norway, the proceedings of which have been published under the title *Who Were the Fascists?: Social Roots of European Fascist Movements* (1980) under the editorship of Stein U. Larsen, Jan Petter Myklebust, and Bernt Hagtvet. Of these, Stein Larsen played a major role as co-convenor and discussant of several of the 1982 panels. Another input came from Martha Crenshaw of Wesleyan University whose project on political terrorism appeared after she served as a discussant at the Washington conference (1982) and who made copies of her project available to us. A third source of inspiration was a major conference of European historians at Bad Homburg in 1979 on "social protest, violence and terror in 19th and 20th century Europe," the proceedings of which have also appeared under this title and the editorship of Wolfgang J. Mommsen and Gerhard Hirschfeld of the German Historical Institute of London. The historical examples presented and discussed there by British, German, and American scholars were later complemented by papers from a two-year seminar on political violence in the Third World and in European history, conducted by W. M. Morris-Jones of the Institute of Commonwealth Studies of the University of London.[8] All these crosscurrents of scholarly endeavor help to demonstrate that, in spite of the presence of a popular literature on the subject, the scholarly study of political violence and terror is still in the process of the inventory of cases and of conceptual development. We present this volume in the hope of having contributed to this process.

NOTES

1. See also Richard Drake, "The Red Brigades and the Italian Political Tradition," in *Terrorism in Europe*, Yonah Alexander and Kenneth Myers, eds. (New York: St. Martin, and London: Croom Helm, 1982).

2. See also Ashkenasi, *Modern German Nationalism* (Cambridge, Mass.: Schenkman, 1976).

3. Such limits appear even within violent organizations when, for example, a particular assassination or bombing is not claimed or specifically disavowed by the organization.

4. Egon Bittner, "Radicalism and the Organization of Radical Movements," *American Sociological Review* 28 (December 1963), 928–940.

5. Statements characterizing a terrorist's social relationships as "normal to the point of being mundane" are interesting in comparison but would seem to call for healthy skepticism. The question is, of course, what is normal? See Clark's chapter, "Patterns in the Lives of ETA Members," below.

6. See this writer's *Political Violence Under the Swastikas: 581 Early Nazis* (1975) and *The Making of a Stormtrooper* (1980), both published by Princeton University Press.

7. Quoted from John Russell Taylor's "Accident," *Sight and Sound* (August 1966), pp. 179–184. Quotation on p. 184.

8. The volume edited by Larsen et al. was published by the Norwegian University Press in 1980. The papers edited by Martha Crenshaw were published under the title *Terrorism, Legitimacy, and Power: The Consequences of Political Violence* (Middletown, Conn.: Wesleyan University Press, 1983); those by Mommsen and Hirschfeld were published by Macmillan, in conjunction with the German Historical Institute in London, in 1982. The papers of the Commonwealth Studies Institute can be obtained from the institute.

PART I

Aspects of Political Violence

———

1

Approaches to the Study of Political Violence

PETER H. MERKL

When Charles de Gaulle returned to France to face "the events" of May 1968, his response to the student riots was direct, if uncharacteristically crude: "*Reforme, oui, le chi-en-lit, non!*" The word *chi-en-lit* reportedly caused some confusion among the foreign correspondents in Paris who could not find it in any dictionary. Eventually, it turned out to be a bit of barracks French, denoting a recruit who messes his bed. The overtones of outrage in de Gaulle's response contain an essential ingredient of the reluctance of most describers of political violence and disorder to define what constitutes violence. Violence breaks powerful social taboos and, while we may watch it with fascination, we are less inclined to be technical about it. Perhaps for the same reason, furthermore, and in spite of the burgeoning literature on particular cases of outbreaks of political violence,[1] there has been little awareness of the many different ways the subject can be and has been treated. The more empirical studies of political violence proliferate, and the more we become aware of the extraordinary complexity of the phenomenon, the greater our need to define it and to categorize analytical approaches along lines suggested by a logical scheme.

AN OPERATIONAL DEFINITION

Setting aside for the moment the common preoccupation with the causes and justifications for political violence, let us attempt an operational definition by which this subject may be distinguished from

19

other kinds of human behavior. According to one thoughtful definition by Ted Honderich:

> Political violence . . . is a considerable or destroying use of force against persons or things, a use of force prohibited by law, directed to a change in the policies, system, territory of jurisdiction, or personnel of a government or governments, and hence also directed to changes in the lives of individuals within societies.[2]

Honderich specifically exempts governmental violence and unjust "social or political policies" as long as they do not involve force and rejects the attempts of "Marxist or other Left" critics to characterize them as violence.[3] Again, the immediate involvement with moral or legal justifications and the purposes of violence is striking and, perhaps, unavoidable. We are left to wonder if it is even possible to define political violence without reference to purpose and justification, although we do of course have to relate it to illegitimate breaches of the political and social order. Governmental violence and even unjust violent policies are exempt as long as we accord a legitimate monopoly of violence to the state and its duly authorized functionaries.

There are additional problems with the degree of what Honderich calls "considerable or destroying use of force." In popular or police parlance, unlawful resistance to a police officer or open defiance, say, of factory discipline need not escalate to acts of force or destruction in order to be perceived as violent. A simple refusal to follow orders or to resume work, or the unauthorized walking away from an encounter with police or the boss in a factory setting can already be construed as a physical act of defiance because it *violates* the bonds of social or governmental control. Some minor acts of force and destruction, however, such as vandalism or pushing and shoving, are frequently not seen as "real violence" even though they may have been clearly intended to make a political point. To be taken seriously, it seems, political violence not only has to *violate* the taboos of the prevailing order but has to give the impression of an attempt not just to nudge, but to overwhelm some persons or objects symbolic of that order.[4]

Even this clarification falls far short of defining the varying degrees and modes of political violence occurring in concrete settings. If we saw an article entitled "Political Violence in the Weimar Republic," for example, we would have no clue to what kind or level of violence was discussed in it: the civil-war-like clashes between left-wing revolutionary armies and the Freecorps of the government of the early years of the republic; individual terrorists and assassins, such as those who murdered Matthias Erzberger and Walther Rathenau; the anti-occupation and antiseparatist violence of the nationalistic under-ground under the French occupation in the West; or anti-Polish violence in the eastern border areas; or the street violence of the paramilitary organizations, the Nazi storm troopers, the communist Red Front, and the republican *Reichsbanner*. It is easy to answer "all of the above," but lumping them together in one category of violence against the feeble public order is not very helpful. Each of the five types of political violence mentioned requires rather different methods of analysis because each is generically different from the others. At-tempts at revolutionary uprising are obviously different from assassi-nations and call for different approaches. And, again, clandestine attacks on members or installations of a military occupation, or ethnic violence, differ drastically from street clashes and meeting-hall brawls between the paramilitary propaganda armies of right and left.

In each case, the persons actively involved and their motivations, the small-group setting, and the larger organizations and their sym-pathizers may vary dramatically. A would-be assassin or bomb-layer is not the same kind of person as one who joins a revolutionary or propaganda army. Even among the recruits of different kinds of private armies there are considerable differences in personality and quasi-military style, ranging from ideologues, proselytizers, propagandists, and congenital brawlers to murderous terrorists.[5] With the differences rises or falls the likelihood of lethal force—many are merely postur-ing—and martyrdom. An organizational context adds important as-pects of small-group dynamics, leader-follower interaction, and symbol-mongering, not to mention ideological beliefs. Fellow group members can supply warm comradeship and reinforce violent impulses. Individual terrorism, in contrast, is highly dependent on the manip-ulation of public opinion, the theater audience of the terrorists, so to speak. The public reaction, whether sympathetic or fearful, is the equivalent of the organizational context of militant groups. The known or imagined sympathy of the larger public audience may give the ethnic or religious terrorists emotional succor just as the fear and powerlessness of the victims may release their aggressiveness.

EXAMPLES OF CONTEMPORARY POLITICAL VIOLENCE

What was true of the variety of political violence under the Weimar Republic is even more obvious in the wide variety of cases of contem-porary political violence that we encounter every day in the news from around the world. Let us take a look at a contemporary sampling on the assumption that the range of empirical phenomena, including the others discussed in this book, may throw some light on the dif-ficulties of defining political violence:[6]

1. A striking example of a politically violent deed was the car bombing of Harrod's London department store complex in the midst of the Christmas shopping season on December 17, 1983, which killed six and wounded ninety-four people. The British police eventually charged twenty-nine-year-old Paul Kavanagh of Belfast with conspiring with others in this and five other terrorist attacks of the IRA.[7] As IRA attcks go, the Harrod's bombing was notable for randomly targeting Christmas shoppers rather than the usual military, police, or political marks of IRA terror. The presumable purpose of the Harrod's bombing was to dramatize the IRA struggle for a British withdrawal from Northern Ireland.

2. Another spectacular case was the kidnapping by the Marxist Eelam People's Revolutionary Front of Sri Lankan Tamil separatists in May 1984 of an American couple who were eventually released unharmed at the home of a Catholic bishop in Jaffna, Sri Lanka. The kidnappers had threatened to kill their victims unless the Sinhalese government of Sri Lanka freed twenty Tamil political prisoners and paid a ransom of $2 million in gold. They had first accused their captives of being CIA spies but let them go after a few days even though the Sri Lankan government refused their demands. The group later claimed that its objective had been to expose U.S. spying and dramatize its campaign for an independent Tamil state just before the impending visit of Sri Lanka President Junius R. Jayewardene to Washington, and that this goal had been met by the brief detention and "humanitarian" release of the hostages who in turn praised the kind treatment provided by their captors whom they described as highly educated.

3. A third recent case is that of the Maoist guerrilla movement Shining Path (*Sendero Luminoso*) of Peru,[8] one of a series of post-Che Guevara movements—Guevara's disciples were more likely to consist only of radicalized middle-class intellectuals and students—of the late 1970s that have sought to build a revolutionary base among Indians and mestizo peasants in the poorest hinterlands. Since 1980, the Shining Path has followed a Maoist strategy of extended guerrilla warfare against the white and mestizo-dominated Peruvian cities and government which involves small-arms attacks on police stations, blowing up power lines, selective bombings, and raids on military detachments. The guerrillas are estimated to number between five hundred and several thousand fighters. They take over whole villages, staging revolutionary trials and executions of local officials, government employees, and "exploitative" shopkeepers or businessmen, and have been known for punitive expeditions against villages that have resisted them. The elected civilian government of President Belaunde Terry sent in the army to reinforce the national police in a similarly violent

campaign of extirpating the Shining Path and its peasant supporters. The military campaign has produced large numbers of killings, "disappearances," and punitive expeditions against villages to add to the casualties inflicted by the *guerrilleros*. And yet, after four years of conflict, it seems unable to keep the insurrection from spreading to an ever-larger rural area or, most recently, from producing bombings and revolutionary incidents in cities. It is worth noting that the underground movement began to make headway only when a democratically elected government replaced twelve years of military rule in Peru.

4. Latin American political violence offers numerous other current examples aside from the ones discussed below by Peter Waldmann. One striking case involved the Colombian groups that in the spring of 1984 agreed to make peace with the government of President Belisario Betancur in exchange for amnesty and an end to military persecution. They included 9,000 men of the communist Colombian Revolutionary Armed Forces (FARC) of Pedro Antonio Marin (Tirofijo), who had carried on guerrilla warfare for two decades, the notorious M-19 terrorists, a left-wing student and middle-class nationalist organization known for its daring raids and kidnappings, and the Maoist Popular Liberation Army, leaving only a Cuban-connected National Liberation Army still in the violent underground. Betancur, a conservative, had been elected two years earlier on promises of bringing domestic peace to his violent land by calling back the country's security forces and letting the guerrillas keep their arms, but it took persistence and the forced retirement of the minister of defense and twelve recalcitrant generals for the program to succeed. Up until the cease-fire, bombs were still exploding almost nightly at Colombian military installations and at American corporate offices and cultural centers[9]—protesting American involvement in Central America—and counterinsurgency killed scores of guerrillas during the last month alone. In rural areas, once the site of *la violencia* of the early 1950s,[10] many hundreds were killed every year as paramilitary death squads massacred "subversive" peasants and agricultural union organizers while the guerrillas killed or kidnapped owners and managers of large farms. Betancur's relative reign of peace is to be policed by a National Verification Commission and its regional subcommittees, which are to investigate violations by both the death squads and the guerrillas and, if possible, keep up the distinction between political cases and the high level of ordinary, violent crime. The president also had to promise major social and political reforms, such as agrarian reforms to enable peasant laborers to acquire their own land, and an opportunity for the former guerrillas to participate without fear in the electoral politics of the country. If he succeeds in the face of considerable

by the government with the machine guns, rocket launchers, and other weaponry found in the fortified complex.

Throughout the state more than a thousand radicals were arrested in a sweep intended to confiscate other weapons caches and to forestall retaliatory violence. Similar arrests were carried out of Sikh leaders in other states who had called for protest demonstrations and strikes. With the death of the extremist leaders in the assault on the temple, the initiative reverted to negotiations between the Akali Dal leaders and the Home Affairs Ministry, which had already granted some concessions to Sikh religious and political demands before the extremists escalated them to the point of crisis.[14]

To understand the extraordinary virulence of Sikh extremism, we need to recall the prominent role that male Sikhs played in the British colonial forces and presently play in the Indian national army where they make up about 10 percent of the total.[15] Their socialization not only involves religious fanaticism but a quasi-military initiation ceremony, which explains the extraordinary group solidarity and willingness to die for the cause of the men who are proud to add "Singh" (lion) to their names. India's troubles with the Sikhs, moreover, were accompanied by major Hindu-Moslem violence in neighboring Kashmir and in Bombay and Bhiwandi where rioting mobs of Moslem and Hindu (*Shiv Sena*) militants with rocks, swords, and knives killed hundreds of people.

8. Religion and militant orders aside, the Sikh case also calls to mind another contemporary European example—other than the Basques, who will be discussed below by Robert P. Clark—of the interaction between a relatively moderate, autonomist movement and a terroristic, separatist underground: Corsica. Evidently triggered in the 1960s by the immigration of French "carpetbaggers" and *pieds noirs* from Algeria who could obtain very favorable government loans—as well as by grand development schemes by outsiders on the island[16]— an autonomist movement, the Action Regionaliste Corse (ARC, later UPC for Unione di u Populu Corsu), was formed in 1967 under the leadership of Max Simeoni and insisted on regional self-government for Corsica. By 1973, ARC agitation had produced a major confrontation involving massive demonstrations and the bombing of an Italian ferryboat,[17] which led to the arrest of Simeoni and rallied mass support to the movement and its manifestos. In 1976, Simeoni was released and his outlawed movement reborn as a more moderate political party that, by 1984, was well entrenched, albeit as a minority, in the new, directly elected Corsican Assembly. Since 1976, also, there has been a separatist Front de la Liberation Nationale Corse (FLNC) which, from its birth, has aimed hundreds of bombings annually at public buildings, police stations, and the property of pieds noirs. The FLNC,

according to its own manifesto, insists on the removal of the French "colonial army and administration" and the pieds noirs, on agrarian reform, and on the confiscation of colonial estates and the property of tourist trusts.[18] Behind the escalation of FLNC violence is a small, shadowy organization presumably composed of a cross section of young Corsicans some of whom are rumored to have been trained in Palestinian camps. Granting Corsica some regional self-government seems to have satisfied the UPC for the time being but has provided only temporary relief from FLNC violence.

9. Our last case—and we have hardly begun to exhaust the gamut of political violence from Lebanon to El Salvador—is the so-called "Greensboro massacre" of 1979, an incident that produced five dead, seven injured, but no convictions in the recent trials of the assailants. The victims were revolutionary communists of the Workers Viewpoint Organization (WVO)—actually all highly educated college graduates, including two with medical doctorates—who had come to Greensboro, North Carolina, in order to organize textile workers. They were armed themselves, had gone out of their way to bait the Ku Klux Klan and, four months earlier, had broken up a Klan rally in China Grove. Before the fatal clash, they had once more challenged the "treacherous scum" and "racist cowards" of the Klan in an open letter to come to their "Death to the Klan" rally in Greensboro. Some forty armed Klan members and American Nazis, calling themselves the United Racist Front, arrived in a caravan at the appointed time and were attacked by armed WVO members pounding on their cars. A brawl turned into a gun battle of less than two minutes with predictable results. A trial of fourteen Klansmen and Nazis in a state court on charges of murder ended in acquittal. A second, federal trial of nine of the defendants on civil rights charges—only one of the dead victims was black—also ended in acquittal. Among other reasons, the failure to convict in both cases was based on the active and provocative role of the WVO group in bringing about the sanguinary confrontation.

What can we learn about the nature of political violence and terror, as we consider this random selection, in addition to the cases mentioned already or treated in separate essays below? The first impression is obviously one of a great variety of situations and activities, a variety so great that it has tempted many a writer to break down the entire phenomenon of political violence into a series of categories, such as, according to J. Bowyer Bell,[19] "psychotic," "criminal," "state," and "revolutionary terror," of which the last-named category alone breaks down further into six categories distinguished by the purpose, the addressee, or the situation.[20] Bell's definition of terror clearly includes revolutionary violence and even counterinsurgency—which we have omitted—unlike Paul Wilkinson who separates political violence and terror and calls the "unintended terror" resulting from mass violence, as in revolutionary uprisings, epiphenomenal. The real or "systematic terrorism"[21] of revolutionary uprisings is clearly intended and planned as "a mode of psychological warfare." This also characterizes most of the cases at hand here, as does Brian Jenkins's definition of terror as "violence for effect,"[22] which does not necessarily imply that it is for effect only. The cases of right-wing terrorism discussed in subsequent chapters (by Leonard Weinberg, Klaus Wasmund, and myself) particularly exemplify "violence for effect."[23]

Of our nine cases, the last, the bloody but very much "intended" clash between the Workers Viewpoint Organization (WVO) and the United Racist Front, is perhaps the least typical of today's political violence. If anything, it reminds us of the continual provocation clashes of Nazis and communists in the streets of Weimar Berlin in the early thirties. There are, however, numerous similar contemporary cases in which violence feeds upon violence: In Arab-Israeli terrorist clashes, among the Christian and various Moslem paramilitaries in Beirut, or between Ulster Protestant and IRA Catholic terrorist groups. Even the Basque ETA now has to cope with counterterrorists and so, of course, does the Corsican FLNC, and the same has always been true of Argentina's violent groups (see Waldmann, chap. 9), not to mention the tit for tat of Latin American death squads and revolutionary organizations.

The process of mutual reinforcement and escalation is so common throughout the world of contemporary political violence that it seems odd that there has not been more of a research focus on this phenomenon. Juxtaposition does wonders for recruitment, motivation, and discipline of a group. If the WVO communists had not had the Klan and the American Nazis, they literally would have had to invent them. And, indeed, inventing a diabolic, virulent enemy is what most violent groups have done, in a manner of speaking, by inventing a believable monster that will galvanize normally lazy, unheroic, and uncooperative young people into coordinated action. The "monster" sometimes takes a religious cast—the "great Satan America"—and sometimes takes the form of ideological "pop" social science, as in vulgar Marxism or fascist ideology. Much of it has been the conjuring up of a monster that allegedly suppresses underdogs or is bent on destroying a people, an ethnos, or a nation about to be born. But there is nothing more helpful to flesh out the myth of hostile unbelievers, shadowy capitalist machinations, or communist conspiracies than a live, violent adversary.

These juxtapositions of the opposing rationalizations for terror render them rather ludicrous as explanations of terrorist activity but, in doing so, they also direct the researcher's attention to the internal group life and the individual motivations of recruits to each violent group, as the authors of this book have tried to do. To understand terrorist motives, we have to start out with the assumption that much in ordinary social life conspires to discourage and inhibit political violence: most people are raised in such a way as to restrain their inclinations toward violence. There is abundant evidence that, even when acting in the well-understood pursuit of legitimatized killing, many police officers and military men experience considerable psychological trauma that may, in the long run, make it impossible for them to carry on and may haunt them for the rest of their lives. Even if we assume that terrorists are somehow more violence-prone[24] than most people, it does not necessarily follow that killing a person, especially a "symbolic victim," does not faze them at all. For this reason, there has to be a very strong motivation supplied by a rationalizing belief, such as a religion, an ideology, or nationalism, and a tightly knit, supportive group that helps the terrorist to maintain the fiction of a world peopled by monsters that deserve to be fought with extreme deeds.

Of these two, the rationalizing beliefs in most of our cases were found to be religious—especially in the Middle Eastern cases, but also with the Sikhs, if not in quite the same manner with the IRA—or nationalist, as with the IRA, the separatists of Sri Lanka, Punjab, and Corsica, not to mention the Basque ETA, and again the Israeli and Palestinian terrorists. The combination of religious fanaticism and nationalism seems to make for a particularly explosive mixture, witness the Shiite terrorists in Lebanon, Iraq, and Iran. This is not necessarily an indictment of religion and nationalism: They can be powerful, community-building, spiritual forces that, in fact, will supply a system of moral beliefs for the communities they build. But there are limits, of course, to the extent to which a violent movement can invoke this moral credit for their fighting deeds. The limits are often ignored both by the protagonists and their sympathizers in the broader public and abroad. And it is easy to demonstrate the presence of these limits whenever a religious or nationalistic cause involves two or more competing organizations, such as Corsican and French-Corsican nationalists, or even competing autonomists and separatists, as in the Basque case.

The interplay between Corsican, Sikh, or Basque extremists and their more moderate equivalents, especially in the presence of other legitimate political forces, produces a complex scenario: We can easily imagine a game of pretense, for example, in which the moderates and extremists appear to be in pitched competition for popular support when, in fact, there may be collusion underneath. The moderate nationalists and their extremist brethren can use one another to expand their appeal to the public. The moderates, moreover, can use their illegal accomplices as a battering ram to make their own demands seem more reasonable, while the extremists use the refusal to grant the moderates' demands as the perfect excuse for extreme actions. The moderates can also help their confreres to raise money, recruit new activists, or to save imprisoned extremists from confinement or the gallows. At the same time, they can maintain and conserve advances and concessions won for the nation by the extremists,[25] because the moderates are already playing a legitimate and recognized role. It is this kind of tacit collusion that demonstrates the inherent legitimacy of nationalist terrorist movements as well, in spite of the extreme means they employ.

This still leaves the Colombian underground movements and the Peruvian Shining Path, as well as other Latin American revolutionaries discussed below by Peter Waldmann. Here the beliefs seem to be a mixture of Marxism-Leninism or Maoism with antiforeign (especially anti-American) nationalism. Cuban or Soviet intrigues rarely play a role, but there is often an underlying, desperate struggle over control of the land. On the one side, there is an arrogant elite of great landowners, old, new, or would-be plantation owners who recoil at nothing to further their interests, not even death squads or military dictatorship. On the other side are villagers, campesinos, mestizos, and Indians, and organized efforts at redistributing the land, or protecting what belongs to the village from the rapacious greed of the landowners. Violent groups emerge mostly from the rural struggle over turf and, less often, from an urban, middle-class or student radicalism as in the case of the Tupámaros of Uruguay. The latter variant is unlikely to pose a major challenge to political stability. Urban guerrillas in Latin America or Italy and Germany are an irritant and their "red fascism," or "violence for effect," to speak with Brian Jenkins, may sometimes provoke repressive measures that weaken democracy but they are not really serious contenders in the revolutionary game. The revolutionary movements struggling for land reform, however, are playing the game for keeps and have a real chance of seizing power if they are not suppressed in time, which in turn may explain the extraordinary and indiscriminate carnage perpetrated against "suspicious" Indians or campesinos, local officials, and farm union organizers in places like El Salvador, Guatemala or, a generation ago, in Colombia. That the killing often involves some students, journalists, and priests as well, should not obscure the tens of thousands of campesinos that have been massacred in cold blood. The rural revolutionaries, for their part, have their own reprisal raids and massacres for villages and officials suspected of collaboration with the repressive efforts of the government.

In most of the cases under consideration, the chief antagonist of the violent movement is indeed the government that, presumably, is in the hands of the enemy. Hence much of the violence is directed against its military and police posts and personnel, or against prominent government officials. But the religious, nationalist, or rural revolutionary movements frequently also take on "the enemy" directly and kill rival religionists—especially militants such as the rampaging Sikhs or Indian Muslims going after Hindu militants—representatives of rival or dominant nationalisms, or capitalists and landowners. And when they do, it is always meant emphatically "for effect" more than anything. The Tamil separatists of Sri Lanka, as the reader will recall, readily dropped their demands for ransom when they saw that their kidnapping of an American couple had achieved more worldwide publicity than they had hoped to receive. They did not have to mistreat or keep their hostages, either. Their real objective in this action had been reached, although they, of course, still needed to win their war against the Sinhalese and their government in Sri Lanka.

We have arranged selected variables of these nine cases in table 1.1 in order to approach the subject more analytically and with the benefit of comparative method. Such qualitative tabulation in such a controversial and underresearched field is always a painful process—forcing us to suppress any tendency to condemn or excuse and requiring operational specifics even where little is known—but it helps to categorize and to establish or confirm patterns by comparison.[26] The first three columns, WHO, did WHAT, to WHOM, require little elaboration except to remind the reader that the character of our nine cases varies from a single incident (e.g., case 1 or 2) to accounts of whole organizations over many years (e.g., cases 3, 4, or 8). The third and fourth columns, furthermore, were used to separate the actual victims of political violence from its "symbolic addressee" who usually differs from them: The symbolic addressee is nearly always a government, quasi-governmental system (capitalism, racism), or foreign governmental influence (imperialism). The actual victims are sometimes officials or representatives of that government, capitalist system, or imperialism (e.g., cases 3, 4, 5, 7, and 8), sometimes merely "civilians" (e.g., cases 1, 2, 6, 7, and 8), or self-chosen counterterrorists (cases 6, 7, and 9). There also seems to be an underlying dimension that runs from an all-out struggle for power, as with the Latin American guerrilla armies (cases 3 and 4) and Sri Lankan Tamil, Sikh, and Corsican nationalists via IRA terrorism to the Communist-Nazi

TABLE 1.1

SELECTED VARIABLES OF CONTEMPORARY EXAMPLES OF POLITICAL VIOLENCE AND TERROR

WHO (Actives)	WHAT (Modus operandi)	TO WHOM (Victims)	Symbolic addressee	Social basis		Organization		WHY (Goals, ideology)
				Claimed	Sympathizers	Small group	Large group	
IRA lone bomber	Car bombing Harrod's department store	Accidentally present "civilians"	U.K. government	Irish Catholics and Republicans	Cross section	Underground cell	Provisional IRA, Sinn Fein	Irish nationalism British withdrawal from Northern Ireland
Tamil separatists	Kidnapping and release	American "civilian" couple	Sri Lankan government, U.S.	Sri Lankan and Indian Tamils	Sri Lankan and Indian Tamils	Commando group	Eelam PRF	Sri Lankan Tamil separatism, freeing political prisoners
Peruvian rural guerrilla army	Bombings, raids, expeditions against villages	Police and military Local officials	Elected government; foreign imperialism	Unmobilized Indian and mestizo peasants, students		Paramilitary groups	Sendero Luminoso	Maoist state; struggle against cities, capitalism, foreign imperialism
Colombian rural guerrillas	Guerrilla raids, assassinations	Police, landowners	Elected government	Unmobilized peasants	Students, middle class	Paramilitary groups	FARC, PLA	Communism, agrarian reform, social revolution
Colombian urban guerrillas	Kidnappings, bombings	Foreign embassies	Foreign (U.S.) imperialism	Urban and rural proletariat		Underground cells	M-19	Struggle against foreign imperialism, capitalism

Shiite religious terrorists	Truck bombings	Foreign embassies (esp. U.S.)	U.S., Gulf states, Israel	Shiite Moslems in Iraq and Iran	3-man cells	Al Dawa (Iran and Syria?)	Islamic Jihad against secular enemies, esp. U.S.
Jewish terrorists	Shootings and bombs on buses	Palestinian "civilians"	Islamic shrines Palestinians	Israeli West Bank settlers	Under-ground cells	Kach movement, network	Struggle for Biblical homeland; defense against persecution
Sikh religious nationalists	Shootings, raids, assassinations	Hindu "civilians," Indian police	Indian government	Sikh religious military community	Paramilitary groups	Akali Dal Auton-omists	Sikh separatism or regional autonomy
Corsican nationalist terrorists	Bombings	Pied noirs, Corsican police	French colonialism	Unmobilized poor Corsicans	Under-ground cells	FLNC—UPC link	Corsican independence; struggle against French colonialism
WVO revolutionary communists	Brawls, shootings	KKK/Nazis	U.S. capitalism and racism	"Workers"/intellectuals	Militant cells	Commu-nists	Proletarian and racial liberation
KKK/Nazis	Intimidations, arson	Blacks, integrationists	Intregrationist "conspiracy"	Whites	Local cells	KKK network	White supremacy, defense against the "conspiracy"

brawls; the civil war guerrilla armies are more likely to attack the police and military of the state, and not mere "civilians," and they are rather more inclined to struggle for keeps and not just for effect.

In the columns on "social basis" and "organization" it was attempted first to dichotomize each into (a) the "claimed" base versus "actual sympathizers," and then into (b) small-group settings and large organizational support. The available information is not quite adequate, however, nor are the categories discrete enough to be entirely satisfactory. The thought behind the dichotomy of the social basis is the separation between myth and reality, but we have no way of measuring the extent to which the "claimed" supporters really support each clandestine group and its often extreme actions. It is a fair guess that, in most cases, only a small cross section of the claimed, but "unmobilized," social base actually supports or sympathizes with the violence, but the extent of this support is too controversial and too crucial to be merely estimated by us. Protagonists and well-wishers are as likely to overstate it as the defenders of the status quo will underestimate it. Dramatic events, moreover, may suddenly mobilize the indifferent social basis in favor of their violent "freedom fighters," especially if the latter manage to bring down the wrath of the state on all the members of their claimed social base, which is often a favorite strategy of such groups.

In the organizational columns attention is called to the small-group dynamics of the small, supportive circle of activists who carry out the actual killings or bombings as contrasted to a larger, often more moderate or legitimate organization that may constitute its "political arm"—as with ETA or the Provisional IRA. Sometimes the larger organization not only helps to raise funds but also provides weapons and explosives, recruits "heavies," and may even direct the tactic and strategy of the militant cell, designating who or what will be attacked at what time and in what manner. The implied division of labor between the small group and the larger organization again goes beyond the available information on most groups, much as we would like to know it. It makes a lot of difference, for example, whether the larger organization is the terrorist directorate and network or merely a political party concerned with somewhat similar goals, as in the cases of the Sikhs and the Corsicans. After an attack, law enforcement can sometimes form a good idea of how the functions were divided. Generally speaking, the division of labor is meant to save the small group from tasks that it cannot perform well and thus to permit it to concentrate on what it does best: to inspire the "heavies" to risk life and limb, not to mention their freedom, in carrying out grisly assignments and to avoid all unnecessary exposure such as might come from having to acquire their own weapons or exploring the specifics of a contemplated action. In some of the cases in our table (e.g., cases 3 and 4), of course, the small group is simply a small detachment, perhaps a platoon of a militarily organized guerrilla army, but even there it has to supply a nurturant environment to keep up the morale of the paramilitaries under trying circumstances. As for the small-group dynamics of terrorist groups, again, there is very little reliable information available aside from the revealing essay by Klaus Wasmund (chap. 7), and a great deal of speculation from other evidence. The contribution of small-group dynamics to the motivation of the active member of a violent group, say to the person in the ski mask holding the submachine gun, is central to the concerns of this book.

The last column, on the ideology or goal of the violent group or action, at first glance seems to require little explanation. The various groups want to realize national, often separatist aspirations, achieve religious fulfillment, or pursue a secular ideology such as the creation of a communist state. We will come back to the subject of various ideological motifs below. On closer examination, however, the question of goals takes on greater complexity. First there are short-range goals, such as the British withdrawal from Northern Ireland or the freeing of political prisoners, and long-range ones, such as the establishment of an independent nation-state, as described in the essay by Abraham Ashkenasi, below. Politics being a complicated business, the short-range goals rarely lead directly or inevitably to the long-range goals. Quite frequently, moreover, either one or both may be very problematical in their likely outcomes, as is for instance a British withdrawal from Northern Ireland.

A third caveat lies in the fact that sometimes the announced long-range goals may turn out to be deceptive: A movement such as the Basque ETA, for example, which started out as a romantic, nationalist reaction to Spanish centralization and is still taken as a movement for a Basque nation-state by most observers, may reveal striking ambiguities beneath this surface appearance. In the 1960s, ETA turned decisively to the far left and eventually found itself in direct competition with the Spanish Communist party (PCE), which also tried to take advantage of Basque ethnic discontents both for furthering its own goals of destabilizing the entire political system, and in regional industrial disputes. ETA's association with the Maoist terrorists of GRAPO and its suspected ties to other far-left terrorist organizations of Europe and the Middle East give added emphasis to interpretations of it as more of an anticapitalist revolutionary than an autonomist force.[27] Although these ideological goals—revolutionary communism and ethnic separatism—may not be entirely incompatible, the addition of communism certainly would give ETA violence and its suppression a different color. If its intention is to destroy the new Spanish democracy and not just to win home rule for the Basques, this would also explain the stepping-up of ETA terror in spite of the granting of regional self-government to the Basques.

CATEGORIZING APPROACHES BY UNIT OF ANALYSIS

The large number of recent empirical studies of past and present political violence can be sorted analytically into meaningful categories when we separate them according to the approach used. Empiricism in social and political research, after all, can have several competing meanings depending on the conception of the nature of the underlying violence and on the methods employed to capture the phenomenon. One way of distinguishing different schools is by the unit of analysis employed.

Many writers on political violence, for example, take large uprisings and entire revolutions, especially successful ones, as their object, which tends to lead them to treat violence as only an incidental, if prominent, part of a larger historical scenario. Typically, an author begins a case study by simply "narrat[ing] what appears to have happened . . ." and with a discussion of "the identity and motives of those who took part in the violence."[28] But these students of revolution are not so much interested in violence per se as in the causes of revolution and perhaps in the phases by which a particular revolution may progress from local discontents to nationwide disorder, civil war, and the eventual consolidation of the new regime. Beginning with Aristotle's Politics, historically oriented sociologists, political scientists, and historians have generalized about such causes of revolution as inequality or excessive equality, "relative deprivation"[29] or arrested economic growth, nationalism or separatism—or home rule—social tensions or class struggle, the perceived impossibility of reform (see Waldmann, chap. 9), the delegitimization of regimes, or a sense of anomie. Frequently, such causes have already been enshrined in the ideology of the revolution.

Another variant that appears when writers take entire revolutions as the unit to be analyzed is their focus, Crane Brinton–style, on the phases of its progression or on the internal dynamic that drives revolutions toward extremes and often results in their destroying themselves. This line of analysis was very popular with post facto interpretations of the French Revolution and its aftermath. The great upheaval and reaction spawned whole philosophies of history that strove to explain in one fashion or another how the great revolution could end with Thermidor. The most prominent of these is the dialectic interpretation of Georg Wilhelm Friedrich Hegel, which has been elevated into a universal philosophy of history. But again, neither

Hegel nor Hegelian disciples like Karl Marx[30] were particularly concerned with violence, although they generally saw it as an indicator of the intensity of social and political conflict. The rise and fall of terrorism in a country can also be described in such stages of action and reaction,[31] although this subject would seem to suggest, more often than not, that the analysis should concentrate on individual acts and individual actors.

There has been very little comparative empirical research so far on the effects of political violence, aside from single-case studies.[32] Such interesting questions as whether and how political violence polarizes a society, especially one already divided along ethnic, religious, or cultural lines, await authoritative generalization. It seems plausible to assume (but it needs to be tested in comparative studies) that violence plays a key role in the ongoing process of revolution. It helps it along, so to speak, by escalating conflict and heightening "revolutionary consciousness" from one stage to the next, delegitimizing authority, and encouraging the rise of new movements and leaders, perhaps even of new concepts of public order and legitimacy. We take it for granted that violence generates counterviolence, but also that societies may react by reining in their violent passions and impulses from a sense of shock. There is a great need for more research on how violence affects both its perpetrators and those they represent, as well as their victims or target populations. There is, of course, much descriptive information in the frequently distorted journalistic accounts of how children, relatives, and friends of victims have reacted among Catholics and Protestants in Northern Ireland, or among Israelis and Palestinians in the Middle East. But the one-sidedness of the reports and the possibly self-serving rationalizations of the activists have obscured the true proportions between those in such situations who react with violent action, or become sympathizers of such actions, and those who recoil or seek to flee from its impact.[33]

Yet another unit of analysis for studies of political violence is the violent organization, or rather the organization within which a specifiable kind of violent act is emotionally supported and ideologically rationalized. There is now considerable literature in which the authors concentrate on describing the genesis and life of such organizations and, frequently, the kind of individuals attracted to and accepted by it. Aside from the rather unusual, and possibly mad, loner, most political violence has such an organizational context, but there has still not been much research[34] into the link between violence-prone individuals and the groups that recruit and socialize them and that may give them the ideological justification, the weapons and training in their use, as well as shelter, legal assistance, and a social-worker kind of care when they are imprisoned for their deeds. At least some violent groups such as the IRA, the West German RAF, or the American Black Panthers have been known to recruit members in prisons. As Klaus Wasmund points out (chap. 7), the care of imprisoned fellow terrorists is also an important vehicle for socializing sympathizers toward deeper involvement with the underground. The Nazi storm troopers of the last years before Hitler's takeover also used to minister to the emotional and physical needs of imprisoned or hospitalized fighters to be sure that they would not leave the fold. All such organizational-centered literature can be a good base for further research on individual members and their violent deeds.

There are, of course, entire methodological schools that use either the violent act or the violent individual as units of analysis. Individual or collective acts of political violence, for instance, are the basis of the work on the changing nature of violence over a century of recent European history by Charles, Louise, and Richard Tilly.[35] The Tillys counted the annual incidence of violent collective actions of a certain severity, that is, involving specified numbers of participants and casualties, in France, Germany, and Italy, and developed a theory of collective violence on this basis. They found that modernization tends to be accompanied by fundamental changes in the extent, duration, and intensity of violent domestic conflicts. Other researchers have tabulated incidents of international and domestic violence and rated various nations accordingly.[36]

At the level of individuals and their acts of violence, there is a growing literature on assassinations and terrorist acts of various sorts. The work of Gerhard Botz on Austria between the wars is also a good example of measuring levels of violence by the number of dead and injured.[37] By the same token, violent individuals of a given level of involvement, say imprisoned assassins and terrorists convicted of causing deaths, can be the basis of various comparisons with, for instance, less seriously involved terrorists or mere sympathizers, or with control groups outside their movement.

The last category is composed of researchers focusing on violent individuals and the process by which they became involved in political violence. There has always been some speculation as to the motives that might drive a person to violent behavior, but relatively little empirical work or empirical theory.[38] In their acceptance of ideological rationalizations or transparent excuses, journalists and even scholars have been all too ready to romanticize the motives of lethal terrorists and assassins. What empirical theory does exist has been derived from individual psychology, which traditionally handles aggression, or frustration-aggression, value conflict, and alienation, not to mention childhood maladjustments that might lead to adult aggressiveness.[39] One of the notable recent interpretations has been that of a psychiatrist, Frederick J. Hacker, who related the terrorist "crusader" type of person to an organizational setting, a sense of belonging, anticipated repression, and a yearning for communal identity. Hacker's theorizing covers ground similar to my work on the early Nazis (psychological and social-psychological), and he also supplies illuminating glimpses of the terrorist as an artist.

IDEOLOGY AND POLITICAL VIOLENCE

The study of politically violent organizations and their members invariably raises questions about the role of political ideologies, in particular of extremist and radical ideologies, among their motivations. Does being a communist, a fascist, or an anarchist make a person or group engage in acts of violence of a political nature? Put in this simplistic form, the question calls for a negative answer. People of normal disposition and a normal degree of social integration are unlikely to become violent solely from reading books or pamphlets, or from listening to a political speech. There have always been thousands of gentle anarchists, little old ladies worshiping *il duce* or *der Führer*, and intellectual communists, none of whom was capable of political violence. And for those who were politically violent, such as the Nazi storm troopers and communist street fighters of the Weimar Republic, ideological considerations may indeed have been, more often than not, "only an afterthought," as I stated in the prologue. And yet, it would be impossible to deny a correlation between extremist ideologies and political violence in the face of the ideological colorings of the Red Brigades, neofascist terrorist groups, and various other contemporary varieties of political "ultraviolence," to borrow a word from Stanley Kubrick's film, *A Clockwork Orange*. The task at hand, then, is to winnow out the complex interactions between violence-prone minds and these ideologies and not just to assume that ideological commitment *causes* engagement in violence. It is just as conceivable that the causal nexus between ideology and political violence goes in the opposite direction: for instance, that violent individuals and groups have made Marxism into a violent faith, or that they have sought rationalizations or good excuses in it for their own violent propensities.

The radical right and its sympathizers in European countries between the two world wars provide illuminating examples of the complex interaction between violence and ideology. There were vast numbers of likely supporters coming from many different directions, various milieus in social and economic decline and from a range of different mobilizing experiences, but nearly all of them from rather unpolitical backgrounds. There were aristocratic officers whose upbringing had not prepared them for the dramatic fall of the old order, the loss of their status, and the rise of those they had always considered their inferiors into politicized masses. There were university students and other scions of the educated middle classes whose impoverished families could no longer promise them the opportunities of advancement implicit in their now discounted status. There were legions of small shopkeepers and free-holding peasants whose livelihood was threatened or destroyed by the long-standing erosion of their economic role in society. Above all, there were millions of patriots—especially among the soldiers of the Great War and the civil servants of the old regimes—whose aroused nationalistic feelings were deeply aggravated by defeat, revolution, and territorial losses, not to mention the loss of close relatives in war or civil war. Long-standing ethnic hatreds of every description had been intensified by war, revolution, and the territorial changes imposed after the war, and were fanned to searing heat by the changed power relationships among the ethnic components of the successor states to the fallen Russian, German, Hapsburg, and Ottoman empires.

Most of the people affected and disoriented by these dramatic changes were not accustomed to responding to threat or deprivation in a political way, having grown up in traditional, authoritarian settings. Their philosophical values and political attitudes prior to the great collapse had been *immanent in the old order*, especially in their loyalty to its spiritual and secular authorities. Now that the old order had fallen, their first reactions, characteristically, were attempts to fight back in a military way, that is, by counterrevolutionary action to beat down the revolutionary hosts. They acted as if they could restore their old regimes in new versions even though there usually was no way of going back. By all accounts, these quasi-military rearguard actions of the Austrian Heimwehr, the German Freecorps and Stahlhelm veterans, and comparable reactionary formations in other successor states were characterized by attitudes among leaders and men that were strikingly *unpolitical.* They lacked political orientation in the sense that there was no cohesive idea, certainly no agreement on the goals or the direction of their violent "counterrevolutionary" undertakings.[40] Their violence, in other words, clearly antedated any commitment to a political cause or organization. They tended to reject ideological politicking, and usually rejected even the paramilitary propaganda armies of the growing fascist movements. As individuals, their alienation from the elected, partisan successor regimes of the Weimar and Austrian republics, and the Italian monarchy, continued for the most part to keep them from political participation,[41] even though their political and social values placed them in the vicinity of the more politicized conservatives and fascists.

Many of them probably never found their way into the partisan political life they detested. Those who eventually did, however, tended to enter the political arena in widely varying, unpredictable ways, some as ultraconservatives, some as fascist chieftains or storm trooper officers, and some as silent helpmates of a fascist revolution in high quarters of the armed forces, the police, or the civil service. With the possible exception of storm trooper officers, political violence was not something with which they came in direct contact, although they may have commanded their foot soldiers to engage in it, silently applauded it, or simply failed to restrain it. The link between their political ideology and violence is a distant and rather rational, instrumental one. The young foot soldiers, however, who permitted themselves to be used by their higher-ups for purposes that may not have been clear to them, became directly and voluntarily involved in street violence and attacks for very different reasons. They risked arrest, serious injury, and even death for the dubious pleasure of inflicting death or injury on generally rather obscure enemies.[42] In their case, the attraction of violence was obviously very strong and requires explanations that take into consideration their entire personality makeup, and not just a set of beliefs.

The contemporary far right in Italy, Germany, or France has been similarly scattered over a broad range of degrees of involvement, beginning their politicization from such depths of alienation and retreat from political reality as are described in the following essay on Julius Evola.[43] The reader may feel hard pressed just to accept Evola's or J. R. Tolkien's fantasies as the equivalent of ideological writings on the left—which by nature seem more clearly focused on matters political. How can such escapist imagery and myths of adventure inspire anyone to acts of terrorism?

The contemporary far right also has its manipulative, ultraconservative politicians and secret helpmates in army, police, and civil service, especially in Italy, whose ideology may be vague and ill defined though clearly to the right of most responsible politicians. And then there are the young foot soldiers in terrorist groups, or even on their own, whose ideological bent is likely to be buried in violent personal animosities and gross prejudices. It is far easier to relate right-wing terrorist acts to these hostile attitudes than to Tolkien's heroes with whom they are all familiar. Terrorist bombings or fusillades near synagogues or Jewish shops clearly point to the anti-Semitic obsessions[44] of certain French, Flemish, German, Austrian, or Italian groups, just as attacks on Pakistanis in England or Indochinese refugees in West Germany stem from the xenophobic prejudices of certain neofascist groups there. The prejudice in question is a kind of missing link between physical aggressiveness and ideological beliefs. Outrages such as the *Oktoberfest* bombing (1980) or the explosions at the Piazza Fontana (1969)[45] or the Bologna railroad station, in contrast, smack more of rebels without an ideological cause. And yet we may well be dealing with similar phenomena in both cases: murderous minds gathering under the justifying umbrella of an extremist organization that supplies them with weapons and rationalizations for doing what to them comes naturally.

Is left-wing terrorism really all that different? As Klaus Wasmund describes the evolution of some of the Baader-Meinhof terrorists,[46] especially of the earlier generation, their recruitment was generally preceded by a lengthy period of alienation and dissociation from family and friends which, more often than not, ended up in a rather disoriented and directionless state of existence in an urban commune of the "alternative scene." They themselves have described their communal life as a state of painful mental emptiness in which drug abuse was often substituted for political discussion. When they finally did become politicized, it was through the personal influence of new "friends" who were already committed to support of the Baader-Meinhof gang; for example, to the support of imprisoned and presumably suffering terrorists. The recruits, with their insecure personalities and weak egos, were given a sense of political direction solely by these recruiters or protectors who took charge of their failed personal lives (many were student or other dropouts) and told them to read a certain political literature. Commitment to a political cause and ideological beliefs, in other words, entered their lives through the back door and was not the prime mover in their terrorist careers. Frequently, their metamorphosis was also helped along by key experiences such as the martyr death of a notorious terrorist—not necessarily a personal acquaintance—or spectacular terrorist coups. This is obviously a rather different nexus between ideology and political violence from the more straightforward quasi-causal one that impels some militant trade unionists or young members of communist or socialist parties to demonstrate against their antagonists in the streets and, in connection with such demonstrations and strikes, to assault them physically.

Still another version of the nexus between ideology and left-wing terrorism was started when the University of Heidelberg supplied a room for the establishment of a self-help street clinic for—generally nonclinical—mental patients. The room quickly became a dormitory for homeless drug addicts and other troubled souls who formed and operated a Socialist Patients Collective (SPK) until it was closed down after a year and a half. With the help of "agitation therapy," the SPK members learned to reinterpret their unhappy lives into an indictment of the "life-denying force of capitalism" and the "criminal institutions" (schools, hospitals, law enforcement) of the Federal Republic, and to spread the message to others. The SPK pamphlets indeed present a totally upside-down image of life and values of West German society, which is blamed for everything that "hurts" these patients. They are in turn enjoined to make war on and "destroy that which hurts them" and, consequently, thirty-two of some six hundred SPK patients actually joined the RAF terrorists as ideologically motivated fighters acting out their own therapy.[47]

Although political violence between right-wing and left-wing groups has been a ubiquitous and perennial phenomenon of twentieth-century politics, there have been few empirical studies that would enable us to answer the question of the ideological nexus on the basis of broader experience. The street violence of the early 1930s in Berlin between young communists and Nazi storm troopers still lends itself best to comparison, even though there may have been some unique features present that would detract from its exemplary value.[48] For one thing, the storm troopers and communists learned from each other and began to emulate each other in style and forms of attack. According to accounts on both sides, the street fighters were motivated far more by the escalating physical confrontations than by ideological beliefs. In many cases, violent antagonists came from the same neighborhoods and knew one another. The young communists were frequently recruited from street-corner society and juvenile gangs in these tenement districts and slum neighborhoods. Eve Rosenhaft's brilliant study of the reactive violence of young neighborhood communist street fighters brings out the vast gap between the party's ideological struggle and the continual need to battle the storm-trooper raids with rationalizing attitudes of *wehrhafter Kampf* (quasi-military battle spirit). Even though Lenin had talked about "individual terror," and the party proposed to meet the Nazi challenge with something called "mass resistance" and "mass terror," the reality of the clashes had a great deal more to do with aroused emotions, brawny fists, and weapons than with these ideological concepts. Communist agitation was far more realistic when it stressed personal heroism and martyrdom, and focused on portraits of injured comrades and funerals of the fallen to galvanize the neighborhoods for an appropriate, violent response. With the Red Frontfighters' League (RFB) outlawed in 1929, the communists also had to organize new militant shock troops composed of small five-man cells to match the storm-trooper challenge. And all along, the communist leadership itself regarded its own "freedom fighters" as socially and politically rather marginal, as they were mostly unemployed, and neither politically nor industrially trained, often belonging to marginal trades and occupations from which they were also recruited by the Nazis, and frequently with considerable criminal records, including violent offenses. The leaders may have been too quick to judge their own violent foot soldiers, much as they needed them, but they clearly distinguished between their own ideology as a motivating force and what seemed to be the motives of many of the communist toughs of the Berlin streets.

Communist street fighters and Nazi storm troopers in Berlin were, after all, largely from the same working-class districts and they probably saw the confrontations more as battles over turf than battles with the political and ideological overtones their parties attempted to give them. The Berlin storm troopers were also heavily proletarian and frequently unemployed. Their "ideology" was mostly a matter of style and uniform, plus the Hitler cult, and not of the abstrusities of Nazi literature, which few of them had ever read. In both cases, the recruitment had been very personal, and loyalty to comrades and group leaders was very important. In fact, the personal angle may have been the major factor—aside from symbolic identification with family attachments to either the organized working class or the patriotic war effort—that made a youngster choose the outlawed Red Front or the storm troopers.[49] The intensity of their involvement in political violence, including lethal force received or dealt out, generally was not proportional to the intensity with which they seem to have held their respective ideological beliefs. On the contrary, more likely than not, the ideologues among them shrank back from the mayhem, while the most violent among them seemed propelled mostly by a mindless yen for murder or martyrdom.[50]

ETHNIC LIBERATION IDEOLOGY

Turning to ethnic terrorist or guerrilla movements, at first glance we may find an equivalent to the role of political ideology in the intense identification with the life and future of one of the unredeemed nationalities—Basque, Kurdish, Palestinian—among a world of established nation-states. To speak with Abraham Ashkenasi (chap. 11),[51] the left-behind ethnic groups are desperately striving to emulate the example of "ethnic core groups" such as the British, French, Germans, Austrians, Spanish, or Israelis who as groups "imperialized" the larger geographic entity they had come to dominate. Left behind, or enclosed in another group's state (or in several, like the Kurds), and exploited or oppressed by their respective core groups, these ethnic minorities may be the external equivalent of the exploited industrial proletariat of the Marxist militants. On closer examination, however, the resemblance between this phenomenon and political-ideological terrorist movements is based on such an accumulation of misconceptions that any effort at comparison becomes confused. On the one hand, none of the major political terrorist groups, such as the Red Brigades, Tupámaros, or the West German RAF, can be said to represent or draw noticeable support from the proletariat they claim to fight for. Ethnic or nationalist guerrillas, on the other hand, have a strong representative claim even though they tend to vary over a wide range in the actual support they receive from their co-ethnics. Rivalry among nationalist guerrilla groups is consequently rare,[52] whereas political terror organizations in the same country are very likely to compete. In Argentina, they have been known to make war on each other even when they belong to the same side of the political spectrum.

Membership and active involvement in an ethnic or ethnocultural group is a part of the universal process of individuation and the establishment of personal identity regardless of whether it expresses itself in political behavior. Among nonterrorist ethnic activists, we can already observe striking differences in the intensity of commitment and political activism. During the great upsurge of ethnic voting in Great Britain in the mid-1970s, for example, the Scottish Nationalist party could boast an impressive mandate of up to 30 percent of Scottish voters, whereas the Welsh Plaid Cymru could never get more than about 11 percent of the Welsh vote. French ethnic parties, with the exception of Corsican autonomists, have done even worse in attracting Occitan and Breton voters because, presumably, asserting one's ethnocultural identity need not necessarily go as far as voting ethnic or supporting ethnopolitical autonomy. Many people of the same ethnic descent may be simply indifferent to this fact. The moderate Basque Nationalist party in the 1984 regional elections received 41 percent of the vote, while the radical Herri Batasuna—a party considered the "political arm" of ETA—polled another 14.5 percent. A third Basque party, the nonviolent left-wing Euskadiko Ezkerra, took 8 percent, leaving only about a third of the vote for the national parties there, the Socialists (PSOE) and the right-wing Popular Alliance (AP). While the three regional parties hardly see eye to eye, there can be little doubt about the regional loyalties of Basque voters, especially vis-à-vis the Spanish army and bureaucracy, the forces most intent on keeping the Basques under central control.

At the same time, ethnic nationalisms can be subject to other insecurities for which, in fact, they may constitute an exaggerated compensation, as we can see in the Basque case: There is little doubt, for example, about the ancient distinctions of language that have set off the four northern Spanish provinces from Spanish and the rest of the Spaniards for 1,200 years. But neither the Basque language nor the population has ever been particularly unified, probably for lack of a central government of their own that could have made them into one people speaking with one tongue. Modern Euskera is a recent revival unifying several tribal languages, but it lacks a literary tradition comparable to that of Catalán or Gaelic. And the Basque population was "imperialized" by both the Spanish and the French nation-states. As in most nationalisms, the historical identity and continuing life of the particular *ethnos* requires an effort to create or recreate, and in the Basque case this was taken on by Sabino de Arana y Goiri, who originated the name Euskadi for the four provinces, developed the Basque ideology and, in 1895, founded the Basque Nationalist party which already in 1918, and again in 1931, had attracted one-third of the Basque vote for the Cortes. The four provinces also had rather different histories—Navarre had its own constitution until the mid-nineteenth century, Vizcaya and Guipuzcoa were the sites of early and rapid industrialization, not to mention the French Basques whose areas had long ago become part of the then-rising French monarchic state. Even during the Spanish civil war of the 1930s, the four provinces were not on the same side, Navarre and Alava siding with Franco.

However doubtful the origins, there is no mistaking the strength of the contemporary Basque nationalist movement, which seems to have started when industrialization and Spanish immigration began to threaten the conservative and devout way of life of small-town and rural Basques. In the meantime, the progress of industrialization and its consequent labor disputes have opened up the romantic, nationalist movement to left-wing agitation which may account for the number of Basque parties. There also has grown a contentious awareness of how the Spanish state redistributes revenues from prosperous Euskadi and Cataluña to the poorer parts of Spain. Such redistribution, of course, is common practice in all modern states, just as the more mobile elements of a country tend to migrate to where opportunity seems to beckon. For the Basque nationalists, however, this is a matter of being bled by the Spanish state, occupied by the Guardia Civil, and invaded by greedy and exploitive outsiders in large numbers.

It is against this background that we need to gauge what it may take to become an IRA or Ulster terrorist, to kill or kidnap for the Basque ETA, or to become a Palestinian guerrilla.[53] A very prominent factor in these cases, and in others discussed in this book, seems to have been the intensity of the confrontation between rival nationalisms: the Catholic Northern Irish against a repressive and increasingly violent Protestant majority, the Basques against the Francoist Spanish state, Zionist terrorists against British rule and an Arab majority, Kurds against repressive Iraqi and Iranian majorities, and so forth (see Clark, Guelke, and Ashkenasi, below). The intensity of the confrontation makes for ethnic identification with and escalation of paramilitary mobilization and violence. It also generates widespread popular support and supplies the rationalization for such grisly deeds as the recent machine-gun massacre of Protestant worshipers in a church near the border by Catholic gunmen. The outrage will un-doubtedly call for, trigger, and rationalize a worse outrage by Ulster Defense Association terrorists.[54]

Unlike the terror of political groups, such as the Red Brigades, such pitched confrontations also contain the potential of a huge following on either side, mobilized by massive and indiscriminate mayhem, which may explain the proportionally far heavier toll of casualties of ethnocultural terrorism which is noted below in the conclusion[55] to this volume. To be sure, there is a strong moment of escalation also in the confrontation of left-wing and right-wing militants in France, West Germany, and Italy but, for lack of a potential mass appeal, the local population is more likely to make a common front against both violent sides than to be provoked into supporting one or the other. In Northern Ireland there were recurrent attempts to break the stran-glehold of the violent escalation by means of peace marches. The hostility to and contempt for these peace marchers shown by both sets of violent terrorists is the equivalent of the "red fascism" of the Red Brigades. Just as the "red fascists" try their best to turn their democratic state into a fascist dictatorship by committing their most horrendous acts of violence so the ethnic terrorists want to bring out the ethnically repressive and confrontational nature of their democratic state. In the early years of the new Spanish democracy, for example, when it was feared that ETA terrorist actions would trigger a right-wing military coup, such a coup was precisely what ETA wanted in order to unhinge the entire Spanish system. And Spain too had its peace marches late in 1983 when tens of thousands were demonstrating against ETA violence. Both sets of terrorists are more comfortable with a repressive, dictatorial state dominated by hostile elements than with a free and open society where pluralistic interests peacefully compromise their differences and follow the precept of live and let live.

There are parallels also in the great care taken by both political or ethnic terrorists to maximize the symbolic impact their violent actions have on the public at large. Whether it is the ETA,[56] the IRA, the Palestinians, or the Red Brigades, the violent act is always a piece of showmanship played to the theater audience of the broader public. This may seemingly reinforce the ideological content of the terrorist message but, in fact, it can have the opposite effect: It casts a lot of doubt on the authenticity of claims made, whether they be the rep-resentation of the true interest of the industrial proletariat or of the eternal soul of the Basque nation. When extreme left or right labels are added for good measure to the ethnic defense claim, moreover, it hardly makes the claim more convincing. Both political and ethnic terrorists also make heavy use of kidnappings for ransom, or bank robberies to bankroll their movements and buy weapons and shelter, and they probably divert some of these proceeds from "proletarian expropriations" into their leaders' pockets, too. As we have seen in the case of Corsica, ethnic terrorists often add to these bankrolling acts elaborate schemes for extortion against moderates or innocent bystanders. Both kinds of terrorists use mortal threats against turncoats and have been known to terrorize or betray to the police those of their recruits who get cold feet halfway through their probation period and to threaten execution for those who wish to drop out of the movement. Once a recruit has been involved in a bank holdup, kidnapping, or killing, the way back to legality is, to all intents and purposes, barred in any case, regardless of the motives that led the person into involvement with the terrorists, including ideological motives.

Progressive involvement with ethnic or ethnocultural terrorists otherwise seems to involve many of the same steps as socialization in a political terrorist group: There are profound dissociative changes, especially in conduct toward family and friends, which precede and accompany the recruitment phase, as if the ties of primary socialization were deliberately undone one by one. Full-fledged ethnic terrorists also develop an intense appreciation of their own ethnic village ways and language, not unlike the nineteenth-century Russian *narodniki*, who had an urge to "go to the people."[57] It should be noted that this seemingly ideological element of ethnocultural consciousness-raising comes not at the beginning of involvement, but later. We could, of course, argue that there is a naive ethnic identity at the outset, but its deliberate pursuit and intensification later is a different matter. Suffice it to say that an ethnocultural terrorist career does not seem to start with the ethnic liberation ideology, but may conceivably end with it. The search for ethnic identity in this context also suggests that the would-be ethnic terrorist needs to associate himself (women are rarer among the ethnic terrorists than among the RAF or Red Brigades)[58] with a "carrier public" no less than the *brigatista* needs the claim of representing the proletariat. The ethnic terrorist, whether Basque, Palestinian, or IRA, however, may then receive the enormous psychological reinforcement of real support from his fellow ethnics, and may in fact be able to go on living an intermittently normal life among them, or to disappear among them like Mao Zedong's fish in the water.[59]

ATTITUDES AND VIOLENT BEHAVIOR

In our attempts to understand politically violent behavior, extremist ideologies are only one subset among the larger universe of attitudes of violent people. Perhaps, what neofascist, "red fascist," and ethnic terrorists have in common—since it is not their ideologies, which may be shared by some nonviolent people—is simply a nasty habit of being violent about many things that annoy them. Many of the pre-1933 storm troopers of the Abel Collection, by their own admission, had substantial records of violent encounters at school with other students and with teachers, at work with fellow workers or the boss, and at home with neighbors, relatives, and especially with the police.[60] Far from the stereotype of authoritarian meekness and docility, they often were born rebels with unruly, violent tempers that had repeatedly gotten them into trouble for entirely nonpolitical reasons before they became involved in political street fighting. The Communist street fighters in Berlin in the early thirties similarly were rebellious in family, school, and at work and often had criminal records. The same may be true of many a terrorist of the groups discussed in this book, although these groups have also included individuals from notably polite and well-mannered backgrounds.[61] In highly organized, advanced urban societies, an unruly or hyperactive child will sooner or later provoke conflict with the persons around him or her and any reluctance to conform to the mores of society cannot pass without notice and censure. Given such disorderly and rebellious, perhaps even violent, propensities, however, an individual may well find a group dedicated to waging war on authority very congenial, and its belligerent, antiauthoritarian rhetoric a welcome change from being the object of constant restraints and reprimands. Such people may also readily adopt an ideology of rebellion as the common coin of a new group of terrorist friends, and they may welcome both friends and ideology as a justification of the surging hostility and violence that have already characterized crucial turning points in their lives.

Social scientists have long wrestled with the problem of relating attitudes and violent behavior and reminded us that, throughout Western industrialized societies, a quantum jump in all forms of political participation has taken place since the 1960s and 1970s, which may well explain the rise of the levels of political violence and terror as well. In national surveys, researchers have attempted to probe at least the "potential for political violence" by asking respondents whether they could imagine themselves reponding with violence to perceived injustice.[62] But while they found levels of about 4 percent expressing such a "potential," the significance of this finding to predict actual behavior seems doubtful. On the one hand, respondents given to verbal hyperbole might easily voice such "potential" in a flash of anger without ever resorting to violence. On the other hand, those actually capable of violence when feeling cornered, or when the provocation is great enough, probably exceed this percentage many times over. Opinion surveys, unless they are targeted on a group known for its

engagement in violence to begin with, are not very helpful in pin-
pointing likely violent behavior.

A more illuminating perspective can be gained from the study of
terrorists in captivity and in the light of ongoing terrorist activities.
With nearly two thousand Italian left- and right-wing terrorists in
custody and over a decade of rampant terrorist violence behind them,
it is two forensic psychiatrists from the University of Rome, Franco
Ferracuti and Francesco Bruno, who have given the most incisive
glimpses of what the personalities of Italian terrorists may be like: No
acceptable general theory in testable form has yet emerged among the
many contenders, such as the blocked expectations of youth, or frus-
tration/aggression, or the exaltation of violence in their respective
ideologies. Ferracuti and Bruno reject sweeping psychopathological
explanations, at least, of the Italian left-winger's choice to become a
terrorist, arguing that "terrorism is, by and large, a normal social
conduct within [this particular "abnormal"] subcultural value system."
The radical left subculture in Italy, they suggest, believed in a "fantasy
war" against the state which, for a decade, legitimized killing or being
killed. The large number of terrorists laying down their weapons, and
even "repenting," however, suggests that the fantasy may have an end,
or at least has limits. At the same time, Ferracuti and Bruno acknowledge that "cold, unaffective, controlled killers coexist [in these
terrorist groups] with intellectuals who organize and manage the movement, establish hierarchies, choose goals and . . . [operate] with passive followers . . . [who] may include seriously disturbed neurotics,
approaching borderline conditions."[63] The latter depend emotionally
on the group and, in this context, may be considered as engaging in
psychopathological and compensatory behavior. In recent years, as
the Red Brigades of the first generation began to attract more and
more such marginal members, including even drug addicts, the quality
of their performance began to decline steeply and they began to lose
their war against the state.

Italian right-wing terrorists, according to Ferracuti and Bruno—
and in the opinion of other observers as well—are not as well integrated into a large supportive subculture as are those of the left.
Instead, they appear to be characterized by an acute, and of course
simplistic, dichotomization of the world into enemies of a bad, even
"subhuman" sort, and heroes of exalted quality. Mentally "borderline
subjects" find it easy to identify with the "good" side, thereby com-
pensating for their own inadequacies. The right-wing terrorists—and
there were nearly five hundred in custody at the time of the report—
tended to be ambivalent toward authority, especially parental, con-
formists about standards of conventional conduct, of poor insight and
vulnerable to stress, superstitious and inclined to believe in "magic,"

given to weapons fetishism, highly destructive of others and themselves, and emotionally detached from the consequences of their
actions.[64] These characteristics may well characterize other violent
right-wingers as well. Some of them may even be found among all
kinds of violent groups, such as the ambivalence toward authority—
both in the form of parent-child conflict and of parental overprotec-
tion—a dichotomization of the world, poor insight and resistance to
stress, superstition, weapons fetish, suicidal tendencies, and emotional
detachment from what they do to their victims.

Some serious accounts and many journalistic descriptions of terrorist
deeds refer to these violent propensities as "madness" or "insanity" on
the part of the perpetrators. Other serious researchers emphatically
reject the attribution of insanity and insist instead that "most *etarras*
are . . . sane human beings" (see Clark, chap. 10). It would appear,
however, that the promotion or rejection of such an evaluation is a
pointless exercise without a definition of the word *insanity*. Nonclinical
meanings aside, most terrorists are clearly able to function, to deadly
effect, in fact, but they are hardly normal, average human beings with
normal needs and desires. Hence, calling them insane or asserting
their clinical sanity is quite beside the point. We should ascertain
instead in what way and to what degree they differ from other people
in order to explain their extreme behavior. Practically all humans at
times show a certain amount of hostility toward others, but terrorists
have probably exhibited a great deal more and, perhaps, have channeled their hatreds, in a prejudicial way against certain categories of
people, such as policemen, capitalists, certain minorities, or against
people representing the power structure of the dominant majority.
Practically all human beings may be *capable* of violence against others
when in a spontaneous rage or when cornered and frightened. But it
takes a violent person to make systematic use of illegal violence as a
political weapon or instrument of political manipulation.

To come back to the subject of violent propensities, there is also
a need to separate the politically violent from other categories of
violent people who may suffer from the same propensity but do not
usually act it out in a political way. Foremost among the latter are
violent criminals who may constitute a separate subculture of violence.[65] There have been other groups as well, including the police
and people inured to domestic violence, who may share this inclination
to violence without necessarily breaking the law.[66] This is of course
an important distinction which we should not obscure in our efforts
to discover the common behavioral sources of the propensity toward
violence. The legal violence of police and soldiers, at least, may
represent a successful effort to bank the destructive fires of aggressive
violence in socially useful ways, whereas terrorist, revolutionary, and

criminal violence is, so to speak, violence on the loose.[67] With regard to the violent individual involved, being on the loose implies in addition a heavy burden of individual moral responsibility for the consequences, whether it is acknowledged or not.

In either type of violence, however, legal or illegal, the most intriguing question has not as yet been conclusively answered: What makes for a violent personality? There are plenty of theories, to be sure, to explain the genesis of violent criminals but only a few dubious speculations about the origins of violent terrorist or revolutionary personalities. Especially the voluntary, individual engagement in violence (revolutionary and police or military violence are rarely voluntary or individual) is beckoning for further analysis. Some of the theories explaining the genesis of the violent criminal (who usually "volunteers" and is of individual motivation) may fit the terrorist as well: Terrorists too, both male and female, and ethnic as well as political, may be products of the failure of the early bonding process in male/female, family, and social roles. Ferracuti and Bruno have mentioned "disturbances in sexual identity, with role uncertainties," among their right-wing Italian terrorists.[68] The prominence of female political terrorists among the brigatisti and RAF, and of machismo patterns in some guerrilla movements has given rise to speculations about sexual role disturbances and abnormalities among some terrorists. Ten years ago at Heidelberg, a group of psychiatrists even suggested possible links between violent political activities and orgasmic release among violent groups, especially of the left. Psychoanalytical speculations about a link between fascist personalities and sexual inhibitions or fears have been around as long as Freudians and Reichians have been writing about this subject.[69] Violent people may have been mistreated as children or come from broken homes or have suffered through other forms of disturbed authority relationships with one or both parents. They may have experienced at first hand the cutting edge of social change and conflict between classes, rural-urban differences, or the erosion of communal-religious life.[70]

Having equated the genesis of the violent terrorist with that of violent but nonpolitical criminals still leaves us with the problem of explaining how the politically violent become politicized. Conceivably, a person of violent propensities could go either way, and it may be a matter of politicizing circumstances and selective recruitment that makes a person emerge as a terrorist. The evidence is confusing as to whether terrorists are more likely produced by a repressive state or by a democratic one as in the cases of pre-coup Uruguay, Italy, Japan, and West Germany. Throughout South America and the Central American republics, repressive dictatorships and unresponsive governments also generated violent counterterror. It is easy to explain political violence as a product of repression. The curious and self-contradictory mixture of terrorist attitudes toward authority further confuses the issue: On the one hand, terrorists direct their rebellion most emphatically against state and social authority in every form. On the other hand, they subject themselves by inclination to extremely authoritarian domination within their terrorist group. Their extreme longing for acceptance and belonging to their small circle makes it almost impossible for the individual terrorist to end his or her dependency on the group. In the second part of this book,[71] the very important small-group dynamics of terrorist movements will be analyzed from this perspective. It appears to be in these small fraternal group settings that the failed bonding of a terrorist's childhood is being repaired or recreated, although under circumstances that, more often than not, will lead to the ultimate self-destruction of the person involved. A terrorist career, in other words, may be nothing less than a death wish realized, perhaps a commitment to self-annihilation, in response to profound frustration and blocked opportunities.[72]

The process of politicization within the dynamics of the small, comradely group also brings us back once more to the role of ideology. Ideological indoctrination is not the only way to socialize new recruits and direct their aggressiveness toward a political target. There is also the uninhibited exaltation of violence and its "moralization," which makes it a self-actualizing value rather than just a means to an end. To the self-denigrating personality of a full-fledged terrorist, violence justifies itself and the terrorist's existence: "I kill, therefore I am." And it may actually be the ideology that becomes a mere means to an end, a way of perpetuating the group and its violent activities for the sake of the terrorist alone.

There is, perhaps, no better way to end this disquisition than by pointing to the paradox of Italian right-wing terrorist initiations in paramilitary encampments.[73] Right-wing youth is never indoctrinated in any ideology but simply trained in the use of weapons and in military operations that seem to prepare them for commando raids on who knows what enemy. They are thus inducted most directly into what Franco Ferracuti has called the "fantasy war" against the left or, for the left-wing terrorists, against the state. As soldiers under orders, the young recruits no longer need to think about the possible death or maiming of victims or innocent bystanders. As long as the subculture of the fantasy war continues—and there have been massive defections and surrenders in recent years—one cannot even consider their warlike conduct irrational or bizarre. Only the emotional detachment from the mayhem they cause, the weapons fetish of the "fantasy soldiers," and their illusionary and paranoid stereotypes remind us that there is madness in the method.

NOTES

1. In addition to the ever-increasing literature on contemporary political violence and terror, there has also been some attention to historical manifestations of it, as in *Social Protest, Violence and Terror in 19th and 20th Century Europe*, edited by Wolfgang J. Mommsen and Gerhard Hirschfeld (London: Macmillan, 1982), containing the proceedings of an international conference of the German Historical Institute of London, and in "Political Violence, the Alternative, and Probability," an article in the *Collected Seminar Papers*, no. 30, of the Institute of Commonwealth Studies of the University of London (1982), which is not limited to violence in Commonwealth countries or former crown colonies.

2. In "Political Violence, the Alternative, and Probability" (see n. 1, above), p. 1.

3. Obvious examples of such characterization are the justifications commonly given to inspire movements of national liberation, colonial revolt, or uprisings against dictatorial rule. In the late 1960s and early 1970s, moreover, it was fashionable to speak of "institutional racism" as a form of political violence against oppressed minorities which had to be countered with overt breaches of the law and, if necessary, violent defiance.

4. The difference between the minor defacing and the destroying of a public monument comes to mind here. The symbolic practices of contemporary terrorism, however, usually favor the destruction of parts of the technological basis of modern society, say power stations, over blowing up patriotic statues of historic figures, in a kind of reverse consumerism of anticonsumerist attitudes.

5. See, for example, the categories used by this writer in *Political Violence Under the Swastika: 581 Early Nazis* (Princeton, N.J.: Princeton University Press, 1975), pt. 4, chap. 4.

6. We may call this the alternative, nominalistic route toward definition, which relies on the direct identification of all politically violent phenomena by the observer rather than on first defining a quasi-Platonic "essence," or concept, of political violence. We shall continue to leave out government-ordered political violence except to distinguish it from some of the examples of anti- or nongovernmental political violence.

7. The other actions included three bomb attacks in London between October 1983 and January 1984—an explosion in an army barracks that wounded four soldiers, one that injured two people, and an unexploded bomb. Kavanagh was charged together with another Belfast man, Thomas Quigley, who was responsible for a 1981 IRA bombing campaign in London which killed three and injured thirty more. Quigley was also charged with the attempted murder of Royal Marine Commander Sir Stewart Pringle and bombing the home of Attorney General Sir Michael Havers.

8. *Sendero Luminoso* derives its name from the writings of José Carlos Mariátegui, an early twentieth-century Peruvian revolutionary writer. Under its leader, Comrade Gonzalo (Abimael Guzman), a former philosophy professor, the group considers itself the true Peruvian Communist party and aims at bringing backward Peru directly into a China-style Communist phase without its passing first through a capitalist stage of development.

9. Four days before the cease-fire, for example, newspapers reported the bombing of the U.S. embassy, the ambassador's residence, two American-sponsored cultural centers, and the Honduran airlines office in Bogotá and Cali. M-19 claimed credit for the last-mentioned of these attacks.

dst of the communist working-class districts of the city. Another
may have been the fact that the city was governed by a social-
ation that made every effort to be equally hard on the violent
the battle.

Eve Rosenhaft in Mommsen and Hirschfeld, *Social Protest*, pp.
book, *Beating the Fascists: The German Communists and Political*
Cambridge: Cambridge University Press, 1983), p. 61, chaps.
The Making of a Stormtrooper, pp. 163–175 and 239–244.
king of a Stormtrooper, pp. 230–231. Most of the storm troopers
were of the second description, men evidently attracted by
cs. Among the party members at large, however, there were
pselytizers for the cause, including large numbers with strong
but little stomach for street confrontations with communist
tical Violence Under the Swastika, pp. 503–505.

low.
cases is the current murderous split in the PLO between the
and the Syrian-backed rebels. IRA groups too have been
ther.
ah, "Learning to Support the PLO: Political Socialization
Kuwait," *Comparative Political Studies* 12 (January 1980),

slaying of three church elders and the wounding of seven
ppers was attributed to a group calling itself the Catholic
cover for the outlawed Marxist Irish National Liberation
earlier slaying of a Catholic in Armagh by a group called
believed to be a cover for the outlawed Ulster Volunteer

w.
by Robert P. Clark, "Patterns of ETA Violence, 1968–

Patterns in the Lives of ETA Members," below, chapter
imination and harassment over the use of the Basque

vation of dominant mother figures among ETA parents
ming overtones of machismo in all terrorist postures.
st side, the less extreme organizations, such as the
German "alternative scene," may also afford members
solidarity in contrast to the RAF and Red Brigades.
Stormtrooper, pp. 194–203.
tistics on juvenile delinquency, truancy, drug abuse,
which can be found in police records of known
ion of the personalities of some like the Red Brigades
ite demeanor while a student at the University of
ng of the violent career to follow.
es, Max Kaase et al., *Political Action* (Beverly Hills:
including the sources cited there, and pp. 543–
nalistic" surveys made in the early 1980s of the
mans, which yielded high percentages that were

ncesco Bruno, "Psychiatric Aspects of Terrorism
the Different, edited by I. L. Barak Glantz and
ington Books, 1981), and their paper, "A Psy-

10. *La violencia* was mostly an extension of liberal-conservative conflict in the back country and, between 1949 and 1953, killed an estimated fifty thousand of both sides in an endless series of escalating raids and retaliations.

11. The club-wielding squads of the Ayatollah, which smashed bookstores, attacked students, and closed down Iranian universities in order to stamp out secular Iranian culture, were also called *hezbollahi*, the "partisans of the party of god." See also the descriptions of life in the Moslem Brotherhood of Egypt, and of the cells (*anqud*) of gama'at el-islamiyeh, the organization that assassinated Sadat, in Mohammed Heikal's *Autumn of Fury: The Assassination of Sadat*, (New York: Random House, 1983).

12. *Washington Post National Weekly Edition* (12 March 1984), p. 17. It is not always clear when these terrorist forces are on their own and when they are clearly in the service of a government.

13. The terrorist network was discovered when an undercover informant tipped off the police about the rigging of explosive devices on five Palestinian-owned buses. The subsequent arrests for the time being forestalled the usual tit-for-tat bombings and assassinations on both sides.

14. The concessions involved protection of the sanctity of their holy city, Amritsar, and making Chandigarh the Punjab capital rather than the capital of Punjab and neighboring Hariyana.

15. After the assault on the Golden Temple, in fact, an estimated two thousand Sikh soldiers mutinied, commandeered trucks, and headed for Amritsar, but after bloody clashes the army soon restored control.

16. In 1971 the French government proposed a major development plan stressing agriculture, tourism, and the development of the coastal regions rather than of the interior. Corsicans also resent their low wages, high unemployment, and the presence of a garrison of the French foreign legion on their soil.

17. The cause of the confrontation was the dumping of titanium dioxide by the Italian Montedison concern off the coast of Corsica. When the French and Italian governments proved slow in responding to Corsican complaints, the ARC took matters into their own hands.

18. There are now also French nationalist groups on Corsica that oppose the UPC and the FLNC, including the violent Francia, which has carried out attacks on the UPC and FLNC and is suspected by the latter of being a tool of the French government. Corsican nationalists also complain that the police and the courts treat violent French nationalists far more leniently than they do violent Corsican nationalists. See especially Robert Ramsay, *The Corsican Time Bomb* (London: Butler and Tanner, 1983).

19. See J. Bowyer Bell, *Transnational Terror* (Washington, D.C.: American Enterprise Institute, 1975).

20. Ibid., pp. 16–19. The subcategories of revolutionary terror are "organized terror" for internal discipline in the group, "allegiance terror" addressed to the masses, "functional," "provocative," "manipulative," and "symbolic terror."

21. See Paul Wilkinson, *Terrorism and the Liberal State* (New York: New York University Press, 1979), p. 48.

22. See Brian Jenkins, *International Terrorism: A New Mode of Conflict* (Los Angeles, Crescent Publications, 1975), p. 1. The effect is not limited and sometimes not even meant for the actual vicitms, but for the wider public audience that may become alarmed and perhaps begin to pressure government, the most likely addressee, to give in to the demands of the terrorists.

23. See also Bruce Hoffman, *Rightwing Terrorism in Europe* (Santa Monica, Calif.: Rand Corporation, 1982), pp. vi–vii, and 13.

24. They are, of course, a self-selected group of persons prepared for dealing out violence, but so are police and military volunteers whose frequent traumas after shootings and wars are familiar to everyone.

25. Extremist organizations, while often capable of changing the perceptions of the public overnight, find it very difficult to maintain their gains. They tend to get caught or they disband and are quickly forgotten.

26. The purpose of such qualitative tabulation on an arbitrary selection of cases is clearly not to make claims of statistical representativeness. Rather, it is a heuristic, model-building device of great flexibility, which can reveal dominant or plausible patterns and, by implication, generate hypotheses about the relationships among the variables chosen. The choice of variables, however, may be its most vulnerable aspect.

27. See, for example, Robert P. Clark, *The Basques: The Franco Years and Beyond* (Reno: University of Nevada Press, 1979), chap. 10; and C. C. Menges, "Soviet Manipulation: Behind Basque Terrorism," *New Leader* 62 (19 November 1979), as well as the occasional press interviews given by ETA spokesmen in Europe, for example to *Der Spiegel* in 1982.

28. From "Self-inflicted Wound: Intercommunal Violence in Ceylon, 1958" by James Manor in *Collected Seminar Papers*, no. 30, p. 15.

29. On equality, see also Ted Honderich, *Violence for Equality: Inquiries in Political Philosophy* (Harmondsworth: Penguin, 1980) and, on relative deprivation, Ted Gurr, *Why Men Rebel* (Princeton, N.J.: Princeton University Press, 1970), and some of the contributions to *Handbook of Political Conflict* (New York: Free Press, 1981), edited by Gurr, especially the contribution by Harry Eckstein, pp. 135–166.

30. Marx's analysis of the mid-nineteenth-century upheaval in France and Germany proceeded from broader economic and class struggle models to the political dynamics of the 1848 revolutions and their aftermath, suggesting among other things stages of progression and regression. See his "Class Struggles in France, 1848–1852," "The 18th Brumaire of Louis Bonaparte," "Germany: Revolution and Counter-revolution," and "The Civil War in France."

31. See also Anthony Burton's introduction to his reader, *Revolutionary Violence: The Theories* (New York, 1978), and several of the essays in *International Terrorism in the Contemporary World*, Marius H. Livingston, ed. (Westport, Conn.: Greenwood Press, 1978). See also the summary in *The Politics of Violence: Revolution in the Modern World*, Carl Leyden and Karl M. Schmitt, eds. (Englewood Cliffs, N.J.: Prentice-Hall, 1968), chaps. 2 and 3; Paul Wilkinson, *Terrorism and the Liberal State* (London, 1977), and Albert Parry, *Terrorism: From Robespierre to Arafat* (New York, Vanguard Press, 1976).

32. But see, for example, Seweryn Bialer, ed., *Radicalism in the Contemporary Age* (Boulder, Colo.: Westview Press, 1977), and Brian Jenkins in the issue on international terrorism, edited by Marvin Wolfgang, in the *Annals of the American Academy of Political and Social Science*, 463 (September 1982), 16–18.

33. To aggravate the danger of bias further, the active recruitment of children as young as eight or ten years, and of women, by the IRA or Palestinian militants makes it even more difficult to separate the impact of violence as a cause from recruitment propaganda and the rationalizations of the recruits about far more complex processes of deciding to join the militant groups.

34. See the approach used in this writer's *Political Violence Under the Swastika: 581 Early Nazis* (Princeton, N.J.: Princeton University Press, 1975), parts III–4, IV, and V, and *The Making of a Stormtrooper* (Princeton University Press, 1980), chaps. 4 and 5. See also Egon Bittner, "Radicalism and the Organization of Radical Movements," *American Sociological Review* 28 (1963), 928–940.

35. See *The Rebellious Ce* 1975) and Charles Tilly and Cambridge University Pres

36. See especially the and the work of Ivo and Haas. Fred R. von der M N.J.: Prentice-Hall, 197 different nations. Harr performance and stabili war" and civil disturba

37. See Gerhard especially chap. 4. A chap. 3; and M. Cl *Assassination* (Engle

38. See, for ex N.J.: Princeton U and A. Storr to L tones. Also Wilk

39. See espe *Analysis* (Engle Psycho-social *A* Origins of Vio *Interdisciplinar* York: John J

40. See University and conser possible tr

41. T as in th by junic there, on the pp. 31

42 viole to tl seri to

troopers into the m unique circumstance democratic administ men of both sides of

49. See especially 342–366 and now he *Violence, 1929–1933* 5 and 6. Also Merkl,

50. Merkl, *The Ma* of the Abel Collection the violence and hero more ideologues and p anti-Semitic prejudices toughs. See also my *Pol*

51. See chap. 11, be

52. One of the rare loyalists of Yasser Arafat known to go after each o

53. See Tawfic E. Fa of Palestinian Children in 470–484.

54. The machine-gun other hymn-singing worshi Reaction Force, probably a Army, in retaliation for the the Protestant Action Force Force (UVF).

55. See conclusion, belo

56. See chapter 4, below 1980."

57. See especially Clark, 10, where experiences of disc language are discussed.

58. Nevertheless, the obse is intriguing amid the overwhe

59. On the political terror Italian *Autonomia* or the West a modicum of social support and

60. Merkl, *The Making of a*

61. We have not seen any sta or other nonpolitical activities, terrorists, but there has been men leader Renato Curcio, whose po Trento apparently gave little inkl

62. See especially Samuel Barr Sage, 1979), chap. 5 and p. 397 550. There were also rather "jou "violence potential" of young Ger subsequently questioned.

63. See Franco Ferracuti and Fr in Italy," in *The Mad, the Bad, and* C. R. Huff (Lexington, Mass.: Lex

chiatric Comparative Analysis of Left and Rightwing Terrorism in Italy," delivered at the 1983 meeting of the International Society for Political Psychology in Oxford.

64. Ferracuti and Bruno, "A Psychiatric Comparative Analysis." This has also been confirmed in interviews by this writer with other Italian social scientists such as S. S. Acquaviva of the University of Padua.

65. See, for example, Marvin E. Wolfgang and Neil A. Weiner, eds., *Criminal Violence* (Beverly Hills, Calif.: Sage, 1982) and Wolfgang and Franco Ferracuti, *The Subculture of Violence* (republished Beverly Hills: Sage, 1982; original edition London: Tavistock, 1967).

66. Legality is of course not always in conformity with morality. See also the essays in *Violence in America: Historical and Comparative Perspectives*, rev. ed., Hugh D. Graham and Ted R. Gurr, eds. (Beverly Hills, Calif.: Sage, 1979).

67. But see also the argument presented by Austin T. Turk in "Social Dynamics of Terrorism," in the issue on international terrorism of the *Annals of the American Academy of Political and Social Science*, 463 (September 1982), 119–140 and in Turk's *Political Criminality: The Defiance and Defense of Authority* (Beverly Hills, Calif.: Sage, 1982).

68. See Ferracuti and Bruno, "A Psychiatric Comparative Analysis."

69. See Wilhelm Reich, *The Mass Psychology of Fascism* (New York: Farrar, Straus & Giroux, 1969; earlier translation 1946).

70. See also the chapters by Gianfranco Pasquino, Leonard Weinberg, and Klaus Wasmund, below. This writer's *Political Violence Under the Swastika: 581 Early Nazis* also contains considerable evidence that many early Nazis came either from marriages between a bourgeois and a proletarian parent or from other pressure points in a rapidly changing class society (pp. 38–48).

71. See especially the chapters by Pasquino and Weinberg, but also chap. 9 by Waldmann and chap. 10 by Clark, below.

72. The rising expectations of Italian youth, according to Franco Ferracuti, have been blocked by unemployment, social disorganization, drugs, and despair, and the unresponsiveness of the democratic state, which has failed to open up paths for the future.

73. See especially Weinberg's essay, chap. 5, below. But such encampments among the militant right and sometimes the left exist also in some form in West Germany, the United States, among Palestinians, and in several other countries.

2

Julius Evola and the Ideological Origins of the Radical Right in Contemporary Italy

RICHARD H. DRAKE

———

The radical left has appeared to dominate Italian politics to such an extent in the last ten years or so that it is easy to overlook the importance if not the existence of the radical right. Difficulty surrounds any attempt to define or to quantify these extremes in Italian political life but, generally speaking, they are represented by the extraparliamentary groups to the left of the Communist party (PCI) and to the right of the Movimento Sociale Italiano (MSI). The true relationships of the PCI and the MSI to the left and to the right extremists are matters of conjecture; both parties, however, repudiate the means of the extremists, if not necessarily their ends.[1] The PCI's Enrico Berlinguer has taken a forthright stand against extremism, and Giorgio Almirante, the leader of the MSI, has been no less outspoken against the violent fanatics to the right of his own extremely reactionary movement.[2]

Conversely, the extraparliamentary groups repudiate the PCI and the MSI. For instance, it is well known that Antonio Negri, the leader of the extraparliamentary left Autonomia Operaia movement, has dismissed the PCI as "a dead loss," hopelessly corrupted by reformism and completely unsympathetic to the essence of Marxism, that is, the violent overthrow of capitalism.[3] Similarly, right-wing extremists, such as Adriano Romualdi, have condemned the MSI as a retrograde party, unequal to the political tasks facing Italy: the containment of the communist menace and the restoration of a sense of destiny in Italian life.[4] In other words, just as the Red Brigades wave of political terrorism, now apparently ebbing in Italy, has been a consequence of left-wing disenchantment with PCI reformism, so recent Italian terrorism of the right has resulted from the radical neofascist rejection of the MSI's parliamentary strategy.[5]

Intellectuals have played leading roles in both of these extremist movements: the ideas of Antonio Negri have served the theoretical purposes of the Red Brigades, and Julius Evola—the source of Romualdi's diatribe—has been the guru of the extraparliamentary right.[6] The intellectuals are, in Antonio Gramsci's words, "the specialized representatives and standard-bearers of society," that is, they articulate the political and cultural aspirations of certain groups in society and, to some extent, influence them.[7] When these groups belong to what Arno Mayer calls the "crisis strata" of society, the function of ideology becomes a crucial part of the revolutionary process, whether on the left or on the right.[8] Tocqueville illustrated this point in *The Old Régime and the French Revolution:* "the vapourings of the *littérateurs,*" he noted, had created the essential preconditions for the events of 1789 by undermining respect for traditional values and customs or, in the idiom of Gramsci, by furnishing the shock troops for the assault of an enlightened "counterhegemony" against the Bourbon "hegemony" of Crown and Altar.[9]

My thesis on the general subject of Italian terrorism is that left- and right-wing intellectuals are performing a function analogous to the one Tocqueville described in *The Old Régime and the French Revolution.* I intend here to discuss my thesis as it affects right-wing terrorism, specifically how the paramount Italian thinker of the extreme right—Julius Evola—developed ideologically in response to certain definite political, social, and psychological realities in twentieth-century Italy. His ideology continues to exist as a basis for the rationale of right-wing terrorism, but, in keeping with our dangerous ignorance about the radical right in general, Evola's particular place in the spectrum of reactionary thought has not been the subject of systematic inquiries. The hegemony of Christian Democratic Italy, to borrow once again from Gramscian theory, is under attack by Marxist intellectuals who have developed an ideological counterhegemony which the political agents of the left seek to realize in fact. This attack is well known to political analysts and increasingly understood by the general public. It is just the opposite with the counterhegemony of the right, which opposes the Christian Democratic center and the Marxist left. The ideological basis of the right's counterhegemony is my subject, and because Evola remains the single most creative and influential thinker in this tradition I will focus my attention on him.

Evola was born in 1898, the scion of an aristocratic Roman family. A brilliant student with a critically recognized talent for art, the young baron fought as an artillery officer in World War I and then became the leading representative in Italy of the Dada movement in art and literature.[10] Even before the war he had been drawn to the Italian literary avant-garde, then under the high-spirited direction of Giovanni Papini and Giuseppe Prezzolini, and to F. T. Marinetti's Futurist movement in art.[11] Evola ultimately found the Futurist aesthetic "too loud and showy," but the Dada movement of Tristan Tzara and Andrè Breton suited his artistic sensibilities perfectly.[12] After the war he plunged into a whirl of Dada activities: reading his extremely avant-garde poetry—to the accompaniment of music by Schönberg, Satie, and Bartok—in the Cabaret Grotte dell' Augusteo, which was Italy's version of Zurich's Cabaret Voltaire, the birthplace of Dadaism; exhibiting his Dada paintings in Rome's Galleria Bragaglia as well as in Milan, Lausanne, and Berlin; and collaborating on the Dada journal, *Revue Bleu.*[13]

His avant-garde notoriety after World War I has caused many of his contemporary admirers to conclude that Evola went through a decadent period before discovering his true conservative voice, but he always resisted this interpretation of his early life. Visitors to his Roman *palazzo* home on Corso Vittorio Emanuele could hardly fail to notice the numerous Dada paintings always on display, and Evola strongly insisted in his autobiography that Dadaism could not be dismissed as a "sin of my youth."[14] The Dada movement, Evola recalled, spearheaded a frontal attack on the rationalist cultural values of the bourgeoisie, always the true enemy of conservative elites.[15] The Dadaists intended to excise all passé art forms, and in 1920 this meant the Victorian-Edwardian residue of middle-class culture and morality. Only with such an excision would a new and better world be possible. For Evola, then, Dada was not art, but the dissolution of art as a preparatory stage for "a superior state of liberty."[16]

Evola, recognizing that avant-garde art was rapidly becoming undermined by commercialism and hardened into an academic convention, anticipated Marcel Duchamps's extreme Dada gesture and, in 1922, gave up painting completely. At the same time he followed the example of Rimbaud and renounced poetry as well. Evola then began those "trans-rational" philosophic studies that would occupy him for the rest of the 1920s: *Saggi sull'idealismo magico* appeared in 1925, *L'individuo e il divenire del mondo* and *L'uomo come potenza* in 1926, *Teoria dell'individuo assoluto* in 1927, and *Fenomenologia dell'individuo assoluto* in 1930. All purported to defend philosophical idealism, which in Evola's parlance meant that "the world is my representation," or "the ability to be unconditionally whatever one wants."[17] In practical terms these ideas signified that the limits of the "real" world were self-imposed and could be eliminated easily by the "absolute individual" who had achieved complete control over himself through wisdom.[18] Hegelian and Schopenhauerian concepts made a deep impression on him, and Evola concluded that through a hierarchy of stages a society of absolute individuals could achieve unity with the One, that is, "the ultimate synthesis" or "the perfection of perfection."[19]

Evola's shift from painting and poetry to philosophy suggests something of the restlessness that characterized the "lost" generation of 1914.[20] Like so many other artists and intellectuals of the postwar period, Evola failed to adjust to civilian life, and his artistic-intellectual career during the 1920s may be summarized as a series of experiments in what he called "transcendence." He rejected the same bourgeois social and cultural values that had alienated Robert Graves, John Dos Passos, Ernst Jünger, and Julien Benda—only in Evola's case this alienation assumed a totally uncompromising form. His postwar quest for a personal philosophy of transcendence led him to Oriental studies, and he became a student of magic, the occult, alchemy, and Eastern religions.[21] In 1927 Evola founded the "Gruppo di Ur," an association of Italian intellectuals who wanted to treat "the esoteric and initiate disciplines with seriousness and rigor."[22] His three-year affiliation with this highly unconventional *cénacle* of spiritualists gave him a lifelong reputation for eccentricity.

At just about this time he had a fateful encounter with the work of a French Orientalist named René Guénon (1886–1951) whose *La Crise du Monde Moderne* (1927) inspired Evola to organize his fragmentary and increasingly dyspeptic thoughts around a central concept, the critique of modernity.[23] He called Guénon "the Descartes of esoteric studies" and "the true master of modern times."[24] Certainly, the Frenchman's aggressively antimodern philosophy was the point of departure for *La rivolta contro il mondo moderno* (1934), Evola's most important book. This last fact did not prevent Evola from suffering the worst possible fate for any writer: neglect.[25] As a belated compensation, *La rivolta* eventually became and remains a cult book on the extreme right—not only for Italian reactionaries but, in translation, for their political counterparts nearly everywhere in Europe.

Evola wanted to explain "the decadent nature of the modern world," with decadence understood as a decline in spiritual values and a corresponding rise in materialism.[26] Where did this decadence begin? he asked. Evola pointed accusingly at the intellectuals—first in the Greece and Rome of antiquity—who, by their relentless questioning, had brought about the decline of traditional values. However, the massive disorientation of the West, Evola asserted, resulted mainly from the Humanist movement, the Renaissance, and the Protestant

Reformation.[27] Renaissance anthropomorphism signaled the demise of organic medieval society, and Western man has been trapped in a modern version of Plato's cave of shadows ever since.[28] According to Evola, the Enlightenment had vastly augmented the triumph of liberal humanism, and the whole sorry process had achieved an apotheosis with the French Revolution: democracy, socialism, and communism had become inevitable after that, and with them the eclipse of order, culture, and tradition. World War I, the Russian Revolution, and World War II were merely addenda to the disaster of 1789, but by 1945, he pointed out in a later edition of the book, it could be said that modernity had eliminated Europe "as a subject of great world politics."[29]

Italy had the contemptible distinction of inaugurating this decadent dialectic. Even before the Humanist movement and the Renaissance, medieval communes had sabotaged the idea and then the physical existence of the Ghibelline Empire. Evola deeply admired Frederick I who had affirmed "the supranational and sacred principle" of empire against the anarchy of the communes.[30] Far from celebrating the patriotic legend of the communes, Evola denigrated it, insisting that Werner Sombart was right to call Florence "the New York of the Middle Ages."[31] For Evola the rising of the communes had been essentially a movement of the Third Estate and therefore a preview of the French Revolution. More immediately and in strictly Italian terms the revolt against the empire plunged Italy into a long night of chaos, civil war, and regionalism at the expense of organic unity. While Spain, England, and France emerged from the Middle Ages under the guidance of strong national monarchies, Italy tore itself apart during the reign of the *signorie* and of a cynical, opportunistic Church.[32] The subjugation of the peninsula by foreigners irrepressibly followed, and when, after four centuries, national unification did occur, it came about as a conquest by Piedmont, not from any desire on the part of the Italian people. Now, seventy-five years later, Italy was still struggling to establish a true polity.

The victim of the historical process by which Europe, under Italy's lead, had modernized itself was the world of Tradition. Evola thought of this world in essentially Platonic and Nietzschean terms of transcendence. Claiming the authority of these thinkers, he asserted that "progress" is powerless to change certain fundamental truths about men and society, especially the need for hierarchy, caste, monarchy, race, myth, religion, and ritual—categories subsumed in *La rivolta contro il mondo moderno* under the rubric, *viriltà spirituale*. To lose this spiritual virility was to become incapable of generating true order; hence the retreat of modern man from cosmos to chaos. Evola cited Toynbee with approval: when the spiritual center is no more, civilization begins to disintegrate, and by 1934 the disintegration of Europe had proceeded very far, with Russia and the United States menacingly poised on its flanks.[33]

The obvious question here is, did Evola view fascism as a cure for the ailments caused by American capitalism and Soviet communism? Up to a point he did. At about the time that *La rivolta contro il mondo moderno* appeared, Evola began his collaboration with Roberto Farinacci's radical fascist Cremonese newspaper, *Regime fascista*. He edited a page entitled "Diorama filosofico" where some of the most important thinkers on the international right discussed problems of fascist philosophy. Included among the contributors were Paul Valéry, Gottfried Benn, Gonzague De Reynold, Sir Charles Petrie, Prince Karl Anton Rohan, Othmar Spann, Edmund Dodsworth, Friedrich Everling, and Albrecht Erich Günther.[34] René Guénon authorized the translation of his essays and of passages from his books for publication as articles in *Regime fascista,* and Farinacci himself set the tone for Evola's third-page section of the newspaper by writing the first "Diorama" piece, "Formare l'Italiano Nuovo," in which he called upon fascist intellectuals to consecrate their work to "a new classical mission."[35] Evola's own contributions to this page often stressed the need for a more aggressive, imperialistic foreign policy; for example, on the eve of the Ethiopian war he counseled Mussolini to transform Italy into a "warrior nation," one that would appreciate and admire "the sacred valor of war."[36]

Even earlier, in 1930, Evola had founded the fortnightly review *Torre* to give voice to an authentic, elitist conservatism in opposition to what he denounced as the demagogic tendencies rising to the surface of official fascism. "We would like," he wrote in a *Torre* editorial, "a fascism more radical, more intrepid, a truly absolute fascism, made of pure force, inaccessible to any compromise."[37] These views endeared him to the reactionary Farinacci, but not to the considerably more pragmatic Mussolini, whose censors, according to Evola, ruthlessly suppressed the journal and subjected its staff to a campaign of character assassination. For months Evola felt compelled to maintain a group of bodyguards, made up of like-minded radical fascists. The journal died out after five months and ten numbers, the last one published on 15 June 1930. Italian fascism, it seems, had as little tolerance for opposition on the right as on the left, but with Farinacci's protection Evola resurrected the *Torre* idea in *Regime fascista.*

The fanatically anti-Semitic editor of *Vita italiana,* Giovanni Preziosi, who had deeply admired the *Torre* experiment, introduced Evola to Farinacci, the fascist chief of Cremona and, after 1933, the cynosure in Italy for pro-Nazi sentiment.[38] Evola became the editor's candidate to succeed Giovanni Gentile as the philosopher of true fascism.[39] The succession never took place, but Evola's relationship with *Regime fascista* lasted until the fall of fascism in July 1943. On the day that Italy formally defected from her alliance with Germany, 8 September 1943, Evola was in Berlin, and he thereafter became actively involved in the creation of the fascist Republic of Salò. Indeed, he was among the first to see Mussolini after the dictator's liberation from prison by Otto Skorzeny. However, his aristocratic sensibilities were injured by the ostentatious efforts of Mussolini's new government to soil fascism with the catchwords of democracy and socialism, as interpreted by the highly inconsistent intellect of yet another socialist turned fascist, Nicola Bombacci.[40] The Congress of Verona, where the ideological patchwork of fascism in extremis took place, elicited Evola's stern disapproval, and yet he had to admire "the combattant and legionary side of Salò, the decision of thousands of Italians to remain faithful to [their] ally and to continue the war."[41] He observed that "in the history of post-Roman Italy such a phenomenon was nearly unheard of."[42]

Since the mid-1930s Evola had nevertheless felt that his "natural environment" was in Germany. His books had enjoyed a *succès d'estime* among right-wing German intellectuals, and after 1934, when Evola lectured at the University of Berlin and the city's Herrenklub, he became an increasingly admired and sought-after speaker in those circles. According to him, fascism had attained its most sublime form in Germany because the country's traditional thinkers, such as Arthur Moeller van den Bruck, Ernst Jünger, and Gottfried Benn had been taken seriously by the National Socialist regime. His admiration for Hitler far surpassed any that he ever expressed for Mussolini. The contrast, he thought, between Hitler's SS and the Moschettieri di Mussolini (Musketeers of Mussolini) was or should be a source of acute embarrassment for every virile Italian. What Evola liked most about Nazi Germany was the "attempt to create a kind of new political-military Order with precise qualifications of race," and he longed for an elite organization in Rome comparable to Berlin's Herrenklub.[43]

Returning to Rome with Farinacci on 18 September 1943, Evola began to organize a group called the Movimento per la Rinascita dell'Italia, a forerunner of the radical right-wing groups that would proliferate in Italy after World War II.[44] Rome fell to the Allies in June 1944, however, and he fled to Vienna where, in his own words, "I sought to work in a mode analogous to that in Rome," that is, by continuing to participate in the Nazi struggle against the forces of bourgeois capitalism and Bolshevik communism.[45] During an aerial bombardment of Vienna he suffered a crippling injury, and medical problems resulting from this wound forced him to remain in Austria until after the war was over.

Despite his passionate involvement in various fascist causes, Evola always refused to join the Fascist party.[46] Membership in the party no doubt would have advanced his career, but for reasons clearly set forth in *Il fascismo: saggio di una analisi critica dal punto di vista della destra* (1970) Evola thought that fascism was at best a halfway house on the road to a genuine state.[47] For the sake of clarity it might be best to describe first what Evola found attractive in fascism and then what he found wanting in it.

Evola declared that the greatest merit of fascism was "to have realized in Italy the idea of a State, to have created the bases for an energetic government."[48] The fascist motto, "Everything in the State, nothing outside the State, nothing against the State," met with his enthusiastic approval. Man must belong to a traditional, organic, and hierarchical order, he pontificated. According to him, Mussolini promised such an order and seemed to be working towards its realization; at least *il duce* did get rid of "the *partitocrazia*" of democratic regimes and parliamentary reform.[49] Certainly, Evola continued, fascist corporativism represented a vast improvement over the chaos of laissez-faire capitalism and the regimentation of Soviet Marxism. He could therefore write that whatever flaws may have existed in fascist corporativism, "the direction . . . can be considered as substantially positive."[50] Moreover, Mussolini had persevered heroically in his efforts to instill discipline in the Italian people—"discipline and the love of discipline"—in order to avoid "the perils of the bourgeois spirit."[51] The glory of fascism, Evola believed, lay in its generation-long war against the "bourgeois race" on behalf of Roman ideals, and as late as 1941 he still was hoping that the process of *fascistizzazione* would correct the manifold defects of the Italian people.[52] Even after 1945 Evola maintained that in *theory* "fascist reforms presented a rational and plausible character."[53]

He lamented, however, that *fascismo reale* fell tragically short of these theoretical goals.[54] The regime did not succeed in creating a traditional state, and in fact did everything possible to minimize the roles of the monarchy and the aristocracy. Evola insisted that Mussolini should have been Vittorio Emmanuele III's "loyal counselor," not the king's rival for power.[55] The fascist party itself should have been disbanded in 1922, when Mussolini took office, and have become one with the state instead of continuing to function as a parallel state.[56] Not only did the party remain in existence but it also became a mass organization and increasingly demagogic. The cult of the Duce offended Evola, and he observed that the longer the party held power the more fatuous its slogans became; for example, "the Duce is always right" appealed to the lowest common denominator in Italian society, not to the elite where fascism should have aimed its message.

In addition, fascism compromised itself in an entente with the Catholic church. In 1928 Evola had declared: "The identification of *our* tradition with the Christian and Catholic Church is the *most absurd of all errors.*"[57] The Lateran Accords of the next year confirmed his worst fears about fascism, and he called it a "laughable revolution."[58] Most damaging of all to fascism from Evola's point of view was "a heavy bureaucratic centralism," characterized by extreme inefficiency and venality. The regime simply did not produce "a sufficient number of men who were equal to certain high exigencies . . . and capable of promoting the development of the positive potentialities . . . contained in the system."[59] In other words, Mussolini had promised the right things, but had only managed to make a start on delivering a few of them when the calamitous finale of World War II overtook him.[60]

Because Evola influenced the regime's racial laws directly, he felt obliged in *Il fascismo* to comment on his reputation as a racist. As early as 1935 Mussolini had enthusiastically noted Evola's articles on race, beginning with "Razza e cultura" in *Rassegna italiana*. When Mussolini read his book-length treatise on the subject, *Sintesi di dottrina della razza* (1941), the duce was so favorably impressed by it that a subsequent printing carried the title, *Sintesi di dottrina fascista della razza.*[61] The two men at last met in September 1941, and Mussolini promised to support Evola's projected Italian-German journal, *Sangue e spirito*. By then, however, the Italian dictator was already caught in a vortex of defeats that would smash his regime and leave fascism hardly more than a phantom of its former self. *Sangue e spirito* never appeared.

Evola wrote *Sintesi di dottrina della razza* with two fundamental problems in mind: the Jews and Ethiopia. While not an anti-Semite in the formal sense of the term, Evola did loathe Jews.[62] The distinction in his thought between anti-Semitism and anti-Jewishness is worth noting: he had a horror of the "corrosive irony" in Jewish culture and bewailed its effect on Europe; however, he did not then leap to the main anti-Semitic position, that Jews are responsible for what is wrong with the world.[63] Evola believed that there would always be a problem with the Jews as long as they retained a preponderance out of all proportion to their numbers in the political, economic, and intellectual life of the West.[64] Moreover, Jewish intellectuals had played a large part in demolishing the foundations of Europe's traditional culture, and Evola did not choose his words carefully in condemning them for this.[65]

Although Evola concurred with the anti-Semites on their assertion concerning the strongly marked Jewish tendency to denigrate lofty ideals by ascribing every human activity to economic and sexual mo-

tives, à la Marx and Freud—the two archetypal Jewish intellectuals—
he nevertheless charged that Hitler's theories about Jews, inspired by
gross misconceptions of history, amounted to a "demagogic aberra-
tion."[66] In his judgment Nazi musings on the race question never rose
above a low level of polemicism and expediency. The Nazis were right,
Evola thought, in claiming that through a combination of money and
guile the Jews worked to subvert Aryan spirituality, but he rejected
the conspiracy theory for this subversion.[67] He contended that the
Jews, especially now that Judaism had degenerated into a secular ethic
of professional advancement and mammonism, felt both envy and
hatred for the Aryan ideals of faith, loyalty, courage, devotion, and
constancy; however, this feeling, he believed, was an instinctual reaction, that is, they compulsively "poison, soil, and debase all that is
held to be high and noble" (per la sua stessa natura, cioè senza pro-
priamente volerlo).[68] Certainly the Jews had risen to lofty heights of
power and influence in the modern world, but for Evola this was merely
a symptom of modern decadence, not its essence, as Nazi anti-Semites
claimed. The real problem, as he had written earlier in La rivolta contro
il mondo moderno, began with the rise of rationalism, first in Antiquity
and then, more tragically, in the Renaissance: Humanists and Protestants had dramatically accelerated the historical process of which
Jews had merely taken advantage. For Evola the Jewish problem was
just one element in a much larger phenomenon.[69]

Leaving aside Hitler's paranoia on the question of the Jews, Evola
insisted in Sintesi di dottrina della razza that racism could have positive
results, if the concept were interpreted primarily in Nietzschean terms
of spirit rather than in biological terms of blood. For example, Ary-
anism, like Semitism, was not a race, as the Germans untenably
claimed, but an attitude, an idea, a vision of the world.[70] Evola did
not doubt that there were inferior peoples, and his remarks about the
Ethiopians, lately terrorized into colonial subjection by Mussolini's
legions, revealed how fully he shared the vision of fascist imperialism.
The most elementary powers of observation, he wrote, should con-
vince any honest person that some races possessed a "dominant" character while others were intended by Nature to be slaves. The principles
of social Darwinism, updated and streamlined by fascism, should therefore be applied to all areas of what would later be called the Third
World. Although biology did, in fact, matter to Evola, his precise
position was that race must not be understood solely as a biological
condition; it was a spiritual condition as well.[71] Like Evola, Mussolini
worried about the problem of race-mixing in Ethiopia, but the dictator's main racial preoccupation from 1921 on was to create "a new
type of Italian," that is, to introduce a higher civic consciousness in
the Italian people and thereby create a new breed of man in Italy.[72]

Evola's achievement in his writings on racism was to have provided Mussolini with a theory of "Nordic *Romanità*," which the duce was then to have used selectively for his own ends.[73]

Another point must be added, then, to Evola's list of positive fascist features—the regime's attempt to create a race imbued with "a traditional and antimaterialistic conception of human nature."[74] As so often happened with Italian fascism, however, theory did not presage practice, and he complained that nowhere did Mussolini fail more conspicuously than in his attempt to improve the race. He doubtlessly would have agreed with Hindenburg's remark, that Mussolini would never be able to make anything but Italians of Italians.[75] Evola theorized that in Italy Nordic elements coexisted in perpetual anarchy with Africo-Mediterranean elements, and for him this complete absence of psychic equilibrium was the key to understanding the complex, creative, and infuriating history of the Italian people.[76]

Evola concluded his analysis of racism in fascist Italy by affirming, "it was not fascism that acted negatively on the Italian people, on the 'Italian race,' but vice-versa: it was the people, this 'race' that acted negatively on fascism."[77] For Evola the betrayal of Mussolini on 25 July 1943 by the Fascist Grand Council and then the horrible confusion of the country, culminating in a desolating civil war between the communist partisans and the fascist loyalists, "fully revealed the inconsistent and damaged human component [that] had been hidden behind the façade of fascism."[78] How utterly unlike the Germans, who because of their "love for discipline" fought on "until the end without a lament and without a rebellion," he caustically remarked.[79] Croce had been right about fascism: it was a "parenthesis" in Italian life but, Evola believed, a "heroic" one for all its shortcomings.

Evola regarded the Allied liberation of Italy as an unmitigated disaster because it meant that the country had fallen again into the mainstream of liberal development, and yet at the same time he was pleasantly surprised, upon returning home, to find so many young people interested in him and in his books.[80] This belated recognition should not have been completely surprising to him, however. As Mario Tedeschi noted in his memoir, *Fascisti dopo Mussolini*, the very completeness of official fascism's failure opened the door wide for right-wingers whose reputations had not been ruined during the war.[81] By this standard the noncommittal and elusive Evola was perfectly situated to play an important role in the postwar intellectual and political life of the extreme right.

Although he shared the antiliberal and anticommunist resentments of Guglielmo Giannini's ephemeral right-wing Uomo qualunque (Common Man) party in the years immediately following the war, Evola continued to reject party labels.[82] This rejection even applied to the extreme right-wing Movimento Sociale Italiano, with its symbol of a flaming tricolor above Mussolini's funeral bier, founded on 26 December 1946 by ex-fascists who had been active in the Republic of Salò, typically at the second and third echelons.[83] For the most radical of the *missini* leaders the resolutely antiparty Evola existed as an oracle. Giorgio Almirante hailed him as "our Marcuse—only better."[84] Pino Rauti, the leader of the *evoliani* in the MSI, exalted Evola as the paramount intellect of the age and based much of his own writing on *La rivolta contro il mondo moderno.*[85]

Through articles in the MSI's leading newspaper in the late 1940s, *La rivolta ideale,* and other party publications, Evola goaded the missini in the same way that he had the fascists, always toward a more reactionary theoretical position.[86] On 1 June 1951 the government arrested him, along with twenty other neofascists, for trying to revive the Fascist party. Their sensational trial, described by Evola as "a comic episode," lasted from June to November 1951, and in the end they all received either light or suspended sentences.[87] Evola for his part had little trouble proving that he had never belonged to the Fascist party or to any neofascist organizations, and the government case against him came to nothing.[88]

He continued to agitate for radical right-wing causes, and in 1956 Rauti's founding of Ordine Nuovo, whose members had been repelled by the increasingly moderate line of the MSI, came about as a result of Evola's inspiration and was modeled on the Nouvel Ordre Européen.[89] Ordine Nuovo was not without precedent in Italy's postwar politics. For example, Fasci di Azione Rivoluzionaria (FAR), founded in September 1946, was a violent shadow organization of the fledgling MSI. FAR implemented the radical right's strategy of tension, characterized by indiscriminate explosions and acts of aggression against communist organizations.[90] Ordine Nuovo continued that violent tradition and, by the late 1960s, this radical right-wing organization, with its fasces and double-ax symbol, boasted five to six thousand adherents in dozens of provincial groups, with particular strength in the Veneto, Campania, and Sicily. Evola later referred to Ordine Nuovo as the only political group in Italy "that doctrinally had held firm without descending to compromise."[91]

During these postwar years Evola remained an independent intellectual, but he exerted a definite and historically verifiable influence on those right-wing Italians who despaired at the prospect of an Italy in thrall to American capitalism and endangered by Soviet Marxism.[92] Militant right-wing youths in post-Fascist Italy compared their fate with that of Dante who had lamented the collapse of the Ghibelline order.[93] They—the generation of 1945, as they called themselves—hailed Evola as the "celestial warrior" whose work made sense of what for them were ruinous times.[94]

It was for this generation that in 1953 Evola summed up his thoughts about the Christian Democratic regime, in a book entitled *Gli uomini e le rovine*.[95] Prince Junio Valerio Borghese, a fascist war hero, the supreme idol of neofascist youth groups, and one of the most influential postwar figures on the extreme right—first as president of the MSI and then as a tireless promoter of extraparliamentary right-wing organizations and coups—wrote an introduction for the book, accurately describing it as "a cry of protest."[96]

Evola argued that the fundamental right-wing task in the postwar period was that of counterrevolution or, more accurately, of conservative revolution.[97] The task entailed two objectives, one political and the other ideological. The political objective involved outmaneuvering the Italian agents of American capitalism and Russian Marxism, for this is how Evola described, respectively, the Christian Democratic party (DC) and the PCI. As for the ideological objective, Evola, in effect, took a leaf from Gramsci's *Prison Notebooks*, namely, the ideas of hegemony and counterhegemony. The results of World War II had left the DC and the PCI in political and intellectual control of Italy; this for Evola was the hegemony of the hour. He proposed a counterhegemony, however, led by men capable of saying "no" to all the ideologies that were derived from "the immortal principles of 1789," that is, the world of ideas from liberalism to bolshevism. Such men would be a minority—only a few would listen to "the word of order"—but fortified by "a general vision of life and by a rigorous political doctrine" these reactionary supermen could retrieve the world that fascism had lost.[98] This is what he meant when he addressed his appeal to those men who "are rising from the ruins" to constitute a new order.

Evola could not counsel his readers to look for leadership from existing political organizations. Even the right, "as presently constituted," offered authentic conservatives little solace and no hope for ultimate victory.[99] Evola took enormous pleasure in pointing out what he called the obnoxious and tendentious assumption of Marxists, that they alone were motivated by a selfless pursuit of truth and justice, whereas conservatives merely acted from class interests. For him this was the fairy tale at the heart of scientific socialism, and he insisted that Marxist "realism" was in fact nothing more than a mythology. Here Evola reminded Marxists of a point made earlier by Karl Mannheim in *Ideology and Utopia*, that Marxism was itself only a hypothesis, an ideology, not an irrefutable Truth that entitled its spokesmen to adopt an attitude of disdainful arrogance toward the spokesmen of all other ideologies.[100] This was not even to mention the laughably coarse oversimplifications at the core of Marxist psychology, with its unreal and unbelievable emphasis on the mode of production in human affairs, Evola complained.

The depressing truth nonetheless—polemically analyzed in *Gli uomini e le rovine*—was that Italian conservatives had played into the hands of the left by attaching their cause to the destiny of "capitalist piracy and cynical, antisocial plutocracy."[101] Evola insisted that the conservative revolution should be based, not on bourgeois sociopolitical structures, but on "a general conception of life and of the State, . . . on values and interests of superior character, clearly transcending the levels of economy and of 'classism.'"[102]

For the rest of his life Evola continued to diagnose the problems of Europe in a manner consistent with his analysis in *La rivolta contro il mondo moderno*: Western man was sick unto death from an existential dread of the future. In *Cavalcare la tigre* (1961) he revealed himself to be more depressed than ever.[103] "The desert is growing," he averred, quoting his adored Nietzsche.[104] It seemed irrefutable to him that the farther along man progressed into the modern period—the more "liberty" he enjoyed—the worse things became. Such liberation as modern man had experienced since the death of God had failed to satisfy his deepest wants, and Evola interpreted the widespread abuse of alcohol, drugs, sex, and work itself as feverish attempts to compensate for inner loneliness; these abuses obviously reflected a negative psychic and existential situation. As for women's liberation, that most progressive of all modern developments, he tersely defined it as "the renunciation by woman of her right to be a woman."[105]

Above all, the conspicuous decline of the modern city proved to him that the values of modernity had failed; they had taken away from man his dignity and his very identity in exchange for the dubious benefits of debauching himself and ruining his environment. The invalidating flaw in these values lay in the assertion that all men are created equal. The attempt to design social, economic, political, and cultural institutions in conformity with that primordial error resulted in cruel and perpetual frustrations for the masses who neither could be nor wanted to be free. The most visible consequences of the false and pernicious freedom characteristic of the modern world, Evola contended, was a degree of cultural and psychological disorientation not seen since the collapse of the Roman Empire. He concluded that there was a fundamental dishonesty at the core of democratic theory, an unwillingness or an inability to test its philosophical abstractions against what we knew—by the middle of the twentieth century—to be true about man and society. For Evola, the complete disjunction between democratic theory and reality condemned democratic society to an endless round of crisis, chaos, and terror.

To document his thesis about progressive democratic societies, Evola cited the well-known brutality of American life. A country like Switzerland could be democratic, though even there a pall of bourgeois sameness had been the most noticeable result of democracy; however, in a heterogeneous country like the United States, where "the most degenerate people from Europe had gathered," such an absurd political theory, he thought, had produced the hideous urban jungles made world famous by American novels and films.[106] Evola studied the literature of the "beat generation," and he derived extremely pessimistic social conclusions from the books of Jack Kerouac and the young Norman Mailer. He felt sorry for the "beatnik" and the "hipster" because instinctively they were reacting in a quite natural, human way to the immoral institutions, social practices, and "culture" of consumer society, but, pathetically, these "rebels without a cause" had failed to develop a coherent philosophy and plan of action. Unlike the "anarchists of the right," Evola criticized, the American dissenters had no serious alternative to the existing state of things, only a petulant, egotistical, and insipid desire to set themselves off from the thickheaded multitude. Their existential despair amounted to nothing but an expression of futility, making them the last pitiful product of bourgeois capitalism, not the point of genesis for a salutary transformation of society, "an object of study in the general picture of an epoch's pathology," not the *Sturm und Drang* alarum for a brave new world.[107]

Evola judged Sartre's terminal disgust with the bourgeois world as the quintessential literary expression of the depersonalized and dehumanized culture of twentieth-century Western man. Existential alienation had been inescapable in a society that deprived man of moral bearings, and these could only be found in the traditional values of courage and honor for the few, obedience and discipline for the many.[108] Ultimately, there could be no hope for the West unless it retraced its missteps and succeeded in creating a sane order based on transcendence, that is, by "confirming spiritual stability against temporality."[109] A serious contemporary philosophy would have to go beyond existentialism, which merely reflected the present crisis without solving or transcending it. Existentialists had only succeeded in creating a new jargon for the philosophical question that they had pretended to solve, the question of authenticity, but, Evola asked, who decides what an authentic existence is? To raise this question implied a metaphysical answer; to solve it necessitated a particular metaphysical answer, the one arising from traditional and antimodern values, or so he believed. Admittedly, few in today's world would be receptive to such a vision of life, for his ideas went against the grain of practically everything sacred and sensible to modern man. Nevertheless, Evola continued to believe in those few people who "by temperament and vocation still think, in spite of everything, about the possibility of a rectifying political action."[110]

Evola's recommendations raise two immediate questions: (1) what, in concrete political terms, did he have in mind by calling for a return to Tradition? and (2) what does any of this have to do with the everyday realities of contemporary Italian politics—was he merely a far from amiable crank, or did his subjective vision of the world and history make a significant impression on society?

First, Evola advised his followers to adhere to a policy of *apolitià*, that is, to withdraw completely from the illusory world of national politics, now dominated by democratic, parliamentary, and socialist forms.[111] By national politics he meant the official institutional life of the nation states, themselves thoroughly conditioned by that most odious product of the satanic French Revolution: nationalism.[112] At first glance, Evola's aversion here seems paradoxical because nationalism is generally viewed as a right-wing force. To view it so, however, requires that we ignore the enormous and largely realized revolutionary potential in European nationalism during the first half of the nineteenth century, as well as in Third World nationalism today. In Europe, nationalism was a ram with which the left of that time battered the old order, and parallel phenomena are now in progress all over the Third World. Evola identified completely with men like Metternich and Bismarck—aristocrats who in his judgment viewed nationalism as a frightful modern development.[113] The premonitions of these Central European leaders had proved tragically correct, but now that Europe's world hegemony had been crushed, Evola invoked Vico's principle regarding cycles in history: when one cycle reaches its nadir another begins.[114] In other words, the very ashes of World War II concealed the materials for a new European order.

Evola found evidence for this assertion in the creation of foreign Waffen-SS units. Tens of thousands of international volunteers had fought alongside German soldiers in defense of the continent against Russian and American invaders.[115] By the end of the war the Waffen-SS had consisted of forty divisions and 594,000 men.[116] As of 1 October 1944 this elite corps had lost 320,000 men.[117] The major foreign units in the Waffen-SS were the French Charlemagne, the Flemish Langemark, the Walloon Wallonie, the Dutch Landstorm Nederland, the Albanian Skanderberg, the Muslim Handschar, and the Croatian Kama. There were also three Cossack divisions, some Caucasian and Turkestan regiments, an Indian legion, two Rumanian battalions, one Bulgarian battalion, and one Norwegian battalion. A number of Arab volunteers served in the Thirteenth Bosnische-Herzegovinische SS Gebirgsdivision. Approximately, 6,000 Danes, 10,000 Norwegians, 75,000 Dutchmen, 25,000 Flemings, 15,000 Walloons, and 22,000 Frenchmen served in the Waffen-SS.[118]

Evola argued that this supranational military organization, reminiscent in his mind of the "ascetic warriors" in the Order of Teutonic Knights, signaled Europe's continued "spiritual virility."[119] It was this kind of international cooperation by European reactionary elites that

Evola had in mind when he called for a new supranational militancy against the postwar Russian and American occupiers of Europe.[120] All men opposed to the bourgeois world of modernity were potential recruits for this army of the conservative revolution, and Evola felt encouraged by the emergence of the British National party and the National Socialist movement in England, the Movimiento Nacional in Spain, the Vlaamse Militanten Orde in Belgium, the Organisation de l'Armée Secrète and the Nouvel Ordre Européen in France, the Legion Europa in Austria, and the Ordine Nuovo and Fasci d'Azione Rivoluzionaria in Italy. The emergence of these Euro-fascist groups signified that a broad constituency for reaction existed, and Evola incited them to confront the left and center in a struggle for power. By revolutionary struggle the Tradition had been lost; by revolutionary struggle—and only by such struggle—could it be restored. In practical terms the restoration of the Tradition thus meant taking the war to the enemy, and by this Evola meant total war.

Second, concerning Evola's impact on the right, it is never a simple matter to determine a writer's influence on politics, but in his case an abundance of fragmentary evidence indicates that the books and ideas under discussion here have not been merely one man's sound and fury, signifying nothing. Evola himself had written that the traditional "vision of the world is not based on books, but on an interior form and sensibility having a character not acquired, but innate."[121] In his own books, however, he depicted this vision by means of powerful symbols and images, thereby providing the radical right in postwar Italy with a distinct intellectual coherence.[122]

Two different generations of extreme right-wing youths identified him as their *maestro segreto*. Giulio Salierno, the communist writer who passed his teenage years in the late 1940s and early 1950s as a right-wing terrorist, has described Evola's influence on him and on his cohorts in the MSI youth section of Colle Oppio in Rome.[123] There is a memorable scene in *Autobiografia di un picchiatore fascista* recounting Salierno's *de rigueur* visit with other young missini to Evola's home as though on pilgrimage to an ancient guru high in the Himalayas.[124] Salierno recalled that the crippled Evola held forth like an oracle in the suffocating heat of a small room, never deigning to look at his audience and frequently falling into long silences. Then the low voice would begin again with Evola giving the wide-eyed boys a firsthand account of how he personally had advised Goebbels on a variety of matters and of what Hitler actually had said about this or that.

The séancelike performance overwhelmed Salierno and his friends. Here sat a man who actually had been a protagonist in "that legendary epic poem of the millenarian Third Reich."[125] Some of Evola's charisma did evaporate, Salierno noted, when in the midst of his rambling discourse a servant brought him dinner, which he unceremoniously devoured, "noisily lapping up the soup."[126] Still, Salierno agreed completely with the two major points of Evola's political analysis: to affirm the aristocracy of superior beings and to extirpate the communist cancer with "iron and fire."[127] This meant that bombs and physical attacks had to be part of their strategy against the communists. "Violence," Evola remarked in answer to a question by Salierno, "is the only possible and reasonable solution."[128]

The generation of 1968 accorded him, if anything, an even more enthusiastic reception. Almirante's comparison of him with Marcuse fit perfectly because Evola became that generation's patron saint of counterrevolution in much the same way that his hated adversary at the University of California, San Diego, Herbert Marcuse—Angela Davis's mentor—came to speak for the New Left. Before his death at the age of thirty-three in an automobile accident on 12 August 1973, Adriano Romualdi, the brightest star in the firmament of the Italian extraparliamentary right, singled out Evola in 1971 as the intellectual hero of the militant right-wing youth movement in Italy.[129] Evola's books, many of which had been out of print for years, were reissued in the late sixties, and while the academic community and the world of official politics ignored him, the young on the revolutionary right found in his philosophy what they were looking for, precisely because, in Romualdi's words, "the teaching of Evola is also a philosophy of total war."[130] *Cavalcare la tigre* in particular, Romualdi noted, was "the breviary" for his generation of alienated right-wing intellectuals, a book to be placed alongside the works of Seneca, Marcus Aurelius, and Epictetus.[131]

Evola's mythopoeicization of "a formation of pure and decisive forces" has been interpreted as a strident call for a violent overthrow of the present order in favor of a "solar civilization."[132] Such myth-making formed part of his larger argument, that an unprecedented degree of heroism would be required in the struggle against modernity, now grown to "monstrous dimensions": his followers would have to be spiritual warriors with "souls of steel," like the chivalrous Teutonic Knights, ready and eager for their "baptism by fire" in a holy war to establish "a metaphysical *Regnum.*"[133] The disorders of the modern world had not happened spontaneously, but had been produced by conscious planning and violent struggle. The conservative revolution could succeed only if it developed a conscious plan of its own and prepared to join in this struggle.[134] Georges Sorel's theories of violence held an irresistible fascination for him, and he completely agreed with the ethical assumption of *Reflections on Violence,* that the highest good was the aggressive heroic action.[135] Violence always had been and always would be the hygiene of history.

When asked in January 1970—four years before his death—how the right could defeat the communists, Evola answered that he did not know because he was far from being a practical man, but at the very least the right-wing public (*la piazza di Destra*) would have to be thoroughly organized and turned into a fighting force. By then he had become extremely pessimistic about the political situation in Italy and observed that it would be impossible to temporize with the modern order: "It is not a question of contesting and polemicizing, but of blowing up everything."[136]

If Salierno's testimony is reliable, we can then conclude that in his private audiences with right-wing youths Evola freely advocated violence without truce. Yet even in his published statements on the question of terrorism, Evola hardly bothered to conceal his true sentiments. He counseled that terrorism should be ruled out only when the odds against its success were overwhelming. However, he added: "if today a kind of operating San Vehme could be organized, to hold the persons responsible for this contemporary subversion in a constant state of physical insecurity, that would be an excellent thing."[137] The message here was plain and, on a tactical level, much like Marx's view of terrorism in *The Civil War in France:* not to be employed indiscriminately, but only when the authentic revolutionary cause will be served effectively by it. As Gottfried Benn had written more than thirty years before, in an idolatrous review of *La rivolta contro il mondo moderno:* Evola appeals to those "black monks" who await the stroke of midnight; "when the time is full they will guide the forces of the resurrection."[138]

The right-wing strategy of tension has been a fact of life in Italy since the end of World War II, and beginning with the Piazza Fontana explosion in Milan on 12 December 1969, we witnessed a surge of this activity before it yielded the headlines in the mid-1970s to left-wing terrorism.[139] Then the Bologna train station massacre of 2 August 1980 emphasized once again the extreme right's power and will.[140] These people had not disappeared for five years; they had gone on with their work in the shadow of the Red Brigades, even benefiting from left-wing terrorism because the neofascist thesis had always been that the democratic state would eventually reveal itself to be incapable of defending society. Mussolini took advantage of just such a political situation in 1922, and today the extreme right hopes, not at all unreasonably, for history to repeat itself. Their best chance for victory depends on continued turmoil in Italy. Therefore, now that the shadow of left-wing terrorism is lifting, if only temporarily, the extreme right-wing organizations—Squadre d'Azione Mussolini, Ordine Nuovo, Ordine Nero, Giustizieri d'Italia, Nuclei Armati Rivoluzionari among numerous others—will in all probability become more visible once again.[141]

The phrase "in all probability" forces us to confront the unavoidable problem in writing contemporary history: the concluding facts of the story are never available. The best that the researcher can hope for is to present the antecedents of the story in historical context and to admit the uselessness of history in predicting the future, even—in Georges Sorel's phrase—"the least distant future."[142] Evola is such an antecedent in the history of contemporary Italy's radical right: he performs the signal service of providing very desperate people with a rationale for what they are doing. Certainly such a rationale does not explain everything that we need to know about the radical right in Italy, but it does provide a mental picture of what motivates or, at least, what sustains these extremists. It remains to be shown, in a systematic way, how this mental picture has been projected from one man's mind to a wider circle of politically motivated zealots and, in turn, how they have been guided by it in a politically unstable Italy that has been overwhelmed by inflation, dispirited by unemployment, undermined by scandal, and traumatized by the Red Brigades.[143] For the present perhaps it has been enough to sketch the picture itself.

NOTES

The research for this study was undertaken with the support of a grant from the American Philosophical Society.

1. Giacomo Sani notes that "few issues in Italian politics have been as enduring as the issue of the 'true nature' of the PCI and the MSI." In "Mass Constraints on Political Realignments: Perceptions of Anti-System Parties in Italy," *British Journal of Political Science*, vol. 6, pt. 1 (Jan. 1976).

2. For Berlinguer, see the following articles by him in *Rinascita:* "Imperialismo e consistenza alla luce dei fatti cileni" (28 September 1973); "Riflessioni sull' Italia dopo i fatti di Cile: Via democratica o violenza reazionaria" (5 October 1973); "Riflessioni sull' Italia dopo i fatti di Cile: Alleanze sociali e schieramenti politici" (12 October 1973). For Almirante, see his *Autobiografia di un "fucilatore"* (Milan: Borghese, 1974): "I invite all Italian youths, but I invite above all the men of thought and culture, the newspapermen and the writers, to a crusade against horror" (p. 136). In this same book he categorically denies the charge that acts of violence are ordered by the MSI. See chap. 10, "La mia gente."

3. Antonio Negri, *Dall' operaio massa all' operaio sociale: intervista sull' operaismo,* ed. Paolo Pozzi and Roberta Tommasini (Milan: Multhipia, 1979). See "La fine dei gruppi: la conflittualità diffusa e la nascita dell' autonomia."

4. Adriano Romualdi, *Julius Evola: l'uomo e l'opera* (Rome: Volpe, 1971). The extreme right sees the MSI as a nostalgic and feckless party that confuses true conservatism with "bourgeois and papal conservatism." P. 86.

5. For the Red Brigades, see Richard Drake, "The Red Brigades and the Italian Political Tradition" in *Terrorism in Europe,* ed. Yonah Alexander and Kenneth Myers (London: Croom Helm, 1982; and New York: St. Martin's Press, 1982).

6. Franco Ferrarotti has noted that "the culture of violence, so alive and important in the Italian intellectual tradition, points to a terrain that is entirely still to be explored and interpreted." In *L'ipnosi della violenza* (Milan: Rizzoli, 1980), p. 15.

7. Antonio Gramsci, *The Modern Prince and Other Writings*, trans. and intro. Louis Marks (New York: International Publishers, 1957). See "Critical Notes on an Attempt at a Popular Presentation of Marxism by Bukharin" and "The Formation of the Intellectuals."

8. Arno J. Mayer, "Domestic Causes of the First World War," in *The Responsibility of Power: Historical Essays in Honor of Hajo Holborn*, eds. Leonard Krieger and Fritz Stern (Garden City, N.Y.: Doubleday, 1967), reprinted in *The Outbreak of the First World War: Causes and Responsibilities*, 4th ed., ed. Dwight E. Lee (Lexington, Mass.: D. C. Heath, 1975).

9. Alexis de Tocqueville, *The Old Régime and the Revolution* (Garden City, N.Y.: Doubleday, 1955). Robert Darnton has argued that the alienated hack writers of the eighteenth century exerted a greater influence on the prehistory of the French Revolution than the highly cultivated and more secure *philosophes* did. In *The Literary Underground of the Old Regime* (Cambridge: Harvard University Press, 1982).

10. Romualdi, *Evola*, pp. 8 ff. For Evola's own analysis of his early years, see the autobiographical *Cammino del cinabro* (Milan: Vanni Scheiwiller, 1972), "Il fondo personale e le prime esperienze."

11. Evola wrote disapprovingly of Papini's postwar conversion to Catholicism and scarcely thought of him as a serious thinker after that. Nevertheless, Evola praised the "paradoxical, polemical, iconoclastic, anticonformist, revolutionary Papini" of the *Leonardo* and *Lacerba* prewar period. In "Papini," *Ricognizioni: uomini e problemi* (Rome: Edizioni Mediterranee, 1974). Prezzolini, too, according to Evola, became a caricature of himself without ever possessing anything like Papini's intellectual power and originality." See "La Destra e la Cultura," ibid.

12. Evola, *Il cammino del cinabro*, p. 17.

13. Evola's poetry from the period 1916–1922 was eventually collected in *Raâga blanda* (Milan: Vanni Scheiwiller, 1969). See also his "La parole obscure du paysage intérieur" (1920), republished by Scheiwiller in 1963. Many of Evola's poems were written in French. It should be noted that, before surrendering completely to the linguistic conceits of Dadaism, Evola wrote some excellent war poetry. See especially "Baracca Alpina al Fronte" and "Reticolati" in *Raâga blanda*. One of his Dada paintings is still on display in Rome's Galleria Nazionale d'Arte Moderna.

14. Evola, *Il cammino del cinabro*, p. 26. In a 1964 essay, "Documenti del Dadaismo," Vittorio Orazi (Alessandro Prampolini) linked Evola's Dada past with the Tradition by claiming that it was necessary to destroy the false "tradition" of art dating from the Renaissance. *Omaggio a Julius Evola*, ed. Gianfranco de Turris (Rome: Volpe, 1973).

15. Evola's hatred of the bourgeoisie remained at white heat as the years passed. In a November 1970 interview with Gianfranco de Turris he exclaimed that the central idea of his work was "to be completely and in every way anti-bourgeois, intolerant of every compromise and bourgeois conformism." Ibid.

16. Evola, *Il cammino del cinabro*, "L'arte astratta e il dadaismo," p. 23. This is exactly what he meant in *Fenomenologia dell' individuo assoluto* (Rome: Edizioni Mediterranee, 1974 ed., p. 184) when he wrote that at a certain level of artistic consciousness "a tram ticket is as artistic as the Mona Lisa."

17. Evola, *Teoria dell' individuo assoluto* (Rome: Edizioni Mediterranee, 1973 ed.), pp. 34, 106.

18. For "the ways by which the complete determination of the self can be actuated," see *Fenomenologia*, especially the "Presentazione."

19. Ibid., pp. 277 ff.

20. For the connection between Evola's art and poetry on the one hand and his philosophy on the other, see *Fenomenologia*, pp. 181 ff.

21. Evola devoted an entire section of *Fenomenologia*, which was written in 1924, to an analysis of Eastern mysticism. See "Epoca della Dominazione."

22. Three volumes of their monographs, which originally appeared between 1927 and 1929, were republished in 1955 under the title *Introduzione alla magia*. Critics have always attacked Evola as a theosophist crackpot, but his own withering criticism of theosophy and related sects should be noted. See his 1932 book, *Maschera e volto dello spiritualismo contemporaneo* (Turin: Bocca, 1949 ed.). Elements of his anti-Theosophy critique are to be found in an even earlier work, *Imperialismo pagano: il fascismo dinanzi al pericolo euro-cristiano* (Rome-Todi: "Atenor," 1928), p. 32.

23. Evola translated this book. See *La crisi del mondo moderno* (Rome: Ediz. Mediterranee, 1972). He wrote extensively on Guénon, but see especially "René Guénon e il 'Tradizione Integrale,'" *Ricognizioni: uomini e problemi*, and the pamphlet "René Guénon," ed. Aldo Perez (Rome: Le Arti Grafiche del Grosso, 1979). Although Guénon argued in *La Crise* that Catholicism was the only proper vehicle for traditionalism in the West, he came to believe that Western civilization lacked the philosophical and religious insights necessary for true transcendence. He then converted to Islam and took the name Sheikh Abdel Wahîd Yasha. For the other major influences in Evola's life, notably Guido de Giorgio, Herman Wirth, J. J. Bachofen, and Otto Weininger, see *Il cammino del cinabro*, "L'esplorazione delle origini e la tradizione." See also Alberto Cavaglion, *Otto Weininger in Italia* (Rome: Carucci, 1983).

24. Evola, "René Guénon," *Ricognizioni*. See also "La Destra e la Tradizione," ibid.

25. *La rivolta contro il mondo moderno* did meet with success in right-wing German circles, however. For example, see Gottfried Benn's March 1935 review of the book, reprinted in the appendix of Evola's *L'arco e la clava* (Milan: Scheiwiller, 1968), p. 237. After reading *La rivolta*, Benn wrote, "we feel ourselves transformed."

26. Evola, *La rivolta contro il mondo moderno* (Rome: Edizioni Mediterranee, 1969, ed.). See his "Introduzione."

27. For example, in his view of history Calvin was "the pimp" who introduced the odious idea of money as a sign of man's worth in God's eyes. Ibid., p. 404.

28. With the Renaissance, Evola argued, Western civilization ceased to have a unitary axis: "The center no longer commands the individual parts, not only in political life, but in cultural life as well. A single organizing and animating force no longer exists." Ibid., pp. 377–378.

29. Ibid., p. 417.

30. A February 1970 interview of Evola by Enrico de Boccard in *Playmen* was entitled "Conversation without Complications with the 'Last Ghibelline.'" In *Omaggio*.

31. Cited by Evola in *Gli uomini e le rovine* (Rome: Edizioni dell' Ascia, 1953), p. 109. Evola held Sombart in great esteem. See "La potenza e l'infantilismo" in *Ricognizioni*.

32. Evola rarely missed an opportunity to attack the Catholic church, and his own thought was the antithesis of "Semitic" Christianity. See his *Imperialismo pagano*, which was published on the eve of the Lateran Accords as a warning to Mussolini about "the Euro-Christian peril." In this book Evola claimed that neoguelfism was "the principal danger [threatening] the resurrection of true *Romanità* in a regenerated Italy." See the Introduction. For a sample of his heated rhetoric against Catholicism in the Vatican II era, see his "Quo Vadis Ecclesia?" *L'Italiano* (June–July 1963):6–7. Reprinted in Dennis Eisenberg, *L'internazionale nera: fascisti e nazisti oggi nel mondo* (Milan: Sugar, 1964), Appendix. He believed that the modernizing of Catholicism

had brought about the triumph of the Protestant Reformation. See also "Il mito di Oriente e Occidente" and "L'incontro delle religioni" in *L'arco e la clava*. Here he scorns "the ecumenical euphoria" of the Vatican Council.

33. Evola, *La rivolta*, p. 83. See also his "Americanismo e Bolscevismo," in *Nuova antologia*, n. 1371 (1929). Later in life he found little to choose between America and Russia. He thought that the Cold War was "devoid of every spiritual significance," i.e., the West was based on a negation of traditional values, and Marxism was a negation of the negation. Nevertheless, because of Italy's vulnerable political situation he argued that the Russians represented an even greater immediate danger than the Americans. Evola, *Cavalcare la tigre* (Milan: Vanni Scheiwiller, 1961), p. 249.

34. See Mario Tarchi, ed., *Diorama: problemi dello spirito nell' etica fascista (Antologia della pagina speciale di "Regime fascista" diretta da Julius Evola)*, vol. 1, 1934–1935 (Rome: Ed. Europa, 1974). In the early years of Evola's collaboration on *Regime fascista*, "Diorama" appeared biweekly and later on a monthly basis.

35. Roberto Farinacci, "Formare l'Italiano Nuovo," ibid.

36. Evola, "Metafisica della Guerra" I–IV (25 May–12 August 1935), ibid.

37. Evola, "Cose a Posto e Parole Chiare," *La torre* (1 April 1930). The other principal contributors to *La torre* were Guido de Giorgio, Emilio Servadio, Leonardo Grassi, Guido Ferretti, Girolamo Comi, Roberto Pavese, and René Guénon. See Julius Evola, *La torre* (Milan: Società Ed. Il Falco, 1977), "Introduzione" by Marco Tarchi. Evola had no compunction about challenging Mussolini on policy as well as on principle. For example, he criticized the duce's demographic campaign, arguing that "the maximum number of births" idea was inherently antielitist and demagogic. Italy needed quality, not quantity—"a handful of leaders and rulers" instead of a still larger mob than the one already in existence. "Le Razze Muoiono," *La torre* (1 March 1930). The government reacted to Evola's article by sequestering this issue of the journal.

38. Evola contributed a number of articles to Preziosi's *Vita italiana*.

39. Evola later admired Gentile's courage and fidelity in standing by Mussolini after 25 July 1943, an action that cost the philosopher his life. Nevertheless, Evola always criticized Gentile's ideas as essentially antitraditional and even implicitly Marxist. See "Il Caso di Giovanni Gentile," *Ricognizioni*. For more on how intellectuals became objects of factional intrigue in fascist Italy, see Alastair Hamilton, *The Appeal of Fascism: a Study of Intellectuals and Fascism 1919–1945* (New York: Macmillan, 1971). Part I, "Italy."

40. For Bombacci's influence on the Salò regime, see F. W. Deakin, *The Brutal Friendship* (London: Weidenfeld and Nicolson, 1962), chap. 5, "The Congress of Verona."

41. Evola, *Il cammino del cinabro*, p. 162. Evola maintained that while the war was being fought the "institutional question" had to be suspended.

42. Ibid.

43. Evola, *Sintesi di dottrina della razza* (Padova: Edizioni di Ar, 1978 ed.), p. 224.

44. Tarchi, ed., *Diorama*. See his "Introduzione," p. lxxvii.

45. Evola, *Il cammino del cinabro*, p. 162.

46. Evola boasted that never in his life had he voted or joined any political party. Ibid., p. 72. He complained that all parties were "residues of democracy and of mass organizations." In "the anti-party and organic state" of his heart's desire there would be no room for such relics of the "modern past," and in the meantime he would only consider joining "orders," not parties. See Gianfranco de Turris, "Incontro con Julius Evola," *Omaggio*.

47. This volume also contains his essay "Note sul Terzo Reich." Evola criticized Hitler's government, too, but he gave the Nazis credit for at least recognizing that the modern world was the enemy.

48. Evola, *Il fascismo: saggio di una analisi dal punto di vista della destra* (Rome: Volpe, 1970), pp. 17 ff.

49. Ibid., see chap. 6. In his memoirs Evola added this note about Mussolini: "Certainly, I could not fail to sympathize with someone who struggled against the forces of the left and against the democratic regime." *Il cammino del cinabro*, p. 76.

50. Evola, *Il fascismo*, p. 76. See his *Uomini e le rovine* for an analysis of why fascist corporativism failed, p. 114.

51. Evola, *Il fascismo*, p. 67.

52. Evola, *Sintesi di dottrina della razza*, p. 245. To the duce's delight, Evola celebrated "the race of fascist man or the race of Mussolini's men." P. 266.

53. Evola, *Il fascismo*, pp. 76–77.

54. Giuseppe Gaddi has observed that nearly all Italian neo-fascists today attempt to put some distance between themselves and Mussolini's regime and thereby escape the onus of his debacle in World War II. See his *Neofascismo in Europa* (Milan: La Pietra, 1974), "Introduzione." Along the same line of argument, F. W. Deakin writes, "The collapse of the whole Party machinery throughout Italy, silent and total, in the course of the morning of July 26, 1943 without a gesture in defense of the Duce and Fascism, had indeed been a decisive historic event." *The Brutal Friendship*, p. 581. However, Evola—always the maverick—insisted that Mussolini was right to fight by Germany's side in World War II. Mussolini's mistake, in Evola's opinion, was to be timorous and vacillating at home.

55. In *Il fascismo* Evola theorized that if the king had been strong "fascism would never have arisen." P. 49.

56. On this point Evola was as naive as Marx who also thought that men of power, instead of always seeking to augment it, would freely give up their position under the right historical circumstances. The fascist state was no more likely to wither away than its communist counterpart.

57. Evola, *Imperialismo pagano*, pp. 17 ff.

58. Ibid.

59. Evola, *Il fascismo*, p. 113.

60. Even so, Mussolini's Italy "was one of the most socially progressive and advanced regimes of its time," Evola asserted. Ibid., p. 91. He always maintained that the ideas of fascism should be defended, though not necessarily fascist practice. See *Gli uomini e le rovine*, p. 26.

61. See Benito Mussolini, "Commento a *Sintesi di dottrina della razza*" in Giorgio Pini and Duilio Susmel, *Mussolini: l'uomo e l'opera* (Florence: La Fenice, 1958), IV, 145. In the aftermath of this success Giuseppe Bottai, minister of National Education, asked Evola to give a course of lectures at the universities of Milan and Florence on racial policy. For more on Mussolini's favorable reaction to this book, see Renzo De Felice, *Mussolini il duce II: Lo stato totalitario (1936–1940)* (Turin: Einaudi, 1981), p. 316.

62. Earlier he had written that "an anti-Semitism is not out of the question," but anti-Semites were not yet in possession of a systematic and rational critique of Jewish culture. See *Tre aspetti del problema ebraico* (Rome: Edizioni Mediterranee, 1936). For a discussion of Evola's racial ideas, see Renzo De Felice, *Storia degli ebrei italiani sotto il fascismo* (Turin: Einaudi, 1972) and Giorgio Pisanò, *Mussolini e gli ebrei* (Milan: F.P.E., 1967).

63. *Tre aspetti del problema ebraico* fully reveals his antipathy toward the Jews, e.g., "As the germinating force of a seed does not fully manifest itself until [its

introduction into the soil] so Hebraism did not begin to universally manifest its destructive and ethically subversive power until its political fall and the dispersion into the world of the 'Chosen People.'" P. 33.

64. For Evola modernity meant, in part, "the hebraization of the economy." *Gli uomini e le rovine*, p. 164.

65. See especially his "Introduzione" to *I "Protocolli" dei "Savi Anziani" di Sion* (Rome: La Vita Italiana, 1938) in which he adopted Henry Ford's line of reasoning about the Jews, i.e., whether or not the *Protocols* was an authentic historical document it did describe present reality. For Evola Judaism meant "a systematic and practical work of destruction" in the West. However, even in his introduction to this notorious fabrication, Evola insisted that he "personally could not follow . . . a certain kind of anti-Semitism that sees the Jew everywhere as a deus ex machina. . . ." P. xiv. In addition, see his introduction to E. Malinsky and L. De Poncins, *La guerra occulta: armi e fasi dell' attacco ebraico-massonico alla tradizione europea* (Milan: Hoepli, 1939). Evola also translated this book which purported to analyze Jewish subversion from 1848 down to the triumph of bolshevism.

66. In his earliest articles for "Diorama filosofico" Evola condemned Nazi race theory. See Evola and Roberto Pavese, "In margine al IX Congresso Filosofico," *Regime fascista* (1 November–2 December 1934), in which they declared that "Racist and Nazi Germany gives us an instructive lesson regarding the dangers and the deviations . . . of biological materialism or nationalism more or less deified." Also see Evola's "Sorpassamento del Superuomo" (16 November 1934), and especially his "Critica della Teoria dell' Eredità" (13 December 1934), for more on the "superbiological character of Evolian race theory.

67. Evola, "Introduzione" to *I "Protocolli."* See also *Il mistero del Graal e la tradizione ghibellina dell' Impero* (Bari: Laterza, 1937), p. 185.

68. Evola, *Tre aspetti del problema ebraico*, p. 43. He made the identical point in *Sintesi di dottrina della razza*, p. 118. In his "Introduzione" to *I "Protocolli"* he asserted that the Jew hates "as fire burns." P. xxvii.

69. Evola, *Tre aspetti*, p. 40.

70. Evola, *Sintesi*, p. 118. However, Evola was never prepared to discount the value of blood altogether, and he later wrote: "a certain balanced consciousness and dignity of race can be considered healthy, especially if one thinks where we are going in our time with the exaltation of the Negro and all the rest, with the anticolonialist psychosis, with the 'integrationist' fanaticism: all parallel phenomena in the decline of Europe and the West." *Il fascismo*. See "Note sul Terzo Reich," p. 179.

71. For example, a beautiful Aryan woman could degenerate and become "full of bourgeois limitations." She would then belong to "another race" and, apart from romantic "adventures," a true Aryan male should have nothing to do with such a creature. Certainly, he should not have any children by her because they would be half-breeds. In *Sintesi di dottrina della razza*, p. 240. Incidentally, Evola never married. He defined marrriage as the surest means of forging iron links with bourgeois society. See "La gioventù, i Beats e gli anarchici di destra," in *L'arco e la clava*, p. 221.

72. For more on Mussolini's racial policy in Ethiopia, see Denis Mack Smith, *Mussolini's Roman Empire* (New York: Viking, 1976), chap. 5, "The Ethiopian War." Angelo Del Bocca enumerates the fascist government's racial atrocities in Africa, carried out by Mussolini's express command, in "Sterminateli tutti!," *Il messaggero* (11 April 1983).

73. Evola, *Sintesi di dottrina della razza*, p. 234.

74. Evola, *Il fascismo*, p. 110.

75. Cited by Deakin, in *The Brutal Friendship*, p. 557.

76. Evola, *Sintesi*, p. 237.

77. Evola, *Il fascismo*, p. 113. In *Gli uomini e le rovine* he added that "in spite of everything [fascism] remained bourgeois or became bourgeois by contagion," p. 155.

78. Evola, *Il cammino del cinabro*. See "Ricerca di uomini fra le rovine."

79. Evola, *Il fascismo*. See "Note sul Terzo Reich," p. 164. In *Gil uomini e le rovine* he severely criticized the country's weak national character, symbolized by the image of "chiaro di luna in gondola" (p. 212). Since World War II, he asserted, the worst instincts of the Italians had been exaggerated, especially their "rather primitive sexualism." Ibid.

80. This is what "liberation" meant to Evola: "Italy has returned to itself, that is, to the little Italy of mandolins, of museums, of 'Sole Mio,' and of the tourist industry, having been 'liberated'; liberated from the hard task of giving itself a form inspired by its highest [Roman] tradition," *Gil uomini e le rovine*, p. 206.

81. Mario Tedeschi, *Fascisti dopo Mussolini* (Rome: Arnia, 1950), p. 84.

82. Though destined to disappear from Italian politics by 1948, Giannini's conservative catch-all party enjoyed a fantastic success in the immediate postwar period. In August 1945 his newspaper, *L'uomo qualunque*, was selling 850,000 copies per issue. See Petra Rosenbaum, *Il nuovo fascismo: da Salò ad Almirante (Storia del MSI)* (Milan: Feltrinelli, 1975), chap. 3.

83. Leonard B. Weinberg, *After Mussolini: Italian Neofascism and the Nature of Fascism* (Washington, D.C.: University Press of America, 1979), chap. 2, "Neofascism in Postwar Italy."

84. Cited by Giorgio Galli, *La crisi italiana e la destra internazionale* (Florence: Mondadori, 1974), p. 20.

85. Pino Rauti, *Le idee che mossero il mondo* (Rome: Europa, 1976). See Thomas Sheehan, "Myth and Violence: The Fascism of Evola and Alain de Benoist," in *Social Research* (Spring 1981) for an analysis of Evola's impact on this book. Sheehan argues that this influence extended to wholesale plagiarism. Certainly, Rauti's view of the historical process is the same as the one that we find in *La rivolta contro il mondo moderno*. See Giulio Salierno, *Autobiografia di un picchiatore fascista* (Turin: Einaudi, 1976), chap. 4, in which Rauti is described as the chief of the *evoliani*.

86. Evola was not alone in wishing to purify fascism of all corrupt elements. For example, see Alberto Giovannini on "chilantismo," after Felice Chilanti who fantasized about assassinating the major hierarchs of the regime, "liberating Mussolini and obliging him to make a "total revolution." In the "Prefazione" to Mario Tedeschi's *Fascisti dopo Mussolini*.

87. See Pier Giuseppe Murgia, *Ritorneremo!* (Milan: Sugar, 1976) for more details regarding this trial.

88. See Evola, "Autodifesa (al processo dei F.A.R.)."

89. Gaddi, *Neofascism in Europa*, p. 35. Giampaolo Pansa notes in *Borghese mi ha detto* (Milan: Palazzi, 1971) that Ordine Nuovo was founded after the tempestuous MSI congress of 1956 in which the radicals chanted "Fewer double-breasted suits and more cudgels!" See the material on Ordine Nuovo in the section entitled "Documenti." For the historical background of the Nouvel Ordre Européen, see Jean-Marc Théolleyre, *Les Neo-Nazis* (Paris: Temps Actuels, 1982).

90. For an account of FAR by an active member, see Mario Tedeschi, *Fascisti dopo Mussolini*. According to him, factionalism between moderates and radicals had destroyed FAR by 1947.

91. Evola, *Il cammino del cinabro*, p. 212.

92. Fausto Gianfranceschini, "L'influenza di Evola sulla generazione che non ha fatto in tempo a perdere la guerra," in *Testimonianze su Evola*.

93. Vintilă Horia, "I poeti e il simbolo della patria," ibid.

94. Silvano Panunzio, "Iniziati e metafisici della crisi," ibid.

95. For the impact of *Gli uomini e le rovine* on the radical right, see Romualdi, *Julius Evola*, pp. 78 ff.

96. Junio Valerio Borghese, "Presentazione" in Evola, *Gil uomini e le rovine*, p. 7. For more on Borghese, see Giampaolo Pansa, *Borghese mi ha detto*. Borghese's Fronte Nazionale would espouse many of Evola's ideas. See ibid., "Documenti." F. W. Deakin's *Brutal Friendship* also contains useful information about Borghese's background, particularly during World War II when he was the commander of the dreaded *Decima mas* (Tenth Motor Torpedo Boat Flotilla). See Part III, "Salò: the Six Hundred Days." See also Borghese, *Decima flottiglia mas*, trans. into English by James Cleugh as *Sea Devils* (Chicago: Regnery, 1954).

97. Evola agreed with Joseph de Maistre that conservatives needed more than a counterrevolution; they needed "the contrary of a revolution," i.e., something positive with which to oppose revolution. See *Gil uomini e le rovine*, p. 16.

98. Ibid., p. 218.

99. Evola argued that Italy had never enjoyed a right "worthy of the name." Ibid., p. 22. For the same argument, see "Las Destra e la Cultura," *Ricognizioni*.

100. Karl Mannheim, *Ideology and Utopia: An Introduction to the Sociology of Knowledge* (New York: Harcourt, Brace & World, 1936), chap. 2, "Ideology and Utopia." Mannheim argued that Marx's greatest achievement lay in his discovery of political rhetoric as a cover for interest, but this discovery applies to the Marxists, too, whose interest, on the political level, is power.

101. Evola, *Gli uomini e le rovine*, p. 59. He believed that corporativism was the only way to control "the disorders and subversion of capitalism." Ibid., p. 161.

102. Ibid., p. 18.

103. In this book Evola employed many of Ernest Jünger's ideas about the modern world, particularly those found in *Der Arbeiter: herrschaft und Gestalt* (1932) and in *An der Zeitmauer* (1959). On the first, see Evola's *L'"Operaio" nel pensiero di Ernest Jünger* (Rome: Volpe, 1974 ed.); on the second, see his "Al Muro del Tempo" in *Ricognizioni*. Evola understood Jünger to be saying that only a new type of man could survive in the modern world, i.e., in past times men faced physical threats, but today men, though in some respects physically safer, face a far more deadly peril, which is psychological and moral in nature. Evola's *Cavalcare la tigre* (*To Ride the Tiger*) was intended to be a survival manual for those among his contemporaries who had the wit to understand the evil character of the modern world.

104. Evola, *Cavalcare la tigre*, "Introduzione." Most disappointing of all to him at the start of the 1960s was the rapid modernization of the East. See "Il Tramonto dell' Oriente" in *Ricognizioni* for a further elaboration of his argument that by abandoning Tradition Oriental societies were setting the stage for their own Western-style decline.

105. Evola, *Cavalcare la tigre*, p. 292. See also his *Metafisico del sesso* (Rome: Atanòr, 1958. On the subject of women, Evola gleefully quoted one of his paramount intellectual heroes, Joseph de Maistre: "Woman cannot be superior except as woman, but from the moment in which she desires to emulate man she is nothing but a monkey." Evola's comment on this observation was "Pure truth, whether or not it pleases the various contemporary 'feminist movements.'" In "Joseph de Maistre," *Ricognizioni*.

106. Evola, "Il fenomeno Henry Miller," ibid.

107. Evola, "La gioventù, i Beat e gli anarchici di destra," *L'arco e la clava*, p. 225.

108. For Evola the very center of Western alienation was the United States. See especially "America negrizzata" in *L'arco e la clava* where he lamented the Americanization of the world. He trembled at the thought of "Negroid America" as the main line of defense against the powerful and disciplined Marxist governments of Russia and China. The only hope for America, Evola believed, was an apartheid

policy. He recommended that one of the states be given to the blacks where they could "do whatever they want without annoying or contaminating anyone," p. 27.

109. Evola, "Civiltà dello spazio e civiltà del tempo," *L'arco e la clava*, p. 12.

110. Evola, *Cavalcare la tigre*, p. 247.

111. Ibid., pp. 248–249.

112. Romualdi pointed out that Evola regarded excessive nationalism as the worst failing of fascism. In *Julius Evola*, p. 60.

113. Evola, February 1970 *Playmen* interview with Enrico de Boccard, in *Omaggio*. See also "Metternich" in *Ricognizioni*.

114. Evola also cited U. Varange's two-volume *Imperium* (London: Westropa Press, 1948) to support his cyclical interpretation of history, in *Gli uomini e le rovine*, p. 232. He made the same argument in *Cavalcare la tigre*, p. 19.

115. See Marc Augier (Saint Loup), *I volontari europei delle Waffen-SS* (Rome: Volpe, 1967 and 1971). Adriano Romualdi translated, edited, and introduced this Italian edition. Augier, a veteran of the Waffen-SS, describes his basic training as a "novitiate" on p. 14.

116. Angelo Del Boca and Mario Giovana, *Fascism Today: A World Survey* (New York: Pantheon, 1969), p. 453.

117. Ibid.

118. Ibid. In all, thirty-two nationalities were represented in the Waffen-SS.

119. For Evola's views on the Order of Teutonic Knights as a splendid example of "the soldierly conception of life," see *Gli uomini e le rovine*, p. 123, and "La Destra e la Tradizione" in *Ricognizioni*, e.g., "Prussianism, with its ethic, was born as a secularization of the Order of Teutonic Knights," p. 241. He was even more enchanted by the SS because it was expressly neopagan. Incidentally, the motto of Ordine Nuovo was the same as that of the SS, "Our honor is called fidelity." Also see his study of chivalrous ideals in the Middle Ages, *Il mistero del Graal e la tradizione ghibellina dell' Impero* (see n. 67). In his memoirs he called this study an appendix to *La rivolta contro il mondo moderno*. Elsewhere he defined the Ghibelline ideal as "the reorganization and unification of the West under the sign of sacred imperialism." *Il cammino del cinabro*, p. 133.

120. Gaddi states that "the European idea" is the cornerstone of neofascism, *Neofascismo in Europa*. See his "Introduzione." Evola's historical ideal was always "Roman and imperial supranationality." See *Imperialismo pagano*, p. 36.

121. Evola, *Gli uomini e le rovine*, p. 157.

122. Furio Jesi makes a convincing argument that fascist and neofascist culture possesses a coherent theory of man, of the world, of history, and of nature. See his *Cultura di destra* (Milan: Garzanti, 1979). For the last thirty years of his life Evola was the major intellectual figure in this tradition.

123. For more on Salierno's testimony concerning the extreme right during this period, see Murgia, *Ritorneremo*, pp. 119 ff. Salierno claimed that he knew Evola's works by heart.

124. Salierno, *Autobiografia di un picchiatore fascista*, p. 137. This book is described in the introduction as "the chronicle of a political conversion."

125. Ibid., p. 139. In answer to a question, Evola described Hitler as "a *magister rationalis* . . . a genius." Ibid., p. 142.

126. Ibid.

127. Ibid., p. 143. Pino Rauti, Evola's foremost disciple in the MSI, had said the same thing in a talk before the Colle Oppio youth section of the party: "We must be wolves and make ourselves known as such." Ibid., p. 88. Interestingly, Mussolini had used identical language in describing his solution for the Partisans in 1944: "We must get rid of this odious plague with fire and steel." Cited by Deakin, *The Brutal Friendship*, p. 723.

128. Salierno, *Autobiografia*, pp. 142–143.

129. Romualdi, *Julius Evola*, p. 7.

130. Ibid., p. 92.

131. Ibid., p. 87.

132. "Civiltà solare" was Evola's way of identifying a superior civilization, and his youthful disciples in *Ordine Nuovo* styled themselves "children of the sun." See Angelo Del Bocca and Mario Giovana, *Fascism Today: A World Survey*. The original title was *I "figli del sole."*

133. Evola, *Il mistero del Graal*, Part I, "Principii."

134. Evola, *Gli uomini e le rovine*, p. 183.

135. Ibid., p. 218. For his favorable critique of Sorel's ideas about violence, see *Imperialismo pagano*, p. 41.

136. Evola, in a 15 January 1970 *Il conciliatore* interview with Gianfranco de Turris, *Omaggio*.

137. Evola, "La gioventù, i Beats e gli anarchici di destra," *L'arco e la clava*, p. 223.

138. Ibid., p. 236. It is highly probable that Benn found this image in Evola's youthful poetry. In "Voyage Morbide" (1916) Evola conjured up a vision of "Black monks who will burn the city." *Raâga blanda (1916–1922)*.

139. Ugo Pecchioli estimates that from 1969 to 1975 there were 4,384 acts of political violence in Italy, with 83 percent of them committed by neofascists. See his "Prefazione" *in* Mauro Galleni, ed., *Rapporto sul terrorismo: le stragi, gli agguati, i sequestri, le sigle 1969–1980* (Milan: Rizzoli, 1981). The two right-wing terrorists eventually implicated in the Piazza Fontana massacre, Franco Freda and Giovanni Ventura, were known admirers of Evola. See Weinberg, *After Mussolini* (see n. 83), p. 47. For more on the terrorist activities of these two radical neofascists, see Cesare de Simone, *La pista nera* (Rome: Riuniti, 1972), chap. 2, "Da Treviso a Piazza Fontana."

140. In this one right-wing terrorist operation alone, 85 people were killed and 200 others were wounded.

141. See Galleni, *Rapporto* for detailed information about each of these groups.

142. Georges Sorel, *Reflections on Violence* (New York: Collier, 1950), p. 124.

143. For some suggestions about the wider context in which modern violence operates, see Franco Ferrarotti, *Alle radici della violenza* (Milan: Rizzoli, 1979) and his *L'ipnosi della violenza* (Milan: Rizzoli, 1980). See also his editor's introduction for the Spring 1981 issue of *Social Research*, vol. 48, no. 1, "On Violence: Paradoxes and Antinomies." Included in this issue is a penetrating analysis of Evola's philosophical advocacy of the suprarational, by Thomas Sheehan, "Myth and Violence: The Fascism of Evola and Alain de Benoist."

3

Loyalist and Republican Perceptions of the Northern Ireland Conflict: The UDA and the Provisional IRA

ADRIAN GUELKE

Hannah Arendt has argued that because violence is by its nature instrumental in character, an implement, a means to an end, there is a constant need to justify its use by reference to the end being pursued.[1] If her view is accepted, it follows that the assumptions justifying the political goal itself and providing the analysis of how that goal is to be achieved are of crucial significance in legitimizing the use of political violence. Further, if one accepts that a process of legitimization is necessary to sustain any campaign of violence, then how violent political movements perceive a conflict is of central importance not merely to understanding the movements themselves but to analyzing the conflict itself, even as to whether the conflict will continue in a violent form. A test of these propositions requires a study of the relationship between perception and behavior and of the effect of changes in perception on behavior. Clearly this can be approached from various angles. In the case of Northern Ireland, a broadly political analysis seems the most appropriate.

For the sake of clarity and manageability, I shall restrict my analysis to the two principal paramilitary organizations in Northern Ireland, the Provisional IRA (Irish Republican Army) on the Republican side of the political divide and the UDA (Ulster Defence Association) on the Loyalist side. Both organizations came into being as a result of the civil disturbances that took place in Northern Ireland in the late

1960s. There is one important formal difference between the two organizations. The Provisional IRA is an illegal organization and the UDA is not, despite frequent demands from political representatives of the Catholic minority and others that it should be proscribed. The UDA has escaped proscription through the expedient of not claiming responsibility for the violent activities undertaken by its members. Claims of responsibility for sectarian assassinations, for example, are issued in the name of the Ulster Freedom Fighters and other noms de guerre. In practice, the relationship of the UDA to these activities is somewhat similar to the relationship between the Provisional IRA and Provisional Sinn Fein, which operates as a political and propaganda support group to the Provisional IRA. Like the UDA, Provisional Sinn Fein is a legal organization. Much of my analysis will draw on material published by the UDA and Provisional Sinn Fein as well as interviews with representatives of the two organizations. While what is published or what representatives are prepared to disclose in an interview no doubt tends to gloss over differences within the organizations and may not fully reflect the opinions of those directly engaged in violent operations, it does provide a reasonably accurate picture of their perceptions and the main changes that have taken place in their thinking over the last thirteen years.

Before embarking on an analysis of their views, however, it is necessary to sketch in briefly the political background to the formation of the two organizations. This entails a description of the onset of "the Troubles," the local name given to Northern Ireland's state of violent instability. The key events themselves are readily identifiable as a series of confrontations, initially as a result of marches organized by the Northern Ireland Civil Rights Association (NICRA), which was formed at the beginning of 1967. On an analogy with the civil rights movement in the southern states of the United States, NICRA sought an end to institutionalized discrimination against the Catholic minority. Its demands included a one-man, one-vote system in local government elections, allocation of council housing on a points system, that is, on an administratively impartial basis, and repeal of the Special Powers Act as an infringement of civil liberties. These formally nonsectarian demands were supported by a broad coalition of socialists and Republicans. A march of 2,500 from Coalisland to Dungannon in August 1968 over the housing issue went off peacefully despite the threat of Loyalist counterdemonstrations. However, a march over the gerrymandering of boundaries for the Londonderry Council was banned. The ban was ignored and on 5 October 1968 there was a violent confrontation between demonstrators and the police in Derry, as Catholics call a city in which they constitute a majority of the population.

The impact on mainland British opinion was considerable especially as the Northern Ireland practices the demonstators were protesting against were anomolous in a United Kingdom context. Further confrontations followed. In January 1969 a group of demonstrators on a cross-country march were ambushed and attacked by Loyalists, including off-duty part-time policemen in the B-Specials, at Burntollet bridge near the village of Claudy. Not merely did the RUC[2] fail to protect the marchers but later that day the police entered the Catholic district of the Bogside in Derry and ran amok. Tension was raised further in March and April by a series of bomb attacks on electricity supply lines and waterworks. It later transpired that these attacks were the work of Protestants attempting to raise the specter of IRA involvement behind NICRA's activities. Disturbances in Derry in April and in Belfast in July underlined the breakdown of law and order in the province. The British government was already seriously considering sending troops to Northern Ireland when a confrontation between Catholics and Protestants following the traditional parade of the Protestant Apprentice Boys on 12 August (marking the anniversary of the lifting of the siege of Londonderry in 1689) led to prolonged rioting in the city. After an official request for assistance from the Northern Ireland government, troops were dispatched from Britain on 14 August 1969 with the inevitable consequence that the British government became more intimately involved in the affairs of Northern Ireland and forced the Unionist administration to enact reforms.

Interpreting these events and explaining why they produced such a violent legacy is a much greater challenge than simply identifying the main episodes that led to the breakdown. Only the briefest outline of some of the reasons is possible here. The civil rights movement itself can be seen in part as a product of the social and economic changes that were beginning to erode sectarian divisions and hence becoming the basis of an uneasy accommodation between the two communities under which Catholics had been forced to accept a marginal position within the province of Northern Ireland. Even before the formation of NICRA, political overtures to the Catholic community by the Unionist government and the social and economic changes, particularly the movement of Catholics into previously Protestant suburbs of Belfast, had given rise to anxieties in the Protestant community that its position was being threatened. These fears were reflected in the emergence in 1966 of a Protestant paramilitary organization, the Ulster Volunteer Force, named after the UVF of 1912–1914 that had used the threat of force to block Irish Home Rule. The new UVF declared its intention to kill members of the IRA. In practice, this led to attacks on Catholics who were unconnected with the IRA but who were "intruding" into Protestant areas.[3] At the same time, the improved position in occupational terms resulted in a few Catholics actually joining the Unionist party while others were attracted by the prospect of class politics displacing the sectarian basis of political divisions and supported the Northern Ireland Labour party, a party committed to the link with Britain.

The violent confrontations of 1968 and 1969, however, enabled the sectarian political blocs to reassert their dominance, though with the difference that there was no prospect that Catholics would accept passively a position as a marginal minority within Northern Ireland. Indeed, the British government's intervention at first significantly raised Catholic expectations of a transformation of their status and was one reason why Catholics so warmly welcomed the arrival of British troops. At the same time, the demonstrated vulnerability of Catholic areas to Protestant mobs created a role as defenders of these areas for exponents of physical force. It was a position that the IRA might have been thought well equipped to fill in view of its traditional advocacy of the necessity for physical force to break the link between Britain and Ireland.

Since the failure of the border campaign between 1956 and 1962, the IRA itself had been moving away from a single-minded pursuit of unification through force and had increasingly involved itself in various forms of community politics including NICRA's marches in Northern Ireland. Consequently, the IRA was hardly in a position to defend Catholic areas when they came under attack and, in the ghettos that had borne the brunt of the Protestant backlash, derisive slogans appeared stating that the IRA stood for "I Ran Away."[4] In these circumstances, criticism of the policies of the leadership mounted. Matters came to a head at a meeting of the IRA's army convention in Decemer 1969. The divide came over the principle of abstentionism that stemmed from the IRA's refusal to recognize the parliamentary authority of Stormont in Northern Ireland, the Dáil in the Republic of Ireland, or Westminster. The leadership was committed to abandon abstentionism in order to facilitate participation in elections. A majority of the convention supported this logical extension of the movement's political strategy reportedly by thirty-nine votes to twelve.[5] The outvoted minority withdrew to form a Provisional Army Council, providing the leadership of what consequently became known as the Provisional IRA, or the "Provos" in popular parlance. By a similar process the body supporting the official leadership became known as the Official IRA.

The same division appeared in Sinn Fein, the political wing of the IRA. At its *Ard Fheis* (convention) in Dublin in January 1970 a majority supported the leadership's resolution to end abstentionism.

The dissenters left and met elsewhere in Dublin in a hall hired in advance where they elected a caretaker executive in support of the Provisional Army Council. *An Phoblacht*, a new paper supporting the Provisionals, came out in February. It contained a wide-ranging statement by the caretaker executive justifying the formation of the new movement. The statement made it clear that the disagreement went far beyond the question of abstentionism. It accused the official leadership of having as its ultimate objective "nothing but a totalitarian dictatorship of the Left."[6] It rejected its "extreme socialism"[7] while describing the new movement's commitment to socialism in the following terms:

> Our socialism envisages the nationalization of the monetary system, commercial banks and insurance companies, key industries, mines, building land and fishing rights. Ours is a Socialism based on the native Irish tradition of *Comhar na g-Comharsan* [neighbors cooperation] which is founded on the right of worker-ownership and on our Irish and Christian values.[8]

Another major area of disagreement was the stance the leadership had taken over the issue of the retention of a parliament in Northern Ireland.

> We find absolutely incomprehensible from any Republican standpoint the campaigning in favour of retaining the Stormont parliament in August, September, and October last when it was in danger of being abolished altogether by the British Government. In any future struggle it would surely be preferable to have a direct confrontation with the British Government on Irish soil without the Stormont junta being interposed.[9]

From the outset, the Provisionals viewed the conflict as being essentially between Britain and the Irish people. They based this claim on the mandate Sinn Fein had won in elections in November 1918 to set up an all-Ireland Republic and, further, on the decision of Republican members of the Second Dáil to transfer executive authority for the new "state" to the leadership of the IRA.[10] The existence of a devolved government at Stormont and the sectarian divisions within Northern Ireland were seen as merely clouding the real issue. For example, in the March 1970 issue of *An Phoblacht* it was argued that "[sectarian] bigotry and hatred are deliberately encouraged by the masters in Westminster."[11] The same issue set out the aims of the Provisionals as being

to end foreign rule in Ireland, to establish a 32-county Democratic Socialist
Republic, based on the Proclamation of 1916, to restore the Irish language
and culture to a position of strength, and to promote a social order based
on justice and Christian principles which will give everyone a just share
of the nation's wealth.[12]

These statements by themselves, however, give an incomplete picture of the reasons for the formation of the Provisionals. To many in
the North the overriding issue was securing the means to defend their
areas, though that was not the limit of their ambitions. Ideological
considerations boiled down to a demand for guns rather than books
and pamphlets. There was also a tactical dimension to the denuncia-
tion of "extreme socialism." This relates to the controversial question
of the role played by members of the Fianna Fail government of the
Irish Republic in the formation of the Provisionals. Before the split,
some government ministers had tried "to get the IRA as a whole to
drop its political activities in the South, and concentrate on military
activities in the North."[13] When this failed they had encouraged the
split with promises of money and guns to a new movement freed from
any association with Marxism or the extreme left. The precise degree
of involvement of ministers remains a murky area. In May 1970 the
Irish prime minister, Jack Lynch, dismissed two members of his government, Charles Haughey and Neil Blaney, because of their alleged
involvement in supplying arms to be used in the North. Subsequently,
however, the two ministers were cleared of the charge of illegally
importing arms.[14] Two other ministers had resigned at the same time
as the dismissals. The significance of the dismissals and resignations
was that they marked the end of a period when the Irish government
appeared ready to give direct support to the armed self-defense of
Catholic areas in the North. This was the context of the Irish government's involvement in assistance to the Provisional IRA. Although
the logic of Provisional ideology pointed toward confrontation with
the British army, there was little expectation at the time of a change
in their perceived role as defenders against Protestant mob violence.
     This was because, in the terms of Northern Ireland's sectarian pol-
itics, the arrival of British troops had clearly been seen as a victory
for the Catholics. The reforms forced on the Unionist government in
the weeks after the dispatch of the troops had provided confirmation
that the Labour government would use its new leverage to improve
the position of the minority. In formal terms, these changes, like the
demands of the civil rights movement, did not have any bearing on
Northern Ireland's status as part of the United Kingdom. As the
Downing Street declaration of August 1969 bluntly put it, "the Border
is not an issue."[15] For many in Northern Ireland on both sides of the

religious divide, the two issues were not in practice separable. The interlocking of civil rights with national aspirations on the Catholic side was formulated in the following modest but perceptive terms by Conor Cruise O'Brien:

> Ulster Catholics are interested in equality—especially in relation to jobs— rather than in unity, although their concept of equality does include the right to wave a tricolour whenever a Protestant waves a Union Jack.[16]

On the other side of the divide, Protestant exclusivism,[17] embodying many of the discriminatory practices Westminster objected to, was widely regarded not as an end in itself but as the means by which Protestants maintained their position as British citizens on an island in which they constituted a beleaguered minority. Of all the reforms, the British government's insistence on the disbanding of the Ulster Special Constabulary, the B-Specials, evoked the most hostile reaction precisely because it was interpreted as an attempt to deprive Protestants of the means to defend themselves from their "enemies."

Just as the violent disturbances of 1968 and 1969 had exposed the vulnerability of many Catholic areas, paving the way for the rise of the Provisional IRA, so in exposed Protestant areas vigilantes had appeared on the streets. They were organized in a number of locally based associations. It was out of liaison and cooperation among a number of these associations in Belfast that the Ulster Defence Association emerged. According to one source, the name had first been suggested at a meeting of representatives of various local associations as early as December 1969.[18] The public first became aware of the existence of the UDA, however, in September 1971 when open recruitment for the organization began and its first newsletter was published. By this time, there had been a marked escalation of violence in Northern Ireland.

The street disturbances that had brought British troops to the province continued sporadically after their arrival. But what gave a new impetus to the conflict was the progressive alienation of Catholics from the British army. The defeat of the Labour government in the British general election of June 1970 and the victory of the Conservative party with its traditional alliance with the Unionist party was a factor in changing attitudes insofar as the army was seen as an instrument of government policy. (Much greater importance was attached to British party labels both by Catholics and Protestants during the early years of the Troubles than is now.) But the most influential factor behind the deterioration was the army's own actions in trying to establish its control over Catholic areas where it was in effect responsible for law and order. It is a measure of the gulf in perceptions

between Catholics and Protestants that the Protestant hostility toward
the army stemmed precisely from what they perceived as the army's
passivity in the face of rebellion. House-to-house arms searches conducted by the army in a vigorous manner in the Falls Road area of
Belfast in July 1970 proved to be a turning point in its relations with
the Catholic community. Provisional propaganda quickly reflected—
and exploited—the new mood of Catholic hostility toward the troops.
The front page of the August issue of An Phoblacht declared "British
Troops are Invaders" and followed the comment with a list: "Budapest
1956—Saigon 1966—Prague 1968—Belfast 1970."[19] There was no
mention of Derry 1969. The transformation of the image of the troops
meant that the Provisional IRA could now be presented in a role
consonant with its ideology as defenders of the community against
the British "forces of occupation," as the army was now dubbed. The
change had far-reaching implications because in terms of this role
offensive, action against the British presence could be justified in
a wide area, the argument being that, by forcing the British to dis-
perse their military resources, pressure was being taken off Catholic
ghettos.[20]

The year 1971 saw this logic of escalation being put into practice.
In February, when a British soldier was killed in a gun battle in Belfast,
he was the first army victim of the Troubles. Three more soldiers were
murdered in March. By the end of the year the total killed was forty-
three (see the tables at the end of this chapter). Bombings also occurred
with increasing frequency. The most damaging in economic terms was
the destruction in July of the Daily Mirror printing plant on the out-
skirts of Belfast. Bowyer Bell succinctly summarizes the Provisionals'
justification of this action:

> . . . the British government had to pay compensation for bomb damage,
> so that the campaign not only destroyed the "artificial economy" of the
> six counties but made London foot the bill.[21]

The bombing of Belfast's city center did more than economic damage. It created terror and, although it was primarily directed at property, there was a rising toll of deaths as a result of explosions.

In its publications, Provisional Sinn Fein derided the notion that
political accommodation within Northern Ireland offered the prospect
of a solution to the conflict. According to Republican News Stormont
had "no autonomy—not a shred of self-determination."[22] It saw these
advantages in direct rule from Westminster:

> British forces of occupation could then be clearly seen as forces of invasion
> on Irish soil. The lines of demarcation could be fairly and squarely drawn
> between those whose wish would be to sell their birthright and nationality
> and those who would strive to maintain it and defend it.[23]

The tactical basis of the Provisionals' opposition to Stormont, however, became obscured when they found themselves part of a much wider Catholic movement demanding that Stormont be abolished. This occurred when the Unionist administration of Brian Faulkner introduced internment in August 1971 after the reforms he had carried through had failed either to secure the cooperation of the Social Democratic and Labour party (SDLP), the party that represented most Catholics, or to end the violence. Far from reducing the level of violence, however, internment united "a large section of the Catholic population behind the IRA Provisionals and recruitment of the IRA became easier than ever before."[24] It was greeted with an explosion of Catholic resentment that further polarized Northern Ireland on sectarian lines.

These were the circumstances in which the UDA was publicly launched. In the first issue of its publication, *UDA*, the organization's aim was simply stated as being "the defence of Ulster against all who would destroy her"; among its rules, "because of the present situation in Northern Ireland, in which a STATE OF WAR exists, no Roman Catholic can become a member."[25] In the second issue, the organization's motto was unveiled: *Cedenta Arma Togae* (Law before Violence),[26] a distinctly odd choice for a paramilitary organization. It reflected not only the UDA's perception of its role as one of acting in defense of legitimate institutions but also its frequent complaint that the security forces failed to uphold the law, which is used as a basis on which to justify its Loyalist violence. "It is simple logic," argued *UDA*, "that if there is no law being exercised, how then can one be guilty of breaking the law?"[27] Another persistent theme of early issues of *UDA* was that no Roman Catholic could be trusted. Typical is an article in the second issue referring to the banning of remembrance parades (as part of a general ban on processions).

> They were banned because the number of Roman Catholics who would have participated would have been less than .001% of the Roman Catholic population. They were banned because the Roman Catholic population do not regard themselves as part of Ulster. They regard themselves as part of the Republic of Ireland. They are on the side of murder, terrorism, intimidation, and the total destruction of all loyalists. The exceptions are so very, very few that we simply cannot trust any of them, despite Mr. Brian Faulkner.[28]

Distrust was particularly focused on Catholics living in or near Protestant areas. Underlying this distrust was a territorialism implicit in Protestant exclusivism, which viewed the movement of Catholics outside their own ghettos as a threat. These perceptions largely explain why the UDA's paramilitary activity, apart from shows of strength of

massed ranks of loosely uniformed men, took the form of random
sectarian assassinations, and why Catholics living in Protestant areas
proved particularly vulnerable.

It should be clear by now that the UDA and the Provisional IRA
had (and indeed have) very different conceptions of the nature of the
Northern Ireland conflict. The Provisional model of the conflict was
of the classical anticolonial liberation struggle. In contemporary terms,
the enemy was British imperialism, and Northern Ireland "Britain's
Vietnam."[29] The UDA model of the conflict by contrast was that
Ulster Protestants were a community under siege, surrounded on all
sides by enemies. As a 1973 UDA press statement put it:

> We are betrayed, maligned and our families live in constant fear and misery.
> We are a nuisance to our so-called allies and have no friends anywhere.
> Once more in the history of our people, we have our backs to the wall,
> facing extinction by one way or another. This is the moment to beware,
> for Ulstermen in this position fight mercilessly till they or their enemies
> are dead.[30]

It may be objected that these models simply form the basis of the
propaganda of these two organizations in attempting to justify their
violence to a wider public. In support of this view, one might point
to acts of violence by both the UDA and the Provisional IRA that
cannot easily be accommodated within the respective models, wide
though the terms of both are, given certain assumptions. According
to Walter Laqueur, "free-floating aggression has been a frequent phenomenon in Irish history," and he argues that "many acts of violence
in the recent Troubles have also been quite motiveless."[31] From the
perspective of an outsider who does not share the view that any of
the paramilitaries have of the confict, this may indeed seem to be the
case. The course of the Troubles over the last dozen years, however,
suggests that the role of perceptions is much more important than
many writers on terrorism seem ready to acknowledge. Moreover, it
is possible to trace the influences of changes in perception on the
activities of the paramilitaries, particularly on the level of violence.
But before attempting to do this, let me briefly deal with a few complicating factors.

First, in raising funds for their activities both the UDA and the
Provisional IRA became involved in rackets of one kind or another
so that from time to time gangsterism has seemed almost an end in
itself. It has resulted periodically in violent purges within each organization as well as clashes with other paramilitary organizations on
the same side of the sectarian divide. Second, both organizations have
acted against ordinary criminals in the ghettos since these pose a

security threat as potential informers if caught by the police. In addition, the Provisional IRA has been concerned that the level of crime in Catholic ghettos should not rise to a point that would facilitate an acceptance of the RUC in these areas. Neither of these forms of violence need concern us here. Their contribution to the overall totals of deaths is in any event relatively small.

There are two more serious objections to the argument that variations in the level of violence can be explained in terms of the perceptions of the paramilitaries. The first is that the degree to which operations of the security forces were and are successful provides an independent determinant of the level of violence. This factor cannot be dismissed, though repeated demonstrations of their capacity to act whenever there have been public claims that the paramilitary organizations have been defeated suggest its limits. Second, it can be argued that the relationship between the level of violence and perceptions is an indirect one, with the amount of support the paramilitaries receive operating as the intervening variable. In other words, the argument is that the level of violence is dependent on how much support there is in the ghettos for the paramilitaries and that this support in turn depends on the view of the conflict held by a much wider public than members of the organizations. There is some substance to this argument, as a measure of support for the paramilitaries is clearly essential if they are to sustain themselves, and it is an issue to which they pay attention. The fact is, however, that the paramilitary organizations have at various times clearly run counter to the trend of opinion within their respective areas. Two rather different examples involving the Provisional IRA can be used to illustrate this point.

When the British government suspended Northern Ireland's parliament at Stormont and imposed direct rule in March 1972 in response to the violence that had followed internment, the SDLP, which had campaigned for the abolition of Stormont, issued a statement appealing to "those engaged in the campaign of violence to cease immediately in order to enable us to bring internment to a speedy end and in order to make a positive response to the British Government's proposals."[32] A representative of NICRA also called for a suspension of activities by Republican paramilitaries. Welcome though the fall of Stormont was to the Provisionals as a first step,[33] in their conception of the conflict there was certainly no place for British mediation in relation to Northern Ireland's sectarian divisions. They were ready to negotiate only about British withdrawal. Bowyer Bell described the Provisionals' attitude as follows:

Many of the Provos, however, felt the struggle was just beginning. In Navan, Mac Stiofain (the Provisional IRA Chief of Staff) announced that the campaign of course would continue, for the IRA demands had not been met. There was instant horror among the self-proclaimed friends and advisors of the Provos as well as a general disappointment in more conventional quarters. All felt that a wee pause might not be amiss, most knew that Stormont was finished, many felt more bombing would simply cost lives and further destroy the fragile stability of the North and could produce a civil war. Mac Stiofain, however, had responded in the traditional Republican manner—concessions be dammed, we want our country.[34]

The Protestant backlash that followed the imposition of direct rule and which so alarmed the political representatives of the Catholic community was regarded rather differently by the Provisionals. They welcomed Protestant hostility toward the British government as improving the prospects for breaking the union with Britain.

In June 1972 the Provisional IRA put forward their proposals for a new Ireland (Eire Nua). The proposals were published by Provisional Sinn Fein in September and were in three parts—a constitution, and two programs, one social and one economic, which were incorporated in the constitution. Most interest was created by the suggestion (made in June) that there should be four provincial parliaments based on the historic provinces of Ireland, that is to say, Leinster, Munster, Connacht, and a nine-county Ulster.[35] It was argued that

the establishment of Dail Uladh would be the first step toward the creation of this new government structure for the whole island. . . . The Unionist-oriented people of Ulster would have a working majority within the Province and would therefore have considerable control over their own affairs. That power would be the surest guarantee of their civil and religious liberties within a New Ireland.[36]

The social and economic programs that formed the bulk of the document were not new.[37] The federal proposals were clearly designed to appeal to Loyalists who felt betrayed by Britain. The disillusion was real enough and the statements it gave rise to were sufficiently double-edged to nourish the illusion for the next few years on the Provisional side of an alliance of extremes that would finally drive the British out. For example, the UDA had issued an appeal to Catholics in June 1972 to join with Protestants "and between us work out a new Northern Ireland which will be suitable and admirable for us both."[38]

That 1972 turned out to be the bloodiest year of the Troubles Northern Ireland has so far experienced (see table 3.1) is not surprising. It contained all the requisite ingredients. In particular, there was ample basis for Loyalists to believe that Catholics had supported

TABLE 3.1

DEATHS IN NORTHERN IRELAND AS A RESULT OF THE TROUBLES

Year	Civil	RUC[a] and RUC reserve	UDR[b]		Army	Total
1969	12	1	—		—	13
1970	23	2	—		—	25
1971	114	11	5		43	173
1972	322	17	25		103	467
1973	171	13	9		58	250
1974	165	15	7		30	218
1975	220	11	3		15	249
1976	243	23	15		14	295
1977	67	14	14		15	110
1978	50	10	7		14	81
1979	51	14		48		113
1980	50	9		16		75
1981	55	21		23		99
1982	22	4		10		36
(January–June)						
Totals	1,565	165		474		2,204
	(71.0%)	(7.5%)		(21.5%)		

[a] Royal Ulster Constabulary

[b] Ulster Defense Regiment

NOTE: These figures originate from the RUC as do those in table 2. I have extracted them from a number of sources. No detailed breakdown of the figures into Protestants and Catholics has been issued that covers the whole period, but from what information is available about civilian deaths, there is an approximate ratio of five Catholic deaths to every three Protestant in that category.[95]

the bombing out of existence (as they saw it) of Stormont. The SDLP's very appeal once Stormont had fallen that the violence should stop was open to that interpretation. At the same time they felt betrayed by a British government that was now wholly in charge of security in the province. On the other side, *Republican News* had dubbed 1972 "The Year of Victory."[39] (It was a slogan that was to be repeated in subsequent years, most forcefully in 1974.) The fall of Stormont had seemed to lend weight to the prediction. The mixture of the two sets of expectations was potent. Alarm on both sides of the sectarian divide that the province was being plunged into civil war failed to restrain either the UDA or the Provisional IRA.

The twelve months following the hunger strikes by Republican prisoners, which came to an end at the beginning of October 1981, provide the second example of Provisional activity running counter to the trend of opinion inside the Catholic community. Despite the immense emotion generated by the hunger strike deaths during 1981, resulting by all accounts in a flood of new recruits into the Provisional IRA, there was no escalation in the level of violence (see table 3.1). It would be inaccurate to suggest that Catholic opinion favored an increase in Provisional activity. Rather, the point is that the Provisionals might reasonably have expected greater tolerance for their actions, yet if this was the case it was not translated into the onslaught that many thought would follow the ending of the hunger strike. But before it is possible to analyze why the Provisionals did not launch a major offensive, more needs to be said about the evolution of perceptions since 1972.

The most important change that took place among the Provisionals was that their expectation of an early victory for their campaign for British withdrawal had evaporated. A frank speech by the leading Provisional figure, Gerry Adams, at the Wolfe Tone commemoration at Bodenstown in June 1979 argued that "the aims of the movement could not be achieved simply by military means and their failure to develop a strong alternative to constitutional politics had to be continually analysed."[40] A British army assessment in the same year described the Provisional IRA as being "deeply committed to a long campaign of attrition,"[41] but perhaps the most impressive evidence of the change in mood among the Provisionals was an internal Provisional IRA staff report in 1977 explaining why the structure of the organization had to be changed to the cell system: "We must gear ourselves to Long Term Armed Struggle based on putting unknown men and new recruits into a cell structure."[42] The support generated by the hunger strike campaign has not changed this conviction. In the August 1982 issue of *Magill*, Vincent Browne described current Provisional strategy as envisaging "the continuance of the campaign until well into the next century."[43]

Three factors had helped to sustain the earlier optimism; the readiness of the British government to negotiate directly or indirectly with the Provisional IRA; evidence of the British public's disillusionment with the problem of Northern Ireland; and the hopes attached to the political trends within the Loyalist community. Negotiations with the British government had taken place during 1972, through intermediaries in 1974, and in 1975. It can be argued, partly with benefit of hindsight, that the British government's principal motive for entering into these negotiations was to extract, albeit temporary, cease-fires to assist in wider political initiatives. At the time, however, the ultimate intentions of the British government were far from obvious and the negotiations played a significant part in fueling the suspicions of the Loyalist paramilitaries and stimulating their violence, particularly dur-

TABLE 3.2
PARTIAL BREAKDOWN OF DEATHS 1972–1978

Year	Killed in explosions		Sectarian, intrafactional and interfactional assassinations	
	(Number)	(Percent)	(Number)	(Percent)
1972	143	(30.6)	122	(26.1)
1973	69	(27.6)	87	(34.8)
1974	57	(26.1)	95	(43.6)
1975	76	(30.5)	144	(57.8)
1976	71	(24.1)	121	(41.0)
1977	13	(11.8)	42	(38.2)
1978	25	(30.9)	14	(17.3)

ing the long cease-fire in 1975 (see table 3.2). At the end of 1975 the incident centers that had been established to maintain a channel of communication through Provisional Sinn Fein with the IRA were closed down and it became the settled policy of the government not to negotiate with "terrorists."

The British public's disillusionment with the problem of Northern Ireland has not significantly dimmed over the years. Opinion polls throughout the Troubles have shown majorities in favor of withdrawal. What has diminished, however, is the Provisionals' expectation that such sentiment is likely to bring about a radical shift in government policy. Moreover, the process of Ulsterization of the security forces has undermined the salience of a simple "Brits out" or "Troops out" position. An article in *Fortnight* in response to Tony Benn's advocacy of withdrawal of British troops at the time of the 1981 hunger strikes pointed out that, whereas the level of British army manpower in Northern Ireland was approximately eleven thousand, the total of local security forces amounted to some nineteen thousand.[44] The implications of this position have been acknowledged by the Provisionals insofar as they have added to their demands for a British withdrawal the demand that the RUC be disarmed and the Ulster Defence Regiment disbanded.[45] While the logic of this refinement cannot be faulted, it has much less credibility as an achievable goal than the simple slogans once had.

The hopes of an alliance of the extremes with the Protestant paramilitaries were at their height during the period from 1972 to early 1975 when David O'Connell was the dominant political figure within the Provisional IRA. He had hoped that the federal proposals in *Eire Nua* would provide the basis of accommodation with the Ulster nationalism that seemed to be emerging out of disillusion among Loyalists with what they saw as their betrayal by Britain. O'Connell was even willing to welcome the Ulster Workers Council (UWC) strike that brought the downfall of the power-sharing executive in May 1974 as being in the "Wolfe Tone tradition,"[46] though this was not a view that enjoyed unanimous support within the Provisional movement. But the moment at which the prospect for an alliance of extremes appeared most credible was before the strike when the imperative of undermining the Sunningdale agreement with its proposals for a Council of Ireland created a tactical basis for cooperation. In January, Desmond Boal, a lawyer and politician with links to the Loyalist paramilitaries, put forward proposals for a federal Ireland under which the old Stormont system might be restored in Ulster. To An Phoblacht it appeared to be the breakthrough the Provisionals had been seeking since the June 1972 proposals. It headlined its report of the Boal plan: "Loyalists and Republicans on way to peace."[47] However, once the UWC strike had removed the threat that Loyalists saw in the Sunningdale agreement, the lack of any fundamental basis for agreement became more apparent, although some contacts between the Provisionals and the Loyalist paramilitaries were maintained, for the most part indirectly. Tim Pat Coogan refers to talks proceeding through intermediaries as late as April 1977.[48] It is doubtful, though, that they had much political substance.

After the UWC strike in which the UDA had been able to demonstrate its muscle on the streets, another aspect of Loyalist paramilitary activity began to loom larger in Provisional thinking. This was their continuing campaign of sectarian assassination. The issue illustrates very well the different perceptions the two sides had of the conflict and the different bases on which they legitimized acts of violence. The Provisionals' view of the conflict disposed them to suspect that the assassinations were the work of the British army.[49] Insofar as the role of Loyalist paramilitaries could not be ignored, the Provisionals focused on evidence of cooperation between the killers and the security forces. There was a reluctance on the part of the Provisionals to respond in kind, though here differences in perceptions were most telling. As far as the Loyalists were concerned, the Provisional IRA had from the beginning been engaged in sectarian warfare. They did not recognize the distinction the Provisionals drew between civilians and the security forces, members of the legal system, and other agents of British rule. As a leading figure in the UDA put it in an interview in 1981:

> . . . the Protestants copied the Provisional IRA and we became involved in very deep sectarian violence which lasted for a number of years. In 1972 almost 500 people were killed and we have little doubt now that

most of these people died, whether they were Protestant or Catholic, because they were of the wrong religion in the wrong place at the wrong time. Such was the deep sectarian division and fear within Northern Ireland. [50]

On the Loyalist side, there was thus an element of "tit for tat" underlying the killings from the beginning.

Up to late 1974, there were very few killings attributable to the Provisional IRA that can unambiguously be put into the category of random sectarian assassinations. [51] Eventually, the Provisional IRA did respond in kind, though ideological qualms about such action meant that they rarely claimed responsibility for such murders. It is not difficult to find reasons why the Provisionals should have departed from their own norms of what constituted legitimate violence. The most important was that the random assassinations were drying up Catholic support for the Provisional IRA's campaign of violence. In particular the killings were undermining the Provisionals' claim to be effective defenders of the Catholic community, if not of Catholic areas. The disproportionate toll of Catholics among the civilian victims of the Troubles was influencing opinion and putting the Provisionals themselves on the defensive. The first area to be affected by retaliation in crude sectarian terms was North Belfast, an area where Protestant hostility toward what they saw as widespread Catholic encroachment on their domain had provided a powerful stimulus to random sectarian assassination. [52] At the end of 1974 the Provisional IRA hit back so that for a time more Protestants were dying in North Belfast in random sectarian attacks than Catholics. [53] The retaliation continued across the province during 1975 and 1976. In 1975 sectarian, intrafactional, and interfactional assassinations accounted for a majority of those killed in the Troubles that year (see table 3.2). In January 1976, the day after five Catholics were killed in two attacks in the Provisional stronghold of South Armagh, ten Protestant workmen from Bessbrook traveling in a minibus were stopped by a Provisional IRA unit and murdered by the side of the road. The impact of the resort to sectarian killings on the political thinking of the Provisionals was that it effectively ended the illusion of the alliance of the extremes. O'Connell's arrest in the spring of 1975 assisted the process of change by removing him from a position of leadership. When the period of "tit for tat" killings ended, there was no significant revival of the idea. By that time Provisional thinking was developing in a new direction as a Northern group of radicals, the most important of whom was Gerry Adams, increasingly began to shape policy.

Three trends have been apparent within the Provisional movement since 1976; secularization, radicalization, and politicization. Secularization is the most difficult to pinpoint. On the one hand, conflict between the Roman Catholic church hierarchy and Republican advocates of physical force has been a permanent feature of the Irish political landscape. A deterioration in relations with the Church therefore does not by itself indicate a secular trend. Insofar as the Church's denunciations of Provisional violence have become more strident it can be argued that this has been facilitated by the trend in lay public opinion. On the other hand, the religious symbolism employed during the 1981 hunger strike campaign hardly seems in keeping with a process of secularization. However, emphasis on "Christian principles"[54] and on a "theology of violence,"[55] which were features of early Provisional Sinn Fein publications, is no longer evident, and in recent interviews Provisional Sinn Fein spokesmen have consistently stressed the secular nature of the movement.[56] The old dictum that the Provos went to mass once a week whereas the "Stickies" (the Official IRA, their rivals in the early 1970s) went once a year,[57] dubious as it was from the beginning, no longer enjoys any credence.

Radicalization has led to a much greater emphasis on the socialist aims of the movement, and even to a limited growth in the influence of Marxist ideas on members' thinking. However, while they have moved to the left, the Provisionals have strongly denied that they have become a Marxist organization.[58] The most obvious by-product of radicalization has been that anticommunism, which was a prominent feature of early Provisional Sinn Fein publications, has faded. Criticism of Cuba as a totalitarian dictatorship has given way to a much more sympathetic view of Castro as a Third World leader, and propaganda directed against the Official Republican movement no longer portrays Official leaders with pictures of Lenin or copies of *Pravda.*[59] In policy terms one of the most important results of radicalization has been the ditching of federalism as a sop to Loyalism and an obstacle to socialist planning. The change, which was first voted through at the 1981 Ard Fheis, and confirmed by the 1982 Ard Fheis, was a defeat for those, like David O'Connell, who still wanted to keep open the possibility of an eventual accommodation with Loyalist Ulster nationalism, an idea derided by the Northern radicals. Their view of the Protestant paramilitaries was that they simply represented Loyalist muscle and that there was little substance to their political ideas.

The trend of politicization is a product of a number of factors, not all of which need concern us here. Fundamentally, it has stemmed from the recognition that a single-minded concentration on the "military" campaign is no longer appropriate, given their acceptance of the long-term nature of the struggle. This has meant a subtle change in the importance attached to public support. It had always been recognized that a fall in the level of support jeopardized the campaign of violence and increased the vulnerability of the Provisional IRA to the security forces. This was especially the case before the reorganization from a locally based pyramid structure to the cell system. Indeed, the loss of support from 1975 on had necessitated the reorganization. However, while the cell system has to some extent solved the operational problem of sustaining the campaign of violence with minimal support, the issue of support has acquired a wider political significance. Support is seen as needed to give meaning to the campaign, especially insofar as it is recognized that violence by itself will not bring about a British withdrawal, let alone end partition. This point has been articulated in Provisional publications in a number of ways, including emphasis on the need to pursue "the struggle for national liberation on a successful multifaceted front,"[60] assertion that armed struggle alone cannot succeed, and criticism of a "militaristic" tendency in the past.[61] Although propaganda along these lines often contains an element of empty rhetoric that is by no means new, these arguments are part of a trend of politicization that has some substance.

The area of policy where their influence has been most apparent is that of participation by Provisional Sinn Fein in elections. With the minor exception of elections to local councils in the south, the previous policy was to boycott elections. When the seat of Fermanagh and South Tyrone became vacant in March 1981 as a result of the death of the sitting M.P., Frank Maguire, the opportunity presented itself to highlight the Republican prisoners' hunger strike campaign by putting up a prisoner as a candidate in the by-election, and it proved irresistible. The victory of Bobby Sands in the by-election prompted further participation in elections over the H-block issue both in Northern Ireland and the Republic. The one significant exception was the local council elections in Northern Ireland in May 1981. Many Provisionals regretted their failure to seize this opportunity to challenge the SDLP at a moment when passions were running high within the Catholic community over the H-block issue. While their forays into the electoral process during 1981 can be regarded as tactical, since they were over a single issue, a more fundamental change in policy followed.

Provisional Sinn Fein announced in April 1982 that it would contest elections under its own name to the Northern Ireland Assembly proposed by the British government. A campaign during the summer for a nationalist boycott of the election put this decision in doubt until the SDLP's decision to take part in the elections enabled the Provisionals to reaffirm that they would participate. One further minor change took place before polling for the Assembly on 20 October. Provisional Sinn Fein became simply Sinn Fein, a change in name made possible by the decision of the Workers party, the political heirs of the Official Republican movement, to stop using the term. What did not change was the Provisionals' policy of abstentionism, the original cause of the split in the IRA in 1969. Sinn Fein made clear that it would boycott the Assembly itself, a position the SDLP also adopted.

Sinn Fein achieved a major political breakthrough in the elections to the seventy-eight-member Assembly. Five of its twelve candidates were elected and the party received over 10 percent of first preference votes. This meant that almost a third of Catholic voters had supported Sinn Fein. The implications of the Provisionals' electoral success are distinctly double-edged. On the one hand, the possibility that they might displace the SDLP as representatives of the minority may lead to a greater emphasis on Sinn Fein's involvement in community pol-itics, particularly in the field of housing and in the provision of welfare services, while some restraint is placed on the campaign of violence. On the other hand, the Provisionals may regard the outcome of the elections as providing them with a significant popular base for stepping up the campaign of violence. From the outset, the Provisionals have been careful to make clear that the change in policy does not mean abandoning the campaign of violence. Before the decision on the Assembly elections, Provisional Sinn Fein had first made clear its desire to put up a candidate in West Belfast at the next Westminster general election. A spokesman for Provisional IRA was authorized to express the army leadership's approval. The terms of participation were clearly stated:

> For those who would be concerned that such an intervention in the West Belfast election is a new tendency, or departure, they can be assured that the military struggle will go on with all the energy at our disposal, and, in fact, victory would actually be hastened with the development of a complementary radical political offensive.[62]

At the same time, it is not farfetched to argue that the electoral strategy had an influence on the Provisionals' evident desire to nurture the support gained during the hunger strike as expressed in this extract from an editorial in *Iris:*

> . . . the losses incurred by the nationalist establishment during the hunger strike cannot necessarily be assumed to be republican gains. The Estab-lishment's present instability, lack of credibility and loss of authority may be but a transient thing which can be restored over a period if republicans do not actively and energetically involve themselves in organizing and articulating the just grievances in every area of political, social, economic, and cultural dissidence and disaffection throughout the country.[63]

The low level of violence during the first half of 1982 seems at least partly attributable to deliberate restraint on the part of the Provisionals so as not to alienate potential electoral support. Successes by the security forces as a result of the evidence of informers also probably contributed to the low death toll from the Troubles during this period. In July there were just two deaths, whereas a decade earlier in July 1972, ninety-six people had died. Not surprisingly, those within the Provisional movement who had opposed the electoral strategy because they feared it would lead to a scaling down of the campaign of violence became increasingly vocal.[64] Although there was an escalation in the level of violence in the last three months of 1982, much of this violence was the work of the Irish National Liberation Army (INLA), though the Provisional IRA also stepped up its activities after the Assembly elections. The Provisionals' sensitivity to accusations that participation in elections was undermining the commitment to the campaign of violence was reflected in a resolution of the Sinn Fein Ard Fheis at the end of October requiring candidates in elections to defend the "armed struggle."[65] At the same time, Sinn Fein spokesmen have refused to criticize violence by INLA even though the timing of some of INLA's actions has seemed calculated to damage Sinn Fein politically and despite sharp criticism of the Provisionals' electoral strategy by the Irish Republican Socialist party, the political wing of INLA.[66]

The UDA has also adopted an electoral strategy, but it has reached this position by a very different route. Three broad perceptions formed the basis on which the UDA justified the Loyalist campaign of violence: first, that Catholics in general supported the Provisional IRA; second, that the security forces were incapable of, or were being prevented from, upholding the law; and third, that it was the intention of the British government to sell out the Protestant community. In 1976 the first of these perceptions began to change. In August 1976 the peace movement came into being following an incident in which three children were killed in Andersonstown, a Catholic suburb of Belfast, as a result of a clash between the British army and the Provisional IRA. The demand, articulated forcefully on television by the children's aunt, that the Provisionals end their campaign, brought a dramatic response in the form of large demonstrations for peace, mainly, to begin with, in Catholic areas. There were many reasons why this movement got off the ground where previous attempts had fizzled out. The cumulative impact of seven years of violence after the arrival of the British troops was one factor. The pervasive fear in many areas of Belfast and elsewhere as a result of the sectarian assassinations was another. The fact that a major grievance of the Catholic community had been removed with the ending of internment in December

1975 also may have helped. Last, the government's commitment to the policy of direct rule as, for the moment, the least unacceptable solution, provided a framework of political certainty that met a wide-spread desire for a return to something like normality.

The activities of the peace movement were quickly reflected in the pages of *Ulster*, which had taken the place of *UDA* as the official voice of the Ulster Defence Association. An editorial in the issue of September 1976 entitled "Peace Perfect Peace"[67] was notably sympathetic to the aims of the peace movement, if skeptical about the prospects for success. It readily admitted that "if there was no such thing as the IRA then that would equally apply to the Loyalist paramilitaries."[68] The same issue contained a letter from a Catholic reader hostile to the Provisional IRA. This represented quite a substantial change from the early 1970s when the constant refrain of UDA publications had been "you can trust none of them" and when its supporters had been urged to harden themselves to put aside any friendships with Catholics as "an obstacle to us in the protection and preservation of our community."[69] A partial change was evident before the formation of the peace movement. It was reflected in the terms in which the campaign of sectarian assassination was justified. For example, the July 1976 issue of *Ulster* complained that the media portrayed as random sectarian assassinations what were selective attacks on "known Republicans."[70] It is clear, however, from the list of names they put in this category that the UDA's definition of a Republican was a very wide one, though the UDA was evidently receiving some intelligence from low-level sources in the security forces.

In 1977 the campaign of sectarian assassination stopped altogether, a cease-fire that continued through 1978 and the first half of 1979. In this period there was in fact a general decline in the activities and influence of the Loyalist paramilitaries. Tim Pat Coogan suggests that the cease-fire was a result of a specific agreement made through intermediaries between the Provisional IRA and the UDA,[71] but whether or not such talks played a part in stopping the killings the change in perceptions within the UDA remains an important factor in accounting for the decision and that would seem traceable to the impact of the peace movement. The year 1977 saw a further change in the UDA's political outlook. In May the UDA gave its backing to an indefinite strike called by the Rev. Ian Paisley to demand a change in the government's security policy. The role of the UDA was to provide muscle on the streets as it had done during the 1974 UWC strike. However, despite widespread intimidation, on this occasion the strike was a failure. The UDA's confidence in Loyalist politicians was further undermined by what the UDA saw as the politicians' failure to judge the mood of public opinion. Distrust of politicians had always been close to the surface within the UDA, but in practice it had given its support to Loyalist politicians who had taken a strong stand on the issue of security and British "betrayal" and whose rhetoric came closest to justifying the violence of the Loyalist paramilitaries. The way those same politicians distanced themselves from the cause of Loyalist prisoners was a source of continuing bitterness within the UDA.

After the failure of the 1977 strike, the UDA leadership resolved that the organization should develop its own distinctive position on a long-term political solution to the Northern Ireland conflict. The decline in the level of violence and the British government's commitment to a policy of direct rule created a measure of stability that provided propitious circumstances for a considered examination of the options. In January 1978 the UDA set up the New Ulster Political Research Group (NUPRG) to carry out just such an examination. It was clear from an early stage that the NUPRG would come out in favor of an independent Northern Ireland. It was not a new idea. At various times of crisis in relations with Westminster, the suggestion of a unilateral declaration of independence from Britain had been supported by the UDA. What was different about the NUPRG's thinking was that it envisaged a negotiated independence and that it sought to allay suspicions that the purpose of independence would be to give the UDA a free hand to "clear the decks"[72] on a provincewide scale.

A full statement of the NUPRG's proposals was published in March 1979 in a discussion document entitled "Beyond the Religious Divide."[73] For a paramilitary organization whose members had earlier carried out random sectarian assassinations, it was a remarkable document. Negotiated independence for Northern Ireland was put forward as

> the only proposal which does not have a victor and a loser. It will encourage the development of a common identity between all of our people, regardless of religion. We offer through our proposal, first class Ulster-citizenship to all of our people, because like it or not the Protestant of N.I. is looked upon as a second class British citizen and the Roman Catholic of N.I. as a second class Irish citizen in the South.[74]

Independence was to be on the basis of a new constitution along the lines of the American Constitution with a Bill of Rights, and was to be supported by guarantees from Britain and the Irish Republic, which would withdraw all their claims of sovereignty over Northern Ireland.

Underlying these proposals was "the concept of political unity in Northern Ireland between Protestants and Roman Catholics with the same ideology," which would allow people "to decide their elected Representatives on a political basis rather than religious bigotry and sectarian hatred."[75] It warned:

> Without the evolution of proper politics, the people of Northern Ireland will continually be manipulated by sectarian politicians who make no contribution to the social and economic well-being of the people or the country, but only continue to fan the flames of religious bigotry for self gain and preservation.[76]

The notion of "proper politics" was not defined explicitly but it is clear that what the authors had in mind was the development of class-based politics that would permit the development of working-class unity and the emergence of a broadly based labor party.[77] To buttress the case for independence, the UDA has also set up the Ulster Heritage Agency to conduct research into the historical basis for the notion of a common Ulster identity cutting across sectarian divisions.

Inevitably, despite the evidence of a far-reaching change in perceptions, suspicion lingered that the proposals for independence contained unstated intentions, in particular for retribution.[78] In "Why Independence Is Feared by the IRA," an article in Ulster, it was argued that "it is no secret that if Ulster were to 'go it alone,' the IRA would have their backs to the wall," making possible the destruction of "the hiding places, the rat-holes, the sewers from which they emanate."[79] But the argument that independence would undermine the position of the Provisional IRA did have a more sophisticated basis, which was also quoted approvingly in the pages of Ulster. This was the argument that the Provisionals "could not claim with any conviction that an indigenous government of Ulster politicians would be 'colonial' or 'imperialist.'"[80] The most serious objection to the NUPRG proposals, however, was not that the UDA leadership was insincere in supporting them but that there was little understanding of, or commitment to, the proposals among the rank and file.

The task of promoting the proposals was not made easier by a change in the political climate that followed the election of a Conservative government in May 1979, though the mishandling of a scandal over police interrogation methods under the previous government had already begun to erode confidence in the progress of the return to normality. A new and inexperienced secretary of state for Northern Ireland reduced confidence further in his first months of office by creating an impression of purposeless drift in government policy. The appearance on the streets of Belfast of Provisional IRA gunmen openly displaying their weapons in a propaganda exercise in early August brought a warning from the UDA that it might resume operations.

On 26 August, the *Guardian* published a report, with photograph, of a new Loyalist assassination squad, which claimed that its membership came from the UDA and the UVF and that it was engaged in a professional campaign against selective targets.[81] On the same day a bomb planted by the Provisional IRA killed Lord Mountbatten and three others on a boat in the Irish Republic and, in a separate incident, eighteen British soldiers were killed at Warrenpoint in Northern Ireland in a Provisional IRA ambush. These events were followed by a resumption of sectarian assassinations of Catholics and by a statement from the Ulster Freedom Fighters (UFF) that they were embarking on a campaign against known Republicans.[82] The launching of a new political initiative by the government added to the uncertainty while the mobilization of Catholics in support of the demands of Republican prisoners was increasing tension.

Jack Holland's view of these developments was that it proved that "the old reactive nature of loyalism was too strong to be contained by the confused soul-searching of the New Ulster Political Research Group."[83] The precise role of the UDA leadership in the new situation is a difficult and controversial question. An article by David Beresford in the *Guardian* in August 1980 claimed that the UDA was behind a series of attacks on leading Republican figures.[84] By contrast, Arthur Aughey and Colin McIlhenny have argued that "a more plausible explanation is that we are witnessing independent actions by maverick elements who feel that the military role should be given greater emphasis."[85] However, the two views are not entirely inconsistent. In an interview published in December 1981, the supreme commander of the UDA, Andy Tyrie, explained the relationship between the UDA and the UFF as follows:

> The UFF consist of a group of people who are members or associated members of the Ulster Defence Association and they decided that the only solution to the problem is a purely military one. And their attitude is, well, to remove active Republicans, and active nationalists who are trying to overthrow what exists here in the form of a government—people who are assassinating or bombing Ulster people. The UFF feel they are justified in taking military action against them. Now, if that's the type of action they do stay strictly to, and do bomb and shoot only active Republicans, no way would the UDA disapprove of it. We would have no objection to it whatsoever.[86]

This interview is not the only evidence that the UFF had become more independent of the UDA leadership. Court cases in which individuals were charged with the offense of membership in the UFF, which was illegal, were another indication that a real distinction now

existed between the organizations. At the same time, even allowing
for the largely selective nature of the new Loyalist campaign of violence, the level of violence during 1980, 1981, and most of 1982
suggests a measure of restraint on the part of the UDA itself. What
is more, the UDA adopted a critical stance toward Paisley's campaign
against the Anglo-Irish negotiations initiated at the Dublin summit
in December 1980 and Andy Tyrie even expressed support for Garret
Fitzgerald's crusade at the end of 1981 to alter the Irish constitution
to make it more acceptable to the North.[87] In these circumstances
the gulf between the UDA and militant Loyalists grew wider and
wider. Increasingly, their actions were channeled through smaller, rival
paramilitary organizations. Following Sinn Fein's success in the Assembly elections and an upsurge in Republican violence, the Protestant
Action Force, a front for the UVF, claimed responsibility for a spate
of sectarian attacks on Catholics in the last three months of 1982.

The UDA's political development was taken a stage further with
the formation in June 1981 of the Ulster Loyalist Democratic party
(ULDP). It replaced the NUPRG while adopting the NUPRG proposals as its policy. However, its first significant foray into electoral
politics under its own name was a failure. Its chairman, John Mc-
Michael, stood in the Belfast South by-election in March 1982, receiving a miserable 1 percent of the total vote. Andy Tyrie and John
McMichael were arrested following a police raid on UDA headquarters
in April. They were charged with conspiring to possess information
likely to be useful to terrorists and with conspiracy to possess firearms
with intent to endanger life. A curious episode followed. Originally
refused bail, they were granted bail and released on 14 May after the
intervention of two clergymen who wrote letters of reference to the
court in which, according to the men's counsel, Tyrie was described
as "a moderating influence against more extreme elements in the
UDA."[88] One of the clergymen had previously achieved prominence
as an intermediary in negotiations between the British government
and the Provisional IRA in 1974. Two ULDP candidates stood in the
Assembly elections in October 1982. They received a derisory vote
after conducting a low-key campaign in which little attempt was made
to explain the party's policies to the electorate. While the electoral
failure of the ULDP has not so far reversed the political orientation
of the UDA leadership, it does seem to have weakened further the
leadership's influence over the rank and file. The importance of the
changes in perception within the UDA nonetheless remains considerable. It may be gauged by considering what the organization's reaction might have been at an earlier stage of the conflict to the election
first of a Provisional IRA prisoner, then of a member of Provisional
Sinn Fein, in a constituency with a small Catholic majority and to
negotiations between the British and Irish governments, which in-

cluded the issue of Northern Ireland. It remains to be seen how the organization responds to the new challenge presented by the political prominence Sinn Fein has achieved as a result of the Assembly elections.

In his study of political terrorism, Paul Wilkinson identifies the following as some of the key characteristics: "indiscriminateness, unpredictability, arbitrariness, ruthless destructiveness, and the implicitly amoral and antinomian nature of a terrorist's challenge."[89] The purpose of this study of the Provisional IRA and the UDA is to suggest that their campaigns of violence are altogether more susceptible to rational explanation than Wilkinson's model of terrorism implies. In particular, the role of perceptions in legitimizing violence is much greater than a model of this type would allow and the effect of changes of perception on behavior that I have outlined here suggests that ideological pronouncements cannot be dismissed as mere rationalizations. There are aspects of the two organizations' activities that I have not delved into. In particular, I have not analyzed the Provisionals' extension of their campaign of violence at particular junctures to the British mainland. These gaps, however, do not greatly alter the argument. Another limitation of this study is of course that I have examined in depth only two of the organizations engaged in violence in Northern Ireland. Smaller paramilitary groups were responsible for much of the violence toward the end of 1982.

It may be objected that the terrorist model of the type put forward by Wilkinson is appropriate in some situations but not in Northern Ireland's circumstances of instability. All I can say is that it is not a limitation many writers on terrorism would accept. Wilkinson himself mentions both organizations under the heading of "terror against liberal democracies."[90] Further, it is clear that what might be called the terrorist stereotype has itself had an influence on British policy, particularly in recent years. The point is that the stereotype has rather clear implications for the conduct of government in the face of terrorism. Some of these have been spelled out by Wilkinson in a chapter of prescriptions in a recent collection of essays. His ground rules for liberal democracies include the following:

> No deals should be made with terrorist organizations behind the backs of elected politicians. . . . The Government should not engage in dialogue and negotiations with groups which are actively engaged in promoting, committing, or supporting terrorism. . . . Terrorists imprisoned for crimes committed for professedly political motives should be treated in the same manner as ordinary criminals.[91]

Their relevance to Northern Ireland is obvious. In practice, they are difficult and costly to apply. On a wide but not unreasonable interpretation of the second rule, for example, the government's dialogue with political representatives would be considerably restricted. The government's attempts to uphold the third rule produced the most serious crisis Northern Ireland had witnessed since the fall of the power-sharing executive in 1974.

Not merely was the crisis over the demand by Republican prisoners for political status predictable but its consequences were foreseen. In an essay written in 1978 a colleague of mine argued:

> Any lasting future accommodation has to be based upon the assumption that "men of violence" will be accepted as citizens of the new order, and it cannot be ruled out that such people may achieve positions of elective leadership. However repellant that is, it means in practice accepting the fact that those who commit violent crime for purposes which large sections of the population (whether agreeing with the actions or not) regard as politically motivated, must be treated as a species of political criminal. And a precedent having once been established that political criminals be confined in circumstances different from those of other criminals, it is a mistake to attempt to reverse that. The limited but nonetheless real bond of sympathy between the agents of political violence and a large part of the people who support their objectives but not their means will be strengthened rather than weakened by the official denial of political status of the former.[92]

Despite these strictures, I think a defense can be made for the government's decision to phase out special category status in 1976. It was part of a package that included the ending of internment and a commitment to a policy of direct rule. The policy of criminalization meant reliance on the courts, though courts operating without a jury. In turn, this led to giving primacy to the police over the army in combating political violence and involved an implicit admission that it could not be eliminated completely any more than one could expect to eliminate ordinary crime. In short, it was a policy of containment. Politically, it presupposed a gradual return to normality and the acceptance by both communities that direct rule did not threaten the essential interests of either. That meant the government's refraining from political initiatives that would create uncertainty and raise the level of tension. Between 1976 and 1978 this combination of policies achieved a measure of success. Whether they could have been sustained over a longer period is open to argument.

In any event, the Conservative government launched a new political initiative in October 1979, partly in response to American pressure. At the same time, other aspects of the previous set of policies came under strain. How far this was the result of the government's repudiation of the policy of direct rule is difficult to establish. The most serious challenge to the government was the mobilization of large numbers of Catholics in the campaign against criminalization. It is arguable that this would have happened anyway, but the uncertainty created by the initiative probably assisted the campaign's momentum. The mobilization of Loyalists against the Anglo-Irish negotiations initiated in December 1980 further contributed to polarization while the hunger strike deaths in 1981 increased tensions between the two communities. The seriousness of political divisions, however, was masked by the relatively low level of violence that accompanied the polarization of the communities. At a distance it was even possible to view the low level of violence as a vindication of the government's firmness during the hunger strike campaign and as an indication that support for violent organizations, and most particularly the Provisional IRA, was on the decline.[93] Sinn Fein's showing in the Assembly elections in October 1982 dispelled this complacency but not before it had done considerable damage. In particular, the British government contributed to a marked deterioration in Anglo-Irish relations by frivolously making an issue of the Republic of Ireland's neutral stance during the Falklands war.

That the extreme political polarization of the two communities in Northern Ireland has not had a greater impact on the level of violence can best be explained in terms of the evolution of the perceptions of those engaged in violence—in particular, their recognition of the limited efficacy of violence as a political instrument in present circumstances. By contrast, the thrust of the terrorist stereotype is that harsh measures by government offer the best hope of stamping out terrorism.[94] The adoption of draconian measures in the situation that Northern Ireland faces at the moment, however, would be more likely to precipitate civil war than to bring the violence to an end. Ironically, in Northern Ireland the British government has often been a victim of its own promotion of the terrorist stereotype. It is constantly accused by Loyalists of lacking the political will to defeat terrorism and its failure to take "effective" measures frequently forms the justification of Loyalist terrorism as counterterrorism. That the government has by and large resisted these pressures is a tribute to its recognition of the likely consequences of more repressive policies. This chapter will have fulfilled its purpose if it has shown that Hannah Arendt's emphasis on the instrumental character of violence and hence the constant need to justify its use with reference to the end being pursued provides a more promising starting point for analysis than the conception of terrorism that has become established in recent years. Northern Ireland's prospects for peace, such as they are, are less likely to depend on the techniques employed by government to deal with terrorism than on the evolution of perceptions of those engaged in political violence.

NOTES

1. See her essay on violence in Hannah Arendt, *Crises of the Republic* (Harmondsworth: Penguin, 1973), pp. 33–146.

2. The Royal Ulster Constabulary, Northern Ireland's police force.

3. See Martin Dillon and Denis Lehane, *Political Murder in Northern Ireland* (Harmondsworth: Penguin, 1973), pp. 28–30.

4. See, for example, Conor Cruise O'Brien, *States of Ireland* (St. Albans: Panther, 1974), p. 193.

5. The figures are given in J. Bowyer Bell, *The Secret Army: The IRA 1916–1979* (Dublin: The Academy Press, 1979), p. 366.

6. Quoted in *An Phoblacht* (Dublin), February 1970.

7. Ibid. (A heading of one section of the statement.)

8. Ibid.

9. Ibid.

10. See Provisional Army Council statement, December 1969, quoted in Bell, *Secret Army*, p. 366.

11. *An Phoblacht*, March 1970.

12. Ibid.

13. Cruise O'Brien, *States of Ireland*, p. 197.

14. Blaney was not sent to trial. Haughey was acquitted. Charles Haughey later became prime minister of the Republic of Ireland. He lost office in December 1982.

15. Quoted from the Downing Street Declaration. The full text can be found in Richard Deutsch and Vivien Magowan, *Northern Ireland: A Chronology of Events*, vol. 1, 1968–71 (Belfast: Blackstaff Press, 1973), p. 152.

16. Cruise O'Brien, *States of Ireland*, p. 277.

17. See Frank Wright, "The Ulster Spectrum" in David Carlton and Carlo Schaerf, ed., *Contemporary Terror* (London: Macmillan, 1981), pp. 153–157.

18. Jack Holland, *Too Long a Sacrifice: Life and Death in Northern Ireland Since 1969* (New York: Dodd, Mead, 1981), p. 50.

19. *An Phoblacht*, August 1970.

20. See Frank Burton, *The Politics of Legitimacy: Struggles in a Belfast Community* (London: Routledge and Kegan Paul, 1978), p. 82.

21. Bell, *Secret Army*, p. 381.

22. *Republican News* (Belfast), March 1971. A Provisional Sinn Fein Publication.

23. *Republican News*, April 1971.

24. *Fortnight* (Belfast), 12 January 1972. An independent review for Northern Ireland.

25. *UDA* (Belfast), vol. 1, no. 1, n.d.

26. *UDA*, vol. 1, no. 2 (19 October 1971).

27. *UDA*, vol. 1, no. 3, n.d.

28. *UDA*, vol. 1, no. 2. Faulkner was the prime minister of Northern Ireland at the time. What was being referred to were the tentative moves he had made earlier in the year toward a political accommodation with the Catholic community.

29. See, for example, *Republican News*, 30 October 1971.

30. Quoted in Dillon and Lehane, *Political Murder*, p. 282.

31. Walter Laqueur, *Terrorism* (London: Weidenfeld and Nicolson, 1977), pp. 188 and 189.

32. Quoted in *Fortnight*, 13 April 1972.

33. See, for example, *Republican News*, Easter Sunday 1972.

34. Bell, *Secret Army*, p. 387.

35. Northern Ireland consists of six counties. The other three counties of historic Ulster form part of the Republic of Ireland.

36. *Eire Nua*, (Provisional) Sinn Fein, Dublin 1972, p. 56.

37. It had been published on its own under the same title of *Eire Nua* in January 1971. What is more, apart from a few revisions, the program had been written before the division of the IRA at the end of 1969. The two sets of constitutional proposals had simply been tacked on to a reprint of the social and economic program.

38. Quoted in Dillon and Lehane, *Political Murder*, p. 191.

39. *Republican News*, 2 January 1972.

40. Reported in W. D. Flackes, *Northern Ireland: A Political Directory 1968–69* (Dublin: Gill and Macmillan, 1980), p. 17.

41. Quoted in Holland, *Too Long a Sacrifice*, p. 143.

42. Quoted in Tim Pat Coogan, *The I.R.A.* (London: Fontana, 1980), p. 579.

43. Vincent Browne, "The Provos Settle Down for a 20 Year War," *Magill* (Dublin), August 1982.

44. *Fortnight*, July/August 1981.

45. See the interview with Danny Morrison, editor of *An Phoblacht*, in *Marxism Today* (London), December 1981.

46. Quoted in Holland, *Too Long a Sacrifice*, p. 133.

47. *An Phoblacht*, 18 January 1974.

48. See Coogan, *I.R.A.*, p. 559.

49. See, for example, *An Phoblacht*, October 1972.

50. John McMichael interview in *Marxism Today*, December 1981.

51. See the chapter on the IRA killers in Dillon and Lehane, *Political Murder*, pp. 245–263. Their study covers the Troubles up to the end of June 1973.

52. See R. Murray, *"Doorstep Murders" in Belfast*. Paper presented at the Annual Conference of the Institute of Geographers, University of Lancaster, January 1980. He describes the attitude of Protestants in North Belfast as one of "holding the line," preventing areas "going" Catholic. A slightly different justification of "clearing the decks" occurred in areas of overwhelming Protestant predominance.

53. Holland, *Too Long a Sacrifice*, p. 138.

54. From the Caretaker Executive Statement quoted in *An Phoblacht*, February 1970.

55. See, for example, *An Phoblacht*, June 1970.

56. See, for example, Danny Morrison interview in *Marxism Today*, December 1981.

57. See Burton, *Politics of Legitimacy*, p. 103.

58. *Belfast Telegraph*, 29 October 1979, contains a typical denial in response to a speech by a government minister.

59. For the earlier view, see, for example, *Republican News*, January/February 1971.

60. Editorial in *Iris* (Dublin), November 1981, p. 4. *Iris* is a new Provisional Sinn Fein quarterly.

61. See *Iris*, November 1981, p. 94.

62. Statement in *An Phoblacht*, 5 September 1981.

63. *Iris*, November 1981, p. 4.

64. See, for example, "The Provos have second thoughts," *Fortnight*, July/August 1982.

65. *The Irish Times* (Dublin), 1 November 1982.

66. *Saiorse* (Newspaper of the Irish Republican Socialist Party), 26 November 1982.

67. *Ulster*, September 1976.

68. Ibid.

69. *UDA*, vol. 1, no. 5, n.d.

70. Article headed "Those 'Innocent' Cats" in *Ulster*, July 1976.

71. Coogan, *I.R.A.*, pp. 558–560.

72. See note 52, above.

73. NUPRG, *Beyond the Religious Divide*, Belfast, March 1979.

74. Ibid.

75. Ibid.

76. Ibid.

77. See, for example, Arthur Aughey and Colin McIlhenny, *UDA: Paramilitaries and Politics*, Ulster Polytechnic, 1981 Seminar paper.

78. Ibid. They also quote the article below.

79. *Ulster*, October 1978.

80. Professor Cornelius O'Leary, quoted in *Ulster*, December 1979.

81. The *Guardian* (London), 27 August 1979. The UDA issued a denial that its members were involved.

82. *Fortnight*, December 1979/January 1980.

83. Holland, *Too Long a Sacrifice*, p. 119.

84. The *Guardian*, 26 August 1980.

85. Aughey and McIlhenny, *UDA: Paramilitaries and Politics*.

86. Andy Tyrie interview with *Marxism Today*, December 1981.

87. *Fortnight*, December 1981/January 1982, referring to a television appearance by Tyrie in November 1981.

88. Quoted in *Belfast Telegraph*, 14 May 1982.

89. Paul Wilkinson, *Political Terrorism* (London and Basingstoke: Macmillan, 1974), p. 17.

90. Ibid., pp. 116–120.

91. Paul Wilkinson, ed., *British Perspectives on Terrorism* (London: Allen & Unwin, 1981), pp. 164–165.

92. Wright, "The Ulster Spectrum" in Carlton and Schaerf, *Contemporary Terror*, p. 207.

93. See, for example, Paul Wilkinson, "The Provisional IRA: An Assessment in the Wake of the 1981 Hunger Strike," *Government and Opposition*, 17, 2 (Spring 1982), 140–156.

94. See, for example, Wilkinson, ed., *British Perspectives*, pp. 163–165.

95. See Magne Haugseng, *Violent Deaths as an indicator of denominational conflict in Northern Ireland*. Paper presented to the Political Studies Association work group at the University of Wales Institute of Science and Technology, September 1980.

4

Patterns of ETA Violence: 1968–1980*

R O B E R T P. C L A R K

Like all insurgent organizations, Euzkadi ta Askatasuna (ETA) differs from conventional political groups by the fact that its principal objective is to inflict (or threaten to inflict) damage on people and property. In this essay, I wish to focus on patterns in ETA's use of violent attacks to further its own (and its constituents') objectives. The key assumption here is, simply, that we gain important insights into the character of any insurgent organization by examining empirically what they *do*, as opposed to what they *say* they *intend to do*.

I believe that we can study patterns in ETA violence for important clues to the nature of the organization. I am convinced that we see in ETA's attacks not random, senseless killing and wounding, but rather acts carefully chosen with great attention to their potential impact on their surrounding political environment. Even since ETA's Fourth Assembly adopted the action-repression-action spiral theory in 1965, the organization has demonstrated a very great concern for the instrumental role that violence plays in its overall strategy. Despite a fairly small number of unfortunate and tragic mistakes, there is considerable evidence that ETA plans its attacks with great care to maximize the symbolic and communicative aspects of the violence while minimizing its adverse impact on bystanders and other noncombatants.

*This chapter appeared, slightly modified, in chapters five and eight of Robert P. Clark, *The Basque Insurgents: ETA, 1952–1980* (University of Wisconsin Press, copyright 1984 by the Board of Regents of the University of Wisconsin System) and is included here by special permission. The chapter also appeared in an earlier version of *Terrorism* 6, 3 (1983) and is reprinted by permission of Crane, Russak & Company, Inc.

We have some evidence that ETA attacks are discussed in substantial detail by high-level policymaking bodies of the organization before the assignment is sent down to a local cell, or *comando,* for execution; and the historical record of selected *comandos* suggests that considerable time goes into the planning of an attack, at least three months and, at times, as much as a year. No doubt there have been some random killings and other attacks connected with ETA's struggle. It would be unrealistic and naive to presume that a clandestine insurgent organization can control events perfectly to ensure that all attacks go according to plan. Data to be discussed below suggest that there have been increased numbers of revenge assaults in recent years as ETA and ultrarightists have battled back and forth with killing and counterkilling. Despite these attacks, and some fairly costly mistakes, I believe that ETA's record in this regard has been relatively free of such unplanned or unsystematic violence, especially when compared with other insurgent groups active in the 1970s. This chapter, then, is organized around the basic tenet that ETA's attacks make sense and fit into some larger plan that defines the character of the organization, and, further, that we can discern much about that character by studying the patterns of the attacks.

There is here, however, a methodological problem of considerable proportions. What we have before us is a classic example of an attempt to capture for social science analysis event data that resist being captured. In order for an ETA attack to show up in some data file, it must follow a complicated path of communications. First, an attack (an assassination, a wounding, a kidnapping) must occur in such a way as to warrant its being reported by the Basque and/or Spanish news media. It is obvious, for example, that the media will devote more coverage to some attacks than to others, depending on such factors as the time and place of the attack, the status of the target, and so forth. Second, the characteristics of the attack must be such as to justify news media or police speculation that ETA was involved. In the case of attacks involving machine guns and submachine guns, for example, much is usually made about the kind of ammunition casings left behind, since media observers in Spain believe that ETA has a tendency to use only a certain kind of ammunition (9-mm "Parabellum"). Discovery of casings of this type at the attack scene is usually regarded as one of ETA's "trademarks" and is so reported in press accounts. Third, some person claiming to represent some branch of ETA must contact some news agency and claim that ETA was responsible for the attack. On occasion, these communications have gone to local Basque radio stations; but predominantly the contacts are made with one of the two major Basque newspapers, *Deia* of Bilbao or *Egin* of San Sebastián. Obviously, one has no way of knowing whether or not these claims are legitimate, but they occur frequently enough to create a certain pattern, and an expectation that ETA attacks that are genuine will be followed by such a telephone call. There are, nevertheless, many obvious ETA attacks that are not claimed in this way, so we must infer their authorship by their characteristics. Fourth, the claim of responsibility must be duly reported by the news media, a step that seems to present little problem since their being reported is precisely the reason why ETA goes to the trouble of making the claim in the first place. Finally, these media reports must come to the attention of the social scientists who are gathering data on ETA attacks. Many social scientists will use Madrid newspapers such as *El País, Informaciones,* or *Diario 16* for their data, but these newspapers will never cover events in the Basque country to the same degree as, say, *Deia* of Bilbao. Choice of source documents is thus of critical importance.

It is not surprising, then, to discover that even experts disagree on the exact number of attacks committed by ETA over the period 1968 to 1980. In table 4.1, we see the range of expert opinions on just one kind of attack, the kind that resulted in the death of the target. For this reason, as well as to provide the data needed for other kinds of analysis, I have created my own data base, which will be used for all analysis here.

The data set from which my analyses are derived contains information on 287 killings, 385 woundings, and 24 kidnappings committed by ETA (or which can reasonably be attributed to ETA) from 7 June 1968 through 31 December 1980. There is a small amount of duplication in this enumeration resulting from the practice of double-counting a kidnapping/wounding or a kidnapping/killing. However, an attack that wounds a victim who dies some days later from the wounds is treated as a killing only. The data have been drawn from nine primary sources, including two Basque newspapers and one Basque newsmagazine, and seven secondary sources.[1] Given the inherent ambiguities that exist in data collections of this sort, the enumerations derived from this data set are reasonably close to those provided by both official and unofficial sources. For example, after the assassination of Spanish Army General Constantino Ortín Gil, military governor of Madrid, on 3 January 1979, the Spanish government released its official count, which showed ETA as responsible for killing 137 persons.[2] My count at the same time showed 130 deaths from ETA attacks. Soon after the end of the year, the *Washington Post* estimated the number of ETA killings for 1980 at 85.[3] My count for the year was 88. While no one really knows the exact number of victims of ETA attacks, I estimate that my data are no more than 3 to 5 percent away from the real figure.

TABLE 4.1

VARYING ESTIMATES OF ETA KILLS, 1968–1980

Year	Cambio 16 3-30-81[a]	Diario 16 11-19-79[b]	Portell[c]	New Statesman[d]	Hewitt[e]	Gunther[f]
1968						
1969						
1970			8			
1971						
1972						
1973				134	4	
1974			36		17	
1975					21	
1976			19		20	
1977					10	
1978	67	64			55	53
1979	75				65	40
1980	98				42	

[a] Cited in Peter McDonough and Antonio Lopez Pina, "Continuity and Change in Spanish Politics." Unpublished Ms, p. 1.

[b] Cited in Juan Linz, "The Basques in Spain: Nationalism and Political Conflict in a New Democracy," in W. Phillips Davison and Leon Gordenker, eds., Resolving Nationality Conflicts: The Role of Public Opinion Research (New York: Praeger, 1980), p. 46.

[c] José María Portell, "E.T.A.: Objetivo, La Insurrección de Euzkadi," Blanco y Negro, 29 June–5 July 1977, p. 27.

[d] Julie Flint, "A Democracy under threat," New Statesman, 12 January 1979, p. 46.

[e] From list provided author by Dr. Christopher Hewitt, Department of Sociology, University of Maryland, Baltimore County.

[f] From data provided author by Dr. Richard Gunther, Department of Political Science, Ohio State University, Columbus. These figures include only those killings clearly attributed to ETA by Gunther.

PATTERNS OF VIOLENCE: AN OVERVIEW

From June 1968, through December 1980, ETA's violence affected directly slightly fewer than 700 persons, of whom 287 were killed. Compared with brutal guerrilla wars in other countries, ETA's casualty levels are rather low. In Argentina, for example, more than 2,300 persons were killed between July 1974 and August 1976. In Northern Ireland, more than 1,600 persons were killed in the seven-year period between 1969 and 1976. In many major American cities, there are more criminal homicides in a year than ETA has killed in its entire history. In 1981, in the Greater Washington, D.C., metropolitan area (with a population of approximately the same as that of the Basque provinces), there were 364 homicides, including 226 with firearms. The significance of ETA's violence is a function of the psychological impact of its attacks, as opposed to the actual physical damage done by them.

In addition to the 287 killed, ETA's attacks have also left 385 persons wounded (including one person wounded on two different occasions separated by a two-year period). The treatment of woundings from a statistical standpoint may be misleading. On the one hand, to include wounded casualties along with those killed, to count them, in other words, as essentially a measure of the same level of ETA attack, may inflate the figures unrealistically. One might argue that in many of these attacks, ETA really did not intend to cause any casualties at all, much less large numbers of killed or wounded. Particularly in the case of bombings that caused high casualty levels, the intent of the assailants (not to mention their identity or organizational affiliation) may be legitimately questioned. Such would appear to be the case in at least five such events:

—The bombing of the Café "Rolando" in Madrid on 13 September 1974, which left nine dead and 56 wounded (responsibility for the attack was subsequently denied by ETA).

—The 17 March 1978 bombing of the Lemóniz (Vizcaya) nuclear plant while under construction, which resulted in two deaths and the wounding of 14 construction workers (ETA claimed it had telephoned a warning before the bomb exploded).

—The bombing, on 21 March 1978, of the motor vehicle pool parking lot of the Spanish government ministries in San Sebastián, which wounded 14.

—The simultaneous bombings of the airport and two railroad stations in Madrid on 29 July 1979, which left 6 dead and about 100 wounded (ETA claimed it had telephoned a warning to the Madrid police some thirty minutes before the bombs exploded).

—The bombing in Logroño on 27 November 1980, which killed 2 instantly and wounded 8, 1 of whom died the following January. Were these five events deleted from the list of ETA attacks, the number killed would be reduced by 20 and the number wounded by 191, which would have the overall effect of reducing the level of ETA-caused casualties by slightly less than one-third.

On the other hand, there are several similar attacks in which it is obvious to the outside observer that ETA fully intended there to be mass casualties. These events include the following:

—The machine-gunning of a group of national police playing soccer on a field adjacent to their barracks in Basauri (Vizcaya) on 20 November 1978, which left 2 killed and 11 wounded.

TABLE 4.2

ETA ATTACK CHARACTERISTICS: GROUP RESPONSIBLE
(percent of victims of each kind of attack claimed by or attributed to ETA subgroups)

	ETA before 1974	Unknown branch of ETA after 1974	ETA(m)[a]	ETA(p-m)[b]	Comandos Autónomos
Killed (N = 287)	2.8	32.1	55.0	5.6	4.5
Wounded (N = 385)	0.5	26.0	41.8	31.2	0.5
Kidnapped (N = 24)	8.3	12.5	12.5	62.5	4.2
Total (N = 696)	1.7	28.0	46.3	21.7	2.3

[a] ETA(m) = ETA militar
[b] ETA(p-m) = ETA politico-militar

—The machine-gunning of a café in San Sebastián during lunch hour on 8 October 1979, which resulted in the wounding of 8 national police and 3 construction workers.

—The bombing of a Guardia Civil convoy in Logroño on 22 July 1980, which killed 1 Guardia Civil lieutenant and wounded 34 troops. Moreover, whether or not a particular attack results in death, injury, or no harm at all is a function of a number of factors, not all of which are under the control of the assailants: the accuracy of their aim (if the attack is by firearms); the killing radius of the weapon (if it is by explosive); the density of the crown within which the explosive is detonated; the speed with which the injured can be rushed to well-equipped hospital facilities; the overall health or physical condition of the victims; and so forth.

Given all these ambiguities, it seemed appropriate to give readers as much information as possible and let them make the judgment as to how to interpret the data. For that reason, in the analyses that follow, I provide the data in both aggregated and unaggregated form to facilitate informed interpretation and analysis.

Let us examine first the authorship of ETA-caused attacks. Table 4.2 portrays the percentages of victims caused by the various branches of ETA, divided according to whether they were killed, wounded, or kidnapped. It will be noted that ETA(m)—ETA militar—accounted for more than half of the killings recorded during the period, while about one-third were blamed simply on ETA (without distinguishing among subgroups), or were of unknown origin. ETA(p-m)—ETA

TABLE 4.3

ETA ATTACK CHARACTERISTICS: WEAPONS
(percent of victims caused by each)

| | Firearms | | | | |
	Pistols	Automatic weapons	Other/ unknown	Bombs/ explosives	Other/ unknown
Killed (N = 287)	15.7	27.2	22.6	14.3	20.2
Wounded (N = 385)	2.9	18.2	7.3	68.3	3.4
Total (N = 672)	8.3	22.0	13.8	45.2	10.6

politico-militar—in contrast, was held responsible for only a little more than 5 percent of the killings. ETA(p-m) was, however, responsible for nearly one-third of the woundings charged to ETA (here the Madrid train station and airport attacks bulk very large in the statistics), while ETA(m) caused only slightly more than four out of every ten injuries. The balance of responsibilities was reversed for kidnappings, with ETA(p-m) accused of more than 60 percent, while ETA(m) caused only about one-eighth. Two additional points should be made from that table. First, the Comandos Autónomos committed relatively few assaults of any kind during the period; and second, a substantial number (about one-third of the killings and about one-fourth of the woundings) were committed by persons with unknown affiliation.

Let us next consider some important characteristics or features of ETA attacks, such as the kind of weapons employed, the site of the attack, and the size of the attacked group. Our purpose here is to analyze the available data on these characteristics to determine the extent to which ETA sought to inflict casualties on innocent bystanders, or whether it sought to avoid such casualties. We will return to this theme again later in this chapter when I present data on the characteristics of the victims chosen by ETA for assault.

Table 4.3 portrays statistics drawn from my attack data set which deal with weapons used in the attacks. (This table, in contrast to the others, deals only with killings and woundings since the weapons used in kidnappings are rarely reported and, in any case, seldom used.) It would appear that the favorite weapon of ETA is the automatic firearm, the machine gun or submachine gun (also called the machine pistol). More than one-fourth of all killings were the product of such weapons, as opposed to about 15 percent caused by pistols and 14 percent caused by bombs or other explosives. Bombs and explosives, however, caused many more woundings than did the firearms, although automatic weapons caused about nine times as many woundings as did pistols. Overall, ETA casualties were divided about evenly between firearms and explosives, each category having caused about 45 percent, leaving 10 percent of unknown origin. The reader is reminded, however, that if we deleted the fewer than half-dozen high-casualty bombings referred to earlier, the balance between firearms and explosives would change dramatically.

The choice of weapons by an insurgent group is not a matter of random selection, or even of availability, so it can be assumed that ETA has access to any sort of pistol, submachine gun, or explosive available generally. Rather, different weapons possess different operating characteristics and have different impacts on intended (and unintended) victims. Pistols, for example, are much more precise weapons and the risk of wounding a bystander with one is much reduced. The problem with pistols is that some expertise in marksmanship is required, and generally the assailant must approach the victim much more closely than is true with the other weapons. Machine guns and submachine guns have much greater range; and their higher rate of fire makes it less necessary to have pinpoint accuracy against the intended victim. The major disadvantage of automatic weapons is that they tend to spray a wider area with lethal projectiles, so the chances of wounding a bystander are greater with submachine guns than, say, with pistols. Bombs are the worst weapon in this regard. Since there is usually some considerable lag of time between the placement of the explosive and the time it is actually detonated, it is difficult if not impossible to predict how many people will be within its killing radius when it explodes. On the one hand, many bombs go off harmlessly, or at most damage property without harming persons. In the worst cases, however, such as the Madrid train station bombings, the bombs exploded in the midst of a large crowd of people. Whether or not ETA actually intended these explosions to inflict mass casualties is a subject of much polemic debate, and can probably never be determined. It appears, then, that a tendency to use pistols during attacks would signify some effort by the group to control its violence and to protect bystanders. The use of bombs, on the other hand, lies at the opposite end of the spectrum of controlled violence, in that the assailants have relinquished a large degree of their control over the effects of the weapon, and it may or may not cause considerable casualties when detonated. Automatic weapons fall somewhere in between these two extremes, in that the assailants have greater control over the adverse effects of the weapon than they do with bombs, but less than they do with pistols.

TABLE 4.4

ETA ATTACK CHARACTERISTICS: SITE OF ATTACK
(percent of victims attacked at each type of site)

Site	Killed	Wounded	Kidnapped	Total
City street, park, airport, train station	19.5	35.1	0.0	27.4
Automobile, bus	19.5	21.8	4.2	20.3
Bar, cafe, hotel	13.2	20.3	0.0	16.7
Rural road	2.8	1.6	0.0	2.0
Guardia Civil road block	1.7	0.5	0.0	1.0
Military or police installation	1.7	5.2	0.0	3.6
Private home	7.0	1.6	50.0	5.5
Work place	5.6	6.5	12.5	6.3
Unknown	28.9	7.5	33.3	17.2
Total	99.9 (N = 287)	100.1 (N = 385)	100.0 (N = 24)	100.0 (N = 696)

Let us turn, next, to the site of ETA attacks. Table 4.4 portrays the available data on the location of ETA attacks, together with the proportion of victims assaulted in each site. We notice immediately that a majority of those killed (52.2 percent) and more than three-fourths of those wounded (77.2 percent) suffered their attacks in a public place in an urban area. About one out of every five persons killed and wounded by ETA was assaulted while in an automobile, jeep, Land Rover, bus, or other form of transportation as it moved along a city street. A second group, consisting of about one-fifth of those killed and more than one-third of those wounded, was attacked while walking on a city street, or while in an airport or railroad station. About 13 percent of those killed and 20 percent of those wounded were attacked while in a bar, cafe, restaurant, or hotel. In contrast, relatively few ETA victims were attacked while on country roads, or in their homes or places of employment. (The exception to this latter observation lies, of course, in the category of kidnapping, in which exactly half of all victims were taken from their homes.) Not surprisingly, there were almost no casualties inflicted by ETA during direct attacks on military or paramilitary installations, police stations, Guardia Civil barracks or road blocks, or the like. It is a rather widely accepted rule among urban insurgent groups like ETA that such direct assaults and confrontations with a target group like the Guardia Civil

TABLE 4.5

ETA ATTACK CHARACTERISTICS: SIZE OF TARGET GROUP
(percent of victims in each target group)

	Single individual	Small group (2–5)	Medium group 6–10)	Large group (11<)
Killed (N = 287)	49.8	38.3	4.9	7.0
Wounded (N = 385)	9.9	23.1	4.7	62.3
Kidnapped (N = 24)	100.0	0.0	0.0	0.0
Total (N = 696)	29.4	28.6	4.6	37.4

when it is on its home "turf," so to speak, and can defend itself with greater effectiveness, should be avoided. A group that focuses its attacks so heavily on public places like city streets, bars, or train stations, however, is not really doing all it can to avoid harming bystanders.

The third attack characteristic I examine here involves the size of the victim groups. That is, we want to know whether ETA's victims were attacked individually while alone, or whether the attacks were on small groups, or on large crowds. Table 4.5 shows our findings on this dimension. We see from these data that about half (49.8 percent) of all persons killed by ETA were attacked when they were by themselves, and another 38.3 percent were killed in small groups of fewer than six persons. Very few killings involved medium-sized or large groups of people. In contrast, more than 60 percent of all woundings took place when large groups were attacked, such as in the Café Rolando bombing and the Madrid airport and train station explosions. Overall, about two-thirds of all casualties were suffered by persons when they were alone or in small groups, while the remaining one-third were in large crowds. (Again, the statistical importance of the half dozen or so bombings in crowded places should be noted.)

What is one to make of these data? It seems to me that ETA attacks can be generalized about in this way. Most of the time, ETA attacked either single individuals or small groups of two to five persons. These attacks were carried out with firearms, mostly automatic weapons such as submachine guns but with a considerable number involving pistols. The majority of these attacks took place in public places in cities, such as on public streets, or in bars, cafes, or restaurants. Despite the lack of control the assailants had over the killing radius of their weapons in crowded public settings, these attacks (which account for the bulk of ETA's victims) resulted in relatively few injured bystanders.

TABLE 4.6
DISTRIBUTION OF ETA VICTIMS OVER TIME (1968–1980)

Year	Year	Killed Cumulative	Year	Wounded Cumulative	Year	Kidnapped[a] Cumulative	Year	Total Cumulative
1968	2	2	0	0	0	0	2	2
1969	1	3	0	0	0	0	1	3
1970	0	3	0	0	1	1	1	4
1971	0	3	0	0	0	1	0	4
1972	1	4	1	1	0	1	2	6
1973	3	7	1	2	1	2	5	11
1974	11[b]	18	58[b]	60	0	2	69	80
1975	16	34	5	65	0	2	21	101
1976	17	51	0	65	2	4	19	120
1977	9	60	7	72	1	5	17	137
1978	67	127	91	163	4	9	162	299
1979	72[c]	199	141[c]	304	8	17	221	520
1980	88	287	81	385	7	24	176	696

[a] Victims killed or wounded after kidnapping counted in both columns. Kidnapping does not include motorists whose seizure was incidental to the theft of their automobile.
[b] Includes 9 killed, 56 wounded in Café Rolando bombing.
[c] Includes 6 killed, 100 wounded in Madrid airport and train station bombings.

ETA did make a few (between five and ten) serious and tragic mistakes, however, which involved the placing of bombs under uncontrolled conditions in crowded public sites. The consequence of these errors was massive casualties in the range of two to ten killed and ten to a hundred wounded. I conclude from these observations, then, that most of the time ETA was careful to avoid harming civilian bystanders in its attacks, but its record is not flawless in this regard, and several very serious mistakes did result in the killing and wounding of numerous bystanders.

PATTERNS OF VIOLENCE:
DISTRIBUTION OF ATTACKS OVER TIME

Let us turn, then, to a consideration of the way in which ETA's attacks have been distributed over time. In other words, does the pattern of attacks show they are spread more or less evenly through the 1968 to the 1980 period, or are they concentrated in one or more parts of the period?

Table 4.6 shows the distribution of ETA attacks over time, from 1968 through 1980. Through 1973, ETA was still relatively restrained (or weak, depending on how one looks at it), and accounted for only

TABLE 4.7

LEVEL OF ETA KILLINGS RELATED TO POLITICAL DEVELOPMENTS
CONNECTED WITH BASQUE AUTONOMY

Year	Number of ETA killings	Principal events
1968–1975	34	Franco regime in power: near total suppression of Basque nationalist sentiment.
1976	17	First Suárez government appointed; Cortes approves laws paving way for democracy; popular referendum approves transition.
1977	9	First democratically elected Cortes chosen; Cortes begins drafting of new constitution.
1978	67	New constitution approved, giving legal status to autonomous regions; Basques submit proposed Autonomy Statute.
1979	72	Second Cortes elected; municipal governments popularly elected; Basque referendum approves Autonomy Statute; Cortes subsequently approves.
1980	88	First Basque parliament elected; Basque government chosen and formally begins its work.

seven killings (although one was the Spanish prime minister, Admiral Luis Carrero Blanco). Through the turbulent years of 1974 and 1975, ETA accounted for twenty-seven killings, to bring their total to thirty-four by the end of 1975. By the end of the Franco era, ETA had thus accounted for only about 12 percent of the total number of killings for which it had been held responsible during the 1968 to 1980 period. It should also be kept in mind that police or Guardia Civil killed at least thirty ETA members during this same period.

In table 4.7, we can examine in somewhat greater detail the rate of ETA killings from 1976 through 1980, and relate these attacks to developments in Spanish and Basque politics that had a bearing on Basque self-governance. It should be noted here that the level of assassinations reached during the last two years of the Franco regime (13–14 per year) was maintained, and even declined a little, during the first two years of the post-Franco period, when the Spanish government initiated the transition to parliamentary democracy and a constitutional monarchy. It was only after the election of the first democratically chosen Cortes, in July 1977, that ETA began to increase its level of violence: to sixty-seven killings in 1978 and seventy-two in 1979. And, most paradoxical of all, it was in 1980, when the Basques elected the first regional government they had ever enjoyed, that ETA killings reached a peak of eighty-eight. It has thus been precisely during the time when Basques were attaining most of their

objectives regarding regional autonomy that ETA has been most violent. This trend has confounded attempts at analysis of the ETA
phenomenon and has proven especially frustrating to Basque and Spanish political leaders in their search for a stable political order in the
region.

PATTERNS OF VIOLENCE: CHOICE OF TARGETS

Certainly a key ingredient of this study must be to discover how ETA
members define their political world, how they characterize the sources
of their oppression, and how they separate the political universe into
heroes and villains, friends and enemies, those to be attacked and
those to be defended. I have examined the historical record for this
kind of elusive detail by looking at the kinds of victims targeted for
attack by ETA's assassination squads and kidnap teams. If, as I have
argued, ETA's attacks are not random but in fact carefully chosen and
planned, then the victims selected should reflect the organization's
definition of its enemies. This kind of analysis is central to an understanding of how ETA's ideology is made operational through the
attacks of the members. ETA is an organization whose ideology defines
as the enemy both industrial capitalism (Basque or Spanish) and Spanish political domination, or internal colonialism. The data show, however, that ETA does not choose its victims in strict accord with this
formula.

Table 4.8 shows the way in which the victims of ETA attacks have
been distributed according to profession or occupation (if one can
reasonably infer the motivation for the attack from this fact), or some
other motivating factor behind the attack (if profession or occupation
are not appropriate indicators of motivation).

Overall, it appears that ETA has divided its targets about equally
between military and law enforcement personnel on the one hand,
and civilians on the other. The former category accounts for slightly
more than 50 percent of all victims; the latter, about 46 percent, with
the remainder unknown. However, with the specific attack categories
(killed, wounded, kidnapped) the balance changes dramatically.
Within the killed category, fully two-thirds of the victims were from
the military or law enforcement occupations, or were directly related
to the military or paramilitary struggle against ETA. As far as wounded
victims are concerned, however, the very large number of wounded
bystanders injured by the several mass bombings discussed earlier causes
the balance to shift markedly, so that about six out of every ten
wounded victims were civilians (more than half being bystanders). In
contrast, virtually all of those victims who were kidnapped were civilians, the overwhelming majority being industrial or business figures.

TABLE 4.8

Distribution of ETA Attack Victims by Profession/Occupation or Motivation for Attack
(percent of victims in each class)

Target characteristics	Killed	Wounded	Kidnapped	Total
Military, law enforcement	68.0	40.5	0.0	50.4
Guardia Civil	31.7	23.4	0.0	26.0
National police	14.6	13.5	0.0	13.5
Municipal police	9.1	1.8	0.0	4.7
Military	7.0	1.8	0.0	3.9
Spies/informers	5.6	0.0	0.0	2.3
Civilians	25.1	59.0	95.8	46.2
Political figures/government officials	8.0	1.8	20.8	5.0
Industrial/business figures	2.4	2.9	70.8	5.0
Revenge/retaliation/intimidation	4.2	0.3	4.2	2.0
Bystanders	9.1	53.5	0.0	33.3
Accidents	1.4	0.5	0.0	0.9
Unknown/others	7.0	0.5	4.2	3.3
Total	100.1	100.0	100.0	99.9
	(N = 287)	(N = 385)	(N = 24)	(N = 696)

Let us focus, then, with more precision on each specific subcategory. Apart from the large number of bystanders wounded by the half dozen or so mass bombings, the single most heavily victimized category has been the Guardia Civil. Nearly one-third (91) of those killed and nearly one-fourth (90) of those wounded have been Guardia Civil troops. Most of these attacks were against single Guardia Civil members or small groups on patrol, either on foot or in an automobile or jeep. The favorite ETA tactic was to attack a Guardia Civil contingent in a vehicle while it was parked or stopped at a street intersection, or in an ambush on a country road. By far the most Guardia Civil victims were in the enlisted ranks. The only officers of the Guardia who were killed were two lieutenants, one in Guernica (Vizcaya) in May 1975, and the other in Logroño in July 1980. This latter officer was killed in the bombing of the Guardia Civil convoy that left thirty-four wounded, the most massive assault on the Guardia in ETA's history. Given these data, it is easy to see why the Guardia Civil has felt compelled to offer special bonuses in extra pay and vacation time to its enlisted personnel who serve in the Basque provinces.[4] It is also easy to understand why it is the Guardia Civil that is most restive and impatient with the seeming inability of the Spanish government to deal effectively with the ETA threat.

After the Guardia Civil, the next most popular ETA targets were the police, both national police (called, variously, Policía Armada, Policía Política-Social, and so forth), and municipal or local police. (The division made in table 4.8 between national and municipal police is somewhat artificial, since in a number of cases the exact identification is not apparent.) In all, ETA has killed sixty-eight police (23.7 percent of all killed) and wounded fifty-nine (15.3 percent of all wounded). Slightly less than one victim in every five was a police official or in the enlisted ranks. As was the case with the Guardia Civil, most of these victims were attacked singly or in small groups while they patrolled on foot or in automobiles. In contrast to their targets in the Guardia Civil, however, ETA has killed a number of senior officials in the police force, including the municipal police chiefs of Pasajes (Guipúzcoa) in December 1978; of Munguía (Vizcaya) in February 1979; of Beasain (Guipúzcoa) in March 1979; of Amorebieta (Vizcaya) in September 1979; of Vitoria in April 1980; and of San Sebastián in November 1980; as well as the ex-chief of police in Santurce (Vizcaya) in December 1978.[5] In addition, ETA killed the commander of the national police in Navarra in November 1977, and the chief of the provincial police in Alava in January 1980. Both these latter officials were also active duty Spanish Army majors at the time of their killings.

Although the military victims do not bulk as large in the statistics as do other categories, their assassinations have probably caused more disruption of the Spanish political scene than those of any other kind of victim. Because of the crucial importance of the Spanish armed forces to the democratic government, the assassination of one or several senior military officials does more to jeopardize the Spanish democratic experiment than the killing of an equal number of Guardia Civil enlisted personnel. It is probably for that reason that ETA has concentrated its attacks in this category almost entirely on senior officers. Enlisted military personnel have been killed or wounded only when they have been caught in an attack on an individual or group of senior officers, as was, for example, the driver of a military automobile that was ambushed. Thus, although ETA has killed only twenty members of the armed forces, they include the prime minister of Spain, Admiral Luis Carrero Blanco, killed in December 1973; the military governors of Madrid (January 1979) and Guipúzcoa (September 1979); the aide to the military governor of Guipúzcoa (January 1979); two active duty army generals (July 1978 and May 1979); three army colonels and one navy captain (two killed in May 1979; one in September 1979; and one in October 1978); two army lieutenant colonels (September and October, 1980); and two army majors (September 1979, and February 1980). In addition to these active duty officers, ETA has also killed two retired army colonels, one retired army lieutenant colonel, and one retired army major. The organization has also wounded one army general, two air force colonels, and four army lieutenant colonels.[6]

The last category under the military and law enforcement heading consists not of uniformed personnel in the armed forces or the police but rather of persons identified by ETA communiqués as spies or informers, and as having been executed for that reason. By my count, some sixteen ETA victims fit into this category, all killed. These attacks were usually directed against single individuals walking alone on city streets or driving home alone or to work in their automobiles. These victims represent a wide variety of professions or occupations. At least three were former ETA members who were shot by their former comrades for having allegedly given information to the police. Another group of about half a dozen or so was made up of bar owners or taxi drivers, and the remainder were from various occupations—a tailor, a jewelry store owner, a grave digger, an automobile mechanic, and so forth. It must be emphasized that the only evidence we have that shows that these people were indeed spies and informers is that contained in the ETA communiqués issued after each killing. In almost every case, the family of the deceased denied the accusations and challenged ETA to provide the evidence in the public media.

Turning to civilians, it is evident that the largest single category of victims consisted of 26 bystanders killed and 206 wounded. I have already discussed this category in some detail elsewhere in this chapter. Most of these people were victims because they were in the vicinity when a bomb exploded, although a few were caught in cross fires between *etarras* and police or Guardia Civil troops and lost their lives in the exchange of gunfire. The bystander category accounts for fully one-third of all ETA victims of all kinds. We do not have any detailed information about these 232 people, but I have no reason to believe they are anything but a cross section of Spanish or Basque society.

Under the civilian heading, the next most significant category consists of political figures and government officials, of whom ETA has killed twenty-three, wounded seven, and kidnapped five. In addition to Prime Minister Carrero Blanco, this list would include a number of mayors and former mayors, prominent members of the Spanish political party *Unión del Centro Democrático* (UCD), and leaders of provincial governments in the Basque provinces. In particular, ETA killed the mayors of Oyarzún (Guipúzcoa) in November 1975; of Galdácano (Vizcaya) in February 1976; and of Olaberría (Guipúzcoa) in February 1979; and the ex-mayors of Echarri-Aranaz (Navarra) in January 1979; of Bedia (Vizcaya) in September 1979; and of Elgóibar (Guipúzcoa) in October 1980. ETA also wounded the ex-mayor of Bilbao in an attack in March 1979. Two of the more dramatic ETA attacks were those which resulted in the deaths of Juan María Araluce, president of the Guipúzcoa provincial government, who was machine-gunned along with his bodyguards in San Sebastián in October 1976; and of Augusto Unceta, president of the Vizcaya provincial government, who was killed in a similar manner in Guernica in October 1977. The list of political victims also includes five assassinated members of UCD, including a member of the party's executive committee from Alava (killed in September 1980) and two from the executive committee of Guipúzcoa (both killed in October 1980). ETA's only attacks against members of the Spanish parliament have been the wounding of the information secretary of UCD in Madrid in July 1979, and the kidnapping of the UCD secretary for foreign relations in November 1979.

Industrialists and other business and commercial figures have not been prominent in ETA's attack lists except in the kidnapping category. Several kidnappings of industrialists, including those of Felipe Huarte in Pamplona in January 1973, and of Javier de Ybarra in Bilbao in May 1977, were dramatic events in recent Spanish political history. Most kidnappings have ended happily in the sense that the victims were released unharmed, but at least half a dozen have ended tragically with the death of the victim. These deaths include that of Ybarra, and of Angel Berazadi in Elgóibar in April 1976. Beginning in 1978, ETA adopted its own version of the leg-shooting, or "knee-capping," attack made famous in Northern Ireland in recent years. At least six or seven such attacks have been directed against industrialists and businessmen in the Basque region. In addition, several businessmen have been killed allegedly for refusing to pay the "revolutionary tax," but the evidence to suppport these claims is of course sketchy and subject to challenge. The company that has suffered the most in attacks by ETA has been the Michelin Tire Company, which has a factory in Vitoria. In February 1979, a Michelin director was kidnapped and later released unharmed; in May 1980, the company's personnel director was wounded; and in June 1980, another director of the company was killed in Vitoria.

The most difficult category to describe with accuracy is the one I call "revenge/retaliation/intimidation." On a few occasions, the ETA communiqué following an assassination has made explicit reference to another killing for which ETA's was a response in revenge. These are rather rare, however, and most of the time reliance must be put on press speculation about these motivations. Because of the circumstances surrounding the attack, I would definitely include in this category the sensational assassination of Bilbao journalist José María Portell in June 1978, as well as the wounding of Pamplona newpaper editor José Javier Uranga in August 1980. Most of the time, however, these killings involve much more obscure individuals and motivations.

Finally, mention must be made of the accident category, a classification I distinguish clearly from the bystander category because of the obvious mistake or miscalculation that leads to the former kind of death or injury. For example, in March 1980, a young child was killed in Azcoitia (Guipúzcoa) when he accidentally kicked a bomb lying in the street. ETA had planted the bomb beneath a Guardia Civil truck, but the truck had driven off before the charge exploded. On at least two occasions, ETA has killed a person only to find out that it had identified him incorrectly. On one of these occasions, ETA made monetary restitution to the widow. Given the high levels of violence in Basque society in recent years, and the very large quantities of weapons and explosives available to everyone, it is to me rather remarkable that I can find only six clear cases (four killings and two woundings) of accidental attack in the entire period from 1968 through 1980.

I would offer one final observation having to do with ETA targets; ETA has almost never deliberately attacked women. I have found only one killing (that of the girlfriend of a Guardia Civil trooper, both of whom were killed together in his car in January 1979), and one wounding (of the ex-mayor of Bilbao) in which the intended target was clearly a female.

I have not made an in-depth study of insurgent acts by groups other than ETA, but I have the distinct impression that, compared with other such groups, ETA stands out for the almost surgical precision with which it selects the times, places, and targets for its attacks. I believe that the data presented here support one of my basic propositions about ETA, namely, that we are seeing here not random violence, but killings carefully selected for the kind of impact they are likely to make on Spanish and Basque politics. Our data show that ETA violence persists, and even increases, despite clear gains for the Basques in their struggle for self-governance. The threat of ETA to the maintenance of public order in the Basque country has risen in almost perfect correlation with the granting of more autonomy to the Basques. As regional autonomy has been extended to the Basques, the pace of ETA assassinations has risen accordingly. Finally, ETA's attacks have been directed primarily against the agents of the Spanish military, paramilitary, and law enforcement apparatus in the Basque provinces, only secondarily against civilians, and to an even lesser extent against representatives of industrial capitalism.[7]

NOTES

1. The primary sources for the ETA attack data set include *Deia* (Bilbao), the *Washington Post*, *La Actualidad Española* (Madrid), *El País* (Madrid), *Cambio 16* (Madrid), *Diario Vasco* (San Sebastián), *Punto y Hora* (San Sebastián), the *New York Times*, and the *Times* (London). The secondary sources include the data base developed by Dr. Richard Gunther, Department of Political Science, Ohio State University (covering 1978 and 1979), and these books: Edward F. Mickolus, *Transnational Terrorism: A Chronology of Events, 1968–1979* (Westport, Conn.: Greenwood Press, 1980); Ortzi, *Los Vascos: Síntesis de su Historia* (San Sebastián: Hordago, 1978); José María Portell, *Los Hombres de ETA* (Barcelona: DOPESA, 1974); Equipo Cinco, *Las Víctimas del Post Franquismo* (Madrid: Sedmay, 1977); Javier Sanchez Erauskin, *Txiki-Otaegi: El Viento y las Raices* (San Sebastián: Hordago, 1978); and Miguel Castells Arteche, *El Mejor Defensor el Pueblo* (San Sebastián: Ediciones Vascas, 1978).

2. *Diario Vasco* (San Sebastián), 4 January 1979.

3. *Washington Post*, 3 January 1981.

4. *Deia* (Bilbao), 14 October 1980.

5. See *Deia* (Bilbao), 28 November 1980, for a list of police chiefs killed.

6. For lists of armed forces personnel killed at various times by ETA, see the following: *Diario Vasco* (San Sebastián), 4 January 1979; and *Deia* (Bilbao), 26 May 1979 and 20 September 1979.

7. A report by the deputy chief of staff of the Guardia Civil in June 1982 presented the following pattern of ETA victims from 7 June 1968, to 1 May 1982:

	Killed		Wounded		Total	
	Number	(%)	Number	(%)	Number	(%)
Civilians	152	43.5	273	55.5	425	50.5
Guardia Civil	103	29.5	121	24.6	224	26.6
Police	62	17.8	91	18.5	153	18.2
Military	32	9.2	7	1.4	39	4.6
Total	349		492		841	

SOURCE: *Deia* (Bilbao), 13 June 1982.

The report also estimates that during the same period, 64 members of ETA died violently, including 41 killed in gun battles with police or Guardia Civil, 2 executed, 12 killed by rightist counterterrorist groups, and 9 in accidents of their own making (e.g., premature bomb explosions).

PART II

Individual Motifs and Motivations

———

5

The Violent Life: An Analysis of Left- and Right-Wing Terrorism in Italy

LEONARD WEINBERG

It came without warning. On December 12, 1969, at almost precisely 4:30 in the afternoon, a bomb exploded at the Piazza Fontana office of the National Agricultural Bank in Milan. The explosion killed sixteen people and left another eighty-eight injured. At first the police held anarchists responsible for the deed, but after years of investigation this anonymous slaughter of innocent bank customers was discovered to have been the work of a neofascist group.

Designed to provoke a massive law and order backlash among Italians already upset by outbreaks of student protest and labor agitation, the Piazza Fontana bombing was, in effect, the opening salvo that began an era of terrorist violence in Italian political life. Since 1969 Italy has gone through more than a decade in which thousands of acts of political violence—kidnappings, bombings, assassinations, and mass murders—have shocked its citizens, caused consternation among its allies, and attracted the attention of millions of people around the world.

Groups on the left and right, claiming inspiration from Marxist-Leninist, Trotskyite, Maoist, or neofascist ideologies, have sought to throw Italy into a state of turmoil and undermine the incumbent political regime. Why should Italy have become the setting for such a massive outbreak of hatred and violence?

In the late 1960s the country was not suffering from the kinds of nationality problems that have led to terrorist violence in Spain and Northern Ireland. Its economic performance, although uneven, was substantially better than it had been during more tranquil periods in its history. And Italy was not governed by a repressive authoritarian regime that denied adversaries an opportunity to express their views and organize their dissent: quite the opposite. Opportunities abounded for nonviolent and constitutionally protected political protests.[1]

Of course some scholars have argued that the very attributes of modern democracies, like the Italian, have made them susceptible to terrorist attack. References are made to such characteristics as the freedom of movement, ease of access to the mass media, and the difficulty of protecting likely targets in an open society.[2] All this may be true, but the argument does not explain why some democracies have been more subject to terrorism than others. Why have some democracies experienced only a handful of violent incidents while Italy has suffered so many for so long?

There are a number of factors specific to the Italian situation which have promoted the high level of terrorism we have seen over the last fourteen years. For purposes of analysis these factors may be clustered under two broad headings: *preconditions* and *precipitants*. Preconditions are the relatively constant features of Italian political life in whose absence the wave of terrorism probably would not have occurred. The word "vulnerabilities" also comes to mind. The term *precipitants* applies to factors undergoing change immediately before or during the early phases of terrorist activity.[3] They should be regarded as the immediate causes of terrorism as well as the circumstances that have promoted its amplification and diffusion throughout the country.

PRECONDITIONS

In observing French political history Stanley Hoffmann discerns a pattern of alternation in the style in which that country is governed. Hoffmann's well-known formulation distinguishes between long periods of "routine authority" culminating in deadlock and immobilism, and episodes of heroic leadership, when deadlocks are broken and major decisions taken.[4] The Italian style of political leadership exhibits a somewhat parallel type of duality. There is, however, at least one major difference. Whereas in France the styles of leadership alternate over time, in Italy they occur simultaneously.

The Italian leadership style places great emphasis on the framing of political issues in abstract ideological terms. Thus when a new leader of the Socialists finds it desirable to distance his party from the Communists he feels impelled to account for his endeavors by references to Proudhon and other nineteenth-century socialist luminaries.[5] When the Communist party leadership wishes to distance itself from the Soviet Union it does so by seeking to rehabilitate the memory and, by implication, the political ideas of Nikolai Bukharin. Readers of mass circulation newspapers such as *L'Unità* and ordinary voters complain that they are unable to comprehend much of the political commentary to which they are exposed because of the abstract way it is expressed. Not uncommonly political parties and other public organizations hold conferences and create institutes for study in order to pay homage to great ideological thinkers of the past. Instead of building museums of war, the Italian parties, in effect, build museums for ideas.

There is, however, another side to the coin. Giovanni Sartori has argued the existence of two forms of belief systems: ideological and pragmatic.[6] It seems clear from Sartori's account that Italy represents a country where the dominant form of belief system is ideological while Britain and the United States are examples of the pragmatic. Robert Putnam, in an empirical study of British and Italian parliamentarians, found not a dichotomy between ideological and pragmatic approaches but a considerable overlap. Significant numbers of both British and Italian legislators were found to be both ideologically enthused and pragmatic at the same time.[7] What Putnam has documented is, in a sense, the common stuff of Italian newspapers: that is, the pervasive role of pragmatic bargaining between leaders of political parties, *correnti* (factions), and interest groups in Italian life.

It is, of course, decidedly banal to point out that politicians do not always behave in accordance with the lofty ideals they profess in public. But for individuals who take ideologically grounded beliefs seriously, particularly if they live in a society that treats ideologies with a certain reverence, the constant perception of leaders simultaneously making deals and professing broad ideological objectives—which are seemingly contradicted by the bargains—must be especially frustrating. It should be expected that Italian intellectuals and university students would be especially disgruntled by a style of leadership that combines ideological expression with pragmatic bargaining in the day-to-day conduct of politics.

A second precondition for the outbreak of terrorism is the Italian civil war. For most Americans old enough to remember it the fascist regime ended with the death of Mussolini in 1945. While this is literally the case, fascism and the forces organized in opposition to it still represent important sources of memory, myth, and conflict in Italian society.

Unlike France or the United States, Italy lacks a historic revolutionary experience in the name of which contemporary parties or political movements can justify their behavior. For the Italian left the closest approximation to such a heroic episode from the past is the Resistance, the fight of northern partisans against Nazi and fascist forces during the latter phase of World War II. Whatever the authentic contribution the Resistance played in the defeat of the Nazis and fascists, there is no doubt but that in postwar Italy the memory of the

Resistance has been kept alive and indeed has acquired the status of a myth, replete with ceremonies and rituals.

Given the mythology surrounding the Resistance it is not surprising that when Giangiacomo Feltrinelli, the multimillionaire publisher, founded a left-wing terrorist organization in 1970 he gave it the name *Gruppi di Azione Partigiana* (Partisan Action Groups).[8] Similarly, the title selected for an underground publication begun in 1971 to publicize the doctrines of the *Gruppi di Azione Partigiana* and the *Brigate Rosse* (Red Brigades) was the *New Resistance*.[9]

Renato Curcio, a founder of the *Brigate Rosse*, has a personal tie to the Resistance. His uncle, who played a crucial role as a father figure early in his life (Curcio was born out of wedlock), was killed during a fascist ambush while fighting as a partisan. In a letter written to his mother Curcio seeks to make the link explicit and personal:

> Yolanda dearest, mother mine, years have passed since the day on which I set out to encounter life and left you alone to deal with life. I have worked, I have studied, I have fought. . . . While seeking my road, I found exploitation, injustice, oppression. And people who suffered them. I was among these latter. And these people were in the great majority. Thus I understood that my personal history was their personal history, that my future was their future. Distant memories stirred. Uncle Armando who carried me astride his shoulders. His limpid and ever smiling eyes that peered far into the distance towards a society of free and equal men. And I loved him like a father, and I have picked up the rifle that only death, arriving through the murderous hand of nazi-fascists, had wrested from him. . . . What more can I say to you?[10]

Beyond providing postwar generations with a heroic legend, the Resistance also afforded young leftists with the basis of a more global identification. The Resistance could be interpreted as a guerrilla war comparable to revolutionary insurgencies in Asia, Africa, the Middle East, and Latin America.

Keeping the memory of the Resistance alive in the postwar decades has been made easier by the continued presence of the very evil against which the partisans fought: fascism. Despite constitutional and legislative prohibitions, Italy has had a highly visible and sometimes electorally significant neofascist movement throughout its postwar history. In all of these years, the movement has been led by men like Giorgio Almirante, Valerio Borghese, Giulio Carradonna, and "Pino" Rauti who fought for Mussolini's Social Republic against the Resistance.[11] And although the neofascist movement is presently considered outside the "constitutional arc," its presence has served as a constant reminder of the potential need for a revival of the Resistance. On occasion this need has been made manifest. Periodically the neofascists have achieved some political successes by acquiring allies in parliament, the bureaucracy, and among leaders of the military and intelligence services. These "achievements" have also served to compromise and contaminate the state in the eyes of those who regard the Resistance as the symbol of what is best about Italy.

The neofascists have their own set of historical legends which they use in assessing contemporary events. If the Resistance is perceived by most Italians, but especially by those on the left, as a triumphant episode, it is viewed by the neofascists as a source of shame and a reminder of defeat. The historical epoch to which they assign positive and legendary meaning is the post–World War I era when fascism, as they view it, used violence to defeat the menace of Red revolution, and guile to replace a weak and inept liberal state. If Renato Curcio's uncle was a hero of the Resistance, Franco Freda, one of the principal neofascist terrorists of our era, belongs to the same family as the fascist Italo Balbo.[12]

For the neofascists, the fight against communism or the Reds did not end with the collapse of Nazi and fascist regimes in World War II and the inauguration of a new democratic system in Italy. The period between the end of the war and the onset of the massive wave of terrorism in the late 1960s was one during which gangs of neofascist "*picchiatori*" (literally, dive bombers) frequently assaulted the offices of *L'Unità, Rinascita* (the Resistance Veterans organization), and the Communist party.[13] Just as Italians of the left, inspired by the example of the Resistance, saw the need for a continuous struggle against a fascist revival in the postwar decades, so too the neofascists defined themselves as engaged in a perpetual conflict with communism. Each side has been armed with a historical example of its victory through violence over the other.

The last precondition that has contributed to the rise of terrorism is the Italian state. The issue here may be addressed in a variety of ways. But all the ways lead to the same conclusion: massive and long-term popular dissatisfaction with the functioning of the state. Studies of Italian public opinion dating back to the *Civic Culture* sampling in 1959 consistently disclose the existence of the widely held view that the Italian system of government is untrustworthy, unresponsive, and inefficient. What is more, these reactions to governmental performance seem impervious to improvements in the economic and personal circumstances of the individuals included in the samples.[14] In a comparative perspective, Italians rank lowest among the citizens of the ten European community countries in expressing satisfaction with the way their system works and highest among the ten in believing that a European-wide government could do a better job in handling basic problems than their respective national governments.[15]

These popular perceptions of the state are, of course, not distilled from vapors floating in the air. Newspapers, weekly newsmagazines, and television programs provide the public with accounts of a seemingly endless number of scandals involving bribery, influence peddling, and other forms of political corruption. And state officials are not only defined as venal but state institutions themselves are reported to be incapable of either coping with extraordinary events—earthquakes, floods, epidemics—or providing routine public services, such as keeping an adequate supply of coins in circulation.

If the state is widely viewed as large and weak, its partisan political rulers are often seen as unable or incapable of reforming it. Illustratively, the implementation of important provisions of the constitution concerning a constitutional court, regional governments, and popular referendums took decades to accomplish.

The informal rules of political party recruitment have also ensured that the country would be run, by and large, by old men. Its leaders after World War II were largely drawn from its prefascist political elite, and its rulers today are not uncommonly individuals who rose to prominence in the 1940s and 1950s. It is true that Mao Zedong and John XXIII launched sweeping reform movements when they were past seventy, yet their behavior has rarely been duplicated by Italy's aged leaders.

In addition to these elements there is the perpetual blockage in the political system created by the near hegemonial rule of the Christian Democratic party and the problem of replacing it in power with an opposition dominated by the Communists. The literature on this subject is oceanic in volume. Suffice it to say here that massive popular frustration with the way in which the national government is run has not as yet been transformed into an electoral defeat that would expel the Christian Democrats from power.

The foregoing observations should not be understood to mean that Italians, rulers and ruled, do not support the principles of a democratic political order. Support for the constitution, social pluralism, and competitive elections is widely held.[16] It does mean, however, that many Italians believe these principles have been either distorted or never fully realized under the prevailing arrangements.

PRECIPITANTS

Observers of Italian society generally agree that the country has been going through a process of enormous social and cultural transformation over the last twenty years. Certainly among the most profound of these changes has been a decline in religious belief and a weakening of the social bonds related to membership in and obedience to the Catholic church. As the sociologist Sabino Acquaviva argues, the two strongest bonding institutions in Italian society, the church and the family, have suffered dramatic losses of authority.[17] Not only has there been a loss of faith in God but, as Acquaviva contends, there has also been a corresponding loss of paternal authority within the family.

The decline in religious and familial authority has been associated with or made possible a host of other transformations. The list would have to include the more open expression of sexuality among the young; the growth of a militant feminist movement; and the diffusion throughout the country of the various hedonistic artifacts of modern consumer society.[18]

Political scientists have measured the electoral consequences of the breakdown of traditional forms of authority. In general they have observed a growing volatility on the part of the electorate. For most of the post–World War II period the Italian electorate had enjoyed the reputation of being among the most stable in Western Europe.[19] The variations in the levels of popular support given to the various political parties from one election to the next were minute in comparison to those exhibited by other national electorates. The remarkably stable support enjoyed by all parties, the Christian Democrats, the Socialists, and the Communists in particular, was in turn explained by the existence of stable political subcultures located in various regions of the country.

Beginning with the 1974 divorce referendum, the electorate has shown signs of significant shift. The most discussed change has been the weakening in the Christian Democrats' base of support, an electoral decline associated with the decomposition of the country's Catholic subculture and in the diminished ability of Catholic families and Catholic organizations to dominate the upbringing of the young.[20] One should hasten to add, however, that the instability in the Catholic vote over the last decade should not be treated as a precipitant factor in the rise of terrorism. The two phenomena have occurred almost simultaneously. Rather, both developments should be viewed, in part, as symptoms of the more general decline of religious authority.

This erosion of traditional forms of authority has not altered the basically religious way in which many Italians interpret the world. Rather, there has been a massive substitution in faiths, with a secular political faith replacing a sacred one, or, as Raymond Aron put it many years ago:

> In Marxist eschatology, the proletariat is cast in the role of collective savior. The expressions used by young Marx leave one in no doubt as to the Judeo-Christian origins of the myth of the class elected through suffering for the redemption of humanity. The mission of the proletariat, the

end of prehistory thanks to the Revolution, the reign of liberty—it is easy to recognize the source of these ideas: the Messiah, the break with the past, the Kingdom of God.[21]

As the Catholic subculture and worldview have declined the Marxist subculture and worldview have expanded. For many, the proletariat has become the force that will lead to social and personal salvation. And just as Catholicism has its church so too does Marxism—the *Partito Comunista Italiano* (Italian Communist party).

The Communists were in the midst of a change in direction during the period with which we are concerned, the end of the 1960s and the early 1970s (the period immediately before and immediately following the outbreak of terrorism in 1969). As the result of both international and domestic developments, the party's attitude toward capitalism and the existing political system became progressively more reformist and accommodating.[22] As the society was undergoing an explosive radicalization in 1968 and 1969, involving student protest and worker discontent, the party was becoming more conservative in outlook.

The effort by the leadership to reposition it and persuade skeptics of the authenticity of the party's commitment to liberal democratic principles had several major consequences. First, the party began to achieve significant electoral advances particularly in areas and among voters whose support it had never won in the past. In turn, success at the polls allowed the party a far greater role in government at all levels than it had ever played previously. But the Communists had to pay a price for these achievements.

For supporters of liberal democratic institutions the party's ideological temperance and increased participation in governing Italy represented healthy developments. But for those who viewed the party as a church whose faith was Marxism and whose savior was the proletariat, communist behavior smacked of heresy. Analogous to the loss of the Catholic church's authority, the party suffered a loss of authority among the most zealous adherents of Marxism. As a result, in the late 1960s there was a proliferation in number and growth in size of groups like the Partito Comunista Italiano (*Marxista-Leninista*), the Lotta Continua (Continuous Struggle), Potere Operaio (Worker Power), and Avanguardia Operaio (Worker Vanguard), which defined themselves as continuing, in varying ways, the revolutionary objectives abandoned by the Communists.[23] And it was also from among these believers that the left-wing terrorist organizations have drawn many of their members.

It would be impossible to discuss these developments without also describing the cockpit out of which a good deal of this sentiment arose. In the late 1960s the major Italian universities became centers of political turmoil. Motivated initially by academic issues, Italian students were soon inspired by events occurring abroad. The Vietnam War, student protest movements in the United States and France, and the victories of revolutionary movements in the Third World contributed to the rapid radicalization of the Italian universities. This process may be observed from a number of perspectives. First, the universities experienced a swelling of enrollment. Between 1961 and 1968 enrollments more than doubled, from approximately two hundred thousand to over half a million.[24] And after 1969, when the admissions policy was changed to permit the entrance of all secondary school graduates, the growth rate became even more accelerated.

In this social environment and in an institutional setting unequipped to deal with it, students challenged the traditional sources of academic authority. Deference toward senior professors, the traditional curriculum, and examinations was attacked. In short, anything that seemed to promote hierarchy and scholastic differentiation was challenged. To a considerable extent the students achieved their objectives. "Reforms" were initiated that met many of the student demands. If the authority of academic institutions was so susceptible to challenge, why not that of other social and political institutions as well?

The development of student contestation is, perhaps, best illustrated by the case of the University of Trento. Like Berkeley in the United States or the Free University of Berlin in West Germany, Trento's radicalization provided a model to be emulated at other universities throughout Italy.[25]

Intended to be the first Italian institution of higher learning exclusively devoted to the social sciences, the university was created in 1962 and located in a socially tranquil and politically conservative province in the northern part of the country. With a reputation for curriculum innovation and a flexible admission policy, Trento attracted socially concerned students from all over Italy. Strains developed rather quickly between the cosmopolitan student population and the provincial citizens of the community. The latter came to view the students as strangers and outsiders.

The first issue to provoke student resentment arose in 1965 and involved a decision by the national government not to grant an independent degree in sociology. To protest this action students held a general meeting and decided to occupy the university until the decision was rescinded. The authorities in Rome complied with the demand. Shortly after this apparently innocuous victory, the students reoccupied the university and demanded equality of status with the faculty in the drafting of the university's organizational code. The sit-in yielded another student victory. Direct action and unconventional tactics seemed to work.

By 1967 the focus of student concerns widened to include the Vietnam War and imperialism. The same type of direct action tactics used in contesting academic policy questions were now applied to these far more remote issues. Students went out to promote their cause among the conservative citizens of Trento with predictable and frustrating results. The university was then shut down by a student strike. The police were called in. A "negative" university was created to offer "counter-courses" on such topics as the Chinese revolution and the capitalist system. Also during this period, students, drawing on readily available volumes on revolutionary change in the Third World and the situation of the working class in capitalist societies, began talking and writing about the possibility of radical change in Italy. Discussions dwelt on such classic themes as the dangers of revisionism and the nature of a revolutionary situation. When workers at factories in Milan and Turin went out on strike for higher wages in the autumn of 1969, students from Trento were thus ready to take up and transform their cause.

Student political organizations had been linked historically to Italy's major political parties, Communist, Socialist, Christian Democratic, and so forth. With the advent of the protests, however, there developed new student political groups unaffiliated with and frequently scornful of the adult-directed party organizations. And these new groups quickly mutated into political movements that spread from the universities and sought ways of attracting support in plants, factories, and other working-class settings.[26] These efforts were, in effect, attempts to detach workers, young ones especially, from the traditional trade unions and left-wing political parties, and by so doing make the workers available for revolutionary purposes. In short, the evangelical thrust of the movements was to achieve for workers in industry what they had achieved for students in the universities.

For neofascists the events of 1968–1969 bore significant resemblance to 1919–1922. Italy was gripped by political turmoil animated by left-wing political movements whose short- or long-term objectives were revolutionary. And as in the post–World War I period the state seemed unable to cope with the situation.

The largest neofascist organization, the Movimento Sociale Italiano (Italian Social Movement) underwent a change of leadership in 1969. Giorgio Almirante was chosen as its new secretary. Almirante, the longtime leader of the radicals within the movement, sought to take advantage of the opportunities the radicalized political situation afforded neofascism.[27] He did this by following a dual strategy. Under Almirante's direction the movement presented itself to the public as an exponent of law and order, horrified by the country's descent into chaos. Movimento Sociale Italiano spokesmen decried the loss of respect for authority and the contempt for traditional values expressed by the new leftists. The Mussolini era was defined as a time when Italy enjoyed social peace and foreign respect.[28] On the basis of sentiments of this kind, prominent Italian military officers were enticed into joining the movement and running for parliament under its banner.

In addition to this appeal to supporters of traditional authority, Almirante also was able to attract individuals with a more radical understanding of fascism who did not feel constrained by the Movimento Sociale Italiano's public avowal of law and order. Illustratively, a part of the Ordine Nuovo (New Order) group led by Pino Rauti was persuaded to join the movement.

Rauti and his followers derived much of their ideological inspiration from the work of the philosopher Julius Evola. (For a detailed account of Evola's work and influence, see chap. 2 by Richard Drake in this volume.) Evola's views, a mixture of mysticism, "spiritual" racism, and historical pessimism, provided young neofascists with a set of important values. These values, which Evola believed distilled the essence of real fascism, emphasized the importance of heroism, sacrifice, and adventure in personal life.[29] They also represent a radical rejection of capitalism and Marxism, liberal democracy, and the dictatorship of the proletariat. In short, Evola condemned almost all aspects of materialism and modern industrialism, which he saw as having done irreparable harm to European civilization. His objective was a Europe composed of organic and "pedagogic" states such as had existed in Europe before the French Revolution. As farfetched as all of this sounds, Evola's thought offered neofascists critiques of the existing social order and of the evangelical leftists. Crucially, Evola's goals for Italy were to be achieved by means of a national revolution led by a spiritually inspired elite.

In addition to Rauti's contingent from the Ordine Nuovo the Movimento Sociale Italiano also benefited by a growth in membership in its major youth organizations—Giovane Italia (Young Italy), Fronte Universitario di Azione Nazionale (University National Action Front), Fronte della Gioventù (Youth Front)—during the early 1970s.[30] Recruits were exposed to ideological indoctrination which, among other things, emphasized communist barbarism; and many recruits also attended paramilitary training camps.[31]

These developments within the Movimento Sociale Italiano were not the only signs of the revitalization of neofascism in this period. A great many apparently independent neofascist groups were created in major cities all over the peninsula. Other previously existing

organizations like the Fronte Nazionale (National Front), Avanguardia Nazionale (National Vanguard), and Ordine Nuovo stepped
up their activities, particularly in secondary schools and universities.
And, unlike the Movimento Sociale Italiano, these groups did not
suffer from inhibitions imposed by the desire to avoid parliamentary
sanctions.

GENERATIONAL CONFLICT

In the preceding pages an effort was made to describe the factors, both
long-term and more immediate, that have promoted widespread terrorist activity in Italy. The objective now is to analyze and interpret,
to assign meaning, to the events that have created such turmoil.

The language Italian intellectual and political elites employ in interpreting their own political order is that of social class. Their commentaries on politics are framed in terms of the struggles, victories,
or defeats experienced by one social class or another. Further, the fates
of different classes are usually linked to the fortunes of the various
political organizations that seek or are perceived to represent them.

Given this way of understanding the world, it is not surprising that
prevailing interpretations of Italian terrorism have tended to focus on
the social and economic circumstances of those segments of society
(e.g., proletariat, subproletariat, students) on whose behalf the terrorists claim to act. True, some attention has also been paid to the
social backgrounds of the terrorists themselves, and conspiratorial
interpretations of both left- and right-wing terrorism have also been
relatively common.[32] Nonetheless, in recent years even astute observers of Italian terrorists have come to view their activities in terms
appropriate to the phases of guerrilla warfare and national liberation
struggles in the Third World.[33]

It is this writer's view, however, that Italian terrorism is better
understood not as a manifestation of class antagonism but as a conflict
of generations. The preconditions and precipitants described earlier
have not been the sources of class violence but of youthful anger. And
the concepts that will be employed in analyzing the behavior of Italy's
left- and right-wing terrorists will be those that give structure to this
type of generational understanding.

According to Lewis Feuer, certain elements must be present within
a society in order for a conflict of generations to occur.[34] First, and
most obviously, there must be a group of young people who in their
formative years have shared the same kinds of historical experiences,
hopes, and disillusionments that set them apart from the rest of society.
These commonalities contribute to the formation of a generational
consciousness. Next, the society in which the conflict develops must
be one whose norms promote the development of a gerontocracy, a

society in which leadership of all major social, economic, and political institutions is controlled by old people. Further, there must develop as well a widespread belief that the older generation has failed and consequently has lost its right to rule, what Feuer refers to as "moral deauthorization."

Student movements are usually centers from which generational conflicts spread, and countries with strong traditions of intellectual elitism are ones especially prone to the growth of such movements. They are societies in which abstract ideas and the people who articulate them are taken quite seriously.

Organizations that are created to express the interests of different classes in society typically focus on the concrete self-interest of the various classes they seek to represent. Groups structured around generational struggle, in contrast, usually deny self-interest as a motivation. The goals expressed are often abstract, vague, and ill defined. Rather than self-interest, the statements of generational groups usually refer to the virtues of self-sacrifice if not martyrdom.

Student movements, so Feuer argues, characteristically seek to superimpose themselves on "carriers," movements of larger size—peasant, labor, nationalist—with long-standing grievances against the dominant institutions of their societies. The student movements seek to invest the carriers with the kinds of generationally stimulated emotions that have promoted their own activities.

Finally, student movements go through a series of stages. They begin as circles of like-minded young people who discuss, develop, and reinforce a common political perspective. The circles then attempt to act on their beliefs in an independent fashion, usually within the context of a university setting. There then occurs a populist stage during which the youth search out carrier movements. In a number of cases the young people may succeed in dominating the carriers and, if the historical circumstances are propitious, may even come to dominate the carrier and make a revolution. In other instances, however, the student movement may be rebuffed by the carriers and pursue a course based on the initial frustration of their aims. This course will often lead to bouts of mutual recrimination. Alternatively, the frustration may lead the youth movement to the elitist conclusion that its members are singularly enlightened and that they must show the masses the way. This course often leads to acts of individual and small-group political violence—in short, to terrorism. Lastly, in Feuer's judgment, there have been many occasions when the youth movements were simply overtaken by events, lost their enthusiasm, and faded from view.

Anyone familiar with Italy's recent experience with terrorism will recognize a certain similarity between the characteristics of generational conflict Feuer describes and the evolution of terrorist groups from the late 1960s to the mid-1970s. The fit, though, is hardly perfect. Terrorism is indeed best understood as a manifestation of a generational conflict, but a conflict of a particularly complex character. And some additional remarks are necessary to capture the sense of this complexity.

Italy is a country that has been divided into several distinct and mutually antagonistic political subcultures. The largest of these are the Catholic and socialist. It could be argued as well that there is also a distinct fascist subculture, although one that is far smaller and less geographically concentrated than the others (admittedly, though, the Movimento Sociale Italiano's vote has been drawn disproportionately from the south). The generational conflict should be understood against the background of these cultural divisions.

An additional point necessary to introduce into the discussion is that generational rebellion may, but need not, take the form of an outright rejection of the values of one's parents. In his study of young radicals who became involved in the anti-Vietnam protest movement in the United States, Kenneth Keniston discovered that most of the radicals he interviewed continued to share the core values they had acquired from their families.[35] What distinguished the young radicals from their parents was their willingness to put these values into practice. The parents, however, were perceived by their radical offspring as unwilling to take the risks involved in acting on their values.

Still another complicating element is the fact that Italian terrorism has been not only intergenerational but also intragenerational. A good deal of the violence has involved conflicts between left-wing and neofascist groups whose members come from the same youthful age cohort.[36] This pattern is understandable if we keep in mind the country's historic subcultural antagonisms. For neofascists the "Reds" are the enemy and for many youthful neofascists terrorist violence is the appopriate means for dealing with the enemy. Similarly, for many young leftists "fascists," the enemies of the Resistance, are perceived almost as evil incarnate against whom any and all means are appropriate.

With these views in mind Italy's young radicals, left and right wing, can be seen as having two different paths to terrorism. First, there is the path of cross-cultural migration in which the young radicals turn to terrorism after they have rejected their original subcultural identifications and acquired new ones. The movement here is characteristically from Catholic to Red. In some instances the change is mediated by a transitional period of membership in the Partito Comunista Italiano or one of the extraparliamentary left groups. In other cases the migration is direct.

The second path to terrorism has been that of within-culture challenge. That is, young radicals turn to terrorism because they find that the leadership of the established political organizations within their subculture has failed to behave in accordance with their own ideologies. The established organizations, rather like the parents of Kenniston's young radicals, have been too willing to reach accommodations with the subculture's historically defined enemies. Members of both neofascist and left-wing terrorist groups have been drawn from individuals who have followed this path. Some brief biographical observations can be used to illustrate the two different routes.

CROSS-CULTURAL MIGRATION

The two most famous stories are those of Renato Curcio and Margherita Cagol. Husband and wife, founding members of the "Historical Nucleus" of the Brigate Rosse, they both came from Catholic families and were married in church. Commentaries on their early lives emphasize their free-floating idealism (Curcio was drawn to the work of Jacques Maritain) and their reluctance to settle for mundane jobs in hotel management and bookkeeping for which they had received training.[37] They were attracted to the study of sociology and were admitted to the University of Trento. While enrolled there they became caught up in the student movement and went through a prolonged process of conversion to the cause of communist revolution culminating in the formation of the Brigate Rosse.

But the path of cross-cultural migration to terrorism has not been restricted to the Brigate Rosse in northern Italy. There is, for example, the case of Maria Fiore Pirri Ardizzone, whose father was a Sicilian industrialist and whose mother was a baroness.[38] A scholarship student at the University of Calabria, she married one of the leaders of Potere Operaio and went through a process of radicalization. Along with several former university students she was arrested in Naples in 1978 at a terrorist hideout. She and her companions had been organizing a Neapolitan group of *Prima Linea* (Front Line) revolutionaries. "I am a communist combatant," she told the police.

The Nuclei Armati Proletari (Nuclei of Armed Proletarians) was a group formed in Naples in 1973. Its membership was drawn not only from ex-students and former Potere Operaio militants but also from individuals of lower-class background with little to boast about by way of formal educational attainments.[39] Romeo Giuseppe fit this latter characterization.

He was born in 1954 to a peasant family from a small town in the southern province of Avellino. Described by the local police as intelligent, Giuseppe reacted against the discipline imposed by his elementary school teachers. Responding to acts of juvenile delinquency, his parents appealed to the local parish priest for help. The priest was able to have Giuseppe admitted to the archbishopric's boarding school.

Within a year he had flunked out. He returned to a secondary school in his hometown but was expelled within a short time. After this Giuseppe began a career as a petty criminal. Jailed for theft in Naples, he became acquainted with an anarchist while serving his sentence. Giuseppe's previous literary tastes had been limited to comic books and thrillers. Under the anarchist's tutelage, however, he began reading Marx along with such works as *Tupamaros in Action* and *Soledad Brother.*

After his release from prison Giuseppe joined Lotta Continua and continued his political education. Along with comrades he engaged in violent political clashes with neofascist youth in the streets of Naples. Giuseppe helped organize the Nuclei Armati Proletari. He was killed by the police while attempting a politically motivated bank robbery in Florence in 1974. He was twenty years old at the time of his death.[40]

WITHIN CULTURE CHALLENGE: THE NEOFASCISTS

From the point of view of the Italian left the Movimento Sociale is a neofascist organization, pure and simple. From the perspective of many of its younger members and sympathizers, however, the movement often has been viewed as too tepid, too willing to compromise with Christian Democrats, Liberals, and Monarchists. Many radical neofascists have never been comfortable within the Movimento Sociale Italiano despite Almirante's attempts to revitalize it in the late 1960s.

Giovanni Ventura and Franco Freda achieved national notoriety when they were accused of having been responsible for the 1969 bombing of the National Agricultural Bank in Milan. Both terrorists came from families of longtime fascist sympathizers. Both joined the Movimento Sociale Italiano youth organization, Ventura in Treviso, Freda in Padova. Freda opened a bookstore in Padova and organized a youth group called the Aristocrazia Ariana (Aryan Aristocracy). Later he joined the Ordine Nuovo. Ventura, a person of literary enthusiasms (the works of Celine in particular), also opened a bookstore before joining the Ordine Nuovo.[41] With Pino Rauti, Freda and Ventura sought to take advantage of the radicalized atmosphere of politics in the late 1960s by concocting a scheme for destabilizing the constitutional order. Through a series of bombings, disguised to make it appear that left-wing groups were responsible, they hoped to create a popular reaction against the left. The disorder and ensuing reaction would lead, so they hoped, to a political situation that would make possible the intervention of the military and the installation of some type of fascist-military dictatorship. Instead, they were arrested and, after years of delay, brought to trial.

The political career of Stefano Delle Chiaie, known as the Roman Bombardier, has been similar to that of Freda and Ventura. In the 1960s he became the secretary of a Movimento Sociale Italiano section in Lazio. Like Freda and Ventura, Delle Chiaie left the movement because he found it to be an inadequate expression of fascist idealism. After a brief membership in the Ordine Nuovo, Delle Chiaie organized his own neofascist group in Rome, the Avanguardia Nazionale. He and his youthful followers appeared periodically at Movimento Sociale meetings to heckle members, and demand that the movement pursue a more radical course.[42]

Along with other Roman neofascists, Delle Chiaie perpetrated a series of bombings in 1970, including one in front of an elementary school. As in the case of Freda and Ventura, the objective was to make these acts of terrorism appear to be of leftist inspiration. The ruse did not last long, and, like Freda and Ventura, Delle Chiaie and many of his followers were arrested and brought to trial.

A migrant from Naples and a university graduate with a degree in philosophy, Luciano Buonocore played an important role in Milanese neofascist circles in the late 1960s and early 1970s. In fact, he rose to be head of the Movimento Sociale youth organization in the city. But for reasons of political disagreement he left the movement to head his own group, the Comitato Cittadino Anticomunista (Anticommunist Citizen Committee), and edit its periodical, *Lotta Europea* (European Struggle). Italy must choose a new direction if it is to solve its problems, he wrote. This new course requires a rejection of both capitalism and communism; there must be a return to the spiritual values of the Middle Ages. Modern man must be liberated from the demons of money and materialism. Buonocore was arrested on several occasions for participating in violent neofascist activities, including an attack on the Milanese Chamber of Labor.[43]

WITHIN CULTURE CHALLENGE: THE LEFT

One of the most widely reproduced photographs in modern Italian journalism shows three teenage boys in the middle of a street in Milan. Two of the boys, both wearing masks, are running away from the police. The third, who has a pistol, has stopped running; he is shown about to fire at his pursuers.

The three boys in the photograph, whose ages ranged from sixteen to nineteen, were Maurizio Azzolini (holding the gun), Massimo Sandrini, and Walter Grecchi.[44] They were high school students at the Cattaneo Institute in Milan and members of Autonomia Operaio (Worker Autonomy). They came from working- or lower-middle-class families. The school they attended had been a center of leftist political activity from 1968 (the photograph was taken in 1977). The Federazione Giovanile Comunista (Communist Youth Federation), Lotta Continua, and Avanguardia Operaio had all recruited students and held rallies in front of the school. Azzolini, Sandrini, and Grecchi attended the rallies and joined the organizations, but became dissatisfied with both. According to a fellow student they came to see themselves as living in a desperate situation. On the one hand, their social circumstances were intolerable. Unemployment, crime, and drug use were widespread in their neighborhoods. The school curriculum was designed to turn them into unthinking robots. On the other hand, the conventional leftist organizations to which they turned with high expectations seemed to offer very little. Instead of concrete measures, what they got was endless intellectualizing ("mental masturbation") and bureaucracy. In this situation, the three boys abandoned the school's conventional leftist organizations and joined Autonomia Operaio, a group that not only promised but provided opportunities for direct action against the existing order.

Roberto Ognibene is from Reggio Emilia, a city whose politics has been dominated by the left for over thirty years. Ognibene's father had been a longtime Socialist who broke with the party and joined the Communists in the 1960s. His son Roberto (born in 1954) grew up listening to political talk around the dinner table. By the time Roberto was fifteen he had grown tired of the talk. His father recalls:

> Of course we discussed politics. It couldn't have been otherwise in a family like ours. This doesn't mean we shared the same views. After all, he was young and I was not. I had been a member of the Socialist Party, and I went over to the Communist Party, but let's face it, I'm still a reformist, whereas Roberto was against reformism. He wanted action, and to his way of thinking that was not synonymous with reform. He had an enormous eagerness . . . to act, to see things done.[45]

At the technical school he attended and on the streets of Reggio Emilia, Roberto Ognibene met other young people of similar mind. Some, including young Communists, expressed their contempt for the school system and for the community's Partito Comunista Italiano-dominated city government. In 1970 he joined the extraparliamentary group, Sinistra Proletaria (Proletarian Left). He was arrested briefly for participation in a street scuffle with neofascist youth. Less than two months after enrolling in a course to train surveyors, Ognibene dropped out and left Reggio Emilia for Milan in 1973. In Milan he joined the Brigate Rosse and in 1974 he was arrested along with other brigadists. Ognibene had shot and killed a policeman.

Ognibene was only one of the several young radicals to leave Reggio Emilia for Milan and the Brigate Rosse in the early 1970s. His friend,

Alberto Franceschini, was the first to go. And if the roots of Ognibene's radicalism are to be found in his family and community, the same may be said of Franceschini's, only more so. His grandparents had fought against the fascists in the 1920s and 1930s. His father, taken as a slave laborer to Germany during the war, escaped from Auschwitz and returned to Italy to work for the Resistance. After the war he joined the Partito Comunista Italiano and spent his life working for the Confederazione Generale Italiana del Lavoro (General Federation of Italian Labor). Given this background it is not surprising that as an adolescent Alberto Franceschini joined the Federazione Giovanile Comunista. A person quickly perceived as both energetic and intelligent, he gained a place in the federation's leadership committee.

Beginning in 1968 Franceschini began to view the Partito Comunista Italiano as unresponsive to the concerns of his generation as manifested in the student protest movement. After an effort to win the support of the local party organization to his point of view failed, Franceschini resigned from the party, taking a group of like-minded dissidents with him. He and his followers then organized their own group: Collectivo di Operai e Studenti (Workers and Students Collective). Over the next several years the group held an almost endless discussion about Italian society and its political system. In 1972 Franceschini failed to report for the military draft and went underground. He surfaced in Milan where he was arrested, like Ognibene, for terrorist acts committed under the direction of the Brigate Rosse.[46]

Summary and Conclusion

It has been argued in this essay that the wave of terrorist activity in Italy which began more than a decade ago has been, in part, the product of a cluster of cultural and historical preconditions that made the country vulnerable to a politics of violence. These preconditions were (1) the style of national political leadership, decision making based on a combination of ideological expression and carefully calculated self-interest; (2) memories of the country's experience with fascism and of the Resistance movement organized against it; and (3) the enduring and popular perception of the state as a weak and flawed expression of democratic principles, governed by rules that promoted a gerontocracy.

Within the framework provided by these preconditions there were a number of changes in Italian life that occurred in the years immediately before and during the early stages of violence that precipitated and then helped to amplify the scope of political terrorism. These precipitants included, first and foremost, a decline in traditional religious beliefs and a weakening of the authority of the institutions these beliefs had buttressed. It was also maintained that Italy's Marxist subculture was invested with the same kind of popular religious enthusiasm that had previously been reserved for the church at precisely the time that subculture's leading institution, the Communist party, was becoming a more moderate force in society. The resultant rise of extraparliamentary left organizations, with their calls for revolution and displays of mass protest in the streets, provided an opportunity for a revitalization of radical neofascist activity.

The foregoing developments produced and promoted political terrorism. The terrorist activity itself was defined as a complex generational conflict involving a reaction by the young to the leading organizations of their various political subcultures. These organizations were seen by the young and some of their adult mentors as being inadequate in the face of the subcultures' historically defined enemies.

The pattern has been uneven, however. The Communists have pursued a course of moderation while the Movimento Sociale, under Almirante, has been more susceptible to radical appeals. Left-wing dissidents in the Partito Comunista were being expelled from the party at about the same time the Movimento Sociale Italiano welcomed Pino Rauti and a faction of the Ordine Nuovo. There has been nothing remotely comparable to the violence directed against the Communists and the trade unions by left-wing terrorists experienced by the Movimento Sociale from terrorist groups within the neofascist subculture.

So far as the future of Italian terrorism is concerned, there is clearly a pattern of generational succession under way. As older leaders of terrorist groups are caught by the police, new and younger recruits emerge to take their place. And as longer-lived groups are dissolved by the authorities, new groups with similar names emerge to take up the slack. Many of the circumstances that sparked the initial wave of terrorism have not gone away. Nonetheless, there are a number of factors at work that mitigate against the persistence of terrorism.

First, the very success of terrorism is or becomes a source of vulnerability. Small, clandestine organizations committing acts of kidnapping, sabotage, and assassination in vast urban areas are notoriously hard to detect. However, when such groups seek to translate their terrorist successes into political successes by becoming an "armed party" for example, they inevitably run into trouble. They become larger in size and hence more susceptible to police detection and control. Second, the more prevalent terrorism becomes, the higher it rises in priority on the government's policy agenda, and the more resources are devoted to combating it. With more and more resources and longer experiences in dealing with terrorism the better equipped the police become in coping with it. Both of these factors appear to be at work in Italy now.

Finally, the long-run aims of both communist and neofascist terrorists continue to be frustrated. The democratic state has not toppled either to revolution or military coup. If anything, it seems a bit more secure today than it did in 1968. Almost every calamity has occurred and yet the center, unsavory though it may be, still holds.

NOTES

1. Sidney Tarrow, "Italy: Crisis, Crises or Transition?" *in* Peter Lange and Sidney Tarrow, eds., *Italy in Transition* (London: Frank Cass & Co., 1980), pp. 183–185.

2. Paul Wilkinson, *Terrorism and the Liberal State* (New York: New York University Press, 1979), pp. 188–193. Walter Laqueur, *Terrorism* (Boston: Little, Brown, 1979), p. 923.

3. The analysis here approximates a framework suggested by Martha Crenshaw, "The Causes of Terrorism," *Comparative Politics* 13, 4 (1981), 379–399.

4. Stanley Hoffmann, *Decline or Renewal: France Since the 1930s* (New York: Viking Press, 1979), pp. 63–110.

5. Pasquale Nonno, "Quanto piace Craxi," *Panorama* 16, 660 (1978):46–52.

6. Giovanni Sartori, "Politics, Ideology and Belief Systems," *American Political Science Review* 63 (1969), 398.

7. Robert Putnam, *The Beliefs of Politicians* (New Haven: Yale University Press, 1975), pp. 137–156.

8. Stefan Possony, "Giangiacomo Feltrinelli: The millionaire dinamitero," *Terrorism* 2, 324 (1979), 213–230.

9. Soccorso Rosso, ed., *Brigate rosse* (Milan: Feltrinelli, 1976), pp. 89–101.

10. The letter is quoted in Alessandro Silj's *Never Again Without a Rifle* (New York: Harz, 1979), pp. 72–73.

11. See for example, Giorgio Almirante, *Autobiografia di un "Fucilatore"* (Milan: Edizioni del Borghese, 1974); Giulio Carradonna, *Diario di battaglie* (Rome: Europa Press Service, n.d.); Giampolo Pansa, *Borghese mi ha detto* (Milan: Palazzi Editore, 1971).

12. Cesare De Simone, *La pista nera* (Rome: Editori Riumiti, 1972), p. 64.

13. Pietro Secchia, *Lotta antifascista e qiovani generazioni* (Milan: La Pietra, 1973), pp. 80–87; Giulio Salierno, *Autobiografia di un picchiatore fascista* (Turin: Einaudi Editore, 1976), pp. 100–135.

14. Giacomo Sani, "The Political Culture of Italy: Continuity and Change," *in* Gabriel Almond and Sidney Verba, eds., *The Civic Culture Revisited* (Boston: Little, Brown, 1980), pp. 307–310.

15. Ronald Inglehart, *The Silent Revolution* (Princeton: Princeton University Press, 1977), pp. 146, 359.

16. Putnam, *The Beliefs of Politicians*, pp. 226–236.

17. Sabino Acquaviva, *Il seme religioso della rivolta* (Milan: Rusconi Libri, 1979), pp. 16–21.

18. For a discussion of these and other charges, see Antonio Gambino, et al., *Dal '68 a oggi: come siamo e come eravamo* (Rome: Laterza, 1979), pp. 269–427.

19. See for example, Samuel Barnes, *Representation in Italy* (Chicago: University of Chicago Press, 1977), pp. 65–77; Giorgio Galli and Alfonso Prandi, *Patterns of Political Participation in Italy* (New Haven: Yale University Press, 1970), pp. 26–71.

20. Giacomo Sani, "Political Traditions as Contextual Variables: Partisanship in Italy," *American Journal of Political Science* 20, 3 (1976), pp. 375–404; and "Ricambio elettorale e identificazioni partitiche: verso una egemonia delle sinistra?" *Rivista italiana di scienza politica* 5, 3 (1975), 515–544.

21. Raymond Aron, *The Opium of the Intellectuals* (New York: W. W. Norton, 1957), p. 66.

22. Norman Kogan, *A Political History of Postwar Italy* (New York: Praeger, 1981), pp. 39–46; Grant Amyot, *The Italian Communist Party* (New York: St. Martin's Press, 1981), pp. 170–209; Pasquale Nonno, "Siamo ancora comunisti?" *Panorama* 15, 546 (1976), 38–41.

23. Giuseppe Vettori, ed., *La sinistra extraparlamentare in Italia* (Rome: Newton Compton, 1973).

24. Maria Luisa Agnese and Maria Luigia Pace, "Crolla tutto, ma io . . . ," *Panorama*, 15, 575 (1977), 87.

25. Soccorso Rosso, ed., *Brigate Rosse*, pp. 26–34.

26. Luciano Aguzzi, *Scuola, studenti e lotta di classe* (Milan: Emme edizioni, 1976), pp. 7–27.

27. Petra Rosenbaum, *Il nuovo fascismo* (Milan: Feltrinelli, 1975), pp. 122–129.

28. Mario Tedeschi, *Destra nazionale* (Rome: Edizioni del Borghese, 1972); Armando Plebe, *Il libretto della destra* (Milan: Edizioni del Borghese, 1972).

29. Julius Cesare Evola, *Il fascismo visto dalla destra* (Rome: Volpe editore, 1970), pp. 29–37; see also Thomas Sheehan, "Italy: Terror on the Right," *The New York Review of Books* 27, 21 and 22 (1981), 23–26.

30. *Almanacco della destra nazionale* (Cassino: Saipem, 1975), pp. 28–30.

31. Paolo Guzzanti, *Il neofascismo e le sue organizzazioni paramilitari* (Rome: PSI, 1973), pp. 32–43.

32. See for example, Damiele Barbieri, *Agenda nera* (Rome: Coines edizioni, 1976); Claire Sterling, *The Terrorist Network* (New York: Holt, Rinehart and Winston, 1981), pp. 202–227.

33. Sabino Acquaviva, *Guerriglia e guerra rivoluzionaria in Italia* (Milan: Rizzoli editore, 1979), pp. 137–164.

34. Lewis Feuer, *The Conflict of Generations* (New York: Basic Books, 1969), pp. 3–49.

35. Kenneth Kenniston, *Young Radicals* (New York: Harcourt, Brace and World, 1968), pp. 112–113.

36. Leonard Weinberg, "Patterns of Neo-fascist Violence in Italian Politics," *Terrorism* 2, 324 (1979), 231–259.

37. Silj, *Never Again Without a Rifle*, pp. 39–95.

38. Felice Piemontese, "Al sud, intanto, sulle ceneri dei nap," *Panorama* 16, 626 (1978), 44.

39. Ida Fare and Franca Spirito, "Noi con il fucile," *Panorama* 17, 670 (1979), 41–43.

40. Silj, *Never Again Without a Rifle*, pp. 158–164.

41. Marco Sassano, *La politica delle strage* (Padova: Marsilio editoro, 1972), pp. 39–47; Guido Lorenzon, *Teste a carico* (Milan: Mondadari editore, 1976), pp. 15–28.

42. Marco Fini and Ardrea Barberi, *Valpreda* (Milan: Feltrinelli, 1972), pp. 98–103.

43. Cooperativa scrittori, eds., *Rapporto sulla violenza fascista in Lombardia* (Rome: Archivio italiano, 1975), pp. 525–536.

44. Pino Buongiorno and Carlo Rossella, "Convinti che sia guerra," *Panoramo* 15, 580 (1977), 42–45.

45. Silj, *Never Again Without a Rifle*, p. 4.

46. Ibid., pp. 24–38.

6

Interpretations of Italian
Left-Wing Terrorism

GIANFRANCO PASQUINO
AND
DONATELLA DELLA PORTA

———

Italian terrorism has almost dominated the political scene since the 1970s. It has shown a tremendous amount of continuity and organizational effectiveness and has presented different faces and varieties. More often the object of moral and political condemnations, and sometimes of praise, it has rarely been analyzed in scholarly terms. Moreover, its various forms, both organizational and political, have not been clearly differentiated in their overlapping, and the degrees of imitation and contagion have not been highlighted. In sum, a lot of scholarly work needs to be done on left- and right-wing terrorism in Italian politics.

This essay will briefly attempt to present, analyze, and, when necessary, provide critical comments on the major interpretations of left-wing, or "red," terrorism. Two caveats must be kept in mind, however. The first one is that we do not by any means underestimate the impact and virulence of right-wing terrorism in affecting the psychosis of left-wing terrorists. Indeed, if there is a birth date of terrorism in Italy, it is the explosion of a bomb by the right wing in a bank in Milan (12 December 1969) which killed sixteen persons and wounded another forty. Because of its close connection with the Italian state machinery and foreign secret services, understanding right-wing terrorism requires specific methods and knowledge not readily available.

The second note of caution has to do with the goals of this essay. We are not offering new evidence on left-wing terrorism, which is only now surfacing at a relatively high level. We will focus our attention on the interpretations that have been put forward, on their plausibility, and on their logical consistency. Therefore, we will not provide a history of Italian left-wing terrorism nor a full-blown sociological analysis. But we hope to be able to indicate which are the most important problems for sociological analysis, the relevant questions to be asked in empirical research, and the explanations that seem the most fruitful. Due to its unabated persistence over more than a decade, its pervasiveness, and its threatening and deadly activities, Italian left-wing terrorism deserves more than a short essay. This is only the beginning of a series of empirical explorations.

NONSOCIOLOGICAL EXPLANATIONS

As in other contexts, such as in Germany and Japan, nonsociological explanations have been offered for the birth and the development of Italian terrorism. Two are rather frequently used, often without any attempt to relate them to other explanations: terrorism as the result of a conspiracy and terrorism as the product of individual psychopathologies. As we will see, these two explanations are closely connected as well as almost entirely cut off from any broad sociological explanation.

TERRORISM AS A RESULT OF A CONSPIRACY

The very existence of terrorism is sometimes attributed to an international conspiracy organized by foreign secret services to destabilize Italy. Or it is considered the product of the activities of some sectors of the Italian state machinery (of course, a certain amount of cooperation among foreign secret services and the Italian state machinery is never denied nor underestimated). The question often asked is *cui prodest?* that is, in whose interests are terrorist activities carried out? Although in the past the tendency to involve the Central Intelligence Agency in anything that might go wrong in Italy was automatic, in recent times the spectrum of responsibilities has been enlarged.

Briefly, because of its importance in the Mediterranean, Italy can be considered a target both for the Soviet Union and for the United States. A destabilized and weak Italy would present fewer obstacles to Soviet penetration in the Mediterranean. It would not constitute a credible ally for the United States, thus making Israel the pillar of U.S. policy in this area. As a consequence, and also because of the relative amount of public support given to the Palestine Liberation

Organization's (PLO) claims, some have also suspected the penetration by Israeli secret services as a trigger of some terrorist activities.

During the 1967–1974 phase, moreover, a sort of international fascist organization existed, subsidized by the secret services of Greece (then under a military junta), Portugal (then under an authoritarian dictatorship), and Spain (then under Franco's dictatorship). Indeed, right-wing terrorists often found asylum in these countries and evidence exists that they received more than logistic support. Right-wing terrorism subsided somewhat after the overthrow of these authoritarian regimes. From 1974 up to the bombing of Bologna's railroad station in 1980, no major act of "black" terrorism was carried out.

As to the CIA, often demonized and the easy target of all accusations, the explanation that is offered focuses on the interest of American policymakers in preventing Communist participation in any Italian government coalition. A destabilized and weak Italian government, then, is only a first step toward the creation of a tough, authoritarian democracy capable of restoring order, excluding the Communists, and remaining a close and faithful ally of the United States. No direct evidence has been found concerning the involvement of the CIA in Italian terrorism in the 1970s. It is likely that the CIA had a large amount of information on Italian terrorism, even before the Italian government was able to improve its intelligence system, and it is well known that pressures were put by the U.S. government on various Christian Democrat (DC) leaders not to open the way to Communist participation in political coalitions.

The Italian Communist party (PCI), however, improved its position to such an extent that it became part of the parliamentary coalition supporting the government and influencing its policies. Then Moro's kidnapping and murder took place: a phenomenon that cannot be attributed, on the basis of the available evidence, to the CIA or to foreign secret services.

A lot of evidence, on the contrary, is available concerning the involvement of the Italian secret services in the cover-up for right-wing terrorist activities. Although not systematic, this evidence is impressive and indicates the connivance between some sectors of the "unreconstructed" state machinery and the right wing, the responsibility of some politicians in underestimating the phenomenon (or even their willingness to exploit it for political purposes), or the blandness of some sectors of the judiciary in dealing with right-wing terrorists.

All this having been said, it is difficult to subscribe in its entirety to the conspiracy thesis. Examples of lack of coordination, of major blunders, of accidental events are too widespread and frequent to believe that there was (or there is) a mastermind behind all these events. Of course, it is still possible that there is an objective coincidence of goals among various actors. The evidence is not conclusive, however, and it is therefore difficult to speak of someone who pulls the strings. Moreover, the conspiracy explanation can be used in a relatively satisfactory way (but, alas, in a nonsociological way) to explain right-wing terrorism, which has no social support or, at the most, enjoys some geographically concentrated bases, but it hardly seems applicable, in its entirety, to left-wing terrorism.

Though it is difficult to accept the conspiracy thesis as the only explanation of terrorism, both left- and right-wing, it would be wrong to discard it. Too many pieces of evidence seem to suggest that a full understanding of Italian terrorism will also need this perspective and therefore a close analysis of judicial documents, secret service archives (when available), and of the identification of plausible connections through conjecture. One final point is important: Because of their political and organizational dynamics, it is likely that in some instances and in some areas both right- and left-wing terrorists in Italy have been infiltrated by the Italian as well as by foreign secret services. While this cannot be offered as an explanation for their behavior, it must be kept in mind for the understanding of the overall story of Italian terrorists.

TERRORISM AS THE PRODUCT OF INDIVIDUAL PSYCHOPATHOLOGIES

If there is a mastermind, there must be puppets. This explanation is therefore somewhat related to the previous one. The terrorists are seen as puppets dominated by outside forces. And they can be dominated because of their weak, distorted, and aberrant psychological personalities. The explanations of their becoming terrorists are to be found in their individual histories: a divided, destitute family, an unhappy adolescence, incomplete schooling, an unsatisfactory work experience. All the evidence of deviance and alienation is used in order to classify the terrorists as outside the boundaries of civic life.

More often than not, this explanation is applied to cases of individual acts, attempted assassinations, particularly of important political figures, bombings, and hijackings. It cannot, of course, be used to explain a phenomenon that entails the participation of a large number of individuals. Even in the master-puppets relationship, the psychological explanation does not seem satisfactory beyond a certain size of group.

The study of the personalities of the terrorists is, needless to say, extremely important. But the psychopathological explanation in and by itself cannot provide a satisfactory account of the dynamics of terrorists groups, their formation, workings, and dissolution. While popular explanations of terrorism, particularly in the press, continue to focus on the terrorist personality, they may be telling us more about the fears and beliefs of a certain society than about terrorism in that society. This comment does not mean to detract in any way from a sound psychological analysis of the terrorist personality. This kind of analysis is indeed very productive and definitely relevant, but in using it alone and in isolation the risk is run of its becoming either a rationalization of a nonintegrated society or the exorcism for a very complex problem. In the Italian case, analyses of this kind have been so far very rare, perhaps all too rare. But a thorough understanding of the terrorist syndrome does require a comprehension of the types (in the plural) of personalities receptive to certain psychological more than sociopolitical motivations.

From the amount of material collected in the Italian case, two aspects have emerged so far. First, in their interrogations during the trials and in their many declarations, most terrorists have not shown characteristics that can be attributed to psychic diseases or to distorted personalities. Indeed, what has been most striking and was duly re- marked even by the popular press is the "normalcy" of their person- alities, both in their day-to-day behavior and in their upbringing and previous living conditions. Second, in the light of the quantitative and qualitative dimensions achieved by left-wing terrorists in Italy (this point may be less applicable to right-wing terrorists), it is im- possible to resort to an explanation only or exclusively in psychological terms for the terrorist affiliation of large numbers of individuals.

A very interesting issue then arises concerning the mechanisms through which in a certain historical period distorted psychological personalities resort to crime and in another period they join terrorist bands; and furthermore, why the activation of certain psychological distortions should take place in certain specific periods and how it can be maintained for such a long period of time. These are definitely relevant questions. Most of the necessary elements for a satisfactory answer can be found by reversing the perspective: from a sociological analysis of terrorist movements to a psychological interpretation of the motives of individual terrorists.

We now turn to the most important sociological interpretations of terrorism in Italy with specific, if not exclusive, attention to left-wing terrorism. Only a few passing remarks will be devoted to right-wing terrorism, but only because it does not seem to be the product of collective actions.

SOCIOLOGICAL INTERPRETATIONS OF LEFT-WING TERRORISM

There are two main approaches to the analysis of left-wing terrorism from a sociological perspective. The first puts the emphasis and focuses the attention on the variables and the processes that produce the emergence and influence the behavior of collective actors. The second starts from an assessment of the political system and analyzes terrorism as the reaction (or one of the reactions) against the malfunctioning, or at least the weaknesses and the faults, of the political system. Both interpretations have been widely expounded and used in the Italian case as well as in other Western contexts to explain the rise and the consolidation of terrorism. Let us analyze these interpretations and their variants in detail.

TERRORISM AS THE PRODUCT OF THE CHOICE
MADE BY A COLLECTIVE ACTOR

This interpretative trend analyzes terrorism on the basis of the existence of a collective actor willing to resort to violence as an instrument of political struggle. There are three different, but by no means mutually exclusive, levels of analysis. The first level points to the existence of a cultural model that pushes toward the use of political violence and terrorist means and justifies them (Marletti 1979). The ideological roots of terrorism are then sought and identified in the so-called culture of 1968.

It is in the complex and often confused cultural formulations of the various movements that sprang up in 1968, in Europe and Italy, in the United States and in Japan, that some authors have identified the ideology, the beliefs, and the behaviors that produce and have historically produced terrorism. Terrorism, however, is not the inevitable, automatic, and direct outgrowth of the movements of 1968; that is, other currents of thought and action have joined together to produce that outcome. Still the germs of terrorist culture were present in 1968. Specifically, some of the postulates that might justify political violence and create terrorist bands were: the mythology of the coming revolution, democracy as a mask behind which capitalist domination and exploitation of the masses were hidden, the sovereignty of ideology over theory, the contempt for human life, and the strict subordination of the members to the goals of the "movement" (Dalla Chiesa 1981).

While many elements for a terrorist choice might have been present in the movements of 1968, it is not true that all terrorists were members of those movements nor is it true that the movements of 1968 have been responsible for all subsequent events. Terrorism was contained as a potentiality in some of those movements. But the very fact that it materialized in Italy and not in France may signal something of importance for the analysis. Concretely and in practice, cultural predispositions were not enough to produce terrorist movements; they, moreover, cannot account for the different trajectories of the various terrorist groups in Western societies.

In addition to the culture of 1968, some authors have identified cultural roots of terrorism in the traditions of verbal extremism and in the analyses of the crisis of capitalism and Western political systems spread by the Third International. In the Italian context this type of explanation has often been used to embarrass the Italian Communist party. According to some critics of the PCI, the terrorists are the legitimate children of a certain type of propaganda that is based on the premise that the bourgeois state is an obstacle to the emancipation of the working class to be achieved through the establishment of the dictatorship of the proletariat (Colletti, in "Terrorismo e quadro politico," 1978; Alquati, in Alquati et al. 1980). Moreover, these critics add that the PCI often contrasted the situation existing in Eastern Europe favorably with the situation in Western Europe, certainly up to the tragic denouement of the Prague Spring; after which its analysis changed and culminated in the rejection of the progressive potentialities of Eastern societies in December 1981, following the military coup in Poland.

Others have even spoken of the "family album" of the Communist party in whose photographs one could find the terrorists (Rossana Rossanda, in a famous article in *Il Manifesto*), implying a sort of, albeit distorted, ideological continuity between Italian communism and terrorism. Highly controversial, this interpretation catches, however, some important aspects. While one cannot but be struck by the absence of this kind of terrorism in the French case where a sectarian Communist party has operated without renewing its cultural approach to the problems of contemporary capitalism and the democratic system, the answer may well lie in this contrast.

Exactly because the Italian Communist party was renewing its ideological baggage, some groups felt betrayed, since they thought the historical rendezvous with the revolution was being missed. The criticisms leveled against the Soviet "normalization" of Czechoslovakia, the increasing moderation of the Communist party in Italian affairs, and finally the offer of a historic compromise with the historical enemy, the Christian Democrats, in 1973, all seemed to justify the choice to take up arms and to launch a new Resistance (also against a growing right-wing threat). Indeed, some old and young members of the Communist party are to be found among the ranks of terrorist bands. But terrorism is not the direct or inevitable outgrowth of the decisions made or not made by the PCI. It can be considered, in this interpretation, as the outcome of an unresolved contradiction within the ranks of the PCI (which the PCI did not have to face because of its delay in the process of revision, because of its more highly centralized structure, and because of its stricter control over its members). Once more, though, it is important to stress that, while some cultural predispositions existed, by no means did the PCI accept this development without opposing it. Indeed, some critics add that it was too adamant in its opposition and went too far in blocking the channels of expression for some dissenting groups.

Putting the emphasis on the contradictions and delays in the renewal process of the communist subculture, this interpretation spills over into the field of interpretations that stress the willingness of some political groups to resort to violence anyway in order to change the system. This tradition, too, concerning the acceptance of violence may be found in communist ideology and, of course, in other ideologies as well: first of all in the fascist one. But more often than not, this violence was justified only as a defensive reaction against those preventing the promotion of the working class. Indeed, Lenin strongly and repeatedly condemned any form of terrorist activities.

A distorted interpretation of Leninism, however, was widely diffused in the Italian context in 1968 and after. It provided a legitimation of violence in the light of impending revolution thanks above all to the existence of groups willing to preach violence as a form of action in the political system, and later on to practice their own teachings. Highly sensitive in the Italian context, this interpretation would point toward two political groups responsible for this kind of transformation and these kinds of activities: Potere Operaio (Workers' Power) and Lotta Continua (Continuous Struggle).

Various attempts have been made to reconstruct the stages and phases of the formation and expansion of some political groups, specifically the two mentioned above (and more recently the Red Brigades), in order to identify the thresholds in their ideological and organizational dynamics which have led from their advocacy of mass violence to their actual use of terrorism. Or, perhaps said a better way, from the advocacy of political violence in their writings, documents, and newspapers to the practice of violence by some of their former members. So far, the most compelling evidence comes from bulky judicial inquiries.

In this interpretation, terrorism is seen as the product of an organized minority, born in the period of the great and widespread struggle of 1969 (which in Italy was the climax of the process) which, defining itself as the conscious vanguard of the revolutionary transformation, attempts to force the will of the masses (Ventura 1980). According to this interpretation, therefore, terrorism in Italy is the product of the existence of a collective political actor, which legitimates in theory and advocates in practice the resort to the whole repertoire of political violence: first, as an instrument for the unchaining of the crisis (which should then be considered the outcome of the vanguard's political will); second, as the prerequisite for the creation of the insurrectionary party, which will be able to come into existence only after a period of widespread diffusion of violent confrontations and expansion of the areas and groups affected by violence; and, finally, as an instrument to provoke the radicalization of social and political forces and the collapse of the state (Galante 1981).

The process of organization of the so-called armed party has been alternatively explained as the extreme reaction against the transformation of the Communist party, its access to the governmental arena, and of the social integration of the working class; or as the outcome of the decline of "mass social movements" and of the impossibility of absorbing the energies and the projects of all the militants who appeared in the expansion phase. The surplus of militancy therefore found asylum in the "armed party" (for the first thesis, Minucci, and for the second, Pizzorno, both in "Terrorismo e quadro politico," 1978).

The second variant of this interpretation seems more convincing on the basis of the periodization and of the available documents. While it is not entirely established if and when some militants and leaders of Potere Operaio and Lotta Continua decided to turn to armed activities and to the creation of an armed party, the available evidence indicates that such a decision might have come rather early in the 1970s when the PCI was still far away from the governmental arena and when the working class was still actively and combatively engaged in collective actions: by no means could either be said to have "sold out" to the system. The creation of an armed party therefore anticipated the realities against which it was supposed to struggle. It cannot be denied, of course, that later on some additional militants might have been attracted by terrorist groups on the basis of the reaction to the integration of the PCI and the working class into the system, but this cannot by any means be considered the initial or the most important stimulus to the theory and practice of the armed party.

A correct periodization of the terrorist phenomenon in Italy would clearly distinguish among different phases. If this is done—and it can be done on the basis of the classic indicators: number of groups, number of incidents, intensity and scope of violent occurrences—then the second variant of the interpretation based on the existence of a group or series of groups willing to resort to the use of violence can be put in a correct perspective. Indeed, the influx of alienated and dissatisfied members of the great collective struggles of the late 1960s and the 1970s becomes significant exactly when these struggles become subdued. Furthermore, it is right after 1975–1976 that terrorist groups become more violent, better organized, and geographically more widespread. Without the existence of groups already devoted to the use of violence, however, the surplus of energies and militancy would have gone astray. Therefore, in order to comprehend the complexity of the phenomenon in its entirety, the history and ideology of the leading groups at the beginning of the 1970s must be reconstructed.

Together with cultural and political explanations of terrorism, there are many different variants relating terrorism to social issues. More specifically, two variants have been proposed and used in the analysis (both are often and at the same time interpretations *and* rationalizations of the terrorist phenomenon). Both stress the existence of some social strata that are specifically predisposed to select violence as an instrument of defense of their position in the system of stratification. On the one hand, there are those authors who have identified the existence and the diffusion of a new type of industrial worker. Rather young, without any identification with the trade unions or with a political party, engaged in a repetitive working activity from which they draw no satisfactions, personal or professional, and few material gratifications, in a situation in which even their social relations are limited and confined, subject to a sociopolitical manipulation that penetrates their entire life, this new type of worker has only one way out: rebellion. Their enemy is first of all identified in the system of production within the factory and those responsible for it and in charge of it; and second, in those very organizations which do not protect their interests and do not fight for a total overhaul of the system. Violence is, then, if not the only, certainly a very appealing instrument to be used in order to dramatize their identity, to punish those responsible for their working and living conditions and, last but not least, to change things.

An empirical verification of this interpretation with all the convincing evidence it deserves has not yet been carried out. However, on the basis of the preliminary and sketchy biographical data that are available on convicted terrorists, the number of alienated, dissatisfied industrial workers seems to be extremely limited. Some trade unionists are present in the ranks of terrorist groups, and this seems to provide some support to the thesis based on the "surplus of militancy" (particularly if one looks at the dates of their recruitment), but very few workers. Indeed, while some of them may have joined terrorist ranks in the early phase of the phenomenon, in more recent years when, if anything, the syndrome of alienation and dissatisfaction might have made for more casualties, recruitment from this channel almost came to a halt.

This observation leads to the second variant of the analysis of some social strata especially predisposed to political violence and terrorism. This variant would explain the terrorist phenomenon on the basis of the existence and the production of marginal social strata. That is, capitalist development as well as, and not paradoxically, its lack of development produce the marginalization of some social strata. If and when development takes place, it is accompanied by a growing process of automation and replacement of the traditional type of manpower. The old labor force then is thrown to the margins of the socioeconomic system. If development does not take place, large sectors of the new working class will lose their jobs and the newcomers to the labor market will be rejected. Then a large pool of available youngsters will exist to be recruited into groups advocating violence to change an unjust socioeconomic system.

Since the political system is no longer able to legitimate its existence and its functioning with reference to its ability to produce development, jobs, and resources, it will become increasingly easy to challenge the established order. As long as old marginal sectors and new marginal groups do not possess legal means to challenge the system (they are not, or no longer unionized, they are unwilling to be organized by political parties, and they have been deprived of aggregation sites), it is likely that their only form of collective action will be a rejection of the system and, if the avenue is there, a resort to violence. The blockage of the process of industrialization, particularly in societies that have not yet reached modernity, would produce the emergence of a "negative society," characterized by very limited means of subsistence, lack of unifying symbols, and disarticulation of forms and vehicles of political participation. The typical components of this kind of society are uprooted peasants (Ferrarotti 1978).

This thesis lends itself easily to refutation. Once more the available biographies of convicted terrorists show that very few of them belong, by any stretch of the imagination, to the ranks of the marginals. Even a very schematic distinction between Italy's north and south would lead one to expect the presence of many more terrorists of this kind in the south. This is absolutely not the case. One could still save this thesis by resorting to two types of arguments. In the first place, relative deprivation: terrorists in the north are members of the most marginal of those social groups, being the product of the recent industrialization and urbanization processes. Only a more detailed and in-depth exploration can lend substance to this objection. Or, second, the terrorists themselves, more specifically active terrorists, are not marginals. However, their supporting groups, their logistical troops, are supplied by the marginals. The latter are so poorly organized and so deprived of resources as not to be able to participate actively in the process of "reappropriation." Once more, not even this objection seems tenable. Indeed, if anything, the supporting groups seem to come from well-off middle-class strata, those capable of providing money, apartments, cars, and so on, necessary for a sustained terrorist effort.

Less emphasis has been put on the possibility that the terrorists may be marginals but of a different kind from those unable to integrate themselves in the socioeconomic process and the political system.

According to this intepretation, proposed by a well-known communist leader (Giorgio Amendola in 1978), the terrorists of the 1970s resemble the fascists of the 1920s. He even used the expression "red fascists" and identified in them the enemies of the working class. From this perspective, the terrorists might still be considered marginals, but they are the members of displaced middle strata fighting for their social survival, of petit-bourgeois intellectuals affected by a status panic, involved in a process of proletarianization they hate and reject by resorting to violence.

This variant seems more convincing and able to capture some aspects of the social involvement of specific militants and groups. But exactly because it is rather convincing, this variant indicates at its best the limits of a conventional class analysis: Italian terrorists belong to different social groups; no single social class is responsible for their production and reproduction, for their ideology, or for their behavior.

TERRORISM AS THE SYMPTOM OF DYSFUNCTIONS IN THE SYSTEM

Many scholars have attributed the emergence and consolidation of terrorism in Italy to the inability of the major institutions to perform their functions effectively. From this point of view, terrorism can be interpreted as the most important symptom of the dysfunctions of a sociopolitical system. The various interpretations deriving from this perspective can be distinguished according to the level, or sphere, in which they identify the conditions conducive to terrorism. Schematically, since of course there is a certain amount of overlapping among the various interpretations, three spheres are given paramount attention: the cultural, the political, and the socioeconomic.

1. Interpretations that relate the emergence of terrorism to conditions produced in the cultural sphere: According to the authors who rely on this interpretation, perhaps the major prerequisite of terrorism is the appearance of a value crisis derived from the disruption of the "systems of meaning" of the traditional society. The rapid expansion of technological progress destroys the values that allowed the integration of traditional societies (Acquaviva 1979a). Major difficulties follow the state's attempts to integrate its citizens and to legitimize its domination (Stame, in "Terrorismo come e perche," 1979), which the state cannot but attempt to do by a resort to the more or less acceptable use of force at the expense of the consent freely given by the citizens. This triggers a mechanism of further delegitimation of the system.

This intepretation is largely similar to the one, already analyzed (Ferrarotti 1979), which attributes the malintegration of Italian society to an incomplete transition from a rural to an industrial society. It is in the vacuum of values that terrorist inclinations may be nourished and find a favorable ground: the peasants' world is no longer there to give protection and security, industrial culture is not yet consolidated. In between lie the germs of degeneration of the social system.

The presence of many formerly devout Catholics among the terrorists has led some of the scholars adhering to the interpretation stressing cultural dysfunctions of the system to attribute this fact to the incomplete process of secularization of Italian society and, at the same time, to the exaggerated sense of social justice nourished by some believing Catholics and their families. To redress wrongs, to achieve a more just society, some Catholics have been willing to resort to armed struggle in order to implement in practice some of the teachings they believe are or were betrayed by the church itself and by the Christian Democrats.

Cultural explanations, even when linked with some structural elements, have always been too generic or too complex to be accepted *in toto*. It must be said that they are, in the Italian context, often complemented by other explanations as well. To them we now turn.

2. Interpretations that relate the emergence of terrorism to conditions prevailing in the political sphere: Very many interpretations rely on the identification of conditions of this kind as the most important determinants of terrorism and practically all the other interpretations (with the exception of the psychopathological) devote some attention and indeed put the blame on dysfunctions in the political sphere. These interpretations, therefore, must be carefully analyzed and assessed.

Perhaps the most widespread of these political interpretations is the one that attributes the emergence of terrorism to the fact that the Italian political system is "blocked," or in stalemate. Governed for a long period of time by one party (albeit in a coalition with other, very subordinate partners), the Italian political system has not allowed nor experienced alternation in power, or some circulation within the political class. The type of democracy Italy has had is therefore incomplete, unachieved, imperfect. In such a situation, the opposition finds itself in a very weak position and is compelled either to become "irresponsible" or to accept debasing compromises. Either way, the opposition will be unable to function as an effective channel for the communication of sociopolitical demands made on the system or for their translation into policies.

The government will become identified with the state. At the same time, it will be unable to govern effectively because of its limited legitimacy and relatively restricted power base. The opposition will be unable to control the government or to present itself as a viable alternative. Some political opponents of the "regime," entirely disappointed by the malfunctioning of the system, will therefore feel justified in their advocacy of and resort to political violence. Terrorism becomes the desperate response to a situation deprived of alternatives, of any positive outcome, to the stalemate (Bonanate 1979).

Although interpretation based on the existence of a stalemated political system is used to explain the entire experience of terrorism from its beginnings in the late 1960s to the early 1980s, two other interpretations seem more applicable to specific periods. One interpretation explains left-wing terrorism as a reaction against authoritarian tendencies and developments within the Italian state and the real danger of a rightist coup d'état. From this perspective, left-wing terrorism starts as the attempt by left-wing groups to defend themselves and their organizations, to preserve some of their features (Cicchitto, in "Terrorismo e quadro politico," 1978).

It must be stressed, of course, that authoritarian tendencies and the psychosis of a coup d'état were not simply an obsession of some splinter left-wing groups. As a matter of fact, from 1964 to 1970, right-wing sectors of the state, more specifically, some sectors of the armed forces, with the support of some politicians, or with their connivance, and with the financial help of some industrialists, had engaged in covert attempts to prevent the reformist activities of the center-left coalition from being carried out. General De Lorenzo and Prince Borghese, in 1964 and in 1970, respectively, did engage in conspiratorial activities leading to a coup atmosphere.

Furthermore, at the height of organized protests by the student movement and more specifically by the workers' movement, the slaughter at the Piazza Fontana (December 1969)—originally attributed to anarchist and left-wing groups, but organized by right-wing activists and covered up by the Italian secret services with the knowledge and encouragement of some ministers—gave an additional signal to left-wing movements that the situation was rapidly changing. The progress of the neofascist party in local and political elections between 1970 and 1972, the formation of a very conservative government from mid-1972 to mid-1973, and the gloomy political climate that accompanied the so-called strategy of tension by the state are considered responsible for pushing some left-wing groups underground. The perceptions by some former students and some unionists that the conquests of a period of struggle would be quickly reversed, and the conviction of some former members of the Resistance that the republican-democratic constitution was being challenged (besides the fact that almost thirty years of democracy had not wiped out fascism) acted as triggers for various groups, all of whom became willing to fight against what they considered to be creeping fascism and the emergence of the authoritarian face of the state.

Even though by 1974, as the critics of this interpretation would quickly point out, it was clear that once more Italian society and the political system were changing in a progressive direction, it was also clear by that time that some terrorist groups had probably acquired organizational, political, and also psychological dynamics that could not be arrested or, even less, reversed. Indeed, if the information so far collected and available proves anything, it indicates that the major terrorist groups had already come into existence by the end of 1973.

If a further push were necessary, however, for the creation or strengthening of new and old terrorist groups, the slow process of integration of the PCI into the Italian political system and, particularly, the strategy of the historic compromise, provided the background and the impetus. According to some authors, terrorist groups felt reinforced in their conviction that the political system would not change in a meaningful way (Bonanate 1979), that the lack of a powerful opposition would prevent the expression of new demands, and that the PCI had betrayed the working class and abandoned the class struggle.

To some extent the intensification of terrorist activities after 1976, particularly in 1977 and 1978, seems to indicate that some of these motivations were shared by additional groups in the political system. The disappointment due to the limited changes introduced in the political system in the wake of the highest and longest period of social mobilization experienced by Italian society was widely felt and became conducive to exasperation, desperation and, finally, to armed rebellion.

Not yet fully formulated, this interpretation puts the emphasis on the shrinking of the boundaries for the expression of the legitimate, albeit radical, demands for change and on the responsibility of the PCI for the co-optation of the working class and other social movements by the system. Dissenting fringes, then, lost their reference group and became similar to "fundamentalist sects" or, as the Italian jargon would put it, they "turned mad." Some sectors of the new social movements accepted this kind of integration, even though subordinate, into the system; other sectors abandoned altogether any type of further involvement in politics (thus depriving the left as a whole of its bargaining power); some sectors "degenerated." From this point of view, then, the organizational enhancement of some terrorist groups (but not their origin) was due to the decomposition of social movements (Melucci 1978 and 1981). Former activists, unwilling to accept a subordinate integration and unable to abandon politics, found a refuge in terrorist groups where they believed they could continue their struggle for the radical transformation of the political system.

The decomposition of the two major social movements, specifically the student movement whose activities and demonstrations were already in 1977 infiltrated by outside terrorist organizers, and the workers' movements, particularly at the plant level where violence was often practiced, produced therefore a favorable ground for terrorist recruitment and, if not outright support for, at least a large area of indifference to their activities. Against the institutionalization of social movements, then, terrorism presents itself as a surrogate of class struggle (Ferrajoli 1979).

Behind both interpretations, that of the authoritarian tendencies of the Italian state and that of the shrinking of the boundaries for the expression of radical dissent, it is possible to see different, but not incompatible, versions of the thesis of the stalemate system. If the political system prevents change, then it degenerates. It will do so in a reactionary direction, if authoritarian tendencies, always present in Italy, are not checked by social movements and by a mass opposition, or if the major political opposition accepts its subordinate integration into the system instead of collecting the energies of the social movements and the antisystem forces to transform profoundly the very nature of the system. Both of these motivations led to a strengthening of terrorist groups; the first explains more convincingly the origins and the emergence of some groups; the second explains the consolidation and the expansion of terrorist groups.

It is important to stress, however, that without the previous existence of organized groups willing to resort to violence—groups whose ideology was almost totally impervious to reality, whose theory was in no way put into practice, whose convictions remained steadfast even during the various stages passed through by the Italian political system in the 1970s—the second wave of terrorism in the second half of the 1970s would not have taken place. Indeed, we witness the transformation of some terrorist groups in the second phase, not the emergence of new groups newly alienated from the political system and its rhetoric. If we are to look for an identification of the origins of Italian terrorism, we must therefore direct our attention to the 1969 through 1973 period and the motivations, fears, and expectations prevailing in that period. If we look for an explanation of the expansion and the virulence of Italian terrorism from 1976 to 1978, the same procedure must be applied; that is, we must search for specific factors predominant in those years without forgetting for a moment that the organizational space was already occupied.

The Italian political system has not changed very much in the last few years. It has certainly not improved in its functioning, nor has it provided better channels for the communication of radical demands or for the translation of the preferences of the "antagonists" into acceptable and effective decisions. Yet, terrorist activities have considerably abated. There is no paradox involved here. The explanation is a very simple one and has to do with a dialectical relationship between major improvements in the state apparatus, particularly in the information-gathering system, and the political and organizational crisis which has, also because of the increased effectiveness of the state, appeared in the ranks of the terrorists (the joint phenomena of "repentant" and "dissociated" terrorists).

3. One last interpretation with a systemic character has to be taken into account. It is not based on simple references to processes of marginalization of individuals who are unable to remain within the productive sectors of the economic system or to enter into them in a meaningful and satisfactory way. Instead, it calls for a review in an encompassing way of the development of Italian capitalism and the modernization of the economic sector with specific reference to the changes that occurred during a short period of time, at the beginning of the 1960s, for large masses of migrants and social strata. In spite of this development and the accompanying modernization, or perhaps because of that, the Italian socioeconomic system remains characterized by a clear-cut duality. Capitalism is not only unable to modernize Italy but also unable to wipe out archaic conditions and situations, at least not entirely.

A process of distorted modernization not only prevents the solution of ancient socioeconomic problems but generates new ones. It destroys old patterns, but it does not create new, acceptable, and shared ones. Moreover, it produces new forms of deprivation and large pockets of unemployment particularly among the relatively well-educated youth, opening spaces for violent expressions (Cavalli 1977). It does not shape new forms of sociopolitical activity in a linear way to accompany the mobilization of society. Therefore, "the systematic practice of violence, up to the desperate epilogue of terrorism is the result of a process of decomposition of a movement which has been prevented in its expression on its own ground and has been charged with the contradictions of a dual society" (Melucci 1978:261). Finally, all these groups, whose legitimate socioeconomic demands have been frustrated by the lack of reforms or by their failure (under the center-left) but which remain mobilized and disaffected, are pushed along the path of participation, confrontation, and violence outside the political institutions (Tranfaglia 1981).

Not entirely coherent, with its socioeconomic premises somewhat too broad in reference to capitalism and modernization, this interpretation has many points in common with the various versions of the political interpretation of the conditions conducive to terrorism. Indeed, one major conclusion that can be drawn from our quick summary of the interpretations of left-wing terrorism in Italy is that the variants of the political type have identified important elements of the emergence, consolidation, and dynamics of terrorism. More specifically, political interpretations seem to be able to account satisfactorily for the reasons why some terrorist groups appeared, why they moved toward greater organizational efforts, why their activities and their recruitment expanded and, to some extent, even why terrorist groups have recently experienced a political and organizational decline. Having said this, however, much is still unknown about Italian terrorism and we want to devote our concluding remarks to the specification of a research agenda.

TOWARD A RESEARCH AGENDA ON ITALIAN LEFT-WING TERRORISM

No single explanation of Italian left-wing terrorism or, for that matter, of any kind of terrorism (with the exception, perhaps, of state terrorism) can capture the complexity and the pervasiveness of the phenomenon. Although interpretations that focus on the collective actor in its environment seem more promising, the importance of individual motivations in choosing the path of armed activities on the one hand and, on the other, the influence of state responses in defusing or aggravating the phenomenon of terrorism must not be neglected.

If those schematic considerations are correct, the phenomenon of Italian terrorism, and specifically of left-wing terrorism, broadly defined as the outcome of the degeneration and decomposition of collective movements, needs to be put into perspective. We surmise that there are various ways of doing so. First of all, terrorism cannot be studied as one single phenomenon, as a monolithic block of events and actors. Indeed, the Italian case is rich with different examples, different trajectories of different (and sometimes competing) groups, and diverse forms of behavior. The first and most important item on the research agenda must therefore be the identification of the groups in which violent forms of action were accepted and even theorized about and justified. The evidence suggests that the two groups best qualified to provide material for an in-depth study of this kind are Potere Operaio and Lotta Continua.

Since by no means all the members of these groups later joined terrorist groups, in fact only a tiny fraction of them did, the second item on the research agenda must be the identification of the motivations and the rationalizations used by those who went underground. This line of analysis would lead on the one hand to a clear-cut periodization of the phenomenon (to which we have already made reference) and provide important material on the formation of terrorist groups. On the other hand it suggests an in-depth exploration of the social and geographic contexts in which the transition from violent but still open activities to clandestine terrorist actions was made.

According to some authors, for instance, there is a clear connection between the official decision made by Potere Operaio to disband its organization and the expansion of Autonomia Operaia first as a social presence, then as both the recruiting ground and the connecting link among various types of terrorist activities.

The reconstruction of the history of the various terrorist organizations, prominent among them the Red Brigades and Prima Linea (Front Line), can also be conducted with reference to their numerous documents as well as to their activities and, most recently, to the declaration of many of their members who have "dissociated" themselves from the armed struggle. Using this kind of approach will enable the researcher to identify the various stages concerning the building of the organization, its internal dynamics, its expansion, its functioning and, in recent times, its political and organizational crisis. Moreover, using an approach based on the historical reconstruction can provide the seeker with some hints on the relationships among various organizations, possible international connections, or the hypothesized overlapping with otherwise "legal" groups.

While it may be true that, once established, terrorist organizations follow a dynamic of their own and consequently may not be particularly relevant to analyze them in their interactions with the political system, there is no doubt that the evolution of the political system has influenced their actions and their choices, for instance in the selection of targets. Moreover, and more important, the evolution of the Italian political system, its coalitional dynamics, and the changing role of the PCI have all had an impact on the major social movements that appeared and largely dominated the political scene from the end of the 1960s to the late 1970s. Since it is highly likely that terrorist groups are indeed, if not the direct product, at least an outgrowth of social movements, and in any case have been dependent on their ability to recruit from decomposing social movements, the entire history of these relationships is of the utmost importance for a full understanding of the phenomenon.

What then would be a satisfactory, nonideological, and sophisticated explanation of Italian left-wing terrorism from a comparatively framed perspective? At this stage, we can offer only a preliminary, tentative explanation. Left-wing terrorism in Italy is the result of the stalemate in the political system and at the same time of the conscious decision of some groups to resort to armed activities in the belief that legal avenues for the transformation of the system were no longer available and that, indeed, a right-wing, authoritarian threat was in the making. The mass base for this kind of terrorism could be found repeatedly, at any failure of mobilizational efforts after 1974, and after 1976, when the left achieved its best electoral results ever. The relative openness of Italian society provided the channels for mobilization: The relative blockage of the political system prevented meaningful changes from taking place (and those changes that did take place were always below the expectations of many militants who had not yet become terrorists); and the socioeconomic system allowed pockets of relative deprivation to persist in some areas (though not total marginalization). Terrorism has retained a dynamics of its own, relatively impervious to changes in the objective situation, but definitely affected by the increased effectiveness of the state apparatus and by its inability to recruit new members in the light of the many arrests and defections. Although terrorist actions may reappear here and there, terrorism as a form of violent political struggle against the Italian system has entered a stage of decline.

Note: This essay is the first product of a long-term research project sponsored by the Regional Assembly of Emilia-Romagna and carried out by the "Istituto di Studi e Ricerche 'Carlo Cattaneo'" of Bologna.

For further references to our work, at this stage, see Cattaneo, n. 2/1982, which contains our reflections on the explanations of "red" as well as "black" terrorism and our identification of research problems. See also our introduction and conclusion to the volume tentatively entitled Violenza politica e terrorismo nelle società contemporanee (Bologna: Il Mulino, 1983), a collection of the papers presented to an international seminar organized by the Istituto Cattaneo in Bologna, 25–26 June 1982. The following papers were read: Charles Tilly, European Violence and Collective Action Since 1700; Ted R. Gurr, Coercive Politics in the United States: The Use and Consequences of Political Violence and Terrorism; Hiroshi Kawahara, Political Violence and Terrorism in Japan; and Iring Fetscher, Political Violence and Left-Wing Terrorism in the Federal Republic of Germany.

BIBLIOGRAPHY

Acquaviva, S. Guerriglia e guerra rivoluzionaria in Italia: Ideologia, fatti, prospettive. Milano: Rizzoli, 1979a.

Acquaviva, S., ed. Terrorismo e guerriglia in Italia: La cultura della violenza. Roma: Citta Nuova, 1979b.

Alberti, P. and G. C. Caselli. Il terrorismo "rosso." Paper discussed in a conference on "Perche la barbarie non uccida la democrazia," Torino, March 1980.

Allum, P. "Political Terrorism in Italy," *Contemporary Review* 1531 (1978), 75–84.

Alquati, R., Boato, M., Cacciari, M., Rodota, S., and Violante, L. *Terrorismo: verso la seconda repubblica?* Torino: Stampatori, 1980.

Bechelloni, G. "Terrorismo, giovani, mass media," *Problemi dell' informazione* II, 3 (1977), 303–309.

Bocca, G. *Il terrorismo italiano 1970–1978.* Milano: Bompiani, 1978.

Bolaffi, A. "L'intreccio del terrorismo," *Rinascita* XXXVII, 45 (1980), 7.

Bonanate, L. "Dimensioni del terrorismo politico," *in* L. Bonanate, ed., *Dimensioni del terrorismo politico.* Milano: F. Angeli, 1979. Pp. 99–179.

Cavalli, L. "La violenza politica," *Citta e regione* III, 10–11 (1977), 7–45.

Dalla Chiesa, N. "Del sessantotto e del terrorismo, cultura politica tra continuità e rottura," *Il Mulino* XXX, 273 (1981), 53–94.

Feltrin, P., and E. Santi. "Il terrorismo di sinistra: le interpretazioni," *Progetto.* Pp. 48–55.

Ferrajoli, F. "Critica della violenza come critica della politica." *In* L. Manconi, ed. *La violenza e la politica.* Roma: Savelli, 1979. Pp. 39–69.

Ferrarotti, F. "Riflessioni sul terrorismo italiano: violenza comune e violenza politica," *I problemi di Ulisse* XXXII, 86 (1978), 123–136.

———. *Alle radici della violenza.* Milano: Rizzoli, 1979.

———. "Riflessioni e dati su dodici anni di terrorismo in Italia (1969–1981)." *In* M. Gallieni, ed. *Rapporto sul terrorismo.* Milano: Rizzoli, 1981. Pp. 375–475.

Galante, S. "Alle origini del partito armato," *Il Mulino* XXX, 275 (1981), 444–487.

Mancini, F. "Movimento armato e partito armato," *Mondo operaio,* 2 (1979), 11–19.

Marletti, C. "Immagini pubbliche e ideologia del terrorismo." *In* L. Bonanate, ed. *Dimensioni del terrorismo politico.* Milano: F. Angeli, 1979. Pp. 181–253.

Melucci, A. "Appunti su movimenti, terrorismo, società italiana," *Il Mulino* XXVII, 256 (1978), 253–267.

———. "New Movements, Terrorism and the Political System: Reflections on the Italian Case," *Socialist Review,* 56 (1981), 97–136.

Rodota, S. "E'l'essere 'soggetto politico' che accentua i terrorismi," *Pace e guerra* (1980), 1.

———. "Due linee sul terrorismo," *Pace e guerra* (1981), 10.

"Il sindacato contro la violenza," special issue of *Rassegna sindacale* XXVI, 4 (1980), 15–51.

Soccorso Rosso. *Le B. R.* Milano: Feltrinelli, 1976.

Soccorso Rosso di Napoli. *I.N.A.P.* Milano: Feltrinelli, 1976.

Sole, R. *Le defi terroriste: leçon italienne a l'usage de l'Europe.* Paris: Seuil, 1979.

Stajano, C. *L'Italia nichilista: Il caso di Marco Donat Cattin, la rivolta, il potere.* Milano: Mondadori, 1982.

Stame, F. "Terrorismo e crisi dello Stato." *In* L. Manconi, ed. *La violenza e la politica.* Roma: Savelli, 1979. Pp. 21–32.

"Terrorismo come e perche." Debate among S. Acquaviva, L. Bonanate, G. Caselli, and F. Stame, *Mondo operaio* XXXII, 4 (1979), 13–20.

"Terrorismo e quadro politico." Debate among F. Cicchitto, L. Colletti, F. Mancini, A. Minucci, and A. Pizzorno, *Mondo operaio* XXXI, 4 (1978), 5–18.

"Terrorismo e stato della crisi," special issue of *La questione criminale* V (1979), 1.

Tessandori, V. *BR. Imputazione banda armata: Cronaca e documentazione Brigate Rosse.* Milano: Garzanti, 1977.

Tranfaglia, N. "La crisi italiana e il problema storico del terrorismo." *In* M. Gallieni, ed. *Rapporto sul terrorismo.* Milano: Rizzoli, 1981. Pp. 477–544.

Ventura, A. "Il problema storico del terrorismo italiano," *Rivista storica italian* XCII, 1 (1980), 125–151.

7

The Political Socialization of West German Terrorists

KLAUS WASMUND

It may come as a surprise to anyone observing the German political landscape that politically motivated terrorism could develop at all in West Germany in the 1970s. Is terrorism possible in a country where law and order and a marked sense of conformity and obedience were considered for a long time to be the highest values? Is terrorism, then, a paradox within German political culture? When one takes a closer look at German history in the nineteenth and twentieth centuries, it becomes clear that anarchism has never been popular in Germany—not even the nonviolent variety. And even before World War I, during its international heyday, anarchism still could not attract any kind of noteworthy following in Germany.[1]

It would appear that anarchism is in diametric opposition to the German mentality. There was no real chance, in a political culture with strongly bound authoritarian and state-oriented traditions of thought, of either nonviolent anarchism or its terrorist variety ever really developing out of their roles of political sectarianism and gaining popularity. For anarchism has always been considered as something exotic in Germany.

The fact that terrorism has no tradition in Germany and made its breakthrough more or less overnight also serves to explain the extremely severe and rigid reaction by the state authorities and the German public to the terrorist challenge. Compared with people in some other countries, the Germans have been spared a day-to-day life of terror. Precisely because it has remained a rare political phenomenon among the German people and despite the relatively low number of terrorist attacks compared with the number in other countries, terrorism was seen right from the beginning as a serious threat to the political system, although it neither is nor ever was.

THE RESULTS OF TERRORISM

In comparison with other countries, where terrorist attacks have been a daily occurrence, the number of victims claimed and the damage caused by West German terrorists has been relatively low. This has not, however, excluded an exaggerated and to a certain extent hysterical reaction by the public and the political system. The political system at any rate has reacted to the terrorist challenge in the best possible German state-oriented tradition: by taking illiberal legislative measures and enlarging the police force and the police surveillance system (police search based on computer data, etc.). The balance sheet of West German terrorism in the first ten years (1969–1979) is as follows (Neidhardt 1982:437): 69 attacks on people, of which 25 cases resulted in death, 247 attacks of arson and bombing, as well as 69 other serious offenses (e.g., bank robberies, theft of firearms). Figures not included on this balance sheet, however, are those resulting from the active participation of German terrorists in actions carried out by the PLO (Palestine Liberation Organization), for example during the Entebbe operation.

During the same period of time, seven German terrorists were killed while being pursued; another four died while on a terrorist mission. Seven died during imprisonment by committing suicide or as the direct outcome of a hunger strike. Seventy-seven acts of violence were registered in 1980. By 1981 the number of attacks had increased to 129 (2 planned murders, 28 bombings, and 99 attacks of arson).

Among the most spectacular attacks made in recent years was the assassination of Hesse's minister for economic affairs, Herbert Karry, on 11 May 1981 by the Revolutionäre Zellen (Revolutionary Cells), the bomb attack on the American air force headquarters in Ramstein on 31 August 1981, and the abortive attempt to assassinate America's General Kroesen (15 September 1981) in Heidelberg, both of which were the work of the Rote Armee Fraktion (RAF—Red Army Faction). Despite the fact that terrorist groups have taken a heavy blow, with the leading cadres having been arrested or dead, they are still regarded as highly dangerous by the state authorities. Furthermore, they are apparently capable of bigger operations, since they have to a certain extent successfully managed to replace their casualties by recruiting new members.

At the beginning of 1984, a public search was carried out for sixteen terrorists still on the wanted list. The number of terrorists in this group may well exceed sixteen, however. Meanwhile unorganized terrorism, in the form of *Feierabendterrorismus*—groups that are responsible for sporadic, "after working hours" acts of terrorism—has proven to be a greater dilemma for the police than the organized terrorism of the RAF. These are operations carried out by small groups of anarchists who do not live permanently in the underground but lead a legal existence. The activities of these Feierabendterroristen are not concentrated on spectacular events such as kidnappings, but on small, subversive bomb attacks on objects of particular symbolic value, which can then be defended by further acts of revenge. The narrow circle of followers of the RAF is at present estimated by the Ministry of Domestic Affairs to be two hundred persons.

PRECONDITIONS OF WEST GERMAN TERRORISM

West German terrorism can only be explained against the background of the students' protest movement of the 1960s. Terrorism, of course, is not the logical result of the student movement, but one of its offshoots, or a by-product.

The student protest movement was a reaction to political and social developments in the new West German state in the 1950s and 1960s. During the Adenauer era, after the state had been founded, specific developments and conditions left their mark on the political situation in West Germany. Adenauer played a dominant part in shaping the politics of West Germany in the first half of the 1960s. His ideology, and his foreign policy toward the communist systems was based on a definite orientation to the West and on the permanent integration of West Germany into the Western Alliance. On the domestic front, the Adenauer era was characterized by economic prosperity, the "economic miracle," which set in around the middle of the 1950s and led to remarkable social and political stability. The negative aspect of this process of stabilization, however, was its fixation on the status quo. As a consequence, a certain political rigidity set in, most explicitly expressed in Adenauer's campaign slogan of 1957, *Keine Experimente* (No Experiments). A feature of this domestic stability was the three- or rather the two-and-a-half party system with the Christian Democrats, the Social Democrats, and the Liberals.

The election results in 1957 proved disappointing for the Social Democrats (SPD), for they gave the Christian Democrats (CDU/CSU—Christian Democratic Union/Christian Social Union) the absolute majority in parliament. This in turn accelerated the SPD's changeover from a class party to a catchall party, or Volkspartei: Old ideological ballast was discarded with the passing of the Bad Godesberg Program (1959) and this initiated the transformation of the SPD into a reformist party. The process of ridding the SPD of ideological dead-weight, set also against the background of the East-West conflict, led to the expulsion of ideological, that is, Marxist, fringe groups and to restrictions on the democratic decision-making process within the party. After Godesberg, the Marxist leftists were "homeless," to use a popular term of the period, for the KPD (Communist party) had also been banned by the Federal Constitutional Court (Bundesverfassungs-gericht) in 1956. The SPD now was one of the pillars of the estab-lishment and was proud of the fact that the basic tenets of its policy were in accordance with the CDU, above all in politics dealing with foreign policy and the Western Alliance. It promised, so to speak, the same politics as the CDU, only better.

The broad, basic consensus of the established parties was a main characteristic of the West German party system in the 1960s. During the first critical phase, caused by the economic recession in 1966/1967, this consensus consequently led to the "Great Coalition" between the CDU/CSU and the SPD. For many sectors of the population, the Great Coalition seemed to manifest the old German "desire for a synthesis" (Ralf Dahrendorf). During the period of the Great Coa-lition, the role of the parliamentary opposition fell exclusively to the small Liberal party (FDP). Owing to this situation, and in the face of difficult economic (the recession) and political conditions (the passing of the emergency laws), many discerning citizens no longer felt properly represented in the Bonn parliament. This precipitated the formation of a so-called nonparliamentary opposition (Ausserpar-lamentarische Opposition) and the emergence of an antiauthoritarian protest movement, which went down in West German history as the student movement.

TERRORISM—
AN OFFSHOOT OF THE STUDENT MOVEMENT

At the center of the students' protest was, first of all, the emergency law imposed and enforced exclusively by the Great Coalition, the still unassimilated Nazi past, the abuses arising from life in a consumer society, the concentration of the press—"Expropriate Springer," the West German press tycoon—the hierarchical-authoritarian structure of the universities and, last but not least, the American involvement in Vietnam and, as a result, the process of taboos and repression, which affected both the masses and the political elite.

The Vietnam War destroyed the idealized image of America among the younger generation. The protest against the American involvement in Vietnam was bound to result in serious conflicts, especially in a city like West Berlin, where identification with the United States, based on historical experiences (Berlin blockade), was particularly strong among the political elite and the German population. It was particularly the SDS (Sozialistischer Deutscher Studentenbund, the Socialist Union of German Students)—the SPD had already disassociated itself from it in 1961 because of "left-wing deviations"—which tried to fill the ideological vacuum of the protest movement with undogmatic Marxism. The student movement simply opposed the "establishment," a favorite term of the time, and saw itself as being "undogmatic," "antiauthoritarian," and "radically democratic." The protest movement of students was sparked further by the death of Benno Ohnesorg (2 June 1967), a student shot down by the police during a demonstration in West Berlin against a visit of the Shah of Iran. This incident saw an escalation of the student protest, which not only became more radical in West Berlin but spread to many of the other university towns in West Germany. A great many of the students' activities were modeled on those of the American student movement. Due to the escalation of violence, Jürgen Habermas felt it necessary, after the death of Benno Ohnesorg, to warn the students during a teach-in in Hannover of the dangers of a "left-wing fascism." The year 1968 witnessed the culmination of the protest movement. After an attempt on the life of the SDS student leader, Rudi Dutschke, there was an increase in street clashes between demonstrators and the police, occupations of universities, symbolic provocations, intentional violation of the rules, and "violence against property." All of this produced a confused response among the political elite, which, on the whole, lacked self-confidence in the face of this challenge.

The atmosphere in 1969, with the formation of the social-liberal coalition (SPD and FDP), was undoubtedly far more conducive to the fulfillment of the students' demands and they could now join the reform parties. The new government announced an era of "internal reforms," for which the student protest of the 1960s had already prepared the ground. Chancellor Willy Brandt promised the younger generation that an attempt would be made to achieve "more democracy" in all areas of society and politics: "*Mehr Demokratie wagen.*"

Even the initial social and political reforms that were introduced could not prevent a process of radicalization and ideologization in the student movement during the 1970s. It was, above all, "vulgar Marxism" that became popular among students. There was the feeling that the struggle with the political authorities had failed and that the remaining student movement had become isolated. The SDS, which until then had acted as a central leading body, had disbanded. All this caused an ideological and organizational fragmentation of the movement, which finally led to its decomposition. Numerous dogmatic communist groups, such as Marxists, Stalinists, and "prophets of real socialism," tried to salvage the remaining stock of the student movement and gain allies within the working class. Another proof that the student movement had definitely come to an end was the emergence of anarchists of all shades of political muddleheadedness, who gave free rein to their blind actionism, particularly in the university towns. These groupings only formed a small minority among the masses of students, most of whom were fairly unpolitical. The minority became all the more active and carried much political influence in the universities. It would be no exaggeration to maintain that they dominated the academic scene at most of the universities, until around the middle of the 1970s.

Sit-ins, go-ins, teach-ins, the occupation of institutes and faculty offices made up, so to speak, the daily schedule. These activities in turn provoked police intervention, which set in motion a process of escalating violence and counterviolence.

The breakup of the antiauthoritarian student movement had essentially three consequences: Most of the students were integrated, pursued careers or, with the reform parties, joined the "march through the institutions," of which Rudi Dutschke, the student leader, had once dreamed. A second element went into extremely diverse and mostly dogmatic groups of political left-wing sectarianism. The attempt by communist groups, the so-called K-groups, to gain allies among the working class failed miserably. A third, relatively weak element preached open violence against the political system. The call for revolutionary violence through underground leaflets and pamphlets had already been raised in West Berlin at the beginning of the 1970s. Some groups emerging in this atmosphere tried terrorist methods to achieve their goals as urban guerrillas (RAF, Bewegung 2. Juni—2d of June Movement).

COUNTERCULTURE GROUPS IN WEST BERLIN

The development of the student protest movement and its process of radicalization can only be understood in terms of the specific conditions and circumstances of the Berlin counterculture. It is quite certain that in the 1960s Berlin was a center of attraction for nonconformists, outsiders, dropouts, and for a number of young people from the West German *Provinz* (provinces) seeking adventure and an alternative to their boring provincial life. They willingly allowed the glittering and unconventional atmosphere of the Berlin "scene," as it was called, to thrill and fascinate them. This counterculture "scene" was concentrated in certain residential areas in the city center, mostly areas that had previously housed workers and so-called little people and where a subculture of pubs, shops, workshops, underground systems of communication, and communes had formed. New life-styles, a feeling of living and self-reliant existence developed here, with typical codes and rituals of communication, including a special language. It was consciously antibourgeois and, in contrast to the *Bohème* of earlier times, could be defined as distinctly political. I mean here "political" in its diffuse sense; left, socialist, or anarchist. Protest, in such a concentrated social atmosphere, was not just an expression of one's conviction directed against the political elites or system but more a way of life, in which the division between private and political spheres had been removed and protest had become an integral part of one's entire personality.

This specific type of counterculture in West Berlin was not only a unique social experiment comprising every imaginable way of living and doctrine of salvation but also an arena and a sounding board for the most extreme, "way-out" political opinions and ideas, where such radical exclamations as "It's better to set fire to a department store than to own one" (Fritz Teufel) were circulated and became popular from the start.

A strategy of violence, as a reaction to the political system and its policies, could only find a following in a counterculture on a scale and of an intensity as the one existing in West Berlin. Here was the reservoir from which the urban guerrillas hoped to recruit their "fighters" and where, like fish in water, they hoped to find their element.

One cannot, of course, denounce the entire West Berlin counterculture as sympathizers with the terrorist cause. On the contrary, it was precisely in these circles that, for various reasons, a great deal of criticism was voiced. The criticism was partially of a fundamental moral nature and in part merely a political tactic. Already in 1972, after a series of bomb attacks, nearly all groups and opinion leaders of the left spectrum disassociated themselves unreservedly from the RAF, so that the group was forced more and more to take note of this criticism.

In her pamphlet, "The Concept of the Urban Guerilla" (April 1971), Ulrike Meinhof tried to justify the strategy of the RAF, since "many comrades have been spreading lies about us." This article in defense of the RAF (and herself) ends with the conclusion:

We maintain that the formation of armed resistance groups at this point in time in the Federal Republic in West Berlin is right, is possible, and is morally justified. That it is right, possible, and justified to form urban guerrillas here and now.

Discussions of left-wing criticism of the RAF produced accusations and suspicions, which culminated, in the main, in reproaches of cowardice and opportunism. For all the unorganized criticism of the left of the RAF, there still remained, however, something like a diffuse sense of solidarity with the group which did not, for instance, permit the betrayal of terrorists to the police.

THE ORIGIN OF THE RED ARMY FACTION AND ITS SUCCESSORS

On 2 April 1968 fires broke out in two department stores in Frankfurt. The four firebugs were soon arrested but released on bail before and during their trial. The fires in the department stores in Frankfurt can be regarded as marking the birth of the Red Army Faction. This act of arson by Gudrun Ensslin, Andreas Baader, Thorwald Proll, and Horst Söhnlein was not a signal for society, as they wanted people to believe, but rather a signal for themselves, since by this step they had severed practically all connections with "bourgeois society." I start from the assumption that the foundation of the RAF is not to be regarded as a result of political decisions aimed at changing the political situation in the Federal Republic of Germany in a revolutionary way by the use of terror, but rather as a result of a gradual downward slide into violent crime, with political and private motives becoming intermingled.

The first step on the path leading to terrorist actions was "violence against property" in the form of arson; this step was politically motivated as a signal of protest against the war in Vietnam and against the political situation in the Federal Republic of Germany. The second step, however, the liberation of Baader with the aid of firearms, was by no means politically motivated but was based on private or personal interests: namely Gudrun Ensslin's desire to free her boyfriend from prison. The political justification for this act was provided much later.

> Did some pig really believe we would talk about starting the class struggle, the reorganization of the proletariat without taking up arms? (Underground paper "Agit 883," 22 May 1970.)

A crucial point with regard to the beginning of the RAF is that with the liberation of Baader the people involved in this action irrevocably severed their connections with society. The crime was a serious one which, in the event of conviction, would entail a heavy sentence.

While the disappearance of Baader and Ensslin after the department store fires was more in the character of a "cops and robbers" game in which the robbers had the general support of left-wingers, the liberation of Baader was a matter of deadly earnestness. By this act of violence the group became criminal and illegal. From this point on there was no going back but only the "forward escape."

Following the act of arson in the department stores, there remained the possibility that the culprits could serve their sentences in prison and then start a new life, just as the two accomplices, Proll and Söhnlein, had done. One must admit, however, that a return to the so-called normal bourgeois life with ordinary career expectations was not very attractive for the perpetrators because they had to reckon with being liable for compensation for the damages, which amounted to DM 2.2 million (U.S. $800,000). The prospect of paying money for the rest of their lives and living on a minimal, subsistence wage reduced the chances of integration from the very beginning and did not make it appear very tempting to start a bourgeois career within the established system.

With the liberation of Baader, the basic pattern and the central motive for all future actions of the RAF and its successor organizations were established. That is, if one or more members of the organization were in custody, the others were to concentrate all their energies on the liberation of their comrades in prison. In the case of Baader, this aim was realized by a direct physical act of liberation with firearms; later, however, they switched to indirect actions. Specifically, they attempted to free their comrades by kidnappings and blackmail. Because of its shock value, this method was successful at the beginning but was doomed to fail later.

For the second and third generation of terrorists (Bewegung 2. Juni and Revolutionäre Zellen), in contrast to the founding generation of terrorists, one cannot speak of a gradual sliding into the terrorist scene. As far as these groupings were concerned, it was obvious from the very beginning that they made a conscious decision to employ "armed struggle," which might explain the higher levels of violence and aggression in their members.[2]

METHODOLOGICAL PROBLEMS OF RESEARCH ON TERRORISM

Terrorism is extreme, deviant political behavior, which does not come about overnight, but is the result of a longer development. This developmental process is a complex procedure, influenced by various factors. Thus monocausal explanations, concentrating, for example, exclusively on deficits in primary socialization, cannot be considered adequate for explaining the motives behind a terrorist career when such factors as the political environment, situational circumstances, the *Zeitgeist* of a youth cohort, and group-dynamic processes are not taken into account. Research into the cause of terrorism must be based on the development of a political personality as a product of the interaction between personality and political-social environment. Political behavior is a function of personality characteristics, situation, and of the specific interaction between the person and the situation.

There are many variables to consider in an analysis of the environmental influence on terrorism or on the political underground itself. From this complex mesh of influence and effects, I want to concentrate on *one* factor, which is not only important but perhaps even decisive in explaining terrorist behavior: the influence of the group, since terrorists are in many ways "victims of group thinking." And this must be analyzed not only with respect to the periphery of terrorism but also to the underground itself. The concentration on one influential factor in this study—that is, the group-dynamic aspect—is not to be understood as another monocausal explanation but as an analytical tool, or ideal type of construction, in the sense of Max Weber.

Research into the personalities and motivations of West German terrorists is confronted by a methodological difficulty. The most important sources of information for the origin of a terrorist career are the terrorists themselves, since they are best able to give the information regarding their social and political backgrounds and their motives for terrorist activity. But, as long as most of the terrorists refuse to be exposed to an in-depth psychological analysis (because they want to avoid being labeled as psychiatric cases), the most important source of information remains inaccessible. But in spite of these difficulties, there is some material on hand for an analysis, material that can be put together like a mosaic, though we cannot expect it to be as sharp and clear as a photograph. This material basically consists of (1) the biographies of individual terrorists; (2) statements and observations by parents, brothers and sisters, friends and teachers, lawyers, fellow students, and colleagues; (3) written material from the terrorists themselves—pamphlets, ideological writings setting out a program, interviews, statements, circulars among imprisoned terrorists, and letters smuggled out of a prisoner's cell; (4) statements and confessions, "memoirs" of ex-terrorists; and (5) the political environment and the Zeitgeist in which and to which the terrorists react.

The findings presented in this essay are primarily based on written documents, such as the testimonies and confessions of ex-terrorists, as well as on the ideological self-portraits of terrorist groups. When available, items of biographical information are added. The books analyzed as original sources are those by "Bommi" Baumann (1977) and the OPEC assassin, Hans-Joachim Klein (1979), who for a time fought with "Carlos." Both these authors have now disassociated themselves from the terrorist scene. Other sources include a report by Volker Speitel (1980), published interviews with ex-terrorists (Boock 1981), and various statements published by Horst Mahler (1979), who was one of the founders of the RAF, as well as other marginal figures of the first terrorist generation like Hans-Jürgen Becker, Beate Sturm, Peter Homann, and Karl-Heinz Ruhland. The principal ideological self-portraits are identified in (1) a pamphlet of the Sozialistisches Patienten Kollektiv (SPK), the Socialist Patients' Collective, an organization from which the RAF has obtained many recruits, and (2) the collection of texts authorized by the RAF (*Texts of the RAF*, 1977), which are very informative with respect to the political aims and attitudes of the RAF founders. This volume was originally published in Stockholm in German and was banned in the Federal Republic of Germany.

The analysis of individual motives and group processes—central points in this essay which will be discussed later—does not permit the conclusion that the explanation for the origin of terrorist groups could be transferred from a political level to an exclusively private, individual-psychological level. The aim here is to show the complexity of the motives for such deviant political behavior by taking into consideration individual and group-dynamic processes. Finally, it is necessary to emphasize the hypothetical nature of this analysis, which is inevitable as long as there is no representative sample of terrorists for a thorough social-psychological analysis. But before I start to analyze the group processes, I will try to determine briefly the social background of the terrorists.

CHARACTERISTIC FEATURES IN THE BIOGRAPHIES OF TERRORISTS

One of the questions that has preoccupied analysts of the terrorist problem right from the start is whether there are certain characteristics or striking features in the biographies of terrorists which could have influenced or possibly even have determined to a large extent their terrorist careers. As part of a research project backed by the Federal Ministry for Domestic Affairs (Schmidtchen 1981), 227 life histories of leftist terrorists were analyzed. These biographies were taken mainly of members of the RAF and the 2d of June movement, who at the time of the investigation (1979) were either in detention or had already been sentenced. Although according to this investigation there is admittedly no such thing as a typical terrorist or terrorist career, there are nevertheless certain striking features evident in these biographies.

What becomes apparent with regard to the social background of the terrorists is that they come mostly from the upper middle classes.

Nearly every other terrorist (47%) has a father who holds a so-called higher position. The level of education of the terrorists is correspondingly of an above average standard. Hence, nearly every other terrorist graduated from high school and went on to a university. The reason their integration into society, in the traditional bourgeois sense, remained incomplete lies in the fact that, before joining the group, only 35 percent of the terrorists were employed on a full-time basis. Part-time jobs and unemployment are often outstanding features, as is breaking off in the middle of a training program or education—a factor also partly associated with joining the terrorist group.

Concerning the "family constellation" (Alfred Adler), there are a great many cases in which stress and conflict were inherent features of their childhood and youth. Every fourth terrorist, over the age of fourteen, grew up in a broken home. Fifteen percent were fatherless by the time they reached adolescence, 6 percent motherless, and 5 percent orphaned. The number of orphans resulting from divorce (17%) is above average among the terrorists born in the 1950s (Jaeger, Schmidtchen, and Süllwold 1981).

In the cases in which terrorists grew up in complete family units, the relationship to the parents, especially to the father, was often burdened with conflicts, lack of contact, indifference, conventionality and severity, impatience, and lack of attention.

A particularly extreme case of disturbed family socialization in the formative years is that of OPEC assassin Hans-Joachim Klein. After his mother's death, he spent the remainder of his childhood in a foster family, then in a children's home, and finally with his father and stepmother, where he was maltreated by his father in the classical style of authoritarian education.

> He used to beat the daylights out of me—whether it was because I'd wet the bed, which they always said was because I was "too lazy to go to the loo," or whether it was because I came back from playing with dirty (!) hands, or whether it was because I came home too late. On top of everything else, they didn't give me anything to eat then, even if I was only 5 minutes late. And the beatings—first with his hands and then his fists. Then he noticed that this wasn't enough and grabbed anything within reach. What he loved most of all was an electric cable—trimmed extra to form a good length—a rolling-pin and a wooden spoon. If they broke, which was quite often the case, I got another bashing. At one time in the Ostpark in winter, I fell through the ice and someone risked his life to pull me out of danger and took me home. Instead of being happy that I was still alive, I got a terrible thrashing for it. Another favorite was confining me to my room or making me write the same sentence 1,000 times. (Klein 1979:33)

The relationship between the terrorist and the father can be described as trusting and open in only 8 percent of the cases (mother 20%) and as loving in 7 percent (mother 18%) (Schmidtchen 1981). The parents, in spite of the distance and coldness that in actual fact tended to characterize their relationship to their children, were nevertheless exceedingly ambitious with respect to future plans and prospects for their children.

In many cases, a breakup of personal ties preceded the step into terrorism—28 percent left the family home and 12 percent were separated from their partner or even left their children (Schmidtchen 1981). Nearly all the biographies of the terrorists display unusual family and psychodynamic features. Clearly identifiable in the family structure is the combination, found in many homes, of two features—a certain lack of contact and emotion, and high achievement orientation on the part of the parents for their children's careers (Schmidtchen 1981).

According to what is known about the family socialization of terrorists, no single set of circumstances can be identified in the primary socialization process that would necessarily lead to a terrorist career. On the contrary, many terrorists had the same upbringing as other members of their generation who have not become terrorists. Deficits in primary socialization, which deny young people the chance to form their own identity, can, however, produce dispositions—like the longing for security and firm group ties—which, combined with critical encounters later on, political and ideological learning processes, and corresponding opportunities to join various groups, finally lead to the decisive step of joining a terrorist organization. Thus, deviant political behavior cannot only be linked to and explained by particular biographical events. Deficits in socialization are compensated for in many different ways. How and where a person finds his or her identity are also influenced by historical and environmental factors. If primary socialization has not given a person the chance to find an identity, such a person may be receptive to different social or political opportunities—even including countercultural groups and religious sects. Which of these avenues is pursued depends on numerous other social-psychological and environmental factors.

LONGING FOR A COMMUNITY

According to what we know from the biographies of terrorists, they did not immediately leave their previous surroundings in order to enter the terrorist scene. On the contrary, the decision to go underground was generally preceded by a phase in which such a step was prepared for consciously or unconsciously. In the course of this early phase, the decisive processes of disassociation with existing social links, such as the parental home, family, partner, place of residence, and habitual milieu, took place. This process of disassociation consists of several stages: first, the hitherto existing social and emotional ties are generally called into question; then a phase follows in which these ties are loosened and a process of alienation sets in; and, finally, there is a total negation of everything that existed earlier in life. Ultimately, there follows a total break with the existing social milieu (Jäger, Schmidtchen, and Süllwold 1981:17). It is a break not only with internalized norms and values but with the expectations of other people with respect to a "bourgeois" career and future. The break with the past is celebrated then as a form of internal and external liberation, and the process produces the necessary openness and susceptibility to new ties and commitments.

In almost every terrorist career, after the person in question has left the parental home (to study at the university) or has separated from a partner (divorce), there is a phase marked by his or her joining one or another of many different groupings or left-wing subcultures (like political communes) or by friendships with people in direct sympathy with terrorists (i.e., Rote Hilfe [Red Aid] and Gefangenenräte [Prisoners' Councils], groups that have tried to give "political prisoners" both moral and practical support). Most terrorists, in fact, have ultimately become members of terrorist organizations through personal connections with people or relatives associated with appropriate political initiatives, communes, self-supporting organizations, or committees—the number of couples, and brothers and sisters is astonishingly high.

In the search for new life-styles during this disassociation period, the commune plays an important role as an agent of political socialization. The preference given to collective forms of living is not only for the technical and practical organization of social life but also offers the appropriate ideology. More recent investigations show a clear relationship between extreme left-wing political orientations and a preference for communes as a form of living (Krause, Lehnert, and Scherer 1980). By joining a commune—whether political or nonpolitical—a break with the hitherto existing social relations usually takes place. The stronger the integration into the new group, the more radical the act of disassociation from all other relations. In the political subculture, it is the group that replaces the family: the group serves as an emotional sustainer, offering community experiences and security which the prospective terrorists have painfully had to go without until joining such groupings. The group is, at the same time, a place of joint material support, solidarity, and mutual security. With respect to group experiences in the prephase of terrorism, the OPEC assassin Klein thus talks about experiences of

> solidarity, of sticking together, love and respect without competition and
> its anxieties. Help . . . even for the weakest member of the group. . . .
> That really was a fantastic experience for me. (Klein 1979:120)

The longing for the collective, for community, seems to have been
for many of the later terrorists a search for personal contact, sensitiveness, tenderness, and *Geborgenheit* (security)—feelings that were
missing in their own families. They try to make up for these feelings
in the "total groups" of the radical left-wing subculture or in the
company of people who directly sympathize with terrorists. For many
of the terrorists, the commune is a kind of family substitute, which is
supposed to compensate for the deficiencies of their own primary
socialization.

The pseudosecurity of radical groups with their claim to total personal absoluteness has a very strong attraction, particularly for people
with weak egos, or who have difficulties in getting into contact with
other people. In such groups, people find their strong desire for community, personal contact, and human relations satisfied. The lack of
self-confidence is compensated for by a "we-feeling" of common
strength. "The new feeling of security is paid for with the sacrifice of
autonomous thinking" (Adorno 1980:149). In return for the total
handing over of his or her personality to the group, the member obtains
the feeling of absolute group solidarity. And finally, the group provides
a sympathetic ear for those experiences of success and status that were
missing prior to joining the group:

> My first political group made as many demands on me as I made demands
> on it. I . . . was treated there like a comrade among comrades and I felt
> like that. Everytime I was addressed as comrade I was mighty proud of
> that. . . . It was the pride of being acknowledged and accepted as one of
> many. Of equal value. (Klein 1979:113)

The relationship between interpersonal conflicts and political behavior
in the former Sozialistisches Patienten Kollektiv (SPK)—Socialist Patients Collective—in Heidelberg is particularly evident. This group
originally concerned itself with group therapy. It tried to solve mental
problems with answers beyond those of classical psychology and its
approaches, and experimented with new ways and methods of treatment. The case of the SPK is a prime example of a "politicization of
private conflicts" (Habermas)—which suggests nothing other than the
projection of difficulties from the personal level to a political one.
The simple and rather amazing tenet of this group was that if society
makes you ill, it has to be changed by revolutionary means; or, much
more simply expressed, "Destroy what destroys you!" (*Macht kaputt,*

was Euch kaputt macht!) Meanwhile this slogan has become very popular in the West German anarchist community.

One of the main characteristics of the communes and other sympathetic groups toward terrorism is that there is no separation of private
and political spheres. Private needs are subordinated to the collective
political goal, to the extent that all politically engaging questions and
social contacts take place almost exclusively with or among the politically like-minded. This kind of voluntary isolation and renunciation
of communication with the outside world supports the process of a
one-sided formation of consciousness. In this prephase of a terrorist
career, the decisive political crossroads can be found. An observer of
the West Berlin "alternative scene" has explained, by way of an example of a nonterrorist milieu, how such a reduction in contacts with
the outer world comes about:

> The average *Stadtteilindianer* [urban Indian] wakes up in a commune, buys
> his rolls at a collective bakery round the corner, and gets his *Müsli* from
> a macrobiotic shop. While having his breakfast he reads his *Pflasterstrand,
> Info-Bug, zitty* [papers of the counterculture]; he then goes—provided he
> is not a "zerowork" supporter [one who does not believe in working]—to
> work in a self-organized small business or in some sort of alternative project;
> every five days he has to take care of children in a *Kinderladen* [an alter-
> native kindergarten], his two-CV is only repaired in a left-wing collective
> garage, in the evening he watches the film *Casablanca* in an alternative
> cinema; after that he can be found in a *Teestube* [tearoom], a left-wing
> pub, or a disco. His bedtime reading is from a collective book shop. There
> are doctor-collectives and lawyer-collectives, advisory boards for women,
> women's organizations, and groups for men in the "ghetto." Nearly every-
> thing is covered as far as everyday life is concerned. At the same time,
> communication is very intense compared with that between average West
> Berlin citizens. *Stadtteilindianer* and *Spontis* [spontaneous anarchists] talk
> to this [average] sort of person only when they have to, for instance with
> policemen during a police raid. In West Berlin and in Frankfurt there are
> people belonging to this scene who are very proud of the fact that they
> have not spoken a word to anybody outside their scene for two and a half
> years. (Fichter and Lönnendonker 1979:137)

"Bommi" Baumann also describes this process of growing isolation
among like-minded people: first of all, those who conformed had
broken off contact with him, and the next step had been that "you
automatically look for contacts with similar people" (Baumann
1977:10). Klein reports similar experiences: "Through the three comrades and the other I knew, I got to know more and more comrades.
A snowball system" (Klein 1979:123).

IN SEARCH OF MEANING IN LIFE

In the biographies of terrorists from the offshoot generation, a rather unpolitical phase can be found—a phase in which diffuse left-wing sympathies and orientations are built up emotionally, but remain without any consequences for personal everyday behavior. Accordingly, Volker Speitel recounts the time before his entanglement in terrorism:

> At this time I lived . . . in a commune which was absolutely unpolitical. . . . Correspondingly, life was chaotic in that community and as an orientation or aid for solving our conflicts which arose in all spheres of life we smoked a joint or took a trip. (Speitel 1980, 31:36)

He describes the political consciousness of the group as follows:

> In those days we were as far away from the radical left as a Bavarian village-priest. Nevertheless we already felt ourselves to be a part of it; affinities were set up through formal connections, the same appearance, the same music, the same habits, the same catchwords and slogans. (Ibid., 31:37)

The original demand of the group—to try out things like alternative ways of life, a new lifestyle in the commune—failed because of their own inadequacies.

> Everything we tried as alternative forms of working and living in our commune came to a standstill before it had really begun, or because of our laziness, and we gave up hope because of our own contradictions. (Ibid.)

Speitel summarizes how the feeling of life expressed itself in such a diffuse political commune:

> We felt oppressed and on the other hand were free like never before. We wanted to see reality, but we smoked grass. We dreamed of a farmhouse in the country, of nature, love, peace, and at the same time we were delighted at every activity carried out with firearms. We wanted everything and at the same time nothing. (Ibid.)

When the subcultural atmosphere of aimlessness combines with the feeling of having no future, the desire for a radical alternative arises from a feeling of senselessness and disorientation. Politicization thus becomes a value itself:

The process of isolation, in which we had put ourselves, became more and more unbearable, and the logical compensation was the strong will to unite with other groups that also felt to be "outside." (Ibid.)

For Speitel, the next station on the way from an unpolitical commune in an urban subculture to a terrorist group was the Rote Hilfe (Red Aid), which supported political prisoners, the "committees against the torture of isolation," and the activities of lawyers who defended members of the RAF. Commitment to this kind of group is primarily regarded by those who join as an alternative to their own personal life crises, providing them with a prospect for the future and a new political identity.

Through new objects of identification, which help to overcome the intellectual abeyance of senselessness and aimlessness, every member of the group is given the elevated feeling of being a member of the avant-garde who is fighting for a just and extraordinary cause. Speitel says about his first contact with the political scene:

I took part in some sessions of the Stuttgart *Rote Hilfe* organization, and, though this group behaved rather chaotically, it filled at least the emptiness that resulted from my lack of orientation. The group developed an aim and a perspective with which I could finally identify my individual "trip": Destroy what destroys you! (Ibid.)

After this "chaotic time in the commune," Speitel is fascinated by the "attractiveness of such a really functioning and working group which puts an end to everyday frustration by giving a totally new meaning to life" (Speitel 1980, 31:39). By caring for and helping the imprisoned terrorists, the group which, up to then, had been hanging around without any kind of aim, all of a sudden received a meaningful new life task: caring for and helping imprisoned terrorists.

Through this combination of discussion and work our whole life was practically changed within a period of only three or four months. . . . For us something like discipline and order in daily life developed with respect to our activities. (Ibid., 31:38)

In the group not only is there extreme isolation from other political opinions but also a mutual escalation of emotions. Speitel noted that the "situation of the prisoners" had affected him personally very much. "I really saw tortured and ill-treated prisoners in totally isolated cells where it was intended to destroy them slowly by means of scientific methods" (ibid., 31:41).

During the time of helping and caring for the imprisoned terrorists, it was inevitable that humanitarian objectives would no longer remain the main focus of the group, but that the motives, background, and political implications of the RAF would be discussed, which eventually led the group to identify itself with the goals of the "armed struggle." "We did not only talk about the treatment of the prisoners in jail, but also about the question why they were in jail; in other words, the necessity of the armed struggle was discussed" (ibid., 31:38).

Through the correspondence with the prisoners of the RAF "an idea about what the RAF is slowly developed"—an organization about which they had known little up to then. "The letters were very theoretical, indeed, because of the censorship in the prison, but they conveyed a very decisive point: we were involved by being criticized, . . . and we more or less had to decide whether to support the RAF completely or not at all" (ibid.).

PROCESSES OF IDENTIFICATION

The biographies of several terrorists demonstrate that their identification with certain persons who represent and articulate the ideology and goals of terrorist organizations prepares the ground for, and accelerates the step into, terrorism. Such idols suggest a certain ideological competence, which is often combined with intellectual superiority and personal charisma. These persons serve as a standard or model for those insecure and ego-weak group members who want to be like their idols. Such idols have an imposing effect on the admirer, especially when their personal qualities appear in conjunction with a certain protective attitude toward or an affection for the admirer. Idols thus have a considerable personal and political influence, particularly on the less educated, who in the company of students and graduates feel that they experienced gaps in their education, which results in their having difficulties in expressing themselves, and in a general feeling of inferiority. That such influential people have a politically motivating and activating effect on their followers—in which the affective character of the relationship overrides rational scruples or doubts—is also known from what occurs in other dogmatic political groups not associated with the terrorist scene. This is confirmed by reports of "renegades" from West German Marxist-Leninist "avant-garde" groups (so-called K-groups, in left-wing jargon) which mainly recruited students and at no time represented more than political sects.

My politicization . . . did not take place through the discussion of political issues, but through people. If I had been together with different people I would perhaps have developed in a completely different way. If I had met a man whose intention was to marry and have a family, then I would have done that. In those days I did not have an opinion of my own at all. I was politicized because the man I was with was politically active and pulled me into it. . . . I simply had no self-confidence. Through this man or the people who were my friends I became involved in the KSV [Communist Students Organization]. (*Wir warn die stärkste der Parteien* . . . 1978:37).

Another woman says she became involved in the KSV "because there were women there I admired" (ibid., p. 39).

At that time I oriented myself with other women who, I believed, had achieved self-confidence, knew how to appear in public, and were accepted as somebody because of their political work. Those were my idols, and that is why I wanted to join the KSV at all costs. (Ibid.)

In other cases, lawyers who represented imprisoned terrorists (some of whom went underground later) evidently functioned as idols, too. "If it had not been for Jörg Lang, with whom I was on very close terms, I probably would not have stayed there very long . . . " (Speitel 1980, 31:38). While working as assistants in the offices of RAF lawyers, Speitel and others became more and more involved in terrorism:

Through strong leadership [which still existed at that time in form of the Stammheim inmates], a homogeneously operating apparatus, and the continual reaction to one's work in the press, the courts, and the government, the initial adherence to the group developed very easily; and that is the decisive step. If somebody is involved, it is always possible to drag him or her into illegality, either by repression on the part of the judicial machinery or through personal ties with people already engaged in illegal work. (Ibid., 31:39)

KEY EXPERIENCES

Particular political events or personal traumatic experiences can play a key role on the path leading to the underground. This is not the case in the sense that these events are to be regarded as providing the decisive impulse. But if an individual is disposed in this direction, they can eventually prove to be the "straw that breaks the camel's back." In the emotionally overheated atmosphere of a closed group, an external event or particular political incident will often suffice as a key experience and a reason for taking the decisive step into terrorism. The death of a terrorist (in this case, after a hunger strike) may be such a key experience: "Then came the day Holger Meins died. . . . Siegfried Haag, who was Meins' lawyer . . . described Meins's state of health to us. . . . For us this death was a key experience" (ibid., 31:41). Speitel reports further that they felt morally implicated in this death, because "we could not prevent his death by our activities and efforts" (ibid.).

> The death of Holger Meins and the decision to take up arms were one and the same. Reflection was not possible anymore. It was only the emotional outburst of the last few months which reacted. . . . The whole situation favored the idea of going underground. The only thing that was missing was the "connection." (Ibid.)

Klein, too, describes the death of Holger Meins as the "decisive point" at which "to break with the legal policy of helplessness and powerlessness" (Klein 1979:195).

> If all I needed not only to propagate armed struggle but also to take it up myself was the right "kick," then Holger Meins was this "kick." His death made my misery and my powerlessness in the face of this political system reach such a pitch that it became too much for me. I had had enough of legal policy and I was prepared to fight. Definitely. (Ibid.)

The fascination felt by sympathizers for spectacular operations carried out by terrorists may also arouse the desire to join them. A case in point is the successful operation in 1975, when President Lorenz of the West Berlin parliament was kidnapped and later exchanged for several imprisoned terrorists, who were given safe conduct to Yemen. The departure of the "freed" terrorists at the airport was shown on television. The use of the mass media by the terrorists can impress sympathizers; to this extent it is also a piece of political propaganda. The television broadcast of the departure of the terrorists, who had been released in response to the Lorenz kidnapping, and the demonstration of the government's powerlessness can be regarded by sympathizers, as well as by terrorists, as proof that the "right way" had been chosen.

With regard to those sympathizers in particular who exhibit severe political alienation, low political efficacy, and cynicism with respect to the Federal Republic and its political elites, the terrorist offer of violence can be viewed as a "legitimate" model to compensate for personal feelings of powerlessness. In the case of Baumann, who showed his aversion to society by committing several crimes before he slid into the terrorist world, the fire in the Frankfurt department stores in 1968 was an incident that in essence won his admiration for the culprits.

Of course, then I was on the side of Baader, Ensslin, Proll, and Söhnlein, who set fire to the department stores. That was much better than what I had been doing [puncturing tires]. I wasn't against it anymore, I liked it. (Baumann 1977:30)

For Baumann, however, it was evidently not really the crime and the political motives of the wrongdoers (a protest or a signal against the war in Vietnam) that were important, but rather solidarity with the incendiaries whose action was dismissed as "amateurish" and a "psychological failure" by other leftists.

It was precisely this psychological failure that aroused solidarity and sympathy in me, much more than the action itself. I didn't give a shit at that moment whether they set fire to a department store or not. All that mattered was that there were people who acted out the part and did something like that. Above all, everyone in this case should have backed them and said, fine, ok, they're on our side! (Ibid.)

THE STEP INTO THE UNDERGROUND

Going underground is a decisive turning point for all terrorists, since they leave their previous lives and start a new existence. But before disappearing into illegality most of the terrorists go through a phase of semilegality, which means that they are still listed with the registration office, have a more or less proper job, study, take part in legal political activities, and enjoy social life in a pub adopted by the subculture (aside from the commune itself, the pub is the most important place for social communication with like-minded people), and at the same time their support for terrorists takes the form of concrete actions. These emerging illegal activities in the legal phase are, so to speak, the ticket to the terrorist underground.

The step into the underground usually takes place through contact men who first determine whether the "comrade" is really "clean." Thus, Speitel talks of an "emotional push" after the death of Holger Meins, which was conducive to his decision "to start using a gun." What was missing was the "connection."

The "connection" was Haag. In the course of several talks he questioned me about my motives and introduced himself as a contact man for one of the groups living in the underground. . . . Talks of that kind, which I later had quite frequently with others, are carried on carefully at the beginning; that is to say, they are on a rather abstract political level. This is one of the most critical points in the illegal network, since the contact man—in this case Haag—has to make sure that the person he is talking to keeps his mouth shut in the event of being rejected. . . . The basic agreement at that time was that no more prisoners should die in jail, but that they had to be liberated. For that reason an illegal structure had to be built up, in order to mount a commando-style operation later. Haag informed those already living outside the law of the result of this talk, and they then discussed this topic again—without Haag being present— taking into consideration other items of information (what has the person who is to be recruited already done politically, has he got personal problems, etc.) . . . whether to recruit somebody or not. (Speitel 1980, 31:41)

Klein reports similar experiences:

The RAF and other groupings could and still can only survive and work with the support of comrades who are not wanted by the law. And it was one of these "legal" comrades who told the others about me, and then they wanted to meet me some time or other. So I went to see them. First of all we talked about my political development and what I intended to do, etc. And then (name withheld) asked me, whether I would do this and that for them. I made it clear to (name withheld) that I would support them, but had no intention of going underground. . . . First I had to exchange a large amount of stolen foreign currency. . . . The next thing I had to do was to find a flat for one week. (Klein 1979:41 f.)

Helpers and sympathizers are of vital importance for terrorists living underground. Terrorist groups could not survive without them in the long run. They are the potential recruits which the underground uses to inject new blood and replace its casualties. Helpers are needed for life in the underground, as well as for the preparation of attacks. But above all they are used for the menial work that terrorists themselves cannot risk doing, and thus they gradually become increasingly tied to the group and dragged into the illegal structure. This menial work consists of stealing identity cards, passports, and drivers' licenses, or forging them; purchasing arms, procuring explosives, serving as informers and couriers and, finally, robbing banks.

The transition from the periphery of terrorism, the step from sympathy to direct terrorist action, starts with the role of a helper who takes advantage of his legality. The step into terrorism is immediately preceded by logistic errands, which serve as training for illegality. The period spent as a helper is at the same time both the preliminary stage and a test before being received into the group and "disappearing" into illegality. Only those who have stood the test as helpers and who meet the criteria of an "urban guerrilla" have a chance of being accepted by the hard core of the group. The successful participation in a bank robbery functions as a rite of initiation for entering the group.

The bank robbery, however, is considered to be not so much proof of the applicant's courage as it is a way of preventing police spies from being introduced into the group. For participation in a bank robbery combined with the use of firearms is a severe crime and therefore considered taboo for police spies. The formal break with normal life can thus be made through participation in a bank robbery, and from then on the terrorist recruit is at the mercy of the group, for better or for worse.

THE DYNAMICS OF TERRORIST GROUPS

Life in the underground brings about totally new conditions of life for each terrorist and for the group as a whole. Terrorists live in an isolated world, left to their own resources and cut off from many social and intellectual contacts with the outside environment. The closed formation of the group becomes practically the only frame of reference for the terrorists. Their total dependency on the group, its pressures of adjustment, as well as the internal assignment of roles and division of labor lead to the loss of their own needs, interests and desires, and finally of their own identity. External and internal isolation condition each other, forcing terrorists to live in a deeply alienated world. The loss of their own identity is compensated for by the demonstration of collective strength. Only in this way is it possible to mask their own ego-weakness. The diminished reference to reality, found at the beginning of every terrorist career, is reinforced in the underground by the isolation and renunciation of communication. The political socialization of terrorists—as a process of permanent self-indoctrination by the group—finally leads to a total loss of reality and a complete miscalculation of the political and social environment. The precondition for the dogmatic terrorist is the immunization and isolation from ideological influences and criticism from the outside. The hermetic cutting off of the group from the ideological influences of the external world guarantees that the pure, undiluted indoctrination with the group's own political patterns of interpretation is made possible without any external ideological interference. Only in such a confined atmosphere can the intellectual feelings of omnipotence develop, which are a starting point for individual and collective aggression. Ego-weak persons, particularly, succumb to the fascination of a closed ideology, which offers a complete explanation for everything. Those who have settled themselves comfortably in monocausal theories of conspiracy will hardly risk the breeze of competing ideologies and ways of thinking.

Parallel to the immunizing strategies against political alternatives and criticism, even alternative thinking in general, is the development of a clear concept of the enemy. In the cells of the terrorist underground a friend-enemy mentality exists which is typical of all totalitarian political groupings. Certain antisymbols (Freud) become targets and fixed points of group aggression. These targets are typically the elites of the political and economic system and their "underlings," such as judges, business executives, and policemen. In the jargon of anarchists they are called "pigs." For example, after Baader's liberation Ulrike Meinhof wrote in a letter:

> We say the guy in uniform is a pig, he is not a human being, and we have to tackle him from this point of view. . . . It is wrong to talk to these people at all and of course the use of guns is allowed. (Meinhof 1970:75)

Speitel, too, remembers the clear difference made between friend and enemy in the consciousness of the group.

> You feel as if you are in the "enemy's country," enemies were not only Buback [Federal Prosecutor] and the Federal Attorneyship, but almost all those who didn't do anything against their methods. (Speitel 1980, 31:41).

It is the clear definition of the enemy that makes terrorist actions legitimate in the eyes and minds of the group. The conviction of the moral legitimacy of their activities, however, presupposes a reevaluation of traditional values and norms—one strips off "bourgeois" value orientations and subjugates oneself unconditionally to the new morality of the group. By declaring your enemies "nonpersons," and by denying their human qualities, moral scruples are blocked from the beginning. In the process of defining symbolic figures of the political system as the personification of everything evil and bad, terrorists repress their guilt feelings and provide themselves with a "good conscience," justifying their deeds. The liquidation of the political enemy thus does not only become a necessity but also a legitimate act. "It was a moral duty to kill; that's what you can call it." (Mahler 1978:14).

An illustration of the cold-blooded cynicism and contempt for mankind is seen in the attitudes terrorists have toward ordinary citizens who become victims by chance. For example, Klein reports how "Carlos" explained to him the necessity of shooting hostages.

> If somebody shows resistance or doesn't obey an order immediately he has to be shot. . . . All this has . . . nothing to do with killing, but is a military necessity in the political struggle. (Klein 1979:60)

Another pattern in the thinking of urban guerrillas is that they are at war with society and, consequently, terrorist actions are nothing else but acts of war. "In some way we subjectively were at war and accordingly regarded ourselves as soldiers" (Mahler 1979:14). By raising their own terrorist actions and hence the resulting prosecution by the state to the level of a warlike struggle, the entire matter served the urban guerrilla as a vehicle for massive moral support. When the imprisoned RAF members again and again insisted on being treated as prisoners of war, it was not only for tactical reasons during the trial but also the expression of a broader form of consciousness-raising. Within the group the fantasy of being at war with the "imperialist" and/or "fascist" Federal Republic was supported by a militarization of thinking and language: "They only talked about depots, infrastructure, news structure, and battle structure; they talked of cadres, units, and commandos in a military terminology, which suggested at least to me that something like that really existed" (Speitel 1980, 31:41).

The terms *fight, fighter,* and *to fight* are nothing short of key words for terrorist groups, whereas such terms as *terror, terrorist,* and *to terrorize* are understandably avoided, in order not to accept the emotional connotations or implications of these terms from the opponent or critic. The isolation of the group and the resulting constriction of reality promote the process of mutual escalation to more and more radical actions. Horst Mahler retrospectively describes how the unity of the political line in the RAF was promoted by group pressure and compulsion:

> . . . one wanted to do something, that was the determining factor, and what spoke against it was somehow devalued theoretically and morally, and it was not a matter for discussion any more because one feared that one would be regarded as unreliable or perhaps one would even regard oneself as a shirker. (Mahler 1979:14)

Those who did not subjugate themselves to the ideological and strategic concept of the group had to face the verdict of the group and reckon with its most severe sanctions. "They reproached him (Lang) with 'cowardice toward the enemy' because he for instance had not fought with a gun together with the Arabs in Lebanon, and they forbade us to send him a new passport" (Speitel 1980, 31:39). Just how far such subjection can go, because of group pressure, is shown by the example of Susanne Albrecht. She participated in the attempt to kidnap the director of the governing body of the Dresdner Bank, Jürgen Ponto, who was a friend of her family. (Susanne Albrecht's father is a lawyer and former Christian Democratic Union member of the Hamburg parliament.) Ponto was mortally wounded by shots when he tried to defend himself against his kidnappers. Because Susanne

Albrecht had visited the banker's house before, she and her companions were let in immediately after she telephoned to say she was coming. The motivation for her behavior was due presumably to the massive pressure of a terrorist group, which individual members cannot escape, since they are totally dependent on the group. Any sign of passivity or lack of participation is immediately interpreted as treason. "Bourgeois" moral scruples must be left behind, since the liberation of imprisoned comrades is of much higher value in the terrorist value hierarchy than the death of a good family friend.[3]

The pressure of being pursued and the accompanying suppressed fear cannot automatically find compensation or support outside the group, and therefore this strain affects communication within the group. Once members know one another on a personal level, their relationships become characterized less by solidarity, human warmth, and democratic group processes than by an authoritarian division of labor, concealed hierarchies, and by domination-submission behavioral patterns. Peter Boock notes that sensitivity among group members had been subject to a "slow process of erosion" and that he had seen "only a few true emotional relationships in the group" (Boock 1981:120). In his view, there were "different levels in the group" at which discussions took place. "The majority of the group was simply excluded from certain considerations, didn't get any information at all or only sometime later" (p. 114). "The structure was in any case from top to bottom to an extremely harsh extent" (p. 120).

The voluntary surrender to the group hierarchy is well exemplified by Ulrike Meinhof's glorification of Andreas Baader, the dominating figure in the Baader-Meinhof group: "Of all of us he is the one . . . who anticipates what the group wants and is therefore able to lead its process . . . " (unpublished circular). Evidence suggests that the mechanism of adjustment, rigid forms of interactions, privileges, constraints, and the rituals of violence of the group prevent the development of personal identity among group members in the long run. Terrorists are not capable of retaining normal social relations. They organize themselves, as a former member of the RAF called it, as a "gang" (Homann 1971), in which the structure of communication, favored by the enormous pressure of persecution, is characterized by a basic distrust.

In this atmosphere, the original expectations of group members are turned "inside out": there is no development of identity, but instead an identity crisis; rather than self-realization, there is permanent frustration; instead of promoting warm, human communication, the interrelationships within the group take on a depersonalized character; and in place of love and trust there are distrust and desensitization.

As an example of this, "Bommi" Baumann says: "We've never managed to retain the sensitiveness within the group because the pressure from outside is so strong that it catches up with you" (Baumann 1977:127). Speitel formulates a similar view:

> Of course, the pressure of permanent persecution influences the group. All the relationships of the people in the group are eclipsed by this pressure, which finally becomes the only connecting link that holds the group together. They call it the "dialectics of persecution" and believe that it strengthens the unity of the group. . . . But in reality an extreme tension develops, which erupts in quarrels, the forming of cliques, and sneering remarks to one another. (Speitel 1980, 33:35)

The rigid forms of interaction, latent conflicts, and aggressions within the group must inevitably be diverted to the outside.

> The fear and insecurity everybody had became a kind of group syndrome. And, as a means of mastering this, blind action was proposed. (Ibid., 31:49)

"They didn't know any other value or have any other perspective than the 'battle'" (ibid., 33:34). Another problem for the group in the underground is the lack of social contacts with members of the opposite sex, which causes severe frustration, and which also may lead to an increase in the potential for aggression. With respect to this, Klein reports:

> My sexual life ended in Frankfurt where I got into a car at the beginning of November in 1975 in order to drive to Switzerland and from there to Vienna. Since then I've neither kissed, caressed, nor slept with anyone. (Klein 1979:213)

GROUP IDEOLOGY AND GROUP COHESION

The extraordinary energy that terrorists invest in planning and executing their actions would be inconceivable without the rock-hard conviction that their activities are necessary and meaningful in the interest of a higher aim. I shall use the term *group ideology* to describe the system of arguments and justifications, which "as a rule remain immune to falsifying facts" (Fetscher, Muenkler, and Ludwig 1981:29). Group ideology has a twofold function, namely, to give an outward expression of the group's legitimacy and to act as a means of inner rationalization within the group itself.

Complex social matters are compressed with the help of group ideology into what at first appear to be plausible and correct forms of interpretation and explanation. Ideology lends impetus not only to the individual terrorist but to the whole group. It demands total devotion and selfless engagement of the individual in the interest of a "higher cause" and supplies the terrorist with his notorious good conscience. "Ideology lifts the burden of personal guilt, projects it and licenses a righteous anger and aggression" (Davies 1980:114). Political terrorism would not be able to survive without a corresponding ideology. For ideology is the decisive criterion and the one that distinguishes terrorism from organized crime. Group ideology is the moral mainstay and absolute norm for terrorists, which not only permits the violations of norms and laws within the society being opposed but makes it a moral duty.

German terrorists in particular were compelled to develop an ideological argument for their actions, since the political situation in West Germany does not in any way justify a terrorist strategy. Reality therefore had to be molded to fit the group ideology and not vice versa.

As the terrorist Rolf Pohle was being led to the courtroom, he wore a paper cover over his head on which was written, "No revolution without a theory" (*Münchner Merkur*, 5 April 1974). This statement undoubtedly illustrates the need and the pretension to feel obligated to a grand cause, which can only be achieved by a terrorist revolution. Consequently the motives for their actions are automatically glorified and the actions carried out with a kind of "holy consecration."

Through group ideology, a purely criminal act is reinterpreted into a "political act," or rather it is only then that it gains political dimensions. An ideology conveys to the terrorist the conviction that a meaning lies behind his actions. The decisive factor in the process of internalizing group ideology is not the extent to which it corresponds to the reality it is pretending to describe, but the conviction of its justness and the degree of intensity with which the group believes in the cause, factors which are rooted only in the personality of the individual.

Group ideology is a decisive factor in group cohesion. It welds the individuals into a tightly knit community. Those in doubt or resigned to their fate are remotivated by the call to the common belief system and the superior aim. Ideology, as well as acting as the cement that binds the group, is also an instrument for internal discipline. Isolated from the outside world and its intellectual influences, a process of permanent political indoctrination among the members of the group takes place. In fact, the indoctrination and the continual surveillance of members to ensure that the "right level of consciousness" is maintained is essential for the cohesion of the group.

Precisely because group ideology affords terrorists a sense of legitimate and moral justification for their actions—the inhibition to kill is diminished through it and through it alone—it gains as it were a quasi-religious character, with a sacrosanct quality. Doubts are collectively suppressed. Those who doubt are brought back in line through group pressure and disciplinarian techniques. Those deviating from the correct ideological path are made to toe the line by means of criticism and self-criticism. The instrument of self-criticism was practiced (above all, in detention) with an almost self-destructive intensity, as the following extract from a contribution by Ulrike Meinhof taken from a cell-circular indicates:

> My socialization to becoming a fascist, through sadism and religion, caught up with me, because I never really completely broke ties with the ruling class, whose darling I once was, or wiped out without a trace its influence still on me . . . a sanctimonious bitch of the ruling class, that's just what I now realize, everything done "as if" . . . hypocritical is the right word, because that's how it's always been . . . as far back as I can remember— family, socialization, religion, Communist party, my job at *Konkret* (a left-wing journal)—when I joined the RAF that's just how I didn't want to stay, a gasbag. (Quote in Neidhardt 1982:370)

The group cannot afford an honest, self-critical appraisal of its theoretical premises and position; questioning its theoretical assumptions would endanger the group's *raison d'être* and could activate a destabilizing effect on the group consciousness. This, especially among the ego-weak members, could develop into a personality crisis. It is therefore in keeping with and indicative of this way of thinking, that Horst Mahler had to face sanctions (during detention) in the form of expulsion from the group because his theoretical deliberations contained elements that questioned the obligatory group ideology.

THE SEARCH FOR A REVOLUTION

What then are the fundamental elements of group ideology, and which arguments justify the practice of terrorist methods? In contrast to terrorist groups of the Third World, which can give clearly defined reasons for and explain the aims of their activities—like ethnic emancipation, national independence, or the overthrow of a repressive regime—West German terrorists have the difficult task of justifying their actions on a political basis. In order to achieve this for themselves and in front of the public, they first of all have to deny the democratic legitimacy of the Federal Republic. They do this by simply denouncing it as a fascist state. In this way, they surreptitiously obtain legitimacy for their behavior and consequently transform their resistance into a moral duty. This trick of substituting the past for the present enables the terrorists to style themselves as resistance fighters. It does not occur to the terrorists that, by brandishing the most banal forms of "repression" as fascism, they are in fact rendering harmless the atrocities of historical fascism.

Terrorists legitimize their actions by indicating that they do not act from personal but from altruistic motives, in other words in the interest of a third party. The existence of an interested "revolutionary subject" (Fetscher, Muenkler, and Ludwig 1981) is, so to speak, the *raison d'être* of the group. At first the RAF had expected decisive support for their fight to come from the working class. Even after the freeing of Baader and still under this illusion, Ulrike Meinhof appraised the situation:

> The sector of the proletariat, where we believe to find potential revolutionaries, will not have any problems in identifying with the cause. (Natürlich kann geschossen werden, 1970:74)

Since the group soon afterwards had to concede that it was pointless to try and win over the working class in developed capitalistic countries as a "revolutionary subject," they gave up the idea of wooing the proletariat as a possible ally. The dilemma of finding a suitable "revolutionary subject" was aggravated even more by the fact that the Vietnam War had come to an end, the war having been one of the principal means of legitimizing the RAF's activities in its initial stages.

After the industrial proletariat had been written off as the "working-class aristocracy," the RAF devoted itself to what appeared to be in their eyes as other underprivileged groups in West Germany. Instead of the "corrupt working-class," they now concentrated on adolescents, students, and marginal groups, or the *Lumpenproletariat*, in the Marxist sense of the word. In addition to this, solidarity with suppressed people and Liberation movements in the Third World, seen as allies, stood high on the RAF's list of priorities. This was particularly true for the Palestine Liberation Organization (PLO), who trained members of the group in the late sixties. The continual search for a "revolutionary subject" as proof of the group's legitimacy illustrates just how important this fact was for the identity of the group.

THE DECISION TO LEAVE THE GROUP

The chances of leaving a terrorist group are extremely limited, and for most members the prospect is not attractive. Since the terrorists have broken the law and have committed serious crimes, they can expect a rather long term in prison, if not life imprisonment in some cases. To this extent, they have not much to lose by continuing to the bitter end. And, since there is no way back, there remains only the sense of the forward escape or, in other words, escalation to bigger and bigger terrorist operations. "Reports of success concerning us can only mean: arrested or dead. The power of the guerrillas is the resoluteness of each one of us" (Baader 1972:233). Baader thus paraphrased the guerrilla philosophy of the RAF. It is with this resoluteness that terrorists are willing to use their firearms immediately in order to avoid getting arrested.

The question of leaving the terrorist group is frightening to the hard-core members of the group, since their only alternative would be long imprisonment. The state's offer of amnesty or reduced sentences if members of terrorist organizations appear as witnesses for the prosecution is less likely to be of interest to terrorists, since it underestimates the mentality and energy of terrorist cadres and, above all, it disregards the political belief system that binds the group together. It is a time-honored thought pattern of former terrorists that they do not want to betray their former comrades to the police. Using people who turn state's evidence might be successful in cases relating to criminal organizations, but there is hardly any possibility of using them to get at politically oriented criminals. Those persons who turned state's evidence at German terrorist trials have in most cases been minor figures who felt they were outsiders in the group. One can assume that they were not fully integrated into the group's ideological or social structure.

To leave a group with which one has identified oneself totally for some time and with which one has gone "through thick and thin" represents a tremendous psychological effort, since a break with the group is connected with a loss of identity. Although one may be convinced of the objective "rightness" of such a step, one has massive guilt feelings toward the group. "The consciousness of having committed 'treason,' and the prospect of being shot by a person one has liked or even loved was shattering" (Speitel 1980, 33:35). The internal distancing of oneself from the group is the result of laborious and often lengthy processes of detachment which, to some degree, may even extend into the time of imprisonment, even though one is convinced of the necessity of leaving the group. "One cannot cut through the sticky threads the group has covered one with in the course of time. One's whole existence was first of all in the group" (ibid., 33:34).

Boock speaks of an inner distancing process which, for him, "did not begin with the step of leaving . . . but earlier, at a quite different time" (Boock 1981:11). Speitel also underwent a progressive disillusionment with those people whose lives "are governed by the gun." In this connection the bond that ties the person to the group is only based on "loyalty to the people one still knew from earlier times and whom one didn't want to face as the 'swine' that sneaks off" (ibid.). He continues: "In this ambivalence all one can do is 'function.' I still had meetings, and even tried to train new couriers, but I could only do that with a lump in my throat and with a completely confused brain which was unable to pose any alternative to my long devotion to the group or any alternative to its goals" (ibid.).

Besides the subjective reasons that prevent the particular group member from leaving the terrorist scene (loss of identity), there are several other objective difficulties. Since warrants for arrest have been issued against terrorists in the Federal Republic, a legal existence in most foreign countries is not possible because of the threat of extradition. A terrorist, thinking of finding a life with another identity and independence from the group—that is, the beginning of a totally new life in another country—encounters several barriers and technical difficulties that are not easy to overcome. Another problem for potential defectors is that they are completely integrated into the relations and logistics of the group—terrorists mostly operate in twos—so that, particularly from a technical point of view, it is not easy to pull out at any time.

The extreme tension in the underground and the pressure of pursuit intensifies the distrust of the group members toward one another. A careless word or even carefully formulated doubts about the appropriateness of the political and strategic line entails sanctions by the group. Boock thus reports his inner process of detachment from the group, and the fact that its members did not fail to observe it: ". . . [I] in fact had the status . . . of a prisoner in the group" (Boock 1981:118). He could no longer participate in internal group discussions, and was kept away from other people. His gun was taken away and he was guarded day and night.

> I wasn't allowed to do a thing. I wasn't permitted to leave a certain room if others were present, because they weren't supposed to notice that I was there. (Boock 1981:118)

So far in this essay, I have discussed the psychological inhibitions and technical difficulties that make it almost impossible to break away from terrorist careers. I shall now examine briefly what is probably the greatest barrier, namely, the sanctions applied by the group itself. Like all conspiracies, secret societies, clandestine alliances, and underground organizations, the cadres of West German terrorist groups have no mercy for "traitors." Leaving the group is tantamount to treason. This is the answer given by the "quitter" Ruhland when he was asked whether he feared the vengeance of the RAF: "Yes. I'm afraid of the vengeance of group members . . . because it was always agreed that everyone who gives evidence against the group will be liquidated" (Ruhland 1972:68).

The terrorist "dropout" Klein did not feel safe from his former cadres either, although he did not "betray" anybody. Since terrorists have no inhibitions with respect to killing—even when it involves people who used to be their personal friends, such as Susanne Albrecht's participation in the murder of the banker Ponto—and since treason is regarded as the greatest danger of all for the group, they try to counter it by all available means. The liquidation of the "traitors" is considered by terrorists to be the only effective means of punishing them. The threat of liquidation is supposed to guarantee the continuation of the group. At the same time, liquidations are supposed to act as a warning—as in the case of the execution of Ulrich Schmücker—to deter potential traitors and demonstrate to them the sanctions that the group can apply.

Consequently, as it says in the Stockholm "Assassins' Cookbook," an unpublished pamphlet:

> However, there is no real alternative to killing an informer once he has been detected. But in this case, too, what good old grandma Mao said is true: Punish one—and educate 100!

CONCLUSION

West German terrorists are prototypes of the Gesinnungsethik (ethics of conviction), as Max Weber described it in his classic Politics as a Vocation in 1919. Weber made a distinction between the ethics of conviction and Verantwortungsethik (ethics of responsibility). The yardstick for actions of Gesinnungsethiker is "the flame of pure conviction" (Weber 1958:58). The person does not feel responsible for the consequences of his behavior. Finally, he acts according to the motto "The end justifies the means."

As opposed to this, a person who acts according to the ethics of responsibility takes the "average defects of human beings" into consideration. He reflects on the consequences of his behavior and does not put the blame on others. His character is the only adequate type to pursue "politics as a profession" in a democratic political system. According to Max Weber, those who follow the ethics of convictions are religious as well as revolutionary true believers and zealots who want to achieve "absolute justice on earth by means of force" (Weber 1958:62 f.) and intoxicate themselves with "romantic sensations" (p. 65). Weber could just as well have been describing the terrorist scene in West Germany when he warns us that the "Gesinnungsethiker can suddenly change into a chiliastic prophet. That, for instance, those who have just preached 'love as against violence' may call upon violence moments later—the ultimate in violence that would completely wipe out all other forms of violence" (p. 59).

West German terrorists are indeed *Gesinnungsethiker* par excellence. Their group ideology legitimizes their commitment to a cause based on the ethics of conviction. Its substratum is derived from set pieces of Marxist-Leninist theory and theorists of the guerrilla movement in the Third World, such as is found in Carlos Marighella's "Minimanual of the Urban Guerrilla." A real process of reflection on the ideology of the group is never attempted. This fact and the lack of willingness even to discuss the left wing's criticism of the group are rationalized by referring to the group doctrine of "action has the highest priority."

The strong commitment of terrorists, based on the ethics of conviction, would hardly be conceivable without the specific dynamics of terrorist groups. The formation of consciousness and political socialization of West German terrorists have been influenced decisively by group processes. The group alone dominates the ideology and the activities of its members, not only in the prephase of terrorism but also in the underground itself. These terrorists are not lone wolves; they operate in small groups and are completely dependent on them. Only the group makes it possible to endure the external stress of life in the underground. In all the biographies of terrorists we find the strong desire for community, for a group commitment. In the group they find the sense of security they have long sought. And so it would be no exaggeration to say that terrorists are in many ways "victims of group thinking."

NOTES

1. There have been exceptions to the rule, for example, small strains of "primitive rebels" (Eric Hobsbawn) and notorious outlaws, pirates like Störtebecker, highwaymen like Schinderhannes, and poachers like Jennerwein, who lived in earlier times and who received covert popular admiration. The two attempts by Hödel and Nobiling to assassinate Emperor Wilhelm I in 1878 were deeds carried out by individuals not belonging to any particular group or party. Bismarck used these events as a pretext for pushing the antisocialist laws through the Reichstag. The Weimar Republic also had various assassins and outlaws of the extreme left and right who rebelled against law and order and the political system as a whole.

2. The 2d of June movement grew from the spontaneous and antiauthoritarian milieu in West Berlin at the beginning of the seventies. It regarded itself as an alternative to the RAF, and it rejected the elitist self-image of the RAF, its methods, and its hierarchic group structure. Members of the 2d of June felt themselves to be genuine anarchists and upbraided the RAF mainly because the RAF could not convey the purpose of its actions to the public. The Revolutionäre Zellen (Revolutionary Cells) stand more in the anarchist tradition of the 2d of June movement (see also the chapter by Abraham Ashkenasi in this book).

3. Another example of the influence of the ambiguous mixture of group pressure and group loyalty—in this case, in a hopeless situation—is the collective attempt of the four leading imprisoned terrorists Andreas Baader, Jan Carl Raspe, Gudrun Ensslin, and Irmgard Möller (who survived) to commit suicide after the failed hijacking of a Lufthansa jet on 16 October 1977—which was supposed to bring about their release from jail.

BIBLIOGRAPHY

Adorno, Theodor W.
    1980   *Kritik, Kleine Schriften zur Gesellschaft.* Frankfurt/Main: Suhrkamp.

Baader, Andreas
    1972   Brief an die dpa (25 Jan.), pp. 233–234, *in* Reinhard Rauball, *Die Baader-Meinhof-Gruppe.* Berlin/New York: W. de Gruyter, 1973.

Baeyer-Katte, Wanda von, Dieter Claessens, Hubert Feger, and Friedhelm Neidhardt
    1982   *Gruppenprozesse.* Opladen: Westdeutscher Verlag.

Baumann, "Bommi"
    1977   *Wie alles anfing.* Frankfurt/Main: Sozialistische Verlagsauslieferung.

Becker, Jillian
    1978   *Hitlers Kinder? Der Baader-Meinhof-Terrorismus.* Frankfurt/Main: Fischer.

Binder, Sepp
    1978   *Terrorismus.* Bonn: Verlag Neue Gesellschaft.

Boock, Peter Jürgen
    1981   "Im Schützengraben für die falsche Sache. Spiegel-Gespräch mit Ex-Terrorist Peter Jürgen Boock über seine Erfahrungen in der RAF," *Der Spiegel,* no. 9 (23 Feb.), pp. 110–125.

Bowers, K. S.
    1973   "Situationalism in Psychology: An Analysis and a Critique," *Psychological Review,* pp. 307–336.

Braungart, Richard G., and Margaret M. Braungart
    1981   "International Terrorism: Background and Response," *Journal of Political and Military Sociology* 9, 2; pp. 263–288.

Davies, A. F.
    1980   *Skills, Outlooks and Passions.* Cambridge: Cambridge University Press.

Ekehammar, B.
    1974   "Interactionism in Personality from a Historical Perspective," *Psychological Bulletin* 81:1026–1048.

Fetscher, Iring
1978   *Terrorismus und Reaktion.* Frankfurt/Main: Europäische Verlagsanstalt.
Fetscher, Iring, Herfried Muenkler, and Hannelore Ludwig
1981   Ideologien der Terroristen in der Bundesrepublik Deutschland. Pp. 9–271
        in Iring Fetscher and Guenter Rohrmoser, *Ideologien und Strategien.*
        Opladen: Westdeutscher Verlag.
Fichter, Tilmann, and Siegward Lönnendonker
1979   "Von der APO nach TUNIX." *In* Claus Richter, ed. *Die überflüssige Gen-
        eration.* Königstein: Athenäum. Pp. 132–150.
Geißler, Heiner, ed.
1978   *Der Weg in die Gewalt.* München: Olzog.
Homann, Peter
1971   "Andreas Baader? Er ist ein Feigling," *Der Spiegel,* no. 48 (11 Nov.), pp.
        47–62.
Jäger, Herbert, Gerhard Schmidtchen, and Lieselotte Süllwold
1981   *Lebenslaufanalysen.* Opladen: Westdeutscher Verlag.
Kepplinger, Hans Matthias
1974   "Statusdevianz und Meinungsdevianz. Die Sympathisanten der Baader-
        Meinhof-Gruppe," *Kölner Zeitschrift für Soziologie und Sozial-psychologie* 4:
        pp. 770–800.
Klein, Hans-Joachim
1979   *Rückkehr in die Menschlichkeit. Appell eines ausgestiegenen Terroristen.* Rein-
        bek: Rowohlt.
Kraus, Christian, Detlef Lehnert, and Klaus-Jürgen Scherer
1980   *Zwischen Revolution und Resignation?* Bonn: Verlag Neue Gesellschaft.
Mahler, Horst
1978   "Terrorismus und die Bewußtseinskrise der Linken," *Frankfurter Rundschau,*
        no. 59 (22 March), p. 14.
Matz, Ulrich, and Gerhard Schmidtchen
1983   *Gewalt und Legitimität.* Opladen: Westdeutscher Verlag.
Meinhof, Ulrike
1970   "Natürlich kann geschossen werden." Ulrike Meinhof über die Baader-
        Aktion. *Der Spiegel* 25 (15/6/1970): 74–75.
Mischel, W.
1969   "Continuity and Change in Personality," *American Psychologist,* pp. 1012–
        1018.
Mischel, W.
1973   "Toward a Cognitive Social Learning Reconceptualization of Personality,"
        Psychological Review, pp. 252–283.
Neidhardt, Friedhelm
1982   "Soziale Bedingungen terroristischen Handelns." *In* Wanda von Baeyer-
        Katte et al., *Gruppenprozesse.* Pp. 318–391.
Paczensky, Susanne von, ed.
1978   *Frauen und Terror.* Reinbeck: Rowohlt.
Rasch, Wilfried
1979   "Psychological Dimensions of Political Terrorism in the Federal Republic
        of Germany," *International Journal of Law and Psychiatry* 2:79–85.
Rauball, Reinhard
1973   *Die Baader-Meinhof-Gruppe.* Berlin/New York: W. de Gruyter.
Ruhland, Karl-Heinz
1972   "Die Gruppe wird mir ans Fell wollen." Interview mit dem angeklagten
        Ruhland. *Der Spiegel* 6 (31/1/1972): 68.

Schwind, Hans-Dieter, ed.
   1978   *Ursachen des Terrorismus in der Bundesrepublik Deutschland.* Berlin/New York:
            W. de Gruyter.
Speitel, Volker
   1980   "Wir wollten alles und gleichzeitig nichts. Ex-Terrorist Volker Speitel über
            seine Erfahrungen in der westdeutschen Stadtguerilla," *Der Spiegel,* no. 31
            (28 July), pp. 36–49; no. 32 (4 Aug.), pp. 30–39; no. 33 (11 Aug.), pp.
            30–36.
Sturm, Beate
   1972   "Man kann nur zurückbrüllen," *Der Spiegel,* no. 7 (7 Feb.), pp. 57–63.
Texte der RAF
   1977   Malmö: Bo Cavors.
Wasmund, Klaus
   1980   "Zur politischen Sozialisation in terroristischen Gruppen." *Das Parlament,*
            b. Supplement, pp. 33–34, 29–46.
   1981   "Zur politischen Sozialisation terroristischer Karrieren." *In* H. Moser, ed.,
            Fortschritte der Politischen Psychologie. Weinheim/Basel: Beltz. Pp. 307–335.
   1982   "Ist der politische Einfluβ der Familie ein Mythos oder eine Realität?" *In*
            Bernhard Clauβen and Klaus Wasmund, eds., *Handbuch der politischen
            Sozialisation.* Braunschweig: Pedersen. Pp. 23–63.
Weber, Max
   1958   *Politik als Beruf.* 3d ed. Berlin: Dunker und Humboldt.
Wir warn die stärkste der Parteien . . .
   1977   Erfahrungsberichte aus der Welt der K-Gruppen. Berlin: Rotbuch-Verlag.

8

Rollerball or Neo-Nazi Violence?

PETER H. MERKL

"Fans Knock Out Teeth of Policeman," said the headline over the local police report of the respected *Süddeutsche Zeitung*. The article reported that, aside from a few arrests, it had been comparatively quiet at the Sunday game between the leading Munich soccer clubs First F.C. (*Fussball Club*) Bayern and the visiting team of Werder Bremen. Compared, that is, with the spectacular excesses of the recent past when, among other things, the interior and windows of whole trains of the Federal Railways were demolished by soccer fans returning with their team to another city. At the Bayern-Bremen match, a young man had jumped a Bayern fan from behind, torn off his cap, and disappeared into the crowd. A local prosecutor, however, happened to be there, followed him, and had him arrested. The assailant was only sixteen years old. After the game, a group of twelve to fifteen young fans of the Bremen team gathered in the evening at a tavern near the main railroad station. Two of them suddenly and "without any reason" attacked a young policeman with their fists, cutting his upper lip and knocking out his front teeth. Two others were arrested a little later inside the crowded station for firing a flare pistol into the air. The police once more warned the fans that it intended to prosecute even the customary grabbing of the colorful knitted caps and scarves of fans of the opposing team as "strong-armed robbery."

Another issue of the same newspaper reported the arrest of the sixty-third of the "soccer rowdies" who, on 25 September 1982 (almost exactly two years after the *Oktoberfest* bombing by a young neo-Nazi), had stormed onto the soccer field of the stadium of the second major soccer club of Munich, TSV (Turn und Sportverein) 1860, the

"Lions," on the occasion of a game between the Lions and a visiting team from Schweinfurt, and beaten up the referee. All sixty-three were now being tried for aggravated breach of the peace, and some for assault resulting in serious bodily harm. The most recent arrest involved a "skinhead," a sixteen-year-old apprentice who had let his hair grow in order to escape detection. He had been photographed in the act by the police and his picture appeared in all the newspapers. He belonged to a group that sported shorn heads (hence the name "skinhead") and "paratrooper uniforms" which had attempted to hide him.

A RISING TIDE OF VIOLENCE

Aside from soccer rowdies and political violence, the city of Munich, like other European cities, has been plagued by a steadily rising rate of violent crime, including homicides, for some time. Homicides alone rose from seventy-three to ninety-five a year in this city of 1.4 million from 1981 to 1982 and the current annual total of violent crimes— still modest by American standards—is more than twenty-four hundred cases of homicide, serious injuries, robberies, and kidnappings. A reporter of the *Süddeutsche Zeitung* finally interviewed a local forensic psychiatrist, Prof. Werner Mende, about the likely causes of this increase of violence, including soccer-related mayhem. Mende pointed out, by way of explanation, that there had been a significant shift from domestic violence between spouses or friends, which had made up the majority of cases ten years before, to deadly encounters between strangers. "The human threshold to homicide seems to have dropped," said the forensic psychiatrist and pointed to the increased role of alcohol consumption both among violent criminals and in the population at large. Another spur to violent action was the disorderly example set by leaders of groups of young people such as the "skinheads" and "rockers." The fear of being thought cowardly, under these circumstances, might well lead a "mentally volatile" young man into violent deeds. The professor also mentioned the exaggerated desire of some young minds for public recognition, and especially for reports in the media, as a factor that might trigger violence among volatile juveniles. Another reporter of the *Süddeutsche Zeitung* proceeded to interview some of the violent young soccer fans of TSV 1860 in order to "get to the bottom of this phenomenon." He discovered a curious subculture of violence, which he described in a lengthy feature through the first-person account of one Chelsea Andy and his friends.[1]

What is it that makes people like Chelsea Andy, a twenty-year-old Munich shoemaker, break out of their dull workaday world every Sunday during soccer season and turn the stadium into an arena for their aggressions? For ten years Andy has been a Lions fan while his soccer team slowly declined from the national league to the minors— ten years of intense intermission and after-game violence of which he now proudly considers himself a principal initiator hardened with beatings. "I am a guy who likes to brawl," he says, "I am always one of those who start it. You have to stand your ground before the fans of the other team and not back up or run even one step." He looks it, too; large gaps where his front teeth are missing, which are not worth replacing again and again, a shaven head, steel-tipped boots, and an olive flyer's jacket with club insignia, commemorative stickers, and other shiny decorations. At most games of their declining team, the fans begin to drink to drown their sorrows and this also removes their last inhibitions against aggressive violence. Some of his friends have a serious drinking problem. Many of his peers also carry swastika stickers and buttons with the neo-Nazi slogan "Out with the foreigners (*Ausländer raus*)!"

Curiously, his friends nearly all have English nicknames, such as Andy and Gary, and their informal fan clubs[2] have English names such as the Mighty Blues, Blue Soldiers, or Danger Freaks. Some thirty or forty of the Lions fans are skinheads and nearly all of them consider themselves neo-Nazis, unlike Chelsea Andy, who is an admirer of the British monarchy. He picked up his curious identification with the F.C. Chelsea of the Second League during a brief stay in England. He deeply admires the Chelsea fans for their toughness and devotion. His room is decorated with Chelsea pennants, scarves, and pins, and on occasion he will publicly profess his attachment to the British queen and bring a Union Jack to the games in Munich. This is his identity among the fans but it has never interfered with his championship of the TSV 1860.

Andy's stepfather, also a soccer devotee, threw him out over an altercation during a televised world championship in soccer years ago because Andy was cursing the German national team. Now he lives alone, with a picture of his mother on his nightstand, and claims that the TSV 1860 is father enough for him. His relationships with girl-friends are strained because they show little understanding for his violent mania. The police have gotten to know this loner well. Once they locked him up in juvenile prison and made him spend twenty-four hours cleaning the stadium. Another time he was fined first 100 and then 500 marks for illegal possession of a gas pistol. Finally, he received two weeks in jail for inflicting serious bodily injury. He was spared another two weeks because he agreed to attend a psychother-apeutic course. "Total nonsense," he said, but he attended every one of its fifteen sessions without fail, the only probationer to do so. He also recognizes the justice of his punishment and that there have to be police present at the games to watch the likes of him so that the players can continue to play until the end of each game.

Andy has a steady job and so do many of the other fans of his fan club—bank employees, painters, locksmiths. He has become less willing to risk his job "now that the police is leaning on me." He also goes less often to the games of the TSV 1860 now that the soccer team has been demoted and there is no longer the big thrill of "storming the curve" of the playing field before tens of thousands of onlookers and under the eyes of national television cameras. (In the minor leagues, many opposing teams do not have any violent fans.) He and other members of his group have photo albums and scrapbooks with newspaper clippings describing past violence, even tapes with the raucous cheers and jeers of the fans. Perhaps the time has come for Andy to settle down to adult life after all.

ROLLERBALL OR RIGHT-WING VIOLENCE?

To a social scientist accustomed to thinking of political violence in purposive terms, these tales of a violent subculture that evidently accounts for a significant element of neofascists in West Germany and other European countries may come as a surprise. Could the yen for violence be the cause, and extremist politics only a means to an end? Perhaps it depends on the persons involved: in the world of these rowdy soccer fans, their violence is not at all focused on a recognizable political enemy or object, but rather seems a purpose in itself. Occasionally they may vent their violence on foreign "guest workers" or Southeast Asian refugees,[3] not unlike assaults by skinheads on Pakistanis or Jamaicans in Great Britain. Sometimes it is the police who become targets of physical attack but, as we have seen, the likes of Chelsea Andy recognize the need for the restraining tactics of the police and seem to be in basic agreement with the state's aim of keeping order. In the last analysis, the violent propensities of soccer fans clearly grow out of rather private feelings and frustrations: a lonely fatherless youth, a sense of powerlessness and *anomie*, a hunger for comrades and love, and a thirst for recognition by the great big world in brief moments of glory. From all this, rank aggression appears to be triggered by the ritual violence of the game, by the desire to see one's team win at any price, and by the presence of a huge audience in the soccer stadium and at television sets all over the country. These factors seem to galvanize a person's private unhappiness and feelings of worthlessness, possibly into a very public happening, which may even serve as a vicarious release for thousands of spectators as well.

A few years ago, a futuristic motion picture, *Rollerball*, presented a society in which the blood lust and aggressiveness of the populace was continually satisfied by watching a very violent, competitive ball game. The underlying assumption of *Rollerball* was the presence of pent-up aggressiveness both in the public and in the gladiators of the game. But before we can relate the presence of many German National Democratic party (NPD) members among the soccer rowdies to the blood sport of after-game or intermission brawls,[4] we need to set it into the context of the postwar history of the radical right in West Germany. There is no need to retell this history in any great detail, nor is it easy to do so, considering the rapid succession of numbers of small groups, would-be leaders, and ideological variants over the years. The major outlines of right-wing developments and changes should suffice for our purpose as long as they are set into proper relation to the horrendous crimes and catastrophic fall of the Third Reich which, of course, overshadows everything the German radical right thinks and does to this day. Considering the emphasis of this book on the relationship of ideology to political violence, however, it is rather important to perceive the wide range of ideological factions and the competition among them. Nazi doctrines and attempts to defend the Nazi record have long occupied a decreasing role on the West German far right, as the aging principals die off and younger generations seek to overcome the fatal bane.

For our purposes, also, it is equally important to distinguish the more ideologically oriented cultural or sectarian groups and their publications and activities from political, electoral, or violent organizations. While it is true that the right-wing ideologies continue to weave the cloth for what may be at some time in the future another set of storm trooper uniforms, they are rather unlikely to engage in the political violence we seek to explain. The young militants, say, of the Young National Democrats (JN) neither belong among the ideologues nor do they make any contribution to the working out of the ideological doctrines. In fact, as we shall see, they often oppose or rebel against their elders in the NPD and the other organizations of the "old right," and feel frustrated by the attempts of their elders to stay within the rather restrictive laws that the Federal Republic imposes on extremist organizations.

A BRIEF HISTORY OF THE RADICAL RIGHT

The history of the West German radical right after the collapse and denouement of the Third Reich begins with the end of the Allied occupation, which had placed emphatic controls on all political activities suspected of a neo-Nazi character. To be sure, there were large numbers of incorrigibles among the West German remainder of some ten million card-carrying members of the Nazi party.[5] Some politicians and parties, moreover, were espousing beliefs that bordered on or were not easy to separate from national socialism. In particular, the Lower Saxonian German party (DP) and a national-conservative German Right party (DRP) in the fifties included many politicians and followers of this description who legitimized their representation in legislative organs with declarations of loyalty to the democratic constitution. Nevertheless, it was from these two parties that a radical, antidemocratic, neo-Nazi party arose immediately following the founding of the Federal Republic—the Socialist Reich party (SRP)—which soon became the first in a wave of assaults on the diffident new republic. The SRP partisans were motivated, they said, by a sense of oppression by war crimes and denazification trials and their earlier exclusion from political life. In a short time they gathered some ten thousand members and polled up to 5 percent in several states, mostly from among unemployed German ethnic refugees, World War II veterans, and those punished by denazification courts.[6] When the SRP finally received 11 percent of the vote in the state elections of Lower Saxony in 1951, the federal government filed suit and the Federal Constitutional Court suppressed it as a neo-Nazi party "hostile to the constitution" and led overwhelmingly by former Nazis.[7]

The SRP debacle discouraged and disoriented the radical right for a decade[8] while the Federal Republic succeeded beyond everyone's wildest dreams in achieving political consolidation under Adenauer. Its "economic miracle" helped to indemnify and integrate into West German society many millions of refugees and others who had suffered great damage as a result of the war.[9] A gaggle of right-wing splinter groups, including the German Reich party (also DRP) continued to contest federal and state elections, but with diminishing returns. In 1959 the Constitutional Protection Office in Bonn still counted 56,200 members of 85 right-wing groups (including 17,200 in 8 parties). In 1963 there were only 24,600 members in 123 groups, including 9,700 in 14 parties. This splintering on the right, moreover, was accompanied by an increase in nationalistic elements and rhetoric in such government parties as the DP, the Free Democrats (FDP), and the Christian Democrats (CDU/CSU). A short-lived moderate refugee party (BHE) also helped to tie the ten million Eastern ethnic refugees, whose irredentist potential had long been feared, to their new abode in West Germany. It was thus not until late 1963, after the end of the Adenauer era, that the radical right found a new lease on political life with the "Bremen model" of a coalition of the local Reich party, the DP, and the remainders of the refugee party (BHE/All-German People's party) which together overcame the 5 percent minimum of German electoral law. A year later, the same elements joined to form the NPD (National Democratic party), which in a few years rose to a high point of 28,000 members and 4.3 percent (1.422 million votes) of the popular vote in the federal elections of 1969.[10]

Whether the NPD at its high-water mark was a party of the "national right" or a neo-Nazi party is still a matter of controversy, especially among groups of the German "New Right." What is more important are the questions of context: The NPD was the first radical right party that seems to have gone beyond the old ex-Nazi, veteran, and refugee clientele and to have gathered a social and economic protest vote from many sources. In reflection of the recession of 1966/1967, it attracted many independents, Protestant farmers, and white-collar voters and, in each state, whoever seemed unhappy with the state government in office. It also reflected dissatisfaction with the "grand coalition" government in Bonn although surveys disclosed that as many as 80 percent of the NPD voters were not in principle against the West German democratic system.[11] Most significant for our purposes here is the fact that the rise of the NPD coincided with the dramatic increase in political participation by Germans in general, and with the much larger challenge of an increasingly violent "extra-parliamentary opposition (APO)" and student movement from the left. While the older and more conservative generation in the NPD may have reacted to the left-wing challenge in a stereotypical way, younger groups picked up a somewhat different and divisive message: They began to learn from the left how to organize in cadres, "basis groups," action commandos, and to seek violent confrontations at universities and at the local level.

MILITANT ACTION

The NPD itself, however, no longer stood to gain much from this learning process. Even its violent *Ordnerdienst* squads who were to protect NPD rallies and disrupt those of rival parties in the 1969 elections merely brought to mind distasteful comparisons with the storm troopers of four decades earlier.[12] This opprobrium, together with official intervention, hastened the decline of both the NPD vote and its membership, not to mention opening up fissures among the ever-present factions of the German radical right. In a last fling, in the fall of 1970, the party started a militant *Aktion Widerstand,* meaning resistance against the Eastern policies of Willy Brandt, which generated a big rally in Bonn—like the old nationalist mass rallies of Weimar—and regional demonstrations, all of which resulted in violent excesses, disruptions, and "direct action" by uncontrollable Young National Democratic (JN) groups and other right-wing militants. The faltering NPD, after a few months, once more backed away from its own campaign, leaving the young militants to react with violent out-

bursts of impotent frustration.[13] Elsewhere in this book, this phenomenon of how a dying movement generates militant violence has been
identified as the "fire sale theory" of political violence. The fire of the
movement is out and the disappointed militants embark on highly
destructive, even suicidal and quixotic actions to rekindle it. But their
desperate violence really sullies and cheapens whatever constructive
left- or right-wing political ideals and actions may have inspired them
before. The turn of a radical political movement in decline to scat-
tershot violence is thus in a sense its final sellout, a fire sale of ruined
noble intentions.

The decline of the NPD continued throughout the 1970s, and so
did the turn of the radical right to violence. By 1978 its membership
had shrunk to 9,000, one-third of what it had been in 1968, while
there arose innumerable small militant groups totaling about 1,000
activists, including 150 to 200 bent on violent action. The NPD still
contests many elections, but only as a way of keeping the faltering
organization going, not to win seats. When it launches a provocative
slogan, such as "Out with the foreigners," as it did in the 1980 federal
elections, a grand alliance of all democratic parties, the churches, the
media, and the trade unions condemns it in no uncertain terms.
Individual extremist actions of the radical right mushroomed, however,
and ranged from defacing Jewish cemeteries and synagogues, or painting swastikas on public walls, to illegal possession of weapons or explosives.[14] In 1978 the first neo-Nazi raids and holdups occurred to
secure weapons, ammunition, or money. There have been many pros-
ecutions for similar offenses since the government also found itself
prohibiting neo-Nazi meetings, reunions, and rallies on many occasions. One of the best sources for a record of neo-Nazi activities is
the *Allgemeine Jüdische Wochenzeitung,* which not only reports on de-
faced cemeteries and houses of worship but also on other anti-Semitic
incidents, the actions and appearances of prominent ex-Nazis, SS
reunions, and right-wing publications and utterances.[15] Reading even
just one year's collection of such incidents in the late seventies is a
sobering experience.

Who are the young activists who have been taking the initiative from the "old right" NPD? In January 1972 the Bavarian state
NPD convention became the focus for kicking off a new, "national-
revolutionary" secession group, the Action of the New Right (ANR),
which soon fell short again of the expectations of its young followers:
In 1974, they replaced it with first one, then two new groups, the
National Revolutionary Construction Organization (NRAO), and
then the "socialist" Cause of the People (SdV) with about a thousand
members, and the Solidaristic People's Movement with only a
hundred. These groups, while new, have roots in the 1950s and in

the New Right groups of the sixties. Among the older roots is a spin-off from Otto Strasser's German Social Union (DSU), the Independent Workers Party (UAP) of 1961, and Hamburg publications such as *Young Forum* and *Fragments*. In the mid-sixties, moreover, several Berlin groups formed to oppose the New Left challenge from which they also took on the cadre and "base group" form, the antiestablishment posture, the action orientation of the left, and even a non-Marxist kind of "socialism."[16] These leftist New Right groups cooperated for a while with the NPD, supplying something of an NPD left wing while railing against the "reactionary NPD clique" which had no appreciation for "socialism" and, in some notable respects, still seemed to be in the thrall of the old Nazi philosophy. The NPD left even won out in a few state parties while the "old right" continued to control the NPD elsewhere until the dramatic secessions of 1972 and 1974.

IDEOLOGY AND BELIEFS

What do these groups stand for, and what relation does it bear to their actions? The older postwar movements such as the SRP in a way were easier to understand because much of what they wanted centered around undoing denazification punishments and restoring what had been taken from them in property, freedom, or civic rights.[17] This and the attempted defense of their past record are more pragmatic undertakings than pure ideological quests. Many of the pronouncements of radical right parties in West Germany have to be taken with more than a grain of salt anyway because they have to be careful to avoid prosecution for advocating war or expressing hostility toward other nations or minorities. Right-wing politicians and publications are thus wary of expressing the virulent antiforeign (especially "guest worker") or anti-Semitic feelings many of them seem to have. If these prejudices were not present, there would not be such a profusion of aggressive actions as are reported in the press. Right-wingers may even engage in highly misleading talk assuring the object of their prejudice of their goodwill.[18]

The ideology of the NPD has been described as consisting of the following elements: (1) historical national egotism, including the rejection of all criticism of German responsibility for World War II and the conduct thereof; (2) statism, or state absolutism; (3) biological determinism and race collectivism; (4) a mixture of corporatism and plebiscitary democracy; and (5) cultural pessimism.[19] These issues are not far from orthodox Nazi views and policies, but some of the positions of the New Right seem to give them a modern gloss: racism now may be called "ethnopluralism" which, however, denies the universality of

humankind on an allegedly scientific basis. The prejudice against foreign workers is rationalized as a fear that the Germans may be biologically overwhelmed by alien races. Then there are some new, or
not so new elements, such as the movement for a "European nation,"[20]
perhaps *déjà vu* as the "defense of the occident" against alien intrusions
from the Soviet Union or America. The New Right even speaks of a
"European socialism," meaning apparently a solidaristic *Volksgemein-
schaft* of all Europeans.

There are also some entirely new issues which especially the New
Right groups have in common with the New Left. Their hostility
toward the establishment, the older generation, and the bourgeoisie
has already been mentioned. They also take a dim view of consumer
society, of manipulation by the media and by *Fachidioten* (narrow
experts), and of capitalism. Their "base groups" also produce and
distribute political leaflets, agonize over questions of how "theory and
practice" are best combined, and have been known to make up protest
songs.[21] Most strikingly, the New Right developed an early interest
in ecology and environmental issues. In 1968 and 1970, the Hamburg
New Right became involved in organizing environmental protests and
a citizen initiative. In 1978 its small Solidaristic People's Movement
(SVB) was instrumental in the foundation of the Green List Environment (GLU),[22] one of the antecedents of the national Green party
of 1979. The larger Cause of the People (SdV) also got into the
ecological act trying to counter the *Bunte Liste/Wehrt Euch* (Colorful
List/Defend Yourselves) of left-wing elements such as gay, feminist,
and communist K-groups. Günter Bartsch, writing in 1975 or earlier,
had already said:

> The ecological question is like a volcano. If it erupts, its glowing lava
> could flow all over the Federal Republic, over Berlin, even the DDR.[23]

In the meantime, the ecological volcano has indeed erupted in the
form of the Green party, which includes elements running the gamut
from the K-groups to the New Right. The latter has long gone on
record as being against the fetish of economic growth and profit,
against the "automobile society," and against nuclear plants.[24]

Finally, and very intriguing in the context of this book, leaders of
the New Right have departed a considerable distance from the approach of the old right to nationality questions. There is still common
ground on the "national liberation" of Greater Germany, which would
include East and West Germany, Austria, and probably some further
areas as well for they all tend to be Pan-Germans. Many New Right
leaders in fact are ethnic German refugees from Latvia, Silesia, Danzig,
or East Germany. But then they also admire the Provisional IRA, to
their minds the quintessential national liberation movement in a coun-

try "divided and occupied" like their own. They are also favorably impressed by the Basque, Breton, and Corsican movements, which are on the far left, as well as by the Flemish and most Eastern European national movements, including that of Russia. Leszek Kolakowski's call for the liberation of enslaved Eastern European peoples has caught their fancy and they commiserate with the Czechs, Hungarians, and Poles against Soviet intervention.[25] The New Right groups often maintain contacts with Eastern European exile organizations and, in Munich, support a Club Symonenko—named after a Ukrainian nationalist poet—which agitates for the national liberation of Ukrainians, Poles, and the Irish.

THE TURN TO VIOLENCE

The discussion of the beliefs of the German radical right has given few clues to how or why some of them became violent. It is difficult with most of these issues even to think of a direct course of action unless, of course, it be in collaboration with a militant left-wing group. It is possible to imagine that the admirers of the IRA might try to emulate IRA violence directed at the "Soviet occupation power" of East Germany or its domestic communist collaborators. There have been some minor assaults on the Berlin Wall and a lot of slogans printed on other walls about it. There have also been the sometimes violent actions of the *Aktion Widerstand* against Brandt's policies of reconciliation with the East as well as the March on Bonn and the anti-Brandt demonstrations of 1972. The New Right also likes to put on memorial rallies to commemorate days of East German oppression, such as June 17 or August 13.[26] But these are rarely occasions of serious confrontation because they are also sanctioned by the government (especially June 17) and the media.

In May of 1970, when Chancellor Brandt met the East German premier, Willi Stoph, in Kassel,[27] the network of base groups of the New Right went into action against the hapless East German visitors after the NPD had already decided to leave the scene of the confrontation. The young militants, augmented by other right-wing demonstrators, resolved to stay and some 2,000 of them effectively blocked Premier Stoph for hours from depositing a wreath at the monument for the victims of fascism. They claimed later that the victims of Stalinism should have been honored as well. A handful of the demonstrators also managed to pull down the flag of East Germany, which was displayed to honor the visitor, and to tear it into pieces. "Unheard-of Provocations," read the headlines of the official East German communist daily *Neues Deutschland.* The city police of Kassel and the West German government were deeply embarrassed by their inability to cope with the large numbers of demonstrators of the far right and the far left. The right-wing demonstrators were bloodied but victorious in the trilateral showdown with the police and the left-wing demonstrators for diplomatic recognition of the East German republic.

Finally, the New Right may also have engaged in some violent encounters in connection with citizen initiatives for environmental issues, against freeway construction in Hamburg, rent gouging, and land speculation. Most German citizen initiatives do not involve violence, but there are some, both urban and in connection with nuclear plants, that have led to massive clashes between demonstrators and police. Just as in the confrontations with the "extraparliamentary opposition" (APO) and the SDS, a lively or possibly violent police antagonist could involve New Right groups in violence in spite of their propolice attitudes. Judging from some accounts, the number of violent incidents is lower today than in the seventies, but there is a more covert, terroristic strain that is independent of confrontations and far more deadly. One is already somewhat skeptical of statements claiming that New Right followers "are not the type to desecrate Jewish cemeteries or engage in pathological anti-Semitism."[28] A look at the rising tide of left-wing terrorist acts in the mid-seventies (1974–1977) and at the running log of the *Allgemeine Jüdische Wochenzeitung* confirms one's suspicions. There have been too many anti-Semitic incidents, including some in the German army and its staff colleges, which went far beyond bad taste or youthful high spirits.

The press of the extreme right declined slightly in weekly circulation (159,700 from 174,300) between 1979 and 1980 which, however, did not keep the publisher of the *Deutsche Nationalzeitung* (100,000 circulation), Frey, from catering to all shadings of right-wing opinion. In fact, his new political party, the German People's Union (DVU) soon surpassed the declining NPD in size after incorporating Frey's People's Movement for a German Amnesty (for Nazi crimes) and his Initiative for a Limit on Foreign Workers. The NPD, to be sure, still had a reasonably successful paper, *Deutsche Stimme,* although its membership, by 1981, was down to 7,200 and its organization in debt and, according to the Constitutional Protection Office, "so desolate it is impossible to give precise figures." The entire radical right and some Christian Democrats were united in pushing a campaign against foreigners, guest workers, and seekers of political asylum, differentiated only by the severity of barriers and sanctions they wished to impose on these people in the wake of the second oil crisis of 1979.

THE MILITANT HARD CORE

There are also a handful of extremely violent groups of "militants or weapons fetishists" (Hans-Josef Horchem), who at times seem to act in concert. Among them are the Military Sports Group Hoffmann of

Nuremberg with whom the Oktoberfest bomber of 26 September 1980 was indirectly connected. "A caricature of a nationalist-military organization," according to Horchem, the Hoffmann group is quite capable of killing and destruction. The same seems to be true of the Action Front of National Socialists (ANS),[29] of Michael Kühnen, another former federal army officer, or the Viking Youth whose goals have been described by the Constitutional Protection Office in Bonn as "youth training by means of camping trips, encampments, social meetings, and military training." During their camping trips, members of the Viking Youth have been overheard chanting lines such as "Blood must flow as thick as a stick, we shit on the freedom of the Federal Republic." In 1978, 120 members of ANS and Viking Youth met in a village in Schleswig-Holstein under the motto "Justice for Adolf Hitler" to unveil a memorial plaque to the dictator. A policeman, who tried to close down the illegal meeting, was met with cries of rage and thrown objects, one of which, a heavy ashtray, split open his scalp. He returned with twenty officers to the swastika-festooned tavern and, after a free-for-all with the young militants, many of whom wore black shirts, steel-tipped boots, and old German army helmets, the police withdrew with bloodied heads. The police returned a third time with reinforcements, now with helmets and truncheons against the knives, iron bars, and legs of chairs and tables, not to mention heavy beer mugs of the neo-Nazis. In the end, there were five people injured and the police arrested ANS chief Michael Kühnen and nineteen militants all of whom were released the next day while the prosecutor was still investigating charges.

The ANS, like the Miltary Sports Group Hoffmann in northern Bavaria, is known for intensive military training, and is suspected of being a terrorist organization. One of its members, on whose property the military training took place, was charged with raiding an army depot and forming a terrorist group, another with participation in the same raid—presumably to procure weapons and explosives—and with a bank robbery modeled on the way the terrorist left obtained money. Other members were arrested in Kiel with a large collection of weapons and a plan to raid another army depot for explosives with which to blow up the Kiel office of the Communist Federation (KBW). At first glance, all of this may sound like a replay of the latter days of the Weimar Republic except that, this time, the German extreme right, far from having over ten million voters behind it, is reduced to being on the fringe and to a typical reaction of impotent rage: terrorism.[30]

In 1979, finally, ANS/NA (National Activists) leader Kühnen was sentenced to a four-year prison term for incitement to racism and glorification of violence. While in prison, he wrote more than a thousand letters to his followers who, in a kangaroo court in 1981, executed a gay ANS/NA member who had just visited him and was thought to be a traitor. The organization included about 270 members, but was believed defunct when the self-styled successor of the führer was released in 1982 on condition that he neither employ, train, nor shelter neo-Nazis. He reconstituted the ANS/NA as a cadre group, nevertheless, and it was finally banned in 1983.[31] The Military Sports Group Hoffmann was suppressed in 1980 and Hoffmann himself has been in investigative custody in connection with the 1980 murder of the Jewish publisher Shlomo Levin and his companion. Hoffmann's group had also been suspected of involvement with the Oktoberfest bombing of 1980 on which I shall still comment, but the link could not be proven. Another neo-Nazi group banned in 1982 was the People's Socialist Movement of Germany, linked with the New Right Party of Labor (VBD/PDA) and headed by Friedhelm Busse. Busse's organization had been involved in an October 1981 shootout with police in which two people were killed and two more injured. Busse, fifty-four, was sentenced to three years and nine months for aiding and abetting a crime, sheltering neo-Nazi bank robbers, accepting DM 8,000 of their loot, and keeping an arms and explosives cache in his garage. Four other neo-Nazi bank robbers, including members of a French terrorist group, Omega, received prison sentences of between three and seven years. While in custody, two of them reportedly became extreme left-wingers.[32] Early in 1983, five Busse men were arrested for bomb attacks on U.S. soldiers.

These militant neo-Nazi groups all receive support and copious propaganda material from some American Nazis, especially one Gary Lauck and his organization in Lincoln, Nebraska. According to official reports, there were 52 acts of neo-Nazi violence in 1983, including arson, armed assault and robbery, and property damage. There were 1,400 known neo-Nazis, including 300 regarded as militants. These figures represent a modest increase from the 1,300 neo-Nazis of record in 1982, when about 850 were organized in groups and 250 were regarded as lone activists without known group backing.[33] There can be no doubt that right-wing terrorism in the Federal Republic is increasing again at the same time that political right-wing activities, with an estimated 20,000 members in various organizations, have not really expanded as expected under a conservative administration.[34] Left-wing terrorism, from which the neo-Nazi militants seemed to have learned so much in the late 1970s, has also been relatively quiet in recent years.

CARNAGE AT THE OKTOBERFEST

We have saved the Oktoberfest bombing on 26 September 1980 for the end because it appears to be generically different from most of the rest, except for some neofascist parallels in Italy. There had been a spate of antiforeign (guest worker, or Southeast Asian refugee) bombings earlier in 1980, which were attributed to the Deutsche Aktionsgruppen (German Action Groups),[35] and which led to arrests. At the same time, their shadowy leader, Manfred Roeder, was caught. A former CDU member and attorney who used to crusade against pornography, his German Citizens Initiative collects contributions for the right wing. In one of these bombings, two Southeast Asian refugees were burned to death with Molotov cocktails, a poignant end to a year of heated public debate over the granting of political asylum to large numbers of refugees by the federal government in Bonn. The Oktoberfest bombing involved a large pipe bomb placed in a trash receptacle at the main entrance to the festival grounds and at a time, 10:20 P.M., when large numbers of revelers of both sexes, all ages, and probably all political colors were likely to be in the process of leaving in dense crowds through the Oktoberfest gate. Whatever his true intention may have been, the bomber evidently made one mistake with his device. He accidentally set it off in his hands or miscalculated the time of explosion and thus killed himself along with 12 others, not to mention 219 injured passersby. At the moment of the explosion, people within 50 yards were thrown to the ground. Parts of bodies flew through the air and there were large pools of blood under the fallen.

The elaborate police investigations were not able to find any signs of collaborators or conspirators beyond the fact that the perpetrator, a geology student named Gundolf Köhler, had at one time been a member of the Hoffmann group.[36] At the age of fifteen, according to former fellow students, the introverted Köhler had begun to show interest in right-wing politics. (His father is a farmer and former local CDU chairman.) The young man also collected handguns and experimented with explosives which, on one occasion, led to an accidental explosion that gave him facial injuries. As a teenager, he also participated twice in Hoffmann's military exercises and, as an army recruit, asked Hoffmann's help in starting a Hoffmann affiliate in his hometown of Donaueschingen. After graduating from the *Gymnasium,* he volunteered to join the army where he hoped to become an explosives expert (*Sprengmeister*) but had to drop out after three months with ear trouble. Hoffmann apparently told the nineteen-year-old to join a Hoffmann student group, the University Circle of Tübingen Students (HTS), which was known for brutal confrontations with left-wing students, as on the occasion of an HTS rally for friends of the Union of South Africa when a leather-jacketed Hoffmann squad severely injured six counterdemonstrators. At HTS meetings, Köhler must have been exposed to the group's unabashed racist ideology, anticommunism, and a military romanticism reminiscent of the Weimar Freecorps irregulars. The group also became known for its strident

hostility to gays, feminists, and "politicized women," and for its call
for a strongman who would overcome Western "weakness and decadence" and defend Germany forcefully "with tooth and claws," such
as Franz Josef Strauss.

There is a notable difference here between the stress on political
ideology in the HTS and the stress on weapons, explosives, and soldierly camaraderie in the original Hoffmann group, and it is difficult
to say which of the two may have influenced the dead bomber more.
Unlike the elitist student group, the Hoffmann group rather emphasized a proletarian image, and there was plenty of talk about, and even
instruction on, the use of various kinds of bombs—including pipe
bombs—napalm, and Molotov cocktails. In 1976, a nineteen-year-
old Hoffmann acolyte suffered serious injuries in an unsuccessful attempt to blow up the American Forces Network station in Munich.
Hoffmann himself had been busy trying to move army surplus vehicles
across the German-Austrian border for sale in the Middle East at the
time of the Oktoberfest massacre; that was his alibi. He also called it
"senseless to direct a bomb at an amorphous mass of people—unless
one wanted to blame it on somebody else."[37] Since the bombing took
place on the eve of a major election in which one prominent issue
was the campaign against Federal Minister of the Interior Gerhart
Baum for allegedly being "soft on terrorism," this is not an implausible
motive in itself. The question is one of conspiracy—of which there
is no evidence—or whether this particular suspect was capable of such
a monstrous deed for dubious gains by himself.[38]

Interviews with the suspect's family, in particular his three brothers,
predictably produced skeptical denials of most of the circumstantial
evidence. Even Köhler's teenage radicalism was described by them as
"purely verbal" and his contacts with the Hoffmann group, at age
sixteen, as two weekend campouts allegedly followed by deep disillusionment with the brutality of the group. According to his brothers,
he became rather unpolitical as he grew up and in the last state
elections voted for the Green party. He drove to the Oktoberfest simply
to have a good time, they claimed, and the reason he was found to
have no blood alcohol was his conscientious attitude. He never drank
while driving his parents' automobile. Press interviews with neighbors,
teachers, and acquaintances in Donaueschingen produced other dimensions of disbelief. Most people described him as small and rather
ordinary, but shy and closemouthed. Local newspaper editors related
his numerous efforts to place with them articles about his small geo-
logical discoveries and minor local events, none of them political. No
one remembered his talking about politics or showing favor to any
political color. Did this loner have a great need, given his shyness,
to draw personal recognition by seeing himself in print? His fling with

the Hoffmann group, or with right-wing politics, seems to have escaped everyone's attention except for the Constitutional Protection Office.[39] Donaueschingen has no NPD local and no other known right-wing groups. Is it possible that this young closet neo-Nazi harbored a volcano of destructive feelings that hardly anyone ever glimpsed? His Gymnasium German teacher over three years, a local SPD politician himself, thought it "totally unimaginable that [Köhler] would think of such an idea [the bombing] by himself. He was not the type."

Assuming the known facts to be correct, what can we make of such an improbable wimp of a political mass murderer? The most obvious comparisons for his deed are with the Bologna railway station bombing and similar stunts of Italian neofascists, but there is very little known about the perpetrators and their motives. The Oktoberfest and Bologna outrages differ from most other neofascist violence described above in that they were not aimed in their direct impact at any persons marked as targets of hatred by right-wing ideology, such as foreigners, left-wingers, or Jews, Russians, or Americans, or functionaries of the hated democratic system. To speak with the distinctions made in chapter 1, above,[40] the actual victims made little sense and the "symbolic addressee" was unknown. If Köhler had not been pinpointed as the perpetrator by the signs of the explosion on both hands and clothes, even the neo-Nazi character of the deed would be in doubt. The only parallels that come to mind are cases of nonpolitical, multiple killers such as Charles J. Whitman, who killed sixteen people and injured another thirty-one during a 1966 shooting spree from a tower in Austin, Texas, or James O. Huberty who shot twenty-two people to death and injured fifteen in 1984 in San Ysidro, California. According to psychiatric experts, such multiple killers tend to be loners lacking friends and social networks. Frequently the victims of child abuse, they are indifferent or hostile to other people in general, and curiously detached from the human consequences of physical aggression against the people who triggered their anger—a boss that fired them, unfriendly fellow workers, family members, or former lovers. They generally have a weapons fetish and a record of previous violent encounters, going back to their childhood years, which demonstrate both their hair-trigger temper and their tendency to resort to violence. Their inability to adapt to their social environment aggravates their long pent-up anger and frustration until a particular confrontation or provocation lights the smoldering fuse.[41]

This collective portrait, aside from the killing of many innocent bystanders, actually fits quite a few of the violent persons described in this book, including a category of Weimar storm troopers I have elsewhere called "hostile militants." The hostile militant of the brownshirt hosts of the early 1930s was often a maladjusted veteran of World

War I or a sociopath with a lengthy record of violent encounters with parents, school, employers, or police, long before he became politically involved.[42] The portrait does not seem to fit Köhler very well because we know little of relevance about his personality. His father was said to be very strict but there is no record of violent encounters or confrontations. He was a loner with a weapons and explosives fetish, but nothing seems to be known about his private and political self which he hid so well from nearly everybody. The fact that, for at least the second time, he made a self-destructive mistake with explosives suggests a suicidal streak.[43] If he was abused as a child by his father, elder brothers, or peers, this would not be that unusual in German culture. But it is really the weapons and explosive fetish that marks him as a person who has worked out a way to get even with the cruel world, a secret weapon of the helpless and impotent. Like most other multiple killers he did not survive his own grandiose last stand, and the choice of victims hardly mattered to him.

WEST GERMAN YOUTH AND NEOFASCISM

Just like the Nazi storm troopers of the Weimar Republic,[44] today's neo-Nazis are generally under thirty and, in most cases, under twenty-five, which makes them about the same ages as the much larger Peace movement and ecological (Green) protesters.[45] By now, there are few active old Nazis left as compared with the days of the SRP or even the NPD, that is, during the first quarter century after the fall of the Third Reich, and this makes contemporary neo-Nazism very much of a youth and generational phenomenon rather than one of an older generation trying to explain away its monstrous crimes. The huge wave of youth mobilization for nuclear disarmament and against the environmental threats of an urban-industrial society since the late seventies shows that German youth in general is, once more, on the march for political and existential causes. The cross-connections of some New Right groups to ecological movements and, in some cases, to the neutralism and latent nationalism of the peace and ecology movements, only highlights the overwhelming presence of the latter on the youth scene in West Germany. As compared with the peace and ecology mobilization—and even as compared with earlier, political movements of the radical right—the neo-Nazi activists are a small isolated phenomenon indeed. And yet there are broader strata of youthful opinion behind them that should give pause to anyone belittling the significance of this noxious phenomenon.

Recent surveys have given us alarming glimpses of how increasing numbers of young Germans view their own democratic system—the neo-Nazis call it their *Scheissdemokratie*—and various right-wing slogans. A 1979 survey of teenagers in the Frankfurt area presented the respondents with a list of right-wing radical slogans such as "ratifying the Eastern treaties[46] means losing our freedom" or "race mixing ought to be outlawed," which found favor with one out of ten, and at least some support from one-fourth of the mostly thirteen- to sixteen-year-olds. Two-fifths agreed with the NPD slogan "German jobs for German workers," with the proposed reintroduction of the death penalty, and with barring communists from teaching in the public schools. Nearly half endorsed the slogan "Stop the red murder mob *(Schluss mit dem roten Mördergesindel)*," a reference to left-wing terrorists. While the choice of issues and slogans is not beyond criticism (can we really expect a mature attitude toward interracial liaisons from sexually immature youngsters?),[47] it does highlight a certain receptivity to right-wing propaganda at a time when the public was exposed to the showing on German television of *Holocaust,* the parliamentary debate about lifting the statutory limits on Nazi crimes, and the trial of SS guards of the Nazi concentration camp Maidanek. Another survey in 1980 of the Emnid Institute disclosed that 7 percent of adult Germans would be prepared to vote for another Hitler.[48] A study of unemployed youths by the Saarbrücken Institute for Social Research revealed that 35 percent of the respondents felt "democracy did not do them any good."[49] A 1982 survey by *Der Spiegel* newsmagazine finally turned up no less than 7 percent (15% among the Greens) of adults who said they were prepared to use violence against persons and another 19 percent (39% among the Greens) who would use violence "against things" to protest alleged injustices. Only 74 percent (45% among the Greens) forswore violence altogether. The figures speak for themselves: The once so quiet Germans have become volatile, and some obviously more so than others.[50]

A comparison with the genesis of the Nazi movement in the 1920s and early 1930s makes it seem implausible, of course, that a similar movement today would ever attract such mass support in Germany again. But even in the form of terrorism or of small activist groups the neo-Nazi revival is a disturbing phenomenon. As in other European countries or in the United States, even a small activist fringe on the right can cast a pall of intimidation over the media, politicians, and teachers who happen to be singled out for vandalism or verbal or physical attack by the disturbed minds on the right. Worse yet, the whole fabric of public opinion can become distorted when wild charges are thrown—*aliquid semper haeret*—or radical views suddenly become commonplace. Determined resistance and attacks by small minorities on once-accepted policies and people frequently persuade the public to yield and, in small betrayals, to lift its protecting hand from those that are now "exposed."[51] Totalitarian injustice can thus begin in small ways and without a real takeover by an extremist movement.

A RETURN TO TOTALITARIAN OBSESSIONS?

Responsible West German intellectuals, needless to add, have agonized over the implications of this broad upheaval and its violent reverberations on the extreme left and right. Already in 1977, after the (left-wing) assassination of Federal Attorney General Siegfried Buback, on his way to work, and of the chairman of the Dresdner Bank, Jürgen Ponto, at his home—not to mention the kidnapping and murder of Hanns Martin Schleyer, the head of the German Employers Association and the Institute of Industry, and the dramatic rescue operation in Mogadishu, Somalia—large numbers of erstwhile sympathizers and well-wishers of the political goals of the radical left recoiled in horror. Left-wing professors of the "critical school" disassociated themselves emphatically from the excesses of the left. Old student revolutionaries of 1968 professed a lack of understanding for the "chaotics" and "spontis" (spontaneous anarchists) of the violent "scene."

A highly respected political scientist, Kurt Sontheimer, commented on the depths of alienation among German youth, especially among university students and political engagés, which has produced terrorism, drug addiction, high suicide rates, and all manner of escapism into rural oases or sectarian subcultures: a "lost generation," youth counterculture, or "generation of the excluded," and dropouts.[52] At the same time, Professor Sontheimer is as critical of German overreaction to the menace of violence as he is of the mental habits of romanticizing the left-wing terrorist as a hero of needed social reforms, as was long common among sympathizers and in parts of the left-wing press: "Not all terrorists, by any means, are sensitive and idealistic people." The first generation of terrorists, he adds, was already not very convincing as to why the "bloody signal of terrorism" should reveal the Federal Republic as an inhuman system worthy of destruction. The second generation of left-wing terrorists has not even bothered to formulate such an argument.[53] The neo-Nazi terrorists, it would seem, are a third generation spun off from the vortex of violent left-wing action and they seem even less eager to demonstrate the legitimizing rationale of their actions.[54]

Writing after the Oktoberfest bombing of 1980, the foremost German historian of the Weimar Republic, Karl Dietrich Bracher, agreed that, to justify political violence, the terrorists of either side must be able to claim "a more profound legitimacy" than that of the Bonn Republic on their side. Their references to "being the future," and to "the people" or "the masses" ring hollow as long as the West German population showed its strong distaste for their violence.[55]

Comparing Weimar political violence with the extremist movements of Bonn, the historian undertook to characterize the typical, violent Nazi militant of the early thirties as a "warrior ready to fight for the nation's survival, and insistent on absolute internal solidarity" for the sake of this nationalist cause. The contemporary German extremists, perhaps including even the New Right (though hardly the violent neo-Nazis), Bracher characterized as social-salvational, emancipatory, socialist, and dedicated to "total democracy." For the Bonn Republic, he wrote, the early problems of neo-Nazism and the SRP were absorbed by the achievements of the Adenauer era, whereas since 1969, the great menace has been the ideology of revolutionary violence of the left.[56] To Bracher, however, the central problem is still, as it was in the 1930s, that of *totalitarian* movements and ideologies, which perpetrate the misleading fiction of identifying the leaders' will with that of the people, and obliterate all distinctions between idea and reality, or democracy and dictatorship. The totalitarian obsession justifies violence and terror and "all political terror contains totalitarian roots and motives." For the terrorist mentality demands the complete destruction of the political enemy, of compromises, and of constitutional safeguards. Bracher's reflections are meant for the totalitarian terrorists of both, the left and the right, although he rejects the label of "red fascism" by which apologists of the left have tried to expand the concept of fascism and to wash their hands of the stigma of left-wing terrorism. For fascism then, and, in half-hidden form, now, it is aggressive war and the primacy of the necessities of national survival that dominate totalitarian striving. Leninists, by way of contrast, manage to pursue worldwide revolution while advocating universal peace.[57]

THEORY AND PRACTICE?

Throughout this discussion of neofascist movements in postwar Germany, a curious dichotomy has surfaced again and again which, in a left-wing terrorist or extremist setting, may be less obvious and perhaps not even present. It began with the soccer rowdies, at least with those who are neofascist: There is no political purpose in brawling with other young soccer fans, and the raw violence and occasional use of weapons seem to be a purpose in themselves. This is not to say that the same individuals may not engage in politically motivated violence elsewhere, for example in attacks on Turks or Southeast Asian refugees, or that they may not *nonviolently* vote NPD, or participate in *nonviolent* right-wing meetings. In the various postwar right-wing movements, from the DRP and SRP to the NPD, too, violent excesses were somewhat separated from the more purposive political actions organized by the group: the individual actions were perhaps not apolitical, for right-wing ideology includes the personal antiforeign, anti-Semitic, or anticommunist prejudices. Desecrations of Jewish cemeteries and synagogues, vandalism, or attacks on foreigners and alleged "communists" are not entirely wild shots; nevertheless the particular choice of target or victim is extremely arbitrary and, in most cases, not ordered by the right-wing organization according to a well-considered strategy. It is generally a solitary act or one committed by a few inebriates, and often embarrassing to a serious right-wing group.

The rise of New Right groups on the one hand, and of neo-Nazi militant groups on the other presents yet another version of the same dichotomy. The New Right groups have been drawn into the left-wing, group-oriented patterns and, at times, even into violent actions against the police, banks, or the ecological targets of joint citizen initiatives. Some neo-Nazi militants such as the Hoffmann group, by way of contrast, are so preoccupied with weapons, explosives, and military routines that right-wing ideology seems to play second fiddle to playing war in the bogs and bushes of Franconia. They appear to be violent against opponents in almost as unpolitical, if deeply satisfying, a way as the soccer rowdies. Kühnen's ANS/NA was just as violent and, only by degrees, more political than the Hoffmann group in that it used the hoary Nazi slogans mostly to shock and antagonize. Both of these, and other militant groups, seem to be utterly absorbed in their own internal group dynamics, which have been described in terms equally reminiscent of religious communitarian cults or the homoerotic bonds of Weimar Youth Movement groups. Women seem to play no role in these militant neo-Nazi groups, certainly none comparable to the presence of women in the RAF. Some of the groups are stridently hostile to "politicized women," feminists, or gays, which casts a revealing light on the personality problems of their leaders and members.

Unfortunately we lack the detailed information we have on the Weimar storm troopers to compare with the radical right in postwar Germany. But the latter obviously presents a highly differentiated picture when we seek to examine the relationship between ideology and violence. For one thing, the very splintered existence of the postwar right in the form of numerous independent right-wing groups of varying character and beliefs leaves decisions on militant action to various small groups and even to individuals. The Weimar storm troopers, by comparison, were a centrally directed and centrally controlled paramilitary army with rare lapses of discipline.[58] There were undoubtedly some individual transgressions comparable to the postwar desecrations of Jewish cemeteries and attacks on arbitrarily chosen, not really political enemies, but probably fewer since the movement regularly provided massive outlets for group-supported aggression and prejudice. There were probably also men with a weapons or explosives fetish in it, but they were, by and large, no more permitted to indulge in private pursuits of shooting or bombing than their counterparts were in the World War I army.

Although some New Right groups may have been the only voices of the radical right (under the influence of left-wing groups) to talk about the proper relationship between theory and practice, the problem has long been well understood. Among the Weimar storm troopers and Nazi activists, there was never any doubt but that it took active involvement in the struggle to make a youth into a good militant. The theory, or ideology, was neglected or foreshortened into a few slogans, to be sure. But then the eager militant could always delegate this part to the disciplined organization, which would think for him and issue the marching orders, just as in the Imperial army during the war. In the postwar neo-Nazi groups, however, the understanding of the proper relationship between theory and practice varies widely and there is no longer a central organization of acknowledged authority to generate the theory, or issue marching orders. The armies of the right cannot even march separately and triumph together anymore. There thus remains confusion, frustration, impotent rage, and the propensity for "individual terror," or individual acts of drunken spite, which are perhaps more typical of the German neo-Nazis than the seemingly motiveless Oktoberfest bombing, or the clowning of violent, but purposeless, militant squads.

NOTES

1. See Axel Hacke, "Eine Mühlkippe für Gefühle," 29/30 January 1983, and also the *Süddeutsche Zeitung* of 24 January 1983, for the previously cited police reports.

2. These groups are not to be confused with the large official fan clubs, which do not tolerate violent actions by their members. The smaller groups are very loose although they usually do have statutes, presidents, and treasurers. Members drift in or out of the clubs in a very informal way.

3. There have been several recent cases of such violence. In 1982, a German right-wing radical went berserk in a Nuremberg bar frequented by black U.S. soldiers and shot several persons. See also below.

4. The soccer rowdies, to stay with the image of *Rollerball,* are both players and the more bloodthirsty part of the audience. Their actions, in a manner of speaking, demonstrate the aggressiveness of both game and audience.

5. According to estimates, there were still seven million ex-Nazis left in 1982, including about five million in the Federal Republic. A former member, after forty democratic years and considering the frequently opportunistic or compulsory nature of party membership in the Third Reich, is not necessarily still a Nazi today in any case.

6. See especially *Rechtsradikalismus im Nachkriegsdeutschland: Studien ueber die SRP,* by Otto Büsch and Peter Furth, Schriften des Instituts für Politische Wissenschaft no. 9 (Berlin: Vahlen, 1957), pp. 10–19, 95.

7. The West German constitution specifically provides for such cases although most observers believe, in retrospect, that it would have been better to ignore the SRP until it (possibly) declined by itself. The Federal government also instituted a "constitutional protection office" as part of its Federal Criminal Office—generally law enforcement is a subject of state jurisdiction—as early as March, 1951.

8. For a wide-ranging survey of the organizations and publications of the far right in the fifties, see Manfred Jenke, *Verschwörung von rechts?* (Berlin: Colloquium, 1961).

9. Aside from the absorption by a booming economy, there were also the Equalization of Burdens (1952) and the pension reforms of the late 1950s while the conservative rhetoric of the Adenauer government and German rearmament and integration into the Western alliance anticipated other right-wing criticisms.

10. This high point was reached between 1967 and 1969 when the NPD also garnered between 5% and 10% of the vote and seats in one state election after the other. By 1972 the surge had passed. The party only received 0.6% in the federal elections and lost its last Landtag seats in Baden-Wuerttemberg where its 1968 vote had been 9.8%. Of the large literature on the NPD, one of the best accounts is by Lutz Niethammer, *Angepasster Faschismus. Politische Praxis der NPD* (Frankfurt: Fischer, 1969), where the relationship between the party and various kinds of Third Reich personnel is discussed (pp. 32–55). But see also Hans Maier and Gerhard Bott, *Die NPD—Struktur and Idologie einer "nationalen Rechtspartei"* (Munich: Piper, 1968) and Iring Fetscher et al., *Rechtsradikalismus* (Frankfurt: EVA, 1967). In English, there is John D. Nagle, *The National Democratic Party: Right Radicalism in the Federal Republic of Germany* (Berkeley, Los Angeles, London: University of California Press, 1970), and *Rightwing Radicalism and Rightwing Extremism in the Federal Republic of Germany* (Bonn: Inter Nationes, 1968), which contains documentation of the overwhelming presence of ex-Nazis in the NPD leadership (p. 11). Of the membership, 35% are said to have belonged to either the former Reich party or other right-wing parties (including SRP), or were ex-Nazis.

11. See also Erwin K. Scheuch, H. D. Klingemann, and Thomas A. Herz, *Die NPD in den Landtagswahlen 1966–1968,* Institut für vergleichende Sozialforschung, Universität Köln (in manuscript); Willibald Fink, *Die NPD bei der Bayerischen Landtagswahl 1966* (Munich: Obzog, 1969); and Hans Dieter Klingemann and F. U. Pappi, *Politischer Radikalismus* (Munich: Oldenbourg, 1972).

12. See Niethammer, pp. 244, 267.

13. See Hans-Josef Horchem, *Extremisten in einer selbstbewussten Demokratie* (Freiburg: Herder, 1975), pp. 67–68. In the end, NPD chairman Adolf von Thadden resigned and was replaced by Martin Mussgnug in November 1971, only months before the secession of the Action New Right (ANR).

14. The figures were supplied by the Federal Ministry of the Interior for the year 1977. The ministry also reported that there were 448 public employees known to be of the radical right, down from 533 in 1976. Right-wing extremist actions under investigation doubled from 319 in 1976 to 616 outrages in 1977.

15. See Alphons Silbermann, *Sind wir Anti-Semiten?* (Köln: Wissenschaft und Politik, 1982), pp. 151–202, for 50 pages of excerpts from one year of this weekly, September 1977 to October 1978.

16. For details, see Günter Bartsch, *Revolution von rechts?* (Freiburg: Herder, 1975), pp. 93–114. Bartsch also supplies a telling account of how the "national revolutionaries" at the Ruhr University at Bochum became involved in founding the Republican Student Federation (RSB) in order to fight off the Socialist Student Federation (SDS) in physical combat during an attempted SDS lockout, and how the right-wingers adopted "Marxist terminology" to fight the SDS (pp. 134–136).

17. A majority of the founders came directly from imprisonment resulting from trials. See Büsch and Furth, pp. 17 ff. A common denazification ruling for heavily implicated Nazis stripped them of offices, industrial property, and the right to vote or stand for public office.

18. See, for example, Bartsch, pp. 45 f. There are eery memories also in calls combining the expulsion of foreign workers with the repatriation of German ethnics all over the world," *heim ins Reich.*" Ibid., pp. 56 ff.

19. See, for example, Funk, p. 21, or Nagle, chap. 4.

20. See Bartsch, pp. 86–90.

21. See Bartsch, pp. 126–127.

22. See Karl-Heinz Pröhuber, *Die national-revolutionäre Bewegung* (Hamburg: Verlag Deutsch-europäische Studien, 1980), pp. 145–157. See also the "green" title pages of New Right periodicals, ibid., pp. 166, 198, 201–208.

23. Bartsch, p. 179. Another right-wing group, the Working Group of Independent Germans (AUD), also participated with the Green groups in an alliance contesting the European elections of 1979.

24. Pröhuber, pp. 148–151. The New Right also believes in "basic democracy" in organizations, another issue dear to the Greens. No greater contrast with the Nazis' *Führerprinzip* could be imagined.

25. See Bartsch, pp. 74–79, 161–165. There is even talk of a multinational federation of Poles, Czechs, and Germans. See also Pröhuber, pp. 68, 115–117.

26. On 17 June 1953, a revolt broke out in East Germany which could only be quelled by Soviet tanks. August 13, 1961, was the day that the Berlin Wall was erected.

27. This was the return meeting between the two, following a visit of the German chancellor to Erfurt in East Germany.

28. Bartsch, pp. 181–182. Horchem, the director of the Hamburg Constitutional Protection Office believes that violence from either extreme is here to stay (p. 91). See also Horchem, "Terrorism and Government Response: The German Experience," *Jerusalem Journal of International Relations* 4, 3 (1980), 43–55.

29. Karl-Heinz Hoffmann's career began in 1956 at the age of 19, when the police confiscated illegal weapons in his possession. In 1963, he was arrested in Turkey for smuggling arms to underground groups. There are other militant minigroups with national socialism in their names, such as the National Socialist Fighting Group Greater Germany (NSKG) or the Federation of German National Socialists (BDNS) which adheres to the old Nazi program and party statute. Others, such as the German Social-revolutionary National Fighting Community (SNKD) seem not much different. All of these believe in guns and explosives. See Horchem, p. 85.

30. *Der Stern*, 3 August 1978, pp. 92–95. Kühnen is a former army lieutenant who was first arrested in late 1977 along with others painting swastikas on Hamburg shop windows. By that time he had already been in operation for two years with a group named first the Hansa Recreation Club, then NSDAP Gau Hamburg, and published a periodical with the old storm trooper name, *Sturm*.

31. *Mannheimer Morgen*, 8 Dec. 1983.

32. *Frankfurter Rundschau,* 26 Nov. 1983. The ages of the extremist bankrobbers, including two shot by police and one who went insane, were between 20 and 27.

33. *Mannheimer Morgen,* 8 Dec. 1983. Some of the neo-Nazis appear in more than one group. There is also the pathetic figure of Ekkehard Weil who back in 1970 shot and wounded a Soviet guard at the West Berlin victory memorial over the Third Reich and who is now on trial in Austria for neo-Nazi bombings.

34. As the reader may recall, the curve began to rise steeply from 1976 to 1977 when official reports counted 900 neo-Nazi activists including 150–200 militants. For the year 1979, when things really began to turn violent, the Constitutional Protection Office counted 1,400 neo-Nazis and held them responsible for 1,483 felonies, including 117 that involved violence, 8 of them bombings. See *Der Spiegel,* 6 Oct. 1980, pp. 37–46.

35. See Bruce Hoffman, *Rightwing Terrorism in Europe* (Santa Monica, Calif.: Rand Corporation, 1982), pp. 6–7.

36. They arrested Karl-Heinz Hoffmann and five of his followers but had to let them go after a few days for lack of evidence. Since the bombing took place a little more than a week before the federal elections of 1980, some of the campaigning politicians undertook a considerable widening of the circle of likely suspects. Franz Josef Strauss, the Christian Democratic candidate, even suggested there might be East German agents at work inside neo-Nazi groups.

37. *Der Spiegel* no. 41 (29 Sept. 1980), pp. 30–32. There was a case in 1971 when a Cologne professor named Berthold Rubin was abducted by neo-Nazis who pretended that this was another kidnapping of the Baader-Meinhof gang. The event had a significant impact on state elections in Schleswig-Holstein.

38. Even supposing he had had this in mind and that it had succeeded in producing a victory for the Christian Democratic opposition, such a triumph of a moderate conservative party would hardly have advanced the goals of the radical right. Conversely, Köhler might have wished to save Strauss's campaign for chancellor, which had encountered an intensely personal opposition.

39. See *Süddeutsche Zeitung,* 2 Oct. and 4/5 Oct. 1980.

40. Reference is to table 1 of the chapter on "Approaches to the Study of Political Violence."

41. The psychiatrists referred to are Joe Tupin and Stuart Brown, cited by the *Los Angeles Times,* 20 July 1984.

42. See Merkl, *The Making of a Stormtrooper,* pp. 220–222.

43. Many terrorists and some violent criminals have a pronounced tendency toward suicide. James O. Huberty apparently tried to kill himself about two months before the shooting of customers and employees at the nearest McDonald's restaurant. His crisis was brought on by losing his job and hence his roots in Ohio. Mental distress and a domestic argument triggered the final explosion. This case also contains some elements that suggest that the multiple murder could just as well have been aimed at a political target. Huberty apparently blamed the loss of jobs and property on President Carter, the Trilateral Commission, high interest rates, and the Federal Reserve Board. He was also fascinated by survivalist movements and war. When confronting his victims, guns in hand, he claimed to have killed thousands in Vietnam, and half a year before the massacre he tried to turn himself in to police as a "war criminal." The U.S. Army, however, has no record of his ever having enlisted. He was a polio victim and considerably handicapped as a child, aside from his already unhappy childhood, and had suffered neck and spine injuries in a recent automobile accident.

44. See *The Making of a Stormtrooper,* pp. 60, 109–110, 203–210, 218–220. Over two-thirds of the Weimar storm troopers were under 30, a degree of youthfulness

rivaled only by the communist street fighters. Those among the Nazi militants who got involved by the time they were 18 or 20 were the most involved in street fighting.

45. See this writer's "The West German Peace Movement," in Merkl, ed., *West German Foreign Policy: Dilemmas and Directions* (Chicago: Council on Foreign Relations, 1982), pp. 78–91.

46. The reference is to the Mutual Renunciation of Force Treaties between Bonn and Moscow, Warsaw, and Prague of the early seventies which constituted the core of Willy Brandt's *Ostpolitik*. For details, see Merkl, *German Foreign Policies, West and East* (Santa Barbara: Clio Press, 1974), chaps. 5 and 6.

47. They would be likely to project their own sexual insecurity into strange people just as they tend to do with gays. Similar doubts can be voiced regarding the question of jobs, which in such young, inexperienced youths was likely to engender great anxiety in the face of the critical shortage of trainee positions and apprenticeships. Partisan issues such as the Eastern treaties, the death penalty, or the issue of communist teachers, moreover, may measure the division between CDU and SPD rather than flush out a neo-Nazi potential. See Klaus Sochatzy, *Parole rechts! Jugend Wohin? Neofaschismus im Schülerurteil* (Frankfurt: Fischer, 1980), which also features interviews with young members of right-wing groups.

48. This represents a considerable change from Hitler's standing as "the greatest German statesman" throughout most of the years since 1956 when he would receive only 2%–3% as compared to a poll of 30%–70% for, alternatively, Otto von Bismarck or Konrad Adenauer. See Kendall L. Baker, Russell J. Dalton, and Kai Hildebrandt, *Germany Transformed: Political Culture and the New Politics* (Cambridge, Mass.: Harvard University Press, 1981), p. 24.

49. Quoted in *Der Spiegel* 41 (29 Sept. 1980), pp. 45–46.

50. Reported by Jürgen Leinemann, *Die Angst der Deutschen* (Hamburg: Spiegelbuch, 1982), p. 191.

51. In the United States, the story of the rise of Jim Crowism long after the end of the Civil War is probably the best example of this.

52. Sontheimer, *Die verunsicherte Republik: Die Bundesrepublik Deutschland nach 30 Jahren* (Munich: Piper, 1979), pp. 91–96, 111–112. Sontheimer exonerates the "critical left" from responsibility for the turn to violence. Ibid., pp. 114–119.

53. Ibid., pp. 115–117.

54. Bruce Hoffman suggests that the rationale of right-wing bombings like the Oktoberfest outrage, apart from attracting attention to their cause, is "to produce a climate of disorder and despair amenable to an authoritarian or fascist takeover." *Rightwing Terrorism in Europe*, pp. vi–vii. But, unless the neo-Nazis only mean to blame their deed on left-wing terrorists, this is not likely to be the result. Such a desire to "bring out authoritarianism or fascism" in the democratic state sounds more like the motive of the left.

55. The polls cited above on the readiness to use violence against persons or "things" gives this line of argument a curious twist. It would appear, however, that it is the direction of political violence as much as the violence itself that needs popular consent. Bracher, *Geschichte und Gewalt. Zur Politik des 20. Jahrhunderts* (Berlin: Severin & Siedler, 1981), pp. 25–26.

56. Ibid., pp. 26, 109–111.

57. Ibid., pp. 116–122. Bracher's explanation of both varieties of totalitarianism rests on the "over-emphasis on social conflict behavior" at the expense of the institutionalization of limited conflict in pluralistic democracy. Totalitarian movements and dictatorships cannot tolerate conflicts; they eliminate them by force.

58. See *The Making of a Stormtrooper*, pp. 103–107, 160–167, 175–184, for an account of the organization and its rare major revolts against the party.

9

Guerrilla Movements in Argentina, Guatemala, Nicaragua, and Uruguay

PETER WALDMANN

Translated by
Michael R. Deverell and Richard Fleischauer

For two decades the struggle among partisans in Nicaragua had dragged on before it gave rise to a successful people's revolution. The example of Nicaragua not only rekindled all the firebrands who after the collapse of various armed attempts at revolution in this region between 1965 and 1975 had been waiting to take up arms again against an intolerable distribution of power and property but also gave rise to renewed reflection among researchers who pursue with keen interest the social and political development of Latin America. What are the conditions under which the South American guerrilla can be politically effective? Sad to say, the analysts have not made much more progress than the revolutionaries themselves. We still need to cast more light on the prerequisites of the development and success of guerrilla movements on the subcontinent.

Most studies of the guerrilla movements in Latin America can be roughly divided into two main categories. The first of these comprises descriptive studies, mostly cut out to fit one special case. By far the majority of research studies falls into this category:[1] They contain descriptions of the guerrilla organizations of one country and their historical development, with particular attention being devoted to the biographies of founders and leaders, their main ideological and political doctrines, the hierarchic structure of the guerrilla bands, their equip-

ment and tactical methods. The studies also contain analyses of individual guerrilla actions and the results of clashes with the state
security forces. The value of such studies unquestionably lies in the
fact that they provide us with essential information about semiclan-
destine guerrilla groups without which any further analysis would be
futile. In the light of the military collapse of most of these groups,
however, one becomes skeptical and tends to view these studies as
exaggerations. Was the particular strategy adopted by the individual
guerrilla movement within the broad spectrum of radical left-wing
recipes for revolution really an important factor in the defeat the
guerrillas suffered in Latin America? Was it decisive that the movement was divided into strictly isolated subunits or into openly com-
municating groups, that the decision making was carried on
democratically "from the bottom up," or that the important decisions
were made and carried out by a small committee of leaders; or that
the movement was supplied with arms from the United States or
Czechoslovakia? In these studies was there perhaps too much weight
put on the military-tactical aspect, and was the effectiveness of these
organizations overestimated?

The small number of investigators in our second category, who
come predominantly from the school of North American research on
violence, can hardly be accused of having occupied themselves too
much with the ideas of people with violent aims, or of basing their
arguments on the pipe dreams of the *guerrilleros*. On the contrary,
these studies do not contain any explanations concerning the goals
and thoughts of the fighters.[2] They also form in many other aspects
a counterpoint to the firsthand studies just described: the authors do
not select isolated examples but concern themselves with the entire
region. Rather than relating the guerrilla to a specific manifestation
of the political and social seizure of power, they consider guerrilla
warfare one among several forms of a general, characteristically Latin
American tendency to realize political goals with violent methods. Instead of dwelling on noteworthy characteristics of the guerrilleros and
researching their possible motives for using violence, they try to explain the emergence and development of guerrilla movements by direct
recourse to aggregate data (e.g., data on economic growth or state
repression). If it is difficult to generalize from the study of individual
cases, the global analysis of all Latin America hardly makes it easier
to recognize the profile of a particular guerrilla movement or a guerrilla
subcategory.

This simplified categorization may do an injustice to the few investigations that lie on the dividing line between the two types of
research, or even stress just one of them without noticeable shortcomings.[3] This comparison is not primarily to suggest an exhaustive

categorization of every single study of guerrillas in Latin America, but only to draw attention to a gap in research. Because of their one-sided approach, I feel that both of the above-mentioned research strategies will be only of limited use in the long run unless they are supplemented by research that fills in the gap between these two extremes. This research should neither stop at the description and analysis of individual guerrilla organizations, nor expound a theory of all guerrilla uprisings, not to mention political violence and instability in Latin America. While one should inquire into the special historical circumstances concerning the rise and development of guerrilla warfare in the various societies of the subcontinent, one should also be on the lookout for parallel developments and points of comparison that lie beyond one specific country. Such studies need not include detailed analysis of irrelevant ideological differences between various guerrilla leaders and factions but it must not be forgotten that every analysis must have as its starting point the guerrilleros themselves and their motivation.

The following discussion falls within this intermediary category which, I believe, ought to be researched more often. I hope to elaborate some medium-range hypotheses concerning the formation, propagation, and chances of success of guerrilla movements in Latin America. The size of my sample is not large enough to do more than set up hypotheses. I only cover four guerrilla movements: (a) the ERP and the Montoneros in Argentina, (b) the various guerrilla factions of the sixties in Guatemala, (c) the FSLN of Nicaragua, and (d) the Tupámaros in Uruguay. By 1969/1970 the first two Argentinean groups were already in existence, and from 1973 to 1975, during the second "Peron era," they had reached the zenith of their power, only to be rather quickly destroyed after the military coup d'état of 1976. The various guerrilla factions in Guatemala rose to prominence between 1963 and 1966, but shortly thereafter were outflanked and obliterated by a terror campaign carried out by right-wing murder squads. Nicaragua's FSLN operated fairly unsuccessfully for fourteen years after being founded in 1960. It then succeeded in gaining notoriety by means of a large-scale seizure of hostages in 1974, thus provoking the government to severe reprisals. From then on the number of members and adherents rose steadily until the people's uprising of 1979. The last group, the Tupámaros, are still regarded today as the unsurpassed early masters of urban guerrilla warfare, which they used from 1962 onward to make Uruguay's constitutional government look ridiculous and unmask it as being weak and corrupt. They were destroyed in a period of only a few months, however, when at the beginning of the seventies the armed forces finally took over the battle against the guerrillas.

The choice of these four particular examples depended partly on practical, partly on systematic, considerations. Pragmatically, it was important that I had already concerned myself occasionally with one or the other of these organizations. This should not give rise to the impression that I had made my own extensive inquiries into the subject. Most of the following assertions and deliberations derive from knowledge and material assembled by other researchers. Concerning the systematic aspects that determined the selection, care was taken, among other things, to consider countries of varying size, different states of development, of varying geographical proximity to the United States, and ones with not only civil but also military governments. Furthermore, countries where nonurban and/or urban guerrilla warfare had played a role and, last but not least, a country in which guerrilla warfare was successful (Nicaragua), were taken into account.

OVERRATED FACTORS

To begin, some variables will be discussed which are, I believe, often accorded too great an influence in the respective literature. I do not consider them irrelevant, but I am of the opinon that they cannot tell us very much about the causes of the formation and the success or failure of guerrilla movements.

These variables include, for example, as already indicated, the vehement discussions concerning theory and strategy which are carried out within the confines of the guerrilla organizations, as well as in their intellectual spheres of influence far and near. The criticism of the Cuban Focus theory, which has been increasingly pronounced in recent years, has already adequately exposed the folly of assuming that revolutionary situations can be artificially produced by following the right recipe, and that a people's revolution can be caused primarily by the intellectual and physical exertions of a small revolutionary avant-garde.[4] There is therefore no need to repeat the arguments against giving too much weight to the fluctuating ideas and intended aims of the leaders of guerrilla organizations. The decision of a young Latin American to go underground and join a guerrilla group probably does not depend too much on whether its leading cadre adheres to Castroism, Trotskyism, or Leninism, whether it represents a populist syncretism or has avoided adopting a clear ideological stance. The latter attitude even seems, on the whole, the most promising. In this way the Tupámaros' distinct pragmatism and their tendency to avoid hair splitting of dogma have continually been cited as among the main reasons for the consistency and effectiveness of this organization.[5] Similarly the ideological flexibility and openness of the Sandinistas toward the political center has been one of the prerequisites of their success. In Argentina, the Montoneros, a mixture of socialistic and nationalistic elements, have been much more able to assert themselves than the rigidly Trotskyist ERP.

A second category of characteristics often overvalued in the respective literature is formed by questions of organizational structure, instruction, the gathering of information, and tactical and military-technical procedures. Certainly a minimum of infrastructural prerequisites, of knowledge, training, and equipping of members is required to enable a guerrilla group to exist at all and maintain itself over a long period of time. Especially in the precarious initial stages the wrong decisions can have disastrous results; for example, the decision to isolate itself prematurely will often lead to a guerrilla group's disbandment or destruction, even before it can become fully active. In later phases too, tactical problems are of no small relevance; for example, the search for a suitable time and place, whether for a spectacular operation or for the opening of a new center of fighting, is of paramount importance. One has only to be reminded of the meticulousness and imagination with which the Montoneros used to prepare and carry out their kidnapping raids (in one incident, that of the brothers Bunge and Born, they carried off a ransom of no less than $60 million) or of the advantages of the rule constantly adhered to by the Tupámaros that a guerrillero was allowed to communicate only with members of his own task force. This ensured that no valuable information would be revealed should he be arrested. Many of the tactical maneuvers, coups de main, and surprise attacks carried out by the guerrilla groups have at their execution aroused not only general amazement but also a certain admiration, and are looked on today as being an impressive combination of courage, humor, cunning, and ruthlessness. With hindsight, there is a question here in regard to the escalation of isolated incidents into general uprisings as to how far these incidents were correctly identified and whether the necessary conclusions were drawn.

Despite the enormous intellectual display with which the guerrilleros set about their task and the great sacrifices they demanded of themselves, as well as of their environment, it should certainly not be overlooked that for years most of them did not get beyond the stage of political harassment, partly tolerated by their government, partly pursued like bands of common criminals by the police. If they were finally recognized by those in power as a serious danger and challenge to the existing order, they were persecuted with increasing force and, within a short period of time, suffered a shattering military defeat and sank quickly into oblivion.[6] This development can be observed in the case of the Tupámaros after 1972 when the armed forces began their struggle against underground organizations; in that of the Argentinean guerrilla bands, considered to make up a potentially strong military force from 1975 on; and, finally, with the bush guerrillas of Guatemala during the years 1967 and 1968. It is an open question as to how far the FSLN here is an exception. On the one hand it came out better in the fight against Somoza's national guard than most of its predecessors. On the other hand, the decisive turn in events against the Somoza regime was not a result of the Sandinista raids but of a mass uprising of the Nicaraguan people.[7]

A third factor, the significance of which should be relativized, is Castro's Cuba, which has often been looked on as the driving force behind all guerrilla movements in Latin America. Although I admit I have not carried out any special research in regard to this point, I find no confirmation of these conjectures in the four cases I have examined. It is, however, beyond doubt that the example of Castro and the teachings of Che Guevara, Regis Debray, and others, rightly or wrongly based on the Cuban revolt, made a very lasting impression on the revolutionary youth in the four countries. It is furthermore known that delegates from the various guerrilla organizations occasionally visited Cuba and that small groups were both ideologically and practically schooled there for the partisan struggle. Beyond this, Castro may have supported one or another guerrilla movement personally, financially, or through the supply of arms. However, there are no overwhelming figures or evidence to substantiate this. In all likelihood, Cuban assistance in none of the four cases reached an extent comparable to the aid given to Venezuelan guerrillas in the early sixties which, incidentally, is also a matter of dispute.[8]

In general, it seems appropriate to warn against an overestimation of the channels of communication among the various guerrilla bands operating on a national basis. Authors who see a multinational network of revolutionary movements at work[9] have succumbed to the same utopian ideas and wishful thinking with which the guerrillas have nurtured themselves at times. Certainly there are trends and movements among the guerrillas which go beyond their respective borders. The guerrilleros, for example, who, because of increased military suppression fled from Chile and Uruguay to Argentina, had considerable influence on the reinforcement of the ERP and the Montoneros. And at the beginning of the seventies, a multinational center was founded to coordinate all the guerrilla movements of the Cono Sur (including the Bolivian ELN).[10] Viewing the matter as a whole, however, these networks can be regarded as merely a peripheral phenomenon. When studying the guerrilla movements more closely in the four countries under discussion, it can soon be ascertained that their formation, style, and possible development were determined in the context of national conditions, and not by external directives or aid. As for the latter, as is seen in the example of Nicaragua, sympathy and support given to the revolutionaries from neighboring *governments* (in this case Venezuela, Panama, and Costa Rica) in general carry more weight than acts of solidarity perpetrated by sympathetic guerrilla bands. In any case, such an open participation by third-party states can only be reckoned with when the conflict is in a relatively advanced state and takes on features similar to those of a civil war. Until that point is reached—that is, as long as the regime the guerrillas are fighting against is sitting firmly in the saddle—neighboring countries will find it difficult to intervene in the conflict. Consequently, the insurgents must rely primarily upon the forces that are at their disposal within their own country, and which can be mobilized.[11]

SOCIAL COMPOSITION OF GUERRILLA GROUPS

If the strategic concept represented by their leaders is of secondary importance for the emergence and spread of guerrillas (likewise questions of organization and tactics) and if, furthermore, external influences and aid are not of primary significance, then the reader may well ask what factor decisively affects the growth and success of revolutionary movements. The answer lies in the underground fighters themselves and in the reserves of support, active or passive, that they find in the population. The equipment, training, and organization of a guerrilla group may leave a lot to be desired. Should it gain a foothold in the region where it fights, however, it can claim success for a period of years, as is evident in the example of some Guatemalan and Nicaraguan bands. The rapid annihilation of the Argentinean ERP in 1975 and 1976, however, proves that even perfect organization and a highly qualified leadership are only of limited use when the necessary connection between the group and broad sectors of the population is missing.

The observation is not new that the success or failure of guerrillas is primarily dependent on whether enough people in a country are prepared to join them, thereby risking their existence and their lives, or are willing at least to support the revolutionary movement as much as possible. This, however, is seldom the central point of focus, which it deserves to be, in studies on this topic. Strictly speaking, it is logical to conclude that all research into guerrilla movements should start with the following questions: who are the rebels, from what part of the country or from which social class do they come, what induces them to take up arms against the state and the society in which they have grown up, which sections of the population show sympathy toward their slogans and actions, and for what reasons?

That these questions are often treated somewhat perfunctorily in the relevant literature is not necessarily due to an author's lack of insight, but is connected rather to the amount of data available. Secret organizations do not usually provide public access to their membership files. Researchers therefore have to rely on questionable sources if they are to get the necessary information; for example, the reports of clever journalists or lists of names supplied by security forces (in particular police and prison authorities). Most of this information is somewhat distorted and the biggest danger is an overrepresentation of the especially bold and enterprising leading forces in the underground organizations (those whose "behavior is conspicuous"). These objections and shortcomings apply also to the information on the guerrilla movements in Argentina, Guatemala, Nicaragua, and Uruguay. It seems, however, sufficiently reliable and informative to enable me to draw some tentative conclusions concerning the social structure of guerrilla groups.

First, the characteristics that can easily be discerned: The guerrilla groups consist of whites and half-breeds, but no Indians are to be found among them. This is superfluous in the case of Argentina and Uruguay, two almost purely Caucasian societies, but relevant to Nicaragua and above all to Guatemala whose population is 40 percent Indian. All commentators on the Guatemalan guerrillas agree that no support for the guerrillas was found among Indians in the 1960s.[12] Time will tell whether the talk of recent changes concerning this subject is justified or not.

Guerrilla movements are youth movements.[13] Most of their members are under thirty years of age, many under twenty. There are, however, exceptions to this rule. All organizations have their "veterans," men who either joined up with the underground fighters later on in life or who can look back on a particularly long period of militancy. As far as the peasants who have fought with the guerrilla formations are concerned, their average age lies beyond that of the other members. The marked presence of the youthful element is in many respects decisive for the state of mind and level of expectation in these groups. It is therefore possible that the "generation gap" also plays a role in the revolt against the established order. There is the conviction that the older generation has failed and must be violently disposed of. It can at any rate be deduced from this circumstance that the concrete experiences leading to an individual's joining the underground organization were gathered within a relatively short period of time. In addition, this may be the source of the "romantic" trait so often ascribed to the guerrilleros, that is, an inclination to a one-sided, idealistic interpretation of both historical events and their own political role.

The large number of women among the guerrilleros should be noted. It is necessary to differentiate, however, between urban and nonurban guerrilla groups. Only rarely do women take part in the hard physical work needed for partisan struggle in the bush or in the mountains. They are not mentioned in reports, for example, about guerrilla bands operating in eastern Guatemala. They do, however, form roughly one-third of the Tupámaro membership, and even as much as three-quarters, according to information for the year 1972.[14] The percent of guerrilleras in the individual groups may be closely connected with the social class of their members. From previous experience, women from lower social classes are, because of their upbringing and understanding of their roles as women, less prepared to engage actively in a political movement than are women from the middle class. We have thus reached the key category of any sociostatistical analysis, the question of what social class the guerrilleros belong to.

In the relevant literature, this question is occasionally answered in this fashion: the Latin American guerrilla personifies the violent form of protest of the radicalized petite bourgeoisie.[15] I do not contradict this assertion here, but it is difficult to see where the specifically "petite" bourgeoisie characteristic is supposed to lie. From the data, the following picture develops:[16] the relative majority of guerrilleros consists of high school and university students. This applies to both urban and nonurban guerrillas. It has been learned, for example, that of the group under Turcio, which had its base in the mountain areas of eastern Guatemala and which at times was four hundred strong, about 75 percent were university students or youngsters still in school. As for occupational groups, a distinction must again be made between urban and nonurban fields of operation. In the cities, academic professionals like architects, doctors, lawyers, and journalists turn up rather frequently. Beyond this the underground organizations get a rather large number of their members from the ranks of middle- and upper-grade officials and employees. Thus we find among the Tupámaros many teachers, bank employees, and engineers. In rural areas the typically urban middle-class professionals are not so common. In their stead the guerrilla organizations have sometimes been successful in winning for their cause members of the lower peasant classes—small-holders, tenant farmers, laborers. In scarcely any guerrilla organization, moreover, is there a lack of priests, or people closely connected to the church (former seminarians or monks), or members of Christian-Democratic youth organizations and parties. Sometimes, after a failed coup, even military officers join the guerrillas, whereupon they naturally adopt a leading role due to their superior military knowledge. Here the example of the Guatemalan bush guerrillas comes to mind.

Although the goal of the underground fighters is to bring about a social, economic, and political revolution in favor of the rural and urban lower classes, their slogans and actions find relatively little support among those classes. If mention is made of *campesino* (rural) groups who join up with guerrilla bands, this information should not be overestimated. The interest of the smallholders and tenant farmers of Guatemala in the guerrillas, which comes under consideration here, is contained within narrow regional and temporal limits. Not a few of the halfbreeds, who at first fought on the side of the revolutionaries, suddenly changed sides and placed their services at the disposal of the armed services and the extreme right-wing terror squads when the going got tough with the guerrilleros.[17]

Similarly ambiguous is information on the attitude of the population in Tucumán in northern Argentina where the ERP temporarily had a strong foothold. Although the partisans were accepted by a part of the population, there were other groups who rejected them and sometimes helped the armed forces ferret out their hiding places. The FSLN, whose main strongholds lay partly in the north and northwest and partly in the southwestern administrative districts of Nicaragua, seems to have been more successful in this respect. The present state of research, however, precludes any further conclusions.

If the rural population, although occasionally showing active solidarity with the guerrilleros, is inconsistent in its support of their goals and tactics, the revolutionaries' plans have excited only indifference and skepticism among the urban lower classes. In no guerrilla group for which statistical information is available does the number of workers exceed 10 percent. Even within left-wing Peronism, a group that was represented almost exclusively by workers and trade unions within the Peronist movement, there developed a fairly sharp division between the militant workers' wing and the "revolutionary tendency," consisting predominantly of high school and university students from which the guerrilla bands evolved at a relatively late date (1970).[18]

Although the true state of affairs is somewhat more complex, it is therefore correct, in principle, to characterize guerrillas as representative of the militant protest of certain bourgeois groups against the prevalent order. It is questionable, however, whether guerrilla groups are anchored on this initial social basis or whether they may assimilate other sectors of the population in the course of expansive development. The events in Nicaragua at the end of 1977, when the partisan war began to expand into a widespread people's revolt, should be kept in mind. What were the stages of development of the FSLN in the seventeen years of its existence up to 1977?[19] Were there relevant regroupings in the membership structure among the other guerrilla groups during the period of fighting, until they were defeated by the armed forces?

The data on this problem are extremely sparse. They suggest a separation between qualitative and quantitative factors in the historical evolution of the guerrillas. Quantitatively, some groups at times show an explosive rate of expansion. After the election victory of the Peronists in May 1973, the Montoneros were suddenly faced with more applicants for membership than they knew what to do with.[20] The same can be observed of the Tupámaros after 1967 when the emergency measures of the new president, Pacheco Areco, which were incompatible with the feeling for the constitution of many Uruguayans, drove herds of new members to the underground organization. On a purely numerical basis, therefore, it is not wrong to speak of the expansion of one or another of the groups into a mass organization. That, however, does not mean that a corresponding "qualitative" expansion followed. The figures indicate rather a relative constancy in the social composition of guerrilla groups.[21] They drain off support from the layers of the population and income brackets formerly accessible to them, but do not transcend them. If this assertion is correct, it may at a fairly early stage be ascertained which social groups sympathize with the revolutionary ideas and actions of the rebels, and which do not. Perhaps this is one of the keys to the later success of the FSLN, which from its beginning united in itself very heterogeneous elements (among others, conservative splinter groups, old Sandinistas, and socialists).

INCUBATION AND FORMATION

When the origins and conditions for formation of the guerrillas in the four countries under discussion are compared, the expectations and ideas of those youthful groups from the urban middle class, which form the majority of the guerrilleros, stand out. Three levels of motivation will be discussed: the material-economic, the historical-ideological, and the political.

Concerning the materialistic motives for the dissatisfaction of these groups, reference has often been made to the precarious and very unpromising position of Latin American students, who make up the nucleus of all guerrilla bands.[22] In the 1960s, for example, only a third of the students in Montevideo had the financial means to pursue their studies continuously. Two-thirds were employed part time with the result that most sooner or later gave up the prospect of finishing their courses successfully. In 1967, out of all students who had already been studying for four or five years, not more than 3.3 percent had passed a final examination. The rest tried to find work in service industries, with banks, insurance, or in public administration, and had to settle for a modest income compared with their original expectations. In neighboring Argentina the chances for the younger academic generation are no better. In the 1960s this country, with a total of 250,000 students, had a higher percentage of students among the population than did highly industrialized states like France, Sweden, or West Germany. When one considers that in Buenos Aires alone 80,000 students were enrolled, it is not difficult to see how unfavorable their studying conditions were, and how difficult it was for graduates to find appropriate positions suitable to their qualifications. This is especially true of traditionally preferred disciplines like medicine and law, with the more recent addition of the social sciences, for which the need for trainees in the capital is very limited. The dilemma is worsened by the fact that, according to a study, Argentinean students (the same may be true of their colleagues in other Latin American countries) not only view their studies as a source of later income but attend courses with enthusiasm and take special interest in their subjects.[23] How disappointed they must be when they leave higher education and find that almost every opportunity of putting their acquired knowledge and skills into useful practice is barred. Here may lie one of the reasons for the large influx of professionals, generally from the academic ranks, into urban guerrilla organizations.

The set of motivations that leads from material dissatisfaction to an increased preparedness for armed attack on a society that holds back the expected standard of living can be discerned not only at the professional level but is also evident in society as a whole. Once more Uruguay provides an example. The country, which was once called the Switzerland of Latin America, found itself from the mid-1950s onward (after the end of the Korean War) faced with a steady worsening of its economic situation. In the 1960s it had the slowest economic growth rate (at times the gross national product even diminished) of all Latin American countries, but the highest rate of inflation. The international drop in prices of its agricultural products, a massive flight of capital out of the country, and an increasingly negative balance of payments are further symptoms of this decline. Many authors raise the question of how it came to be that in a republic, which for decades was peaceful and stood out for its stable political circumstances, one of the first and most dangerous underground movements could take root. These same authors arrived at the conclusion that it was probably connected with the declining distributive capacity of the state, and with the stagnation or drop in actual income of large sections of the population which greatly disappointed parts of the pampered Uruguayan middle class and led them to acts of defiance.[24] Such a link can also be observed in two other guerrilla cases here under study. Was it a mere coincidence that a whole series of underground organizations suddenly emerged in Argentina in the years 1969 to 1970, just at a time when the Ongania government, which had at first had a very successful economic record, ran into the first difficulties? Is it mere chance that growing resistance to the Somoza regime coincided with the leveling off of Nicaragua's economic growth rate, which had been steadily increasing since the late 1950s? As a whole these facts confirm the view of North American researchers into revolution, that the probability of a political rebellion does not depend so much on the absolute state of development of a nation, but rather on the course of its economic development. Societies which because of earlier experiences expect a further rise in prosperity are more likely to incite aggressive reactions of protest when these expectations are not fulfilled than are nations that remain in a constant state of poverty.[25]

The reason for the rebellion of a section of the urban middle class should not be reduced to a reaction to the threatening danger of economic and social decline. The young age of most insurgents guarantees a great susceptibility to high ethical standards, to illuminating paragons, and an idealistic conception of the future. Fidel Castro, Mao Zedong, and Che Guevara serve as role models in the drive for initiative and improvement. Cuba, Algeria, Vietnam and, after the latest events, Nicaragua, are the corresponding social models. Some organizations stress the high-flying character of their goals by invoking the memory of national heroes or groups who in earlier centuries served the cause well. The term *montoneros*, for example, refers to the hordes of wild and fearless horsemen who at the beginning of the nineteenth century helped to drive the Spanish out of what is today Argentina.

Often, however, reflection on distant times and personages is not required to ignite the desires of the revolutionaries for a better, more just social order. Three of the four countries examined here have recently had political leaders and regimes with whom the revolutionaries could suitably identify. In the case of Argentina, it was the first rule of Juan Perón (stretching from 1943 to 1955 if one includes the rise to power of the former colonel) in which the guerrilleros saw their ideas of greater social justice and political participation of the masses realized.[26] In Guatemala they associate with the terms of office of Juan José Arévalo and, most of all, of Jacobo Arbenz Guzmán (in all, 1944 to 1954). Political parties and free labor unions were permitted for the first time, legislation for social welfare and social services was introduced, the influence of foreign capital suppressed, and a comprehensive land reform program begun.[27] Finally, in Nicaragua, it is the figure of the freedom fighter General César Augusto Sandino who stirs the imagination of the rebels. Relying only on peasants and workers, the incorruptible general would not rest until the American troops, which had occupied the country for decades, had been driven out and room was made for a national government.[28]

Conspicuous parallels can be drawn among these episodes: in each case the protagonists of the reform movements did not voluntarily leave the political scene nor were they constitutionally removed—

they had to yield to force. Perón lost his office as president though a military putsch. Arbenz was driven out by an army of CIA-equipped mercenaries marching in from Honduras. Sandino was murdered by General Anastasio (Tacho) Somoza García, the father of the last ruling president. After the leaders of the national movements had been removed, an attempt was made in each of the three countries to cover the traces of their activity and to restore the status quo. In Argentina the Peronist trade unions were suppressed and persecuted, in Guatemala the land reform was canceled, and in Nicaragua the economic and military ties to the United States were reestablished. These attempts on the part of the victors to turn back the hands of time were only superficially successful. In fact they failed to extinguish among the population at large the memory of the increased advantages and rights they had temporarily enjoyed. After the downfall of the reformist, the newly erected systems of domination rested precariously on the narrow foundations of the approval of the economically well-off, while the rest of the population followed political events with bitterness and apathy or simply ignored them. In other words, the price for the violent termination of experimental reform was in all three countries a fundamental crisis of legitimacy.[29]

Notably, in all three cases the legitimacy crisis was not particularly vehemently expressed by those social groups which were hardest hit by the political change of course, that is, the peasant and urban lower classes. They certainly resisted, in a fashion limited in time and space, a reintroduction of the old social balance of power. I have particularly in mind here the militant Peronist trade unions after 1955. It should also be mentioned, however, that the areas where Guatemala had begun its land reform, and the north-northeast of Nicaragua where Sandino had most of his followers, continued to be centers of extreme social and political unrest.[30] A social group that had neither witnessed the revolution nor suffered its direct consequences, moreover, made itself the leading advocate of past reforms and the resulting economic and sociopolitical about-face of the injured lower social classes: sensitive young urban middle-class intellectuals. The fact that the young guerrilleros today are separated by a generation gap of fifteen to twenty-five years from Perón's first term of office, Sandino's struggle for freedom, and the presidencies of Arevalo and Arbenz, is possibly one of the main reasons that these figures are depicted as leading role models. On the one hand, the painful experience of those who lived through the failure of the reform efforts is lessened. On the other hand, it contributes to a whitewashing of possible black aspects in the portraits of these political leaders—thereby leaving them idealized.

The dissatisfaction due to a lack of material goods, and the emphasis on a possible social order that would be more just, partly discovered in the history of their own countries, partly taken over from other countries, in general are not reason enough to turn young people into underground fighters. In addition, these young people have to be of the opinion that the existing political system excludes the possibility of peaceful transformation. This impression is conveyed above all by dictatorships. It is not absolutely necessary, however, that the rebellious opposition be severely and brutally held in check. Reports on the Somoza regime, made by people who were careful to preserve their objectivity, show that the family clan had exercised force relatively moderately until the beginning of the 1970s. Even the military government of Ongania prided itself on its sparing application of violent measures.[31] It is not an experience of brutality but the knowledge that alternative social and political ideas have no chance of being realized that partly induces young people under a dictatorship to take up arms.

The decision to fight the rule of force with force is made easier for young people by a further feature inherent in dictatorial regimes: the effort exerted by the latter to bring about social and political polarization. The plurality of forces, which as a rule characterizes the political scene in most Latin American countries, yields to phases of the concentration of power in one person or institution and, at least on a superficial level, to a division of the sociopolitical system into two camps. On the one side, the side of those in power, there exists a limited number of people and groups who are permitted to exert their will on the political decision process. On the other side, there is the heterogeneous multiplicity of the remaining sociopolitical interest groups, which are excluded from official policymaking. This dichotomizing of political power gives dissidents aiming for total social change the impression that they do not stand alone in their rejection of the existing social circumstances, but of having the support of a large section of the population. In many cases (e.g., the Montoneros), this impression is a disastrous miscalculation, but can (this variant relates to the Sandinistas) be the starting point for a gradual merger of the rebellious avant-garde and the people, the end result being a general uprising.

It is not only dictatorships that are looked on by young intellectuals as being closed, encrusted systems that can be broken up only by armed force. The Uruguay of the early 1960s hardly seems to have had a different effect on the left-wing students of that time, who were bent on social change. What had once been a functioning parliamentary democracy had at that time been reduced to an immobile, corrupt, corporationlike government, based on the division of state income among the power-holders and escape from all political responsibility, which left no doors open to political splinter groups with alternative programs.[32]

The decision to found or to join an underground organization is not usually the result of sudden inspiration but rather the consequence of a series of escalating, frustrating events. With some guerrilla movements it is possible to reconstruct the chain of events that resulted in increased embitterment and militancy among the young critics of the system. In Uruguay a direct line can be traced from the impeachment of the Colorados in 1958 (leading to no noticeable improvement in the economic and political situation), who had held political power for decades, through the cutting off of the Socialist party in 1962, and the fruitless protest marches of the sugarcane workers from the northern part of the country to Montevideo in 1962, 1964, and 1965, leading to the founding of the Tupámaros.[33] In Guatemala, too, the rise of the guerrillas was the last step in a growing atmosphere of protest which, among other things, found expression in the failed military putsch of 1960 and the futile demonstrations against the suppressive measures carried out by the Ydigoras government.[34]

DEVELOPMENT AND SUCCESS

Of the four guerrilla movements discussed here, only one has up to now been successful. It is therefore difficult to state generally the conditions under which a limited partisan struggle can develop into a broad people's revolution. It was shown by a diachronic examination of the membership structure of the groups that there is no inherent tendency of the guerrillas to expand. Rather it is necessary that a number of erosive factors combine, so that the unjust character of a regime and the socioeconomic structures it is based on are not only denounced by a small, particularly sensitive minority but are all made evident to everyone. As a result, the latent crisis of legitimacy, which was discussed in the last section, sharpens into a deterioration of legitimacy.

In the case of the Somoza government it is not hard in retrospect to reconstruct which variables led to just such a situation.[35] They were partly inherent in the system's power structure from the start, partly related to the conduct of the last dictator, Major General Anastasio (Tachito) Somoza Debayle. Seen as a determinant of the political structure is the circumstance that the exercise of power was not lodged in an institution, like the armed forces, but lay in the hands of a single family. Such a personalization of government can inspire feelings of loyalty in the governed (provided that the rulers are perceived as responsible people), which an abstract, bureaucratic organization could never generate. Correspondingly intensified feelings of hatred are to be expected, however, when those in power are guilty of serious errors. The close relationship with the United States was also one of the structural conditions of the regime. Without the removal of Sandino, the proponent of national independence, without direct control over the National Guard left behind by the United States as evidence of its further desire to influence matters, without the constant economic and military support of the United States, the Somoza dynasty could hardly have stayed in power for more than four decades. In the decisive final stages of confrontation, the dependence on the United States became doubly disastrous for the dictator and his family. On the one hand, it gave a concrete basis to the reproach leveled against the regime, that it had committed itself at the cost of national sovereignty into the sphere of influence of the northern superpower. As is learned from the example of the anticolonial struggles for freedom after World War II, it is in general much easier to motivate the population to active resistance against a government reputed to be a puppet of foreign powers than against genuinely national rulers.[36] On the other hand, the United States failed to supply Somoza with the desperately needed military aid at the decisive moment, that is, when the civil war reached its last climax. This was denied due to the increased consideration for human rights demanded by President Carter, and because the protection of the Central American dictator became increasingly troublesome for the government of the United States.

The downfall of the ruling family is to be ascribed in many respects, however, to the attitudes of the last dictator, who ruled from 1967 on.[37] His first great political mistake took place in 1972 when Managua was devastated by an earthquake. The embezzlement of the rich supply of donations coming in from all over the world, the shameless speculation in plots that should have served as building land and, above all, the callous drive for personal profit in the face of such general desperation, suddenly proved to the public that the ruling family was striving not only after a political but also an economic monopoly on power.[38] The credibility of the government was further damaged when it declared a state of emergency following a successful kidnapping raid by the Sandinistas at the end of 1974, and when the National Guard persecuted in the most brutal fashion all persons and groups classified as undesirable or sympathetic to the opposition. What finally caused the dam to break was the murder of the best known politician of the opposition, probably instigated but tacitly covered up by the government. He led at that time (the beginning of 1978) the bourgeois resistance movement. The murder triggered a week-long general strike and led to the last stage of the conflict, marked by a general uprising of the people.

The strong dependence of the regime on the United States, which nevertheless withdrew its support at the decisive moment; the entanglement of political and economic power; despotic and repressive systems of domination; the diversion of influential bourgeois groups onto a course against the government—these were essentially the conditions which in Nicaragua helped lead to success the struggle of the FSLN against the Somoza government. What about these prerequisites in the other three countries? Which were present, which were not?

In Argentina, the drawn-out conflict of legitimacy because of the suppression of Peronism after 1955 provided a favorable climate, or willingness, for revolution. This became clear with the *Cordobazo,* a spontaneous uprising of workers and students in the largest provincial capital of the country in 1969, which was only with difficulty brought under control by the security forces.[39] The armed forces, however, were able to forestall an extreme intensification of the conflict by becoming more conciliatory after 1970. They promised free elections in which even the Peronists, with their exiled and now aged leader, were allowed to participate—for the first time in eighteen years. This about-face of the armed forces, and the subsequent return to government of the Peronists in 1973, no doubt on the one hand gave an impetus to the Peronist left-wing guerrilla organizations, who saw therein a successful result of their intensive subversive activities. On the other hand, it became a precondition for a division in the Peronist camp and the isolation of the Peronist left wing. The short space of time still remaining to Perón as head of government before his death was sufficient to cause the breakup of the alliance between the moderate populist wing of the movement and its radical leftist groups.[40] Moreover the bourgeoisie for the most part had never been able to reconcile itself to the Peronist goals of social reform. Since there was also a lack of acute American involvement in internal affairs, which would have lent plausibility to the student rebels' slogans concerning the neocolonial exploitation and the imperialistic dominion of Argentina, the rebels found themselves, from 1974 to 1975, fighting for a lost cause.

Some aspects of the development of guerrilla activity in Guatemala parallel the Argentinean situation, and some do not. It should first be remembered that in Guatemala the political power, at least formally, does not lie in the hands of a single person or institution, but is exercised by a few officially sanctioned parties. The armed forces, which have the last word and are thus in control politically, prefer not to expose themselves as having the decision-making authority. Although this deceptive reserve is transparent, its significance for the general state of public consciousness is not to be underestimated. There was thereby no generally recognized object against which, as a symbol of the existing deplorable state of affairs and injustices, the collective anger of the people could direct itself. Guatemala, like Nicaragua, lies directly in the American sphere of influence, but the guerrilla organizations were unable to derive any great profit from this situation. As in Argentina, they were confronted with a cunning preventive strategy of the groups in control at a key moment: In 1966, when the guerrillas achieved maximal influence, a president took office who not only was linked by way of his party affiliation (Partido Revolucionario) with the failed revolution of 1944 but who also offered the insurgents a general amnesty and set up institutions designed to realize some of their social demands. By their refusal to accept this offer, which they underlined with increased attacks and raids, the guerrilleros ended up in a position that was hard to justify to public opinion and which forfeited the sympathy of large portions of the middle and lower classes.[41] Shortly thereafter several radical right-wing death squadrons appeared on the scene in reaction to the violence of the social revolutionaries. Since then the country has been hit by periodic waves of terror with right-wing extremists being responsible for most of the victims.

Uruguay's underground organization, the Tupámaros, was at times so strong that one could speak of a dual power situation.[42] If the Tupámaros failed to gain mass support this may, as in Argentina, be attributed to the lack of a clear-cut enemy or threatening external force. It was, however, decisive that the previous mandate of legitimacy and trust accorded to the conventional parliamentary government was not yet at an end, despite the government's increasingly evident weakness. The majority of the Uruguayan middle class and the entire upper class rejected the Tupámaros as much for their radical approach as for their socialistic goals.[43] For their part the urban guerrilleros overestimated their military potential and underestimated the fighting capacity of the government forces, which proved to be a fatal error when they assumed the offensive after 1970.[44]

The miscalculation on the part of the Tupámaros of their chances of success supplies an opportunity to single out two points that seem to be particularly relevant to the supposition that a partisan struggle in Latin America can expand into a people's revolt. The first concerns the necessity of winning the support of influential middle-class groups for the revolutionaries' plans. The dogma that revolutions are the work of the lower social strata, workers and peasants, often prevents the guerrilleros from acknowledging this necessity. The history of the guerrilla movements in the four countries examined here reveals that the chances for success are slim for a guerrilla revolt unwilling to appeal to the middle classes. The students and intellectuals who form the core of the guerrilla bands rarely succeed in establishing direct contact with the lower classes. The way to a people's uprising leads, unless the incidents in Nicaragua were a fluke, over the mobilization of a current of middle-class opposition to the ruling faction. This current then puts the rebels in a position to ignite a mass rebellion. The second point concerns the scope and selectivity of acts of violence. No idea has damaged the guerrilleros more than the belief that the provocation of the state is to be achieved by means of violent attacks. They feel that such actions, since the state then responds with brutal retaliatory measures that reveal its violent nature, ultimately work to the advantage of the rebels. This mechanism functions only in specific cases, when a series of additional factors favorably affecting an insurrection are present. In such a case, herds of people willing to rebel are driven to the guerrilleros by government reprisals against the escalation of armed attacks on state representatives. These conditions were, for example, only present in Nicaragua, among the four cases examined here. Where they are absent, and where actions are based on blind faith in the immanent logic of the "action-repression-spiral," this proves to be a self-destructive boomerang, which strikes not only the guerrilla groups but the society that was the object of their experiment as well.[45] It is then justifiable to speak of the "fundamental change" of this society—one thinks for example of the developments in Uruguay since 1970[46]—nevertheless in a different sense from what the guerrilleros had originally conceived.

NOTES

1. An example of this stance can be seen in the studies by K. B. Johnson on the guerrillas in Argentina and Guatemala. Cf. Johnson 1973 and Johnson 1975.

2. The studies of Bwy 1972 and Duff, McCamant 1976 come to mind here.

3. Mention should be made above all of the creditable works by Lamberg 1972 and Allemann 1974, which contain detailed studies of individual cases as well as an attempt to draw general conclusions.

4. See Debray et al. 1970 for an exposition of the Cuban Focus theory of the late sixties; cf. Kiessler 1975 and Mansilla 1978 on guerrilla ideology and criticisms thereof.

5. Gerassi 1970, p. 671; Moss 1971, p. 15; Labrousse 1971, p. 168.

6. In point of fact there seems to be a paradox here which up to now has not been sufficiently recognized in the respective literature: the guerrilla groups owe their initial success mostly to the fact that their revolutionary purposes and slogans were not taken too seriously and consequently they were not persecuted with extreme severity. In other words, they profited from the rules of a political system they were out to destroy (especially in the case of Uruguay). As soon as this was clearly acknowledged and defense expenditures considerably increased, it usually turned out quickly that they had seriously overestimated their own effectiveness.

7. Polo-Cheva and Süssdorf 1980, pp. 32 ff.

8. Lindenberg 1968, p. 289.

9. E.g., Janke (1976) argues along the lines of such a theory of conspiracy.

10. Johnson 1975, p. 12.

11. It is at the moment an open question whether this conclusion from the four guerrilla cases studied here will continue to be valid. Recent early regional processes of consolidation among the groups involved in political conflicts in El Salvador indicate a possible lifting of the threshold of external support for the insurgents. See Krumwiede 1980. As for the status quo in relation to questions on national defense it is generally recognized, especially in the Central American area, that military advice and support from the United States has been in full swing for a long time.

12. Allemann 1974, pp. 162 and 178 f.; Lamberg 1969, pp. 161 and 174. Incidentally the same is true of the radical right-wing death squads, where practically no Indians were involved. Terror and counterterror in Guatemala are therefore exclusively a matter of whites and half-breeds (or those who have been integrated into their culture); Aguilera Peralta 1971, p. 44.

13. Nicaragua. "Der Volksaufstand in Nicaragua" (author unnamed) 1978, pp. 7 and 16; Labrousse 1971, p. 161; Waldmann 1978, p. 301.

14. Weil et al. 1971, p. 225; Halperin 1976, p. 42; D'Oliveira 1973, p. 29. Concerning the high total of 77 percent deriving from D'Oliveira's sources, it should be noted that it is possibly related to prisoners arrested in Uruguay at that time under suspicion of terrorism, whose composition is not necessarily representative of the Tupámaros. For Argentina, see Johnson 1975, p. 13, and Waldmann 1978, p. 301.

15. Gèze and Labrousse 1975, p. 89.

16. On the following, see Labrousse 1971, pp. 159 ff.; Gerassi 1970, p. 673; D'Oliveira 1973, p. 29; Weil et al. 1971, p. 225; Gèze and Labrousse 1975, pp. 89 f., 106 f.; Barcia 1975, pp. 43 f.; James 1976, pp. 282 ff.; Waldmann 1978, pp. 320 ff.; Allemann 1974, p. 171; Lamberg 1969, pp. 161 and 165 f.; Aquilera Peralta 1980, p. 95; Jung 1980, p. 96; Polo-Cheva and Süssdorf 1980, pp. 36 f.

17. The main reserve of the guerrilla organizations is to be found among the Ladinist Campesinos in the west of the country. Johnson (1973, pp. 75–78) believes he can explain the discovery in a sociopsychological framework (confirmed also by Allemann 1974, p. 1976) that more than a few of the members of the peasant militias set up by the guerrilla organizations had gone over to the armed forces and the extreme right-wing death squads since 1960. Due to culturally and racially determined identity conflicts, the Ladinos concerned may have taken the side of the stronger party.

18. James 1976.

19. Cf. the quotation by R. Debray in Polo-Cheva and Süssdorf 1980, p. 36: "On the decline, polemics, divisions. At the beginning of 1977 the shares of the Sandinistas, had there been such a thing as a stock-exchange of revolutionary values, would have found no buyers."

20. Waldmann 1978, p. 302.

21. Barcia 1975, p. 44; D'Oliveira 1973, p. 29.

22. On the following, see Labrousse 1979, pp. 79 f.; Halperin 1973, pp. 38 ff.; Waldmann 1978, pp. 320 ff.

23. Nasatir 1972, pp. 686 ff.

24. Duff and McCamant 1975, pp. 92, 183 ff.; Moss 1971, pp. 16 f., 23; Allemann 1974, pp. 313 ff.; Weinstein 1975, p. 115.

25. Feierabend et al. 1972; Beyme 1973, esp. chaps. 4 and 5; Waldmann 1977, pp. 32 f.

26. Barcia 1975, pp. 31 ff.; James 1976, pp. 279 ff.; Waldmann 1978, pp. 299, 319 330 ff.

27. Allemann 1974 pp. 163 ff.; Johnson 1973, pp. 59 ff.; Weaver 1979, pp. 336 ff.

28. Jung 1980, pp. 25 ff.; Allemann 1974, pp. 45 ff.

29. This aspect is evident also from the titles of two studies on Guatemala and Argentina, respectively: *Guatemala: The Politics of a Frustrated Revolution* and *Stagnation als Ergebnis einer Stückwerkrevolution: Entwicklungshemmnisse und—versäumnisse im peronistischen Argentinien.* Weaver 1979, Waldmann 1976.

30. On the development of trade unions in Argentina after 1955, see the recently published studies by Cavarozzi 1980 and James 1978. Information on the regional continuity of readiness to rebel in Nicaragua can be found, for example, by Amnesty International 1977, p. 28. With regard to Guatemala, Booth (1980) concludes in a painstakingly quantitative analysis that the extent of acts of violence is determined by the degree of political polarization in the region concerned; i.e., ultimately by the intensity of the conflict of legitimacy explained above.

31. See, for example, Walker 1979, p. 16, on the relatively modest ruling style of the Somoza family; on the same feature of Ongania's dictatorship, see Waldmann 1978, pp. 312 ff.

32. Puhle 1968, pp. 24 ff.; Nohlen 1976, p. 447; Taylor 1979, pp. 263 ff.

33. Weinstein 1975, pp. 113 ff.; Labrousse 1971, pp. 32 ff.; Moss 1971, p. 17.

34. Aguilera Peralta 1980, pp. 92 ff.; Johnson 1975, p. 113.

35. The following enumeration is largely in agreement with the analysis of Polo-Cheva and Süssdorf 1980, pp. 18 ff.

36. Haffner, in *Mao-Tse-tung,* 1970, pp. 12 and 19; Waldmann 1977, p. 57.

37. Walker 1979, pp. 324 f.

38. See "Comercio Exterior" no. 11, 1978. This report contains the interesting thesis that the Somozas had forfeited the goodwill of the wealthy families who were on good terms with them, when they, ignoring traditional divisions of power, also began to establish themselves after 1972 in the building and banking sectors.

39. Delich 1973.

40. Waldmann 1978, pp. 330 ff.

41. Aguilera Peralta 1980, pp. 96 ff.; Allemann 1974, pp. 183 ff.; Lamberg 1969, p. 169, characterizes the "total, aggressive militarization" of the guerrillas which began in 1967 as "a suicidal undertaking, which can only be counted as one of the main causes for the decimation of left-wing radicalism." The increased military efficiency of the armed forces as well as the "acción civica militar" initiated by them in 1966, where they tried to play the Campesinos off against the guerrillas, were traceable back to increased North American military advice. See also Weaver 1979, p. 341.

42. Moss 1971, p. 16.

43. Labrousse 1971, pp. 158, 182.

44. Since at this point the comparison of the four countries and the conditions therein which enable or prevent a guerrilla victory comes to an end, let us mention one more factor, which is not important enough to figure in the text, but which could equally have some significance: the respective size of the national territory. We presume that it is easier to overturn the balance of power in small states than in countries with large land surfaces where the guerrilla can only win the upper hand in the context of a genuine war campaign. Is it mere chance that the revolutionaries have up to now been definitely successful only in Cuba and Nicaragua, two countries of limited geographical size?

45. The provocation of those in power, without the existence of the requirements necessary for a quick, fundamental overthrow of government, is above all self-destructive, because the capacity to learn of the security forces, especially of the military, in the fight against and the eradication of underground movements is underestimated. Allemann (1974, pp. 398 ff.) convincingly elaborated this factor, which has turned out to be a fatal tactical mistake on the part of the guerrilleros.

46. But see also the accusation of the Uruguayan representative before the Russell Tribunal in Rome in April 1974 in Jerman 1975, p. 112: "We . . . denounce to the whole world . . . the situation of our homeland; the destruction of its institutions, the negation of the laws and rights consecrated in the past, the explosion of persecutions, killings, tortures, and physical and mental mistreatment as standard measures which the dictatorial government and the military have used against their compatriots."

BIBLIOGRAPHY

Aguilera Peralta, Gabriel. "Terror and Violence as Weapons of Counterinsurgency in Guatemala," Latin American Perspectives 7, 2 (1980), 91–113.

————. "El Proceso del Terror en Guatemala," in Estudios Sociales (Guatemala) (1971), pp. 35–66.

Allemann, Fritz René. Macht und Ohnmacht der Guerrilla. München, 1974.

Amnesty International. Die Republik Nicaragua. Bonn, 1977.

Barcia, Pedro A. "Las guerrillas en la Argentina," Interrogations (Paris), 3 (1975), 30 ff.

Beyme, Klaus von, ed. Empirische Revolutionsforschung. Opladen, 1973.

Booth, John A. "A Guatemalan Nightmare: Levels of Political Violence, 1966–1972," Journal of Interamerican Studies and World Affairs 22 (May 1980), 195–225.

Bwy, Douglas P. "Political Instability in Latin-America: The Cross-Cultural Test of a Causal Model." In Feierabend et al., 1972. Pp. 223 f.

Cavarozzi, Marcelo. "Unions and Politics in Argentina 1955–1962," CEDES 63, Buenos Aires, 1980.

Costa, Omar. Los Tupámaros. 3d ed. Mexico, 1975.

Debray, Regis, et al. Guerrilla in Lateinamerika, 11 Aufsätze zur Focustheorie. Berlin, 1970.

Delich, Francisco J. Crisis y protesta social. Cordoba 1969–73. 2d ed. Buenos Aires, 1973.

D'Oliveira, Sergio L. "Uruguay and the Tupamaro Myth," Military Review, no. 4 (1973), pp. 24 ff.

Duff, Ernest A., and John F. McCamant. Violence and Repression in Latin America. New York/London, 1976.

Feierabend, Ivo K., et al., eds. Anger, Violence, and Politics. Englewood Cliffs, N.J., 1972.

Gerassi, Marysa. "Guerrilla Urbaine en Uruguay," in Les Temps modernes, 1970, pp. 665 ff.

Géze, F., and Alain Labrousse. Argentinien, Revolution und Konterrevolution. Berlin, 1976.

Halperin, Ernst. Terrorism in Latin America. The Washington Papers No. 33, Beverly Hills/London, 1976.

Hodges, Donald C. Argentina 1943–1976. The National Revolution and Resistance. Albuquerque, 1974.

James, Daniel. "The Peronist Left 1955–1975," *Latin American Studies* 8, 2 (1976), 273 ff.

———— . "Power and Politics in Peronist Trade Unions," *Journal of Interamerican Studies and World Affairs* 20, 1 (1978), 3 ff.

Janke, Peter. "Guerrilla Politics in Argentina," *Military Review* 58, 1 (1976), 62 ff.

Jerman, William, ed. *Repression in Latin America.* Nottingham, 1975.

Johnson, Kenneth B. "Peronism's Divisive Legacy," *Conflict Studies,* no. 63, London, 1975.

Johnson, Kenneth F. "On the Guatemalan Political Violence," *Politics and Society* (Los Altos, Calif.), 4, 1 (1973), 55–82.

Jung, Herald. *Nicaragua: Bereicherungsdiktatur und Volksaufstand.* Frankfurt, 1980.

Kiessler, Richard E. *Guerrilla und Revolution.* Bonn-Bad Godesberg, 1975.

Kohl, James, and John Litt. *Urban Guerrilla Warfare in Latin America.* Cambridge, Mass., 1974.

Krumwiede, Heinrich W. "Regime und Opposition in Guatemala und El Salvador." Unpublished manuscript of a lecture. Bonn, October 1980.

Labrousse, Alain. *Die Tupamaros. Stadtguerrilla in Uruguay.* Regensburg, 1971.

Lamberg, Robert F. *Die Guerrilla in Lateinamerika. Theorie und Praxis eines revolutionären Modells.* München, 1972.

———— . "Die Guerrilla in Guatemala. Eine Fallstudie," *Vierteljahresberichte der Friedrich-Ebert-Stiftung,* no. 36 (1969), pp. 157–176.

Lindenberg, Klaus. "Zur Krise der revolutionären Linken in Lateinamerica: Das Beispiel Venezuela," *Vierteljahresberichte der Friedrich-Ebert-Stiftung,* no. 33, (Sept. 1968), pp. 281 ff.

Lopez, Julio C., et al. *La Caida del Somocismo y la Lucha sandinista en Nicaragua.* Costa Rica, 1979.

Mansilla, H. C. Felipe. "Gewalt und Selbstverständnis. Zur Ideologiekritik der lateinamerikanischen Guerrilla-Bewegung," *Jahrbuch für Geschichte von Staat, Wirtschaft und Gesellschaft Lateinamerikas,* 15 (1978), 357–384.

Mao Tse-tung. *Theorie des Guerrilla-Krieges oder Strategie der Dritten Welt.* With an introduction by S. Haffner. Hamburg, 1970.

Moss, Robert. "Urban Guerrillas in Uruguay," *Problems of Communism,* Sept/Oct. 1971, pp. 14 ff.

Nasatir, D. "Education and Social Change: The Argentine Case." In T. J. La Belle, ed.: *Education and Development: Latin America and the Caribbean.* Los Angeles, 1972. Pp. 683 ff.

"Nicaragua," *Comercio Exterior (Mexico)* 24 (1978), 462–472.

Nicaragua. "Der Volksaufstand in Nicaragua" (author unnamed), *Lateinamerika-Nachrichten* 1978 no. 63, (Berlin 1978), pp. 3 ff.

Nohlen, Dieter. "Uruguay." In *Handbuch der Dritten Welt,* vol. 3. Hamburg, 1976. Pp. 444 ff.

Polo-Cheva, Demetrio, and Erich Süssdorf. "Nicaragua: Die historischen Bedingungen einer demokratischen Revolution," *Lateinamerika-Analysen u. Berichte* 4 (Berlin, 1980), 15–42.

Puhle, Hans-Jürgen. "Politik in Uruguay," special issue 1 of *Vierteljahresberichte der Friedrich-Ebert-Stiftung,* Hannover, 1968.

Russel, Charles A., et al. "Urban Guerrillas in Argentina: A Select Bibliography," *Latin American Research Review* 9, 3 (Fall 1974), 53 ff.

Taylor, Philip B. "Uruguay: The costs of inept political corporatism." In Wiarda, Howard J., and Harvey F. Kline, eds., *Latin American Politics and Development.* Boston, 1979, Pp. 262 ff.

Waldmann, Peter. *Strategien politischer Gewalt*. Stuttgart, 1977.

_____ ."Ursachen der Guerrilla in Argentinien," *Jahrbuch fur Geschichte von Staat, Wirtschaft und Gesellschaft Lateinamerikas*, 15 (1978), 295 ff.

Walker, Thomas W. "Nicaragua: The Somoza family regime." In Wiarda, Howard J., and Harvey F. Kline, eds., *Latin American Politics and Development*. Boston, 1979.

Weaver, Jerry L. "Guatemala: the politics of a frustrated revolution." In Wiarda, H. J., and H. F. Kline, eds. *Latin American Politics and Development*. Boston, 1979. Pp. 332–345.

Weil, Thomas E., et al. *Area Handbook for Uruguay*. Washington, D.C., 1971.

Weinstein, Martin. *Uruguay: The Politics of Failure*. Westport, Conn., 1975.

10

Patterns in the Lives of ETA Members

ROBERT P. CLARK

―――――――

It seems to be fairly widely accepted among investigators of insurgent groups that their members generally suffer from distorted or distressed personalities, if they are not in fact insane. The prevailing view among students of political terrorism is that terrorists are, by definition, not psychologically stable, that they are not capable of supportive relationships with others, and that they lack a shared standard of rationality with their enemies. Not only are insurgents different but they are different in a pathological way.[1]

Unlike these observers, I have not made an in-depth investigation of all contemporary political insurgencies, or even of a significant portion of them. My scope is reduced to this single case study. Therefore, I have no wish to take issue with their more general observation regarding political terrorists. Nevertheless, my inquiry into the origins of members of Euzkadi ta Askatasuna (ETA) and their life-style while members of the organization leads me to conclude that, whereas insurgents in general may have distorted personalities, most *etarras* are well within the range of functioning and sane human beings; whereas terrorists in general may be seriously distressed, members of ETA suffer from no greater levels of stress than are observed across Basque society generally, and certainly their stress level does not exceed the bounds of what is manageable by normal, functioning men and women; and whereas insurgents in general may have difficulty in establishing and maintaining warm and nurturant interpersonal relationships, etarras have relationships with loved ones that are normal to the point of being mundane. Indeed, one of the sources of ETA's great durability over the past two decades has no doubt been the ability of etarras to seek refuge and solace (as well as material support) from among those whom they love and cherish. Etarras are not alienated persons; they are, on the contrary, deeply embedded in the culture whose rights they fight to defend.

It is always something of a challenge to determine with any precision the important characteristics of the members of a clandestine insurgent organization. One reason for this is the secret nature of the organization and the consequent reluctance of its members to share information with outsiders. As a general rule, membership records or lists are either not kept or are fragmentary and unreliable. Police records are incomplete and may include many persons accused of criminal acts who are not members of the organization. In any case, police files are not ordinarily opened to outsiders; and when they are shared with journalists or social scientists, it is usually in order to influence the way in which the latter interpret the insurgency to the mass media audience or policymaking circles. These are general problems that would affect any serious research into insurgent organizations. In the case of ETA, however, there are additional problems that complicate our analysis.

Before we can begin to sketch out a profile of a "typical" ETA member, we must first grapple with certain ambiguities in defining what it means to be "a member of ETA." For one thing, as I shall discuss shortly, the process by which new members are recruited into the organization is usually a slow and gradual one, and it is difficult to say exactly when a young man crosses the threshold of ETA membership. A second ambiguity in defining ETA membership has to do with the various categories of membership that exist within the organization. There are several classes of etarras, including *liberados, legales, enlaces, apoyos* and *buzónes,* each of which has a specific role to play in the maintenance and support of the organization. Relatively few etarras actually carry weapons and even fewer have actually carried out assassinations or bank robberies. A final definitional problem stems from the fact that there were in 1980 at least three wings of ETA whose members disagreed (sometimes violently) with one another, and which have markedly different goals, strategies, and tactics. These wings are ETA-militar, ETA-político-militar, and the Comandos Autónomos. In addition, there are undoubtedly small groups of armed men who are not etarras in any strict sense of the word since they do not take orders, or receive support, from the ETA chain of command. They are, nevertheless, capable of harming or killing people and then claiming credit for the attack as a subgroup of ETA.

My search for the social and psychological roots of ETA has led me to two quite different kinds of biographical information. The first consists of some forty-eight case studies of a wide range of ETA members that span the history of the organization from the early 1950s to the present. The sources for most of this information were secondary books that contain biographical data about a number of ETA members. In a few instances, newspaper accounts provided me with additional information. The set also contains several interviews which I conducted with ETA members in France in 1973. The studies include some of the principal leaders of ETA throughout its history, such as José Miguel Beñaran Ordeñana ("Argala") and José Luis Alvarez Enparantza ("Txillardegui"), as well as a number of simple rank-and-file members. They include members who founded the organization in 1959, as well as several who are still at large at this writing, and many in between. In short, they include as near to a cross section of ETA members as could be developed using the source materials available.

These 48 case studies have been supplemented where necessary and appropriate by another data set derived from two sources. The first is a list of 245 Basque political prisoners in Spanish prisons as of October 1974.[2] After discarding unusable names, I have been left with a group of 171 etarras in prison during the last years of the Franco regime. While all I know from this list are the name and place of birth of each etarra in prison, it is surprising how much interpretation one can squeeze out of such scanty material. The second source is a list of 228 persons arrested for ETA crimes or for being members of ETA during 1979 and 1980. For these persons, I have somewhat more information, including what sort of offenses they have been charged with committing, their age, occupation (in a few cases), and so forth. According to the Spanish government's own figures, from 4 December 1978, when Spain's Anti-Terrorist Law went into effect, until 5 December 1979, 652 persons were arrested for ETA-related offenses.[3] From that date until mid-1980, 329 etarras were arrested.[4] My data set thus consists of approximately 23 percent of all etarras arrested during the eighteen-month period from January 1979 through June 1980. I use these aggregate data, together with the case studies, to describe for the reader several important characteristics of ETA members: the social origins of etarras (family, language, class, etc.); the process by which a young Basque is transformed (and recruited) into an ETA member; and, finally, what life is like within ETA, and how etarras terminate their relationship to the organization.

THE ROOTS OF INSURGENCY:
THE SOCIAL ORIGINS OF ETA

Let us begin our description of ETA's members with some basic data on age and sex. Table 10.1 provides us with simple statistics on these characteristics.

TABLE 10.1

AGE AND SEX OF ETA MEMBERS

| Sample | Age when joining ETA or when first arrested | | Percent male |
	Mean	Range	
Case studies (N = 41, 48)	24.0	16–35	93.8
Political prisoners, 1974 (N = Unknown, 171)	—Unknown—		95.3
Arrest records, 1978–1980 (N = 89, 228)	25.2	17–45	90.8
Total (N = 130, 447)	24.8	16–45	93.1

There is a prevailing view among many that ETA members tend to be very young, barely emerged from adolescence; and, indeed, some insurgent groups may be forced to recruit youths in their teenage years. Our data show, however, that on the contrary ETA members tend to be in their middle to late twenties when they join the organization.[5] The cases drawn from our individual studies show a mean age of 24 years when joining the organization; the arrest records data show a slightly higher 25.2 years. These figures coincide fairly closely with those reported by Charles Russell and Bowman Miller, who found that the average age of ETA members arrested was 23.2.[6] For the entire sample of 130 etarras for whom I have age data, the range of entering ages spreads from youths of 16 to middle-aged men of 45.

The data on sex taken from table 10.1 reflect ETA's pronounced antipathy toward women in the organization. As one etarra told me in an interview in 1973, ETA opposed women in the organization because "their place was in the home," and "they talked too much, especially to their parish priest." Fewer than one in ten etarras from the samples were female, and the few women who do manage to enter the organization are always found among the support or information cells. We have few if any actual cases of women taking part in a specific armed attack. Traditionally, ETA members have displayed considerable condescension toward women, and this attitude is reflected quite clearly in the data in table 10.1.

The third characteristic of ETA members that concerns us is social and economic background. On this subject, there seems to be considerable disagreement. Using education as an indicator of social standing, Russell and Miller observe that "over 40 percent of the identified leaders and cadre members [of ETA—V] who have been arrested had some university training and many were graduates."[7] This would seem to suggest that etarras were drawn predominantly from the middle and upper classes, those best able to afford a university education for their sons. The Basque social historian Beltza, however, has argued that some 40 percent of ETA's members during the 1960s and early 1970s were from the working class, and another 20 percent came from such lower-middle-class occupations as office workers and technicians.[8] Still another observer, José María Portell, has suggested that ETA derived its early strength from the petite bourgeoisie or the lower middle class, including rural folk and small businessmen. In this connection, he cites (apparently in agreement) this observation by ETA leader José María Escubi Larraz:

> The nationalist ideology that caused ETA to emerge in the 1960s is a typical product of the Basque intellectual strata as representatives of the petite bourgeoisie (pequeña burguesiá). Its characteristics include small-scale production based on a small industrial shop or family craft, or the small property based on small-scale trade, administered by a family. In both cases, with a few salaried workers.[9]

One of the principal historians of ETA, José Mari Garmendia, asserts that ETA's leadership in the early days came from students whose origins were lower middle class, whereas after 1970 (and the Burgos trial) they tended to come increasingly from industrial workers in the small towns of western and central Guipúzcoa and eastern Vizcaya provinces, which are zones of relatively recent industrialization.[10]

The data in table 10.2 allow us to test these assertions with empirical observations, although the test is incomplete because of the scarcity of data. Of the total of 447 etarras in the sample, I can find occupational information about only 81, or only about 18 percent. In particular, the sample drawn from Basque political prisoners in 1974 has no information at all about occupation or social class. We can, nevertheless, make some tentative generalizations based on these partial data.

As far as social class is concerned, the chances are about even that a typical etarra comes from a working-class or a lower-middle-class background (about one-third of the sample of 81 members comes from each class). The probabilities are somewhat lower that the ETA member is a student or priest, and considerably lower that he comes from a middle-class occupation (18.5 and 12.3 percent, respectively). Very few etarras in my sample came from upper-class occupations. Relatively few were unemployed and living on unemployment compensation. If

TABLE 10.2

SOCIAL CLASS/OCCUPATIONAL IDENTITY OF ETA MEMBERS

Sample	Working class	Middle class	Lower middle class	Upper class	Student/ priest	Unemployed
Case studies (N = 46)	28.3	30.4	8.7	4.3	23.9	4.3
Arrest records, 1978–1980 (N = 35)	34.3	28.6	17.1	0.0	11.4	8.6
Total (N = 81)	30.9	29.6	12.3	2.5	18.5	6.2
Average for Basque provinces[a]	47.2	23.6	12.4	6.0	NA	NA

[a] As of 1970. See Luis C.-Nuñez Astrain, *Clases Sociales en Euskadi* (San Sebastian: Editorial Txertoa, 1977), table 27, p. 116. Data exclude 10.8 percent in agriculture and armed forces.

the etarra is an industrial worker, he is not likely to be employed in a very large factory, but rather in a small factory or shop (perhaps in a family-owned firm), or he may even be self-employed as a carpenter, a bricklayer, or in another manual labor occupation. Those from the lower middle class are likely to be small shop owners or employees, office workers for commercial firms or government agencies or banks, or schoolteachers. Those from a middle-class background will probably be lawyers, engineers, or economists, but few of them will still be practicing their professions, having left their careers to go over completely to ETA and its activities. My data are too scanty to permit any analysis of trends in class structure over the years, but it would appear that three classes—working, lower middle, and middle—have been represented within ETA to approximately the same degree that they are in Basque society generally, with the exception that the working class seems slightly underrepresented. In any case, one cannot say that ETA has been dominated by any single class or professional stratum over the years.

Several additional observations are of interest here. In my review of the eighty-one cases cited here, I found not a single instance of an ETA member who had come from a farming occupation or even a farming community. A number (including such well-known cases as Miguel Angel Apalategui ["Apala"]) grew up in the typical traditional Basque homes known as *caseríos* (in Spanish) or *baserriak* (in Basque), which are extended family units located close to small towns. The caserío is typically an agricultural enterprise, somewhat like the family farm in the American Midwest. Crops are cultivated and some farm animals are kept in proximity to the building (usually occupying the ground floor while the family lives on the second floor). Nevertheless, in those few cases where we find an etarra still living in this environment, he almost invariably leaves the caserío during the day to work in a nearby shop, factory, or office, returning in the evening to his traditional home and family.

The second point to be made is this: despite assertions to the contrary that one reads in the popular literature about ETA, I found very few cases of etarras who were unemployed. In about 95 percent of the cases, ETA recruited its members from among persons who were either employed or going to school. Moreover, most of the *legales* continued to work at their regular job even after joining ETA. This finding should put to rest the myth that ETA recruits from among some vast *lumpenproletariat* of unemployed youths who harbor serious grudges against society for denying them honest employment. I find little evidence that such is the case.[11]

From these observations, I want to turn next to a description of the family background within which many etarras grew to adulthood, and out of which they were recruited to ETA. Let us examine, first, their ethnic heritage. Table 10.3 illustrates this dimension of ETA by showing the proportion of my samples with identifiable Basque surnames. This kind of analysis is aided greatly by the fact that Basque family names are quite distinctive from those of Spanish families, and can be easily distinguished.[12] Moreover, because most Basques follow the Iberian custom of using both paternal and maternal surnames, we can in most instances discern whether both parents were Basque, or only one, and if so, which one. We can see from table 10.3 that between four and five out of ten etarras were the offspring of two Basque parents (slightly below the average for the Basque population as a whole), while about one out of six was the son of two non-Basque parents (less than half the average of the population of the Basque provinces generally). Also revealing is the fact that while only about 8 percent of the population of the Basque provinces is of mixed ancestry (with one Basque and one non-Basque parent), fully 40 percent of ETA's members comes from such parentage. The consequence is that more than 80 percent of all etarras have at least one Basque parent, as compared with slightly less than 60 percent of the provinces' overall population.

The forty-eight case studies offer us only tantalizing glimpses of the role ethnicity played in the family life and early years of the etarras. Apparently a number of them, such as Angel Otaegi and Miguel Angel Apalategui ("Apala"), grew up in families where Spanish was seldom spoken, and Basque ethnicity was something taken for granted. Many others, such as Andoni Bengoa, grew up in a family setting where

TABLE 10.3

ETHNIC BACKGROUND OF ETA MEMBERS

| Sample | Identifiable Basque surnames | | | |
	Both parents	Father only[a]	Mother only	Neither parent[a]
Case studies (N = 48)	54.2	27.1	14.6	4.2
Political prisoners, 1974 (N = 171)	40.9	34.5	8.8	15.8
Arrest reports, 1978–1980 (N = 228)	43.0	23.2	14.0	19.7
Total (N = 447)	43.4	28.0	12.1	16.6
Average for Basque provinces[b]	51.0	— 8.0 —		41.0

[a] Includes cases in which mother's surname not known.

[b] As of 1975. See Luis C.-Nuñez Astrain, Clases Sociales en Euskadi: (San Sebastian: Editorial Txertoa, 1977), table 43, p. 168.

Spanish was spoken, but where Basque nationalism was ardently espoused and was the topic of dinner table conversation on numerous occasions. In still other cases, such as that of José Luis Alvarez Enparantza ("Txillardegui"), not only was the family not particularly self-conscious about its ethnicity but the boy himself was not able to learn Basque until he was seventeen, and then it had to be done almost by himself, with little open encouragement or support. In a few cases, such as that of Jon Paredes Manot ("Txiki"), we see the son of two non-Basque parents completely reject his non-Basque ancestry and even change his name (from the Spanish, Juan, to the Basque equivalent, Jon) to fit into a pro-Basque peer group. We should note also that the fathers of the future ETA members did not as a rule suffer much for their nationalist sentiments; that is, they did not suffer to any marked degree more than others of their generation. Only Iñaki Orbeta (whose father spent four years in prison for his pronationalist sentiments) and an anonymous etarra I interviewed in France in 1973 (whose father died in combat in the Spanish Civil War) could be said to be seeking revenge for something done to their fathers. In the great majority of cases, the oppression felt by etarras was experienced by Basques generally, and was not something peculiar to their specific family. We have, thus, something of a mixed picture as far as depicting the family as the cradle of radicalism is concerned. In a few cases, perhaps as many as half, the young etarra learned his ethnic intransigence in the home. In many others, however, the radicalism of the youth far exceeded that of the father, not to mention that of the mother.

Let us linger a moment on this question of parental status in the home. Numerous authors have commented on the strength and dominant role of the mother/wife in Basque homes and families; and what little we know about the early lives of the etarras confirms that what was true of Basque society in general is especially true of etarra families in particular.[13] It is striking to read again and again descriptions of the family in which the father is either deceased, missing, away from home for long periods, or just not mentioned at all in the account. The mothers of the etarras, in contrast, are very prominent in every story, standing solid as a boulder in the midst of turmoil that swirls about the family. Or, as we read in the account of the "Apala" case written by Miguel Castells (Apala's attorney), "At times when everything seems to be coming down around her, she [Apala's mother] remains strong and holds the rudder firmly."[14]

The exact formula of strong mother and subdued or absent father varies, of course, from case to case. For José Luis Alvarez Enparantza, in his accounts of his youth, his father does not appear at all, and it is his mother who puts him on the road to political activism by helping him learn Basque at age seventeen. In a number of cases, including that of José Miguel Beñaran Ordeñana ("Argala"), José Martín Sagardía Zaldúa, and Angel Otaegi, the father died when the son was quite young, and the mother was left with the arduous task of rearing her offspring alone and unaided. Others had the experience of Iñaki Orbeta, whose father spent several years in jail for his political views, and then left home for work abroad (in his case, Venezuela) because the economic conditions in the Basque region offered little hope of his being able to maintain a large family comfortably. Finally, we have cases like those of Miguel Angel Apalategui and Jon Paredes Manot whose fathers stayed with their families but who were not significant figures in the lives of their growing sons. Castells tells us of an interesting account of how Apala's father was made so ill by the news of his son's extradition trial that he had to take several days off from his job to recover from the shock.[15] Virtually the identical reaction was exhibited by the father of Andoni Bengoa, who was so upset by the news that his son had joined ETA that he had to go to bed for several days.[16] One can simply not imagine the mother of one of these young men reacting to such news with illness or collapse, but rather with calm, fortitude, and strength.

Compared with what we know about the social class or occupation of the etarras as young men, we know next to nothing about the social class of the family into which they were born. But of the nine or so cases in which information of this sort is available, it would appear that the families of ETA members span a range of social class origins equally as wide as those we have already described in the case of their sons grown to adulthood. While none of the etarras came from what we call an aristocratic or elite background, at least two had fathers who were employed in upper-class professions: Iñaki Orbeta (lawyer) and José María Escubi Larraz (doctor). Txillardegui's father ran a printing firm which had about forty employees. Argala's father was a construction laborer who started his own construction company with a prize he won in the state lottery. Several etarras, however, came from humble origins. José Martín Sagardía Zaldúa's father worked as a butcher and a truck driver and was working as a garbage collector when a heart attack killed him. Angel Otaegi's mother worked as a waitress in a hotel in San Sebastián and also managed the family tavern in their hometown of Nuarbe. The family of Txiki was extremely poor, and could probably be classified as a peasant class family in the process of becoming working class. Apala's father had started as a *carbonero* (maker of charcoal) working in the mountains of Guipúzcoa, and had managed to build up his modest caserío by virtue of many years of hard labor. The anonymous etarra whom I interviewed in 1973 was the son of a laborer who had died in the civil war, leaving a widow and two sons in desperate financial straits. If there are clear patterns in all this, I have yet to see them.

Let us examine, next, the linguistic character of the towns where etarras come from. In all, we know the birthplace or town of origin of 320 ETA members, drawn from the various samples as shown in table 10.4. As the data in this table reveal, slightly less than 45 percent of these etarras come from towns where more than 40 percent of the population speak the Basque language, Euskera; while slightly less than 40 percent come from towns where less than 20 percent speak Euskera. These figures show that ETA tends to recruit from Basque-speaking regions, since only 19.3 percent of the total population live in towns of more than 40 percent Basque speakers, and about two-thirds of the population live in towns of less than 20 percent Basque speakers. I cannot assert that a person born in a town where, say, 60 percent of the population speak Basque will himself be Basque-speaking, but the probability seems rather great that such will indeed be the case. The opposite proposition (that persons born in towns where no one speaks Basque will not speak the language) seems even more strongly supported by common sense. ETA's membership thus appears to be drawn somewhat more heavily from areas where Euskera is still the predominant medium of communication, or is at least as widely spoken as Spanish. In this instance, ETA's origins appear to be distinctly different from those of the general society within which the organization operates.

TABLE 10.4

LINGUISTIC CHARACTER OF BIRTHPLACES OF ETA MEMBERS

| Sample | Distribution of ETA members by degree of use of Basque language in township of birth[a] | | |
	Less than 20% of town population speak Basque	Between 20% and 40% of town population speak Basque	More than 40% of town population speak Basque
Case studies (N = 34)	29.4	17.6	52.9
Political prisoners, 1974 (N = 151)	39.1	16.6	44.4
Arrest records, 1978–1980 (N = 135)	40.7	16.3	43.0
Total (N = 320)	38.8	16.6	44.7
Average for Basque provinces[a]	66.6	14.1	19.3

[a] As of the early 1970s. All calculations made from data collected by Pedro de Yrizar, "Los dialectos y variedades de la lengua Vasca: Estudio Linguistico-Demografico," *Separata del Boletin de la Real Sociedad Vascongada de los Amigos del Pais*, vol. 29, nos. 1–3 (1973).

Another significant difference in origins has to do with the size of the township of birth. As table 10.5 reveals, about 40 percent of the total population of the Basque provinces live in large cities of more than 100,000 persons, while about one-quarter of the total population live in smaller towns of 10,000 to 50,000 inhabitants. Significantly, the distribution of etarras is exactly the reverse: about four out of ten ETA members come from the small cities; about one out of four, from the large metropolitan areas. (The distribution of etarras among townships of other sizes corresponds almost exactly to that of the Basque population as a whole.)

We can conclude, then, that ETA draws its members predominantly from areas where Euskera is still spoken widely, and from smaller cities between 10,000 and 50,000 in population.

LIFE IN ETA: INSURGENCY AND THE INDIVIDUAL

It may be something of an exaggeration to say that the "making of an etarra" begins in the cradle, but almost certainly it begins quite soon thereafter. The process by which a Basque youth is transformed into a member of ETA is a long one full of detours and the exploration of competing alternatives. Even the actual recruiting process is a gradual one which many potential etarras resist for months or even years before

TABLE 10.5

GEOGRAPHICAL ORIGIN OF ETA MEMBERS, BY SIZE OF TOWNSHIP OF ORIGIN

	Population of township of origin[a]				
Sample	Less than 2,000	2,000– 10,000	10,000– 50,000	50,000 100,000	More than 100,000
Case studies (N = 34)	8.8	29.4	35.3	8.8	17.6
Political prisoners, 1974 (N = 152)	8.6	10.5	43.4	7.2	30.3
Arrest records, 1978–1980 (N = 135)	8.9	14.1	36.3	20.0	20.7
Total (N = 321)	8.7	14.0	39.6	12.8	24.9
Average for Basque provinces[a]	8.0	15.5	24.5	10.5	41.5

[a] As of 1975. See Talde Euskal Estudio Elkartea, *Euskadi: ante las elecciones municipales* (San Sebastian: Ediciones Vascas, 1975), table 1.1, p. 11.

yielding to the call to join. Once in the organization, most etarras live a fairly conventional life punctuated by brief flurries of hazardous activity. For the most part, they continue to live in the protective culture of their home and neighborhood, where they are buffered to some extent from the frustrations and anxieties of a clandestine insurgency. Most of them spend a relatively short time in the organization. Many are hunted down and captured or killed by police or Guardia Civil; but a significant number simply leave the organization and return to a more or less normal life, despite the threat of reprisals for having abandoned the struggle.

> [O]ne of the first requirements for a free man [writes psychologist Erik Erikson about the beliefs of the great Indian leader Mahatma Gandhi] was the ability to express himself well in the language of his childhood. . . . For truth becomes a hazy matter indeed where most official business and much of everyday life of a people must be transacted either in a stilted and often broken [foreign language] or in a multitude of idioms offering no more than an approximation of intended meaning. And since this fact, in the long run, makes it both impossible and unnecessary to say what one "really" means, it supports a form of habitual half-truth such as the English had come to consider "inborn" in all Indians.[17]

So it was that many future etarras first encountered the notion of discrimination and deprivation when they emerged from the home and found themselves in a school setting where they could neither speak nor understand the language of instruction, and were in fact punished for their inability to do so. Miguel Castells, for example, writes of his conversation with a cousin of Miguel Angel Apalategui, who tells us:

> The first shock for a young person from Ataun is when he enters the Spanish national schools, and, whether you want to or not, you have to speak in Spanish. In Ataun we speak only Euskera. But the teacher, in a radical way with punishment and persecution, requires that in school one speaks only Spanish, and really the child when he enters doesn't know it. And later, as the child grows up, he continues to run up against different kinds of repression.[18]

José María Portell, to cite a second case, tells a similar story of José María Escubi Larraz, one of the chief ETA leaders of the 1960s. Escubi was born to the well-to-do family of a doctor in the small village of Leiza, located in Navarra but only twenty kilometers from Tolosa and the Goierri region. At the age of seven, Escubi was taken to Pamplona where he was enrolled in the Jesuit elementary school there. At the time, he spoke only Euskera, the language of his parents and his home. He recalls his encounter with Spanish education this way:

> When I got to the school, I realized that no one talked like me; I felt, then, a feeling of loneliness. I couldn't understand Spanish and the lectures of the teacher. They thought that I didn't want to study my lessons, and they punished me. This marked me deeply. And when I grew up I decided to do something for my Basque country.[19]

Even young Basques who did not speak Euskera as a child still felt the impact of Spanish government policies that suppressed not only this but other expressions of Basque ethnicity. Some, like Txillardegui, began to learn Euskera only at a relatively advanced age (in his case, seventeen), and against formidable odds, which included a proscription of textbooks in the language and an absence of teachers. But it was, after all, the language of his mother, and that fact eventually prevailed over the obstacles. Many others felt the presence of the Spanish government in their inability to enjoy simple expressions of folklore, such as singing of nationalistic songs, the playing of proscribed musical instruments, or the wearing of the prohibited colors (red, green, and white—the colors of the Basque flag) in public. Eduardo Uriarte, for example, one of the Burgos 16, remembered vividly an event from his childhood when several youths were driven out of town by the mayor and the Guardia Civil for playing in public a Basque musical instrument, the *txistu,* an act that required prior approval by the governor of the province.[20] A cousin of Miguel Angel Apalategui tells us this story (related by Miguel Castells):

> Ten years ago [in about 1967. RPC], in the festival in Aya, I was wearing a cap with four clusters of ribbons hanging from it. They [the police] grabbed me, they took off the ribbons and they took away my identity card, and they told me to come to Ataun the next day to get it. I went there, and they made me return home and come back with the cap that I had had on in Aya. I went back with the cap. They slapped me around a little, and yelled at me. And I had to remain quiet. The ribbons were the [Basque] colors. They gave me a fine of 500 pesetas [about U.S. $10] and they let me leave.[21]

Most certainly these were mistaken policies used by the Franco regime to wipe out the last remaining vestiges of Basque cultural distinctiveness, and in truth many of the more irritating decisions were reversed soon after the Generalissimo's death. But while they were in effect, they had a significant impact on Basque youth and on ETA's ability to recruit new members. At one level, these policies served as a constant irritant, an enduring reminder of the oppressive nature of the Spanish state in the Basque country. Moreover, they forced the youth of the region to take their folkloric celebrations to distant mountaintops where they could not be observed by police or Guardia Civil troops. In earlier years, Basque mountain-climbing clubs (which exist in every town, no matter how small) had been used as a cover for clandestine meetings. During the Franco years, they served much the same purpose. And it was during the excursions of these clubs to their remote mountains that ETA chose to make many of its initial contacts, which later led to recruiting activities in earnest.

As Basque youth grew and became increasingly aware of their deprivation, other factors began to come into play, factors that would move them along little by little toward their rendezvous with ETA. A significant number of them began as adolescents to engage in what we might term "searching behavior." During their teenage years, they wandered restlessly and intensely in a search for solutions to the crises that afflicted them as individuals and their culture as a group. There was not much actual travel, and few of these future etarras actually left the Basque country in search of their role in the struggle yet to come. There were, it turned out, quite enough alternatives for them close to home. Their search, instead, focused on the possibilities for social change short of armed struggle. In all the cases for which I have data (very few, to be sure), the future ETA members tried other options first, and turned to ETA only when their earlier searches proved futile.

This searching phase of their young lives nevertheless played a crucial role in the development of rebels in several ways. On the one hand, the wider the search ranged, the greater the likelihood that a random event would touch the life of a rebel and convert him into a revolutionary. In other words, the more a young Basque male looked for trouble, the greater the likelihood that he would find it. The Guardia Civil and the police were, after all, only too ready to play this role in the emergence of radicalized youths. On the other hand, the search made the groping youths painfully aware of those options that were not truly open, but only appeared to be. For those who only dream of revolution, many roads that appear open would close if only they were tested. Without this test, the youth may never know that moderate solutions to oppression are only an image created by the elite defenders of the status quo.

The searching phase in the lives of future etarras assumed many different forms. A few, such as Jon Paredes Manot, became enchanted with dangerous sports such as motorcycle racing and mountain climbing. "If they had not killed him," said one friend about Txiki, "he would have killed himself—against the pavement."[22] Others, such as Argala, were subjected to a very confusing and dissonant childhood, divided in their loyalties between a conservative home and church, on the one hand, and a militant need for rebellion and justice, on the other. Their lives during this period oscillated widely from one extreme to the other, until they finally settled into an acceptable identity as an etarra. But most of those for whom I have data began their journey toward ETA in much less violent and less intransigent groups. Txillardegui helped form a number of illegal Basque youth and student groups during the late 1940s. The police breakup of one of these (Eusko Ikasle Alkartasuna) was a key factor in his radicalization in the early 1950s. Many young future etarras participated in strikes and demonstrations that were, during the Franco era, flatly prohibited. Angel Otaegi worked with militant union organizers as well as with the Partido Nacional Vasco (PNV) youth organization, Euzki Gaztedi (EGI), before joining ETA. Apala participated in strikes and demonstrations on a regular basis, even to the point of being arrested on several occasions. Mario Onaindia was active in various labor movements as a youth, and Jokin Gorostidi had been an active participant in a number of illegal Basque patriotic celebrations. In each case, the police suppression of this early searching behavior played a key role in the psychological development of the etarras. They saw their earlier prejudices confirmed, and they became even more stoutly convinced that only violence would suffice to gain their objectives. They discarded nonviolent options as they saw them prove futile against a much stronger and intransigent enemy. This searching phase led, almost inevitably, to greater interest in ETA, and, as we shall see, greater interest by ETA in the young men who were demonstrating their resolve and their commitment to Basque independence.

In all this change, the family appears to have played a surprisingly minor role. In only one case of the dozen or so for which I have information was the family actually supportive of the youth's decision to join ETA. The widowed mother of an etarra I interviewed in 1973 actually encouraged her sons to join the resistance movement to avenge their father's death. In all the other cases, however, the family was either neutral on the subject, or actually opposed to ETA. The families of several etarras in my sample were supportive of Basque nationalism, but opposed ETA's violent tactics. In several cases, such as those of José Martín Sagardía and Jon Paredes Manot, the family had no overt political connections and little interest in politics. Apala's family was apolitical in the sense that it was not tied to any specific party. Apala hid the news from his mother that he had joined ETA, for she certainly would have opposed such a step, as would the mother of Otaegi have tried to dissuade her son from joining. In at least one instance, that of Jon Echave, his mother did indeed try to persuade the young man to change his mind when she learned of his intention to join the organization. Significantly, then, the families of etarras usually played either no role at all in the radicalization of their young sons, or in some cases they actually opposed it. In contrast, once the youth joined ETA and was caught, killed, or driven into exile for his actions, the family rallied around in a solid show of support for their son and brother.

We come now to the critical event in the making of an etarra: his recruitment into the organization. The process by which new members are recruited into the organization is a slow and gradual one, and it is difficult if not impossible to say exactly when a young man crosses the threshold of ETA and becomes a full-fledged member.[23] The recruitment process typically begins when an older ETA member approaches a young prospective member while they are with a group on an outing or a mountain-climbing expedition. The ETA member who makes this initial contact is the key to the whole process. Throughout the recruitment phase, this person remains the contact between the organization and the prospective member. Once the youth decides to join, the contact etarra becomes his sponsor, and guides him through his first tasks and assignments. Since this recruiter is a critical member of the ETA organization, much emphasis is put on selecting *etarras* for recruiting duty, and they are given a great deal of preparation to help them become proficient in this role. In particular, they must be very skilled at keeping up the enthusiasm and morale of the future etarra, for there will be many moments when the youth's commitment will wane, and the organization will lose a new member if he is not bolstered in his decision.

After the initial contact is made, and the youth expresses interest in knowing more about the organization, the etarra will wait several months and then contact him again to invite him to participate in a simple operation. The first task given to the youth during this novice phase usually consists of something like carrying packages of pamphlets to a drop point or delivering cans of spray paint to someone else for use in painting slogans on walls. The organization is careful to give the potential member very limited information to avoid security leaks. Once the youth has proven his competence in this exercise, the older member may ask him to participate in other operations of increasing danger and complexity such as gathering information on the routine or schedule of bank employees prior to a robbery, for example, or driving a load of weapons to deliver to another ETA member. As the youth demonstrates his ability to carry out challenging assignments, he also invests considerable psychological energy in the operations of ETA, so it becomes increasingly difficult for him to disengage from the organization. In addition, the organization now acquires a certain leverage over him because it can divulge information about these early exploits to police authorities. At this point, which may come as much as a year after the initial contact, the organization is ready to bring the young man into full membership. As far as I can tell, however, there is no formal "oathing" ceremony involved in becoming a member. The older ETA member who made the initial contact will usually escort the younger new member to a meeting of a local cell of the organization and will in effect sponsor his young apprentice, after which the youth is accepted as a full-fledged member.

If ETA takes a very long time in recruiting each member, potential members also tend to take their time deciding to join. Young men approached to become etarras typically resist joining for a very long time before they cast their lot with the organization. Virtually every case study reports that the young man resisted the first invitations to join, sometimes for as long as eighteen months or two years, before finally deciding to become a member. The reasons for delay vary from case to case. Iñaki Orbeta thought that being a member of ETA would interfere with his university studies, which he wanted to complete before joining. Angel Otaegi waited until he had completed his military service. Others, like Jokin Gorostidi or Enrique Guesalaga, were involved in other organizations that were active in clandestine politics and they waited to see what would be the fruits of those labors before finally deciding that ETA promised more results in a shorter span of time. In a few cases, young women joined the organization only after their husbands or boyfriends had joined. But in any case, the story has one constant: they all studied the organization, talked to many people about it, attended meetings of the local cells, and actively debated joining with friends and other ETA members. This process of decision lasted a surprisingly long time, and involved a great deal of soul-searching. We are seeing here, then, not a dramatic conversion of a person from a simple uninvolved citizen to a flaming revolutionary overnight. I find in all the case studies a surprising lack of any sort of "catalytic event," an incident so full of dramatic confrontation with authority that the issue of joining or not joining is made to stand out in stark relief, and the young man is thrust in an instant across the threshold into ETA. Such events may have characterized the passage to revolution of famous rebels like Che Guevara or Lenin, but they are strikingly absent in the lives of my etarras.

It is difficult, if not impossible, to generalize about what life is like for a typical etarra once he joins the organization, for there are many different levels of membership, and, correspondingly, many different degrees of commitment to the life of an insurgent. The great majority of the members of ETA continue to live at home, either with their parents or (if they are married) with their spouse and children, and to work at their regular employment, either in the office or on the factory assembly line. Being a member of ETA is time-consuming, to be sure, and many members report having little time left over for the demands of their personal lives once they join. Yet, at the same time, it is not a commitment that demands 100 percent of a member's waking moments.

There are, in general, three kinds of activities that occupy the time and energy of members of ETA. The first involves what we might call consciousness raising. Young etarras are rather more highly politicized than many other Basques from their age group. The organization nevertheless believes that well-informed or well-indoctrinated members are in the long run more reliable and more competent at their jobs. So the organization has from its inception devoted much of its time to sponsoring study sessions or discussion groups whose purpose it is to raise the participants' level of understanding about contemporary political and economic matters, as well as to raise complicated ideological issues for debate and resolution. Even senior members of the organization attend these meetings and participate in the debates, which are usually spirited. These meetings also afford young non-members the opportunity to see ETA in action and to hear some of its members discuss current concerns. These meetings thus frequently serve the purpose of a recruiting device as well.[24]

The second general type of activity engaged in by ETA members has to do with support services for the armed commandos of the organization. A high proportion of ETA's members are involved in support functions, such as gathering and transmitting intelligence information about potential targets, carrying messages or supplies or weapons from one member to another, providing transportation for other members, offering food and shelter for members who are involved in some sort of armed action or fleeing from police pursuit, or simply in producing or disseminating information about ETA or about political matters generally. Some of these functions are delegated to nonmembers who are serving their apprenticeship, while others are provided by older persons who are not etarras themselves but who desire to be of help to the organization. Most of these critical support functions, however, are performed by ETA commandos or by cells whose assignments do not include armed assaults.

ETA support members are reported arrested almost daily in the local Basque press, so the following are cited merely as examples of the kinds of activities in which these members engage. In May 1980, for instance, police announced the arrest of members of an ETA intelligence cell (*comando de información*) that had conducted the following operations in support of ETA:

For four or five Sundays in a row, this comando monitored the schedule of the former mayor of Bilbao, Pilar Careaga, as she came and went to and from church, with the purpose of giving such information to an ETA assassination team, which subsequently carried out an attack (nonfatal) on the former mayor.

The commando also gathered information on the airports near Bilbao (Sondica) and Vitoria (Foronda), as well as on the Guardia Civil patrols that protect these installations. This information was subsequently given to an ETA commando that attacked one of the patrols and killed one Guardia Civil trooper and wounded several others.

The commando also gathered and provided to ETA photographs, blueprints, and other information about several electric power plant installations in Vizcaya, as well as lists of names of persons who occupied key roles in the power plants.

Finally, the commando also gathered personal information about two national policemen who lived in Algorta, with the presumed objective being to attack them at some later date.[25]

The third kind of activity undertaken by ETA members is, of course, armed assaults on persons or property, with the intention either to kill or injure people, to kidnap them for subsequent ransom, or to seize money, weapons, automobiles, or other needed resources. My feeling is that fewer than half of the ETA members actually engage in violent actions of this sort. But they are the ones that give the organization its special insurgent character, as well as attract all the attention. Let us examine in some detail, then, a few specific examples of ETA's assault cells, or commandos. On 20 November 1980, police arrested all five members of an ETA (militar) commando named "Kioto." Four of the five members lived in Amorebieta (Vizcaya), and the fifth lived in Larrabezúa, about ten kilometers away. This commando was accused of five killings:

On 30 December 1978, a taxicab driver in the small village of Yurre, about six kilometers from Amorebieta.

On 17 May 1979, a night watchman of a cement plant in Lemona, about two kilometers from Amorebieta.

On 30 September 1979, the police chief of Amorebieta in Guernica, about eighteen kilometers from Amorebieta.

On 24 March 1980, a jeweler in Durango, fifteen kilometers from Amorebieta.

On 23 October 1980, a factory worker in Amorebieta itself.[26]

On 7 November 1980, police arrested five members of the ETA (militar) commando, "Besaide." Three of the members lived in Mondragón (Guipúzcoa), one was from Oñate (eleven kilometers from Mondragón), and the other was from Vergara (nine kilometers away). The group was accused of the following four killings:

On 13 March 1977, a Guardia Civil trooper in a bar in Oñate (wounding a second Guardia).

On 30 January 1979, a civilian, accused of being a police informer, in Anzuola, about five kilometers from Vergara.

On 8 February 1980, a Guardia Civil trooper in Oñate.

On 18 July 1980, an automobile mechanic in Vergara.[27]

On 17 April 1979, police arrested two members of the six-person commando, "Urola," based in the Goierri region of Guipúzcoa. Two of the commando's members were from Azcoitia (Guipúzcoa), three were from Ezquioga (about fifteen kilometers from Azcoitia), and the sixth was from Legazpia (about the same distance away). The commando was accused of the following actions:

On 11 September 1978, an attack against a Guardia Civil Land Rover in Ezquioga, which resulted in two Guardia Civil troopers dead.

On 13 January 1979, an attack on a Guardia Civil Land Rover in Azcoitia, which left one Guardia Civil trooper dead and another wounded. The commando left behind a booby-trap bomb that exploded killing two other Guardias.

On 2 June 1979, the assassination of the mayor of Olaberri (Guipúzcoa), about twenty kilometers from Azcoitia and ten from Ezquioga.[28]

From these data, we can conclude that ETA commandos were given orders to conduct armed attacks about once every eight months, the average length of time separating each of the attacks listed above. The shortest period separating one attack from another was about four months; the longest, about twenty-two months. About half the attacks were conducted in the hometown of members of the assault commando; the remainder were carried out in towns between five and twenty kilometers away from the base village of the commando. As a general rule, commandos are composed of persons either from the same town or from nearby towns. These examples and the conclusions derived from them help us understand how ETA can recruit and maintain members who continue to live at home and work at their regular job. Their tasks as etarras, even those that involve armed assaults, never take them far away from their homes. Their assignments are spread out over rather long periods of at least four to five months, and sometimes periods of more than a year separate one attack from another. One gets the impression from reading these examples that service in an ETA commando is rather like working at a temporary part-time job, one that requires supremely dangerous and stressful tasks but one that is assigned so as to interfere minimally with the daily life of the perpetrator.

Let us turn, then, to the question of how being a member of ETA affects the daily life of an etarra. How does a member of ETA deal with family, loved ones, and friends?

There seems little doubt that joining ETA has important repercussions on the ability of members to carry on ordinary relationships with nonmembers. Friends of etarras, like those interviewed by Sanchez Erauskin in his book on Txiki and Otaegi, report that after joining the organization their former friends and comrades seemed totally absorbed by their new organizational responsibilities and duties. Etarras have less time in which to join in the normal social life of a small Basque village. There is less time to make the rounds of bars drinking wine and coffee and catching up on the gossip. In many cases, relationships with friends and family members deteriorate considerably after joining ETA. Light political banter that means little to people with only a casual interest in politics begins to take on new and more serious meaning to a young man who has just joined an insurgent organization. The friends of newly recruited etarras report frequently that they seem distant, more difficult to reach, and much more easily aroused by political conversation. In most cases, however, the former friends and comrades know of their old friends' conversion, and they seldom hold it against them that they have changed somehow.[29]

If relationships with friends and family lose immediacy for new etarras, they paradoxically become even more important in a sort of symbolic sense. Even though ETA members now have less time for their former friends and family members, it becomes even more important for them to know that their cultural origins are still intact, awaiting their return when and if they leave the struggle. No matter how far away from their caserío they travel, and how much time they devote to insurgent struggle, they remain steadfastly bound to the life of the traditional small Basque village. ETA has embedded itself organizationally in the everyday life of the Basque village. This it has done for strategic and tactical reasons, no doubt. Yet, there is a personal and psychological dimension to this decision as well. For it is from small-town traditional Basque culture that individual etarras derive their emotional strength, the unusual mixture of social, cultural, and psychological forces that sustains them in the midst of a constantly failing guerrilla war.

I have already described elsewhere in this chapter the relatively minor role played by the families of etarras in their transformation from simply politically conscious youths to members of an insurgent group. From the bits and fragments I have collected about their later lives, the family seems to play the same kind of role for active etarras. That is, during the phase of their lives when they are engaged in active operations for the organization, the family appears to have little to do with them, and plays only a small role in their maintenance and support. This dimension of the social support for ETA changes dramatically whenever an etarra is captured or killed, for then the entire village, but especially the family, becomes mobilized in a major show of support for their friend and son or brother.

For active etarras, however, the principal source of support seems to me to be the small circle of friends, job associates, and other ETA members who cluster together for mutual psychological support and assistance. This group may contain no more than half a dozen members, usually young men who have been close to one another since their early childhood. One of the most prominent social institutions in small Basque villages is the *cuadrilla*, a small (four to six members) group or gang of young boys who spend all of their time in various kinds of exploits with one another. In their youth, these groups may engage in relatively harmless acts of minor vandalism common to young boys in all cultures, such as breaking street lights or painting obscenities on walls. In Basque villages, however, the cuadrillas find other socially acceptable "targets of opportunity," and their harmless adventures may turn toward something a little riskier, like throwing stones at the passing car of some Guardia Civil troops. The reader can easily imagine how exploits like this can spiral into much more serious matters as the youngsters grow to adolescence. During the teenage years, however, many cuadrillas become more organized, and devote themselves to such group activities as mountain climbing, country outings, and informal discussion or study of important contemporary issues. The boys begin to make the rounds of local neighborhood bars, where they are gradually accepted into adult Basque male culture. As they reach their twenties, Basque men may have stronger ties to the cuadrilla than to their own families. It is easy to see how the commando, or small cell, organization of ETA fits so readily into the youth culture of small Basque towns. For young Basque men have already spent as much as a decade in which the dominant social factor was a small group of intimate friends bound in tight cohesion against strangers from the outside. In this important respect (as in others), the culture of small Basque towns is ideal for the implantation of a clandestine political organization organized around the secret cell concept.

If the relationships of etarras with other men are fairly simple, we can draw no such conclusions about their relationships with women. I have already remarked on the significant role played by Basque women in the family, and the mothers of most etarras seem also to have been major figures in the lives of their sons. One can imagine, then, how a member of ETA would have a life-style and an image of the ideal woman that would combine to impose near impossible demands on any wife, sweetheart, or lover. The significant woman in the life of an etarra must have the strength, resolve, patience, and durability necessary to enable her to carry the entire burden of the relationship. She must manage the family and rear the children, perform the tasks so essential to the day-to-day life of a family unit, see her husband or lover leave home at night never knowing where he is going or even whether he will return, and endure all of this in silence and support, literally for years at a time. Not surprisingly, I found few examples of etarras who managed to maintain a normal family life under these circumstances.[30] Most of the etarras about whom I have such personal data fell into one of two categories. Many had no real lasting relationships with women, even though they might have reached (and gone beyond) the conventional age for courtship and marriage in Basque society. Angel Otaegi, for example, was chided by his friends for being a *mutil zarra*, literally in English, "old boy," but a phrase that connotes a man who has remained a bachelor too long.[31] In the case of others, like Apala and Txiki, we find no mention at all of any love interest or any commitment they might have had to a sweetheart or lover. There were others, however, who solved the problem essentially by courting and marrying women who likewise had committed themselves to revolutionary struggle. Especially during the 1960s and early 1970s, when being a member of ETA did not seem to be such a hazardous matter, husband and wife "teams" were fairly commonplace in the organization. Several of the Burgos trial prisoners were in fact married to one another, including Gregorio Lopez Irasuegui and Arantxa Arruti, and Juana Dorronsoro and Francisco Javier Izco de la Iglesia. Another early ETA leader, José María Escubi, was also married to an ETA member, Mariasu Goenaga. If the combined pressure of ETA membership on these couples was too great, we have no record of it. In fact, most of these marriages survived as long as did the partners themselves, and as far as I know they remained married well into their post-ETA period when they were no longer living a clandestine existence.

I have tried to portray life in ETA as being significant and demanding, even difficult and hazardous, but not necessarily as involving levels of stress that would exceed the limits of normal and healthy personalities. Nevertheless, if we are to know why men (and, on occasion, their women) join ETA, we must also know how they can endure year after year of such a life, filled with a certain degree of danger, and (it must be admitted) rewarded with success only very sporadically, if at all. Analysts of insurgency call these factors the "reinforcers," the elements of life that keep a person going in an organization when rationally speaking he or she should give up the struggle and return to a normal life.

In the summer of 1973, I had an opportunity to question several members of ETA about their life, their problems and successes, what caused them despair and what brought them happiness. I concluded, first of all, that these were not especially happy men. They had been at their dangerous occupation for a number of years at that time, and the thrill (if there ever had been one) had long since died away. They had seen dear friends caught or killed, and they had witnessed the failure of the Basque people to rise up in mass insurrection against the Spanish, even after ETA had shown them the way. They were nostalgic over the life they had to leave behind (this particular group was living in France at the time), and they resented the fact that they were almost constantly on duty, that the organization had the right to call them away from whatever they were doing to carry out some operation on short notice. And, perhaps most of all, they were growing restive at the thought that they were losing some of their most precious years in a struggle that might in the future be regarded as futile and even a bit silly.

But they continued the struggle out of a combination of factors that blends both positive and negative reinforcements. On the positive side, they received solid support from their close friends and from their spouses (if they were married). They lived and moved about in a sort of hermetically closed compartment where one simply did not raise depressing questions or challenge the ultimate victory of the organization. They had also learned to lower their expectations, to resign themselves to a very long struggle with little hope for immediate success. They had learned, in other words, the psychological defense of insurgency, as expressed by one of them this way:

A clandestine organization is living and dying every day. There are people who quit. Tired people leave. New people join, and we train them, and then we do it all over again. You see someone once, and then you never see them again. You don't ask questions, you just do your job.

There are, however, negative forces at work that discourage etarras from leaving the organization, no matter how depressed they may become or how much they may yearn for a normal existence. There is, simply put, a fear of reprisals if they were to abandon the struggle and return to civilian life. The source of the reprisals is disputed. Etarras claim that Spanish secret police pursue ex-etarras after they leave the protective cover of the organization, and settle old scores by gunning many of them down, either in France (where many of them continue to live) or in Spain. The official media and government version of all this is that the killings are perpetrated by ETA gunmen who are punishing their former colleagues for abandoning the struggle, and perhaps for delivering information to the enemy. No one can really know the true story. In all probability, both forces are at work. But speaking realistically, there is some truth to the belief that former members of ETA are frequently the targets of armed attack after they leave the organization and attempt to return to normal life.

In reality, we need not make too much out of the question of reinforcers, however, for the simple fact of the matter is that men usually spend rather brief periods of time as ETA members. I have no way to calculate such a statistic, but I would estimate that the average length of time that an etarra spends as an active member of the organization would be less than three years. What happens to them? Obviously, a number of them are killed during one of the organization's armed attacks, and others (probably fewer) are killed by internecine quarrels within ETA itself. Many, probably the majority, are caught and sentenced to long prison terms, and do not rejoin the organization once they are released. And, of course, there are those countless etarras in insignificant support roles who simply blend back into the environment after they "retire" from the organization. For some young Basques, ETA is a crucial end point in their lives, the determinative factor that gives meaning and purpose to an otherwise disorderly and rather pointless frustration. For many others, however, it is only a way station, a phase through which a youth must pass if he is to move on to other more complex and more conventional forms of struggle. In the long run, ETA's major contribution to Basque and Spanish politics may turn out to be that it served as a crucial link that brought young Basques out of their adolescence, radicalized and trained them, and then sent them back to attack the sources of their grievances through the institutions of conventional politics.

NOTES

1. As examples, see the following: Konrad Kellen, "Terrorists—What Are They Like? How Some Terrorists Describe Their World and Actions." Rand Publication N-1300-SL. (Santa Monica, Calif.: Rand, November 1979). Herbert Hendin, "A Psychoanalyst Looks at Student Revolutionaries," *New York Times Magazine*, 17 January 1971. Bruce Mazlish, *The Revolutionary Ascetic* (New York: Basic Books, 1976). Walter Laqueur, *Terrorism* (Boston: Little, Brown, 1977). Albert Parry, *Terrorism: From Robespierre to Arafat* (New York: Vanguard, 1976).

2. The entire list is found in Julen Agirre, *Operation Ogro*, trans. by Barbara Probst Solomon (New York: Ballantine, 1975), pp. 150–158.

3. *Deia* (Bilbao), 6 December 1979.

4. *Deia* (Bilbao), 19 July 1980.

5. One methodological note on the age data: In many cases, I have the actual age when a person joined ETA. In a majority, however, the age on record is the age when the person was first arrested. Since most etarras are arrested very soon after they join the organization (a fact referred to in the text), there will not be much difference (if any) between age of joining and age of first arrest. Hence, my decision to use one datum as a surrogate for the other.

6. Charles A. Russell and Bowman H. Miller, "Profile of a Terrorist" (Washington, D.C.: Headquarters, Office of Special Investigations, United States Air Force, August, 1977), p. 3.

7. Russell and Miller, p. 14.

8. Beltza, *Nacionalismo Vasco y Clases Sociales* (San Sebastian: Editorial Txertoa, 1976), p. 153.

9. José María Portell, *Los Hombres de ETA* (Barcelona: DOPESA, 1974), p. 64.

10. José Mari Garmendia, *Historia de ETA*, 2 vols. (San Sebastian: L. Haranburu, 1980), II, 142.

11. This is especially unusual given the high rate of unemployment that has wracked the Basque economy during the late 1970s. From a base of almost total employment, the unemployment rate climbed to 5.0 percent in 1977, 11.2 percent in 1978, and 17 percent in 1979. The estimated rate was 14.8 percent as of 31 March 1980, compared with an official rate of about 10 percent throughout Spain. Guipúzcoa (with a rate of 18.6 percent in late 1979) and Vizcaya (17.2 percent) have been the provinces hardest hit by the economic crisis. See, for sources, *Deia* (Bilbao), 16 December 1979; and 17 February and 1 August 1980.

12. The authoritative source on this subject, consulted in this analysis, is Luis Michelena, *Apellidos Vascos*, 2d ed. (San Sebastian: Biblioteca Vascongada de los Amigos del Pais, 1955). In cases of doubt, I consulted my spouse who, being Basque herself, was able to identify questionable names as being Basque or non-Basque.

13. See, for example, Charlotte Crawford, "The Position of Women in a Basque Fishing Community," in *Anglo-American Contributions to Basque Studies: Essays in Honor of Jon Bilbao*, William A. Douglass, Richard W. Etulain, and William H. Jacobsen, Jr., eds. (Desert Research Institute Publications on the Social Sciences, no. 13, 1977), pp. 145–152.

14. Miguel Castells, *El Mejor Defensor El Pueblo* (San Sebastian: Ediciones Vascas, 1978), p. 49.

15. Castells, p. 57.

16. Portell, p. 66.

17. Erik H. Erikson, *Ghandi's Truth: On the Origins of Militant Nonviolence* (New York: Norton, 1969), p. 259.

18. Castells, p. 50.

19. Portell, pp. 147–148.

20. *La Actualidad Espanola,* no. 1326, May 30–June 5, 1977, p. 34.

21. Castells, p. 63.

22. Savier Sanchez Erauskin, *Pxikl-Otaigi: El Vinto y las Raices* (San Sebastían: Hordago, 1978), p. 50 n. 31.

23. Much of the following is drawn from the interesting account of ETA recruiting contained in Portell, pp. 39–45.

24. The story of one such meeting is told in detail in Portell, pp. 47–61.

25. *Deia* (Bilbao), 20 May 1980.

26. *Deia* (Bilbao), 29 November 1980.

27. *Deia* (Bilbao), 9 November 1980.

28. *Deia* (Bilbao), 1 May 1979.

29. I am told reliably that in small Basque villages everyone knows who the etarras are among the young men—everyone, that is, except the Guardia Civil. As soon as a youth joins, most of his friends "know" it, at least in the limited sense that they know something important has happened to him, and they can guess most of the rest.

30. In contrast to members of the Basque Nationalist Party, who, even though they were active in the anti-Franco underground, still kept a family together in remarkably good order. See my treatment of this phenomenon in *The Basques: The Franco Years and Beyond* (Reno: University of Nevada Press, 1980), pp. 121–124.

31. Sanchez Erauskin, p. 220.

11

Social-Ethnic Conflict and Paramilitary Organization in the Near East

ABRAHAM ASHKENASI

Much of twentieth-century history has centered on two elementary clashes: social, and ethnic or national. Such conflicts have erupted as the basic expression of popular dissatisfaction. The nation-state system has been weakened by technological change and ideological mistrust. The myths that bind have unraveled. The legitimacies of social control and the verities of economic structures are under constant assault. Periods of political, social, and economic unrest of this kind are always violent. Dislocated social groups and abused communities seize the occasion to rebel. But the residual strengths of central authorities are always relatively formidable. Armed organizations seem to be the last elements of society vulnerable to collapse. Social and ethnic conflicts are often expressed and maintained through the operations of small groups of armed bands. Terrorists to some, guerrillas to others, paramilitary organizations to still others, these represent, or think they do, a social or national idea, or a class or ethnic group, or a diffuse combination of all of these.

In the post–World War II period, we have witnessed the success of three major sociorevolutionary movements that grew from paramilitarism to national and social dominance. The Chinese, Vietnamese, and Cuban experiences provided and provide a model for successful paramilitary revolutionary activity for a generation of political and social militants. An analysis of these movements and their success is well outside the scope of this paper. The relation of ethnosocial or national frustrations and humiliation to socioeconomic revolutionary zeal is another important but moot and unresolved point. Seemingly similar conflicts in El Salvador and Guatemala and the "revolutionary" success in Nicaragua indicate that the model has an ongoing validity and applicability. This is especially true as an organizational pattern.

The "socialist" paramilitary movements combined popular allegiance and legitimatized leadership with "modern" organizational techniques. A "modern" political organization maintains:

1. Educated and ideologically highly motivated, efficient cadres.
2. Quick lines of communication.
3. Flexible policies and tactics and economically feasible and easily understandable sets of goals.
4. Easy assimilation of potential followers.
5. Geographic mobility: the ability to operate efficiently throughout the broad conflict area.
6. Strong, interlocking ties between socioeconomic units, or segments of society (farming and rural areas, school organizations, urban employees or trade unions), and fighting units.
7. Highly motivated, *permanently available* fighting units, highly mobile and motivated, loyal to ideas, not men, and capable of handling new technologies.

This kind of "modern" organization seems to have functioned successfully in predominantly agrarian or half-agrarian societies. Modern industrial societies have not spawned this kind of movement. Social revolutionaries in industrial societies are by and large urban guerrillas. They have not been able to spread into the countryside. Their ties to a broad social network are tenuous at best. The most prominent of these groups, that is, the Red Brigades in Italy, the Red Army Faction (RAF) in West Germany, or the Weathermen in the United States, proclaim socialistic goals and ideals. These goals remain in the realm of wishful thinking. Indeed, typical urban guerrilla groups are socially as well as organizationally different from their charismatic models. The city guerrilla remains an outsider. Obviously, then, paramilitary organization is not simply paramilitary organization. Operations and policies are a function of social structure.

ETHNIC CONFLICT AND NATIONAL SEPARATISTS

Most modern conflicts seem to be ethnic or national conflicts. Most paramilitary organizations intent on drastic systemic change in this current vale of struggles are ethnic in character. The most volatile of these are in the Near East. Socioeconomic factors are obviously also bound up in these conflicts. The major unifying factor is ethnic, ethnoreligious, or national identity.

Much of twentieth-century history has centered on the clash of national aspirations. As nationalism was the binding ideology for social control, political security, and economic growth, it was almost inevitable that dissatisfaction would be expressed in antinational or neonational forms. In many instances even working-class dissatisfaction could be described as ethnic. This was certainly true of the immigrant and black workers in the United States and to a degree in Great Britain as well where Celts were universally exploited. Indeed much purely social conflict has been expressed as national conflict. The volatility of this conflict was enhanced by asymmetries of development. Conflict increased in intensity in direct relation to the social dislocation inherent in the asymmetry of external and indeed internal development. Nationalism is a volatile ideology that moved eastward across Europe and into Asia. It not only lit the fires of national and social aspirations in the colonialized world outside the European metropolis but left large ethnic or national groups, and not always minorities at that, on the sidelines. While the English, French, or German-Hungarian Austrians might be satisfied, the Irish, Bretons, and various Balkan Slavs were certainly not. At various points in their and their opponents' social and political development, dissatisfaction turned to open defiance.

In some instances new states arose out of the nationalist calamity of World War I. Some did not outlive World War II. Some national groups were only partly successful in establishing a nation-state, and national irredentism persisted and persists. This development was not limited to Europe. The anticolonial struggles of Asia and Africa and indeed America are well documented. But here too some nationalities were left behind in the pell-mell rush to create nation-states. French Canadians, Muslim Filipinos, South Sudanese, Biafrans, Eritreans, among others, joined the ranks of the dissatisfied national groups. These late-blooming nationalisms differ in some significant ways from the established nations.

The most significant difference is that of socioeconomic development. Most late-blooming nationalisms, those nationalisms which had not developed into a nation-state by the end of World War II reflected the political, social, and economic aspirations of a core ethnic group. The ethnic group involved usually had been left behind in the sense that socioeconomic development is asymmetric. This did not imply a lack of cultural, economic, religious, or linguistic homogeneity. Indeed elements of this homogeneity as well as a historical sense of being one group had to be strongly felt and maintained in order for an ethnic group of this kind to articulate its sociopolitical growth and to back it up with resolute action. It meant, however, that the group had not enjoyed the same economic development as the dominant national group. It also implied exploitation. This was true not only of imperialist exploitation from without but also within the "imperialized" geographic entity, the imperialists would find cooperative elements of society. These groups often reflected a certain ethnic or socioreligious homogeneity. Their leadership would help dominate and help exploit and the whole group would to a degree profit. Such groups (Christians in Lebanon, to a degree Zionists in Israel and, for a time, upper-class and Sunnite Arabs in Iraq) would develop the sinews of modern and efficient political and military life more quickly than other ethnic groups in the area. They were often able to promote their national idea more successfully. In order to establish this nationalism successfully, however, all ethnic groupings had to have certain characteristics:

1. A clearly defined geographical area from which to operate and which would develop into the nation-state.

2. Clear lines of operational legitimacy for a leadership group. In most instances various leadership groups competed with one another along distinct sociological and ideological lines. One leadership group, however, always assumed ascendancy and was able to legitimize its control over the bulk of the ethnic group involved.

3. A keen sense of religious and/or linguistic and/or historical ethnocultural and/or economic homogeneity and solidarity usually arising out of economically exploitative and psychologically demeaning conditions.

4. A certain amount of demographic mass relative to other competing ethnic core groups or nation-states.

5. A certain amount of international support. It appears impossible to make a successful national movement out of an internal ethnic conflict without some measure of international sponsorship. This international sponsorship is all the more critical since the goals of core ethnic groups have not changed in three hundred years although the world in which they live has changed significantly. There is embittered opposition to any new attempts to carve out a nation-state.

NATIONAL CONFLICT IN THE NEAR EAST

The nation-state always grew out of a core ethnic group in a well-defined geographical area. This process had a valid function in growing industrial societies where the new bourgeois class sought upward mobility, and a larger geographic unit made economic and military sense. In the twentieth century the nation-state has lost much of its reason for existence. It does not provide much upward social mobility for newly emerging classes. It is not an economically feasible unit. It no longer provides real psychological or physical security. Because of its relative weakness, the left-behind core groups are able to demand their "nationhood." The paradox is complete. The dream's disintegration allows new dreamers to implement the tired emancipatory hope: the nation-state fixed within its own geographical limits with vertical mobility for those adhering to its codes and enjoying full citizenship; in most instances a dominant nationality with its paraphernalia of security-giving symbols and agencies, flags and anthems, armed forces and legends, and so forth. This is the measure of success for ethnic conflict and although much of this conflict is articulated along emancipatory, ideological, or revolutionary lines it remains highly particularistic in its structure and goals. In the early years of the twentieth century, the Balkans were considered the powder keg of the world and the Balkans reflected best the destabilizing power inherent in unfulfilled national goals and involatile ethnic aspirations. After World War II and certainly after the establishment of the many nation-states that grew out of the imperialist experiment of the eighteenth, nineteenth, and twentieth centuries, the focus of ethnic conflict shifted to the Near East. This was so for many reasons:

1. The area maintained within it a large number of ethnic groups that could function successfully side by side under the relatively disinterested and anational Ottoman Empire. The ideas of nationalism and the nation-state had indeed penetrated the area with the British and French incursions, especially into Algeria and Egypt, but for the most part the Ottomans and the feudal social conditions of the empire did not encourage national goals either by their example or by their repressions. This was left for the new Turkish nationalism after 1908 and especially after the growth of Kemalism in Turkey. The Arab armies that fought with the British in World War I were still largely particularistic in aspiration and in structure and represented a preindustrial family- and clan-oriented society. They had little contact with the burgeoning Arab nationalism of a rising intelligentsia in towns like Algiers and especially Cairo. A nationalism like that of the Palestinians did not exist at all, except perhaps in the sense that one may have considered oneself a South Syrian. It is even questionable whether Syria at this time was much more than a geographic hangover of Roman organization. The Zionist movement had begun to function in the area but it was still primarily a non-Near Eastern phenomenon. Only the Kurds could make themselves felt in the early twentieth century and their bid for a nation-state was destroyed by a combination of Turkish, Persian, Iraqi Arab, and British repression. Certain ethnic groups that saw a chance of success in cooperation with the imperialist or colonial powers did so in the period between 1920 and 1948. This

contributed to a lack of emancipatory political organization in many ethnic groups. The Iraqi Arabs who cooperated with the British against the Kurds, and the Christian Maronites who cooperated with the French against Lebanese and Syrian Muslims, have already been mentioned, but smaller groups or clans were also easily co-opted.

2. The lack of industrialization in the area and the continued family- and clan-oriented social structure plus the conservative aspect of Islam made it impossible for many potential national groups to organize along modern lines. This was especially true of the Palestinians and the Kurds, and possibly for the Druze as well. The great exception to this regional axiom were the Zionists, but they organized first in Europe. And they had no powerful Jewish traditionalists or conservative social structure to combat in Palestine.

3. The strategic importance of the area, both in geopolitical and economic senses, made it a prime area of big-power intervention and repression. It was only in the period after World War II, and given the weakness of the European nation-states, that the late-blooming nationalisms of the Near East were able to succeed. The Arabs, however, advanced separately into international recognition and national life. Arab nationalism became fragmented. Various forms of national Arab states were established. The concept of the Arab Nation remained a concept. The Palestinians were left behind by this development. The relatively quick development of nation-states in Syria and Iraq combined with the early national establishments in Iran and Turkey also left the Kurds behind. The Zionist movement originated outside of the Near East, and probably because of this the Zionists were most successful in establishing and maintaining their nation-state. Other groups in the area were either too small or too badly disorganized—such as the Druze—or too associated with colonial powers—such as the Maronite Christians—to establish themselves successfully. The situation as we know it today reflects the conditions of the late forties.

Nationalism, as many of its theorists and analyzers (i.e., Hans Kohn, Carleton Hayes, and Richard Rosecrance) have pointed out, is very much the ideology of the soldier and it is thus not surprising that the ethnic groups striving for a nationalist homeland embedded in a Western type of nation-state should turn to violence to underscore their political agitation. There does not seem to have been an establishment of a national state without conflagration. In most instances this conflagration was initiated by paramilitary groups serving the cause of ethnic emancipation. Perhaps it is stretching a historical point to compare groups like Ethan Allan's Green Mountain Boys in Vermont shortly before the American Revolution or other elements of the American revolutionary army, General Lützow's famous *Wilde Jagd* or

Schwarze Schar in Germany during the Napoleonic period, Garibaldi's Red Shirts in Italy before the establishment of the Italian State, and so on, with paramilitary or guerrilla or terrorist operations today. Nevertheless it seems certain that ethnic groups in conflict with dominating political entities, either imperialist, colonialist, or of another dominant culture on common political turf, have all resorted to the paramilitary option to forward their goals. Legal and logistical support of these paramilitary operations internationally seems quite critical for success. Almost inevitably, the paramilitary organization melts into the political organization of the emerging state, if indeed it does not metamorphose totally into that political organization. This may have been less true in the nineteenth century than it is today. However, it is fair to say that in the twentieth century, paramilitary groups that have resorted to terror as an instrument of their struggle for power have also spawned the political leadership of the nation-states to follow. The Irish give a good example of this phenomenon, but the Algerian and the Israeli experiences are probably the most well documented in this regard in the postwar period. Again the Near East provides the best current examples of this process.

PARAMILITARY ORGANIZATION

In the struggle for national emergence, the fluid lines between paramilitarism and guerrilla activities, between political organization and nascent political structures, are only too evident. This is as true for those who have established their state (Algeria, Israel, etc.) as for those who have not (Kurds, Palestinians). The Near East provides us with good examples of the various types of paramilitary structures. There are several distinct forms of paramilitary organization. They usually reflect elements of the social structure of the ethnic group engaged in its emancipatory struggle. A typical structure for the Near East was the semifeudal, family-oriented paramilitary organization. This reflected basic elements of Islamic society—its landowner and family orientation, and its hierarchically structured social groupings with dominant patriarchal characteristics. This organizational structure was strongly in evidence among the Riff in Morocco, among the Kurds throughout their conflict and into the present, among the Palestinians in the thirties and indeed even in today's PLO structure, and among the Druze in Lebanon. This particularistic and segmented organization belies the national idea while using the concept ideologically. It also favors conservative social structures.

A second type of paramilitary group is strongly petit bourgeois in its social characteristics and tends to be nationalist to the exclusion of social reformist characteristics. It is a right-wing paramilitary organization. Although this type of lower-middle-class paramilitary operation is rarely acknowledged as such, there are many examples of this phenomenon. The best example is probably the Irgun Zwai Leumi in Israel (Bell 1977). This Zionist organization arose out of a clear body of conservative nationalist European thought (Laqueur 1972). Its supporters within the urban middle class and its metamorphosis into a political party left it exactly where it had begun: a nationalist conservative political group. It is highly conceivable that elements of the PLO reflect this kind of structure and ideology and certainly the Maronite Christian forces of the Lebanon are illustrative of this kind of paramilitary ethnic organization in the Near East. The OAS in Algeria, in its day, is the prime example.

The third category of paramilitary ethnic organization is that of the so-called socialist grouping. Very often groups that are not socialist at all will call themselves socialist. Defining a paramilitary organization as socialist can only be done by analyzing the social structure of its supporters. They are usually dislocated farmers who no longer are embedded in the social and economic structure of the area or they are working-class individuals from the urban area. The leadership is often bourgeois, the so-called intelligentsia. These paramilitary organizations not only bring with them a volatile and emancipatory nationalist ideology but also structured social plans based on socialist theory, which are often put into practice before the end of the conflict.

The Israeli Haganah, although not purely socialist, harbored within it a cadre fighting organization, the Palmach group, which maintained strong elements of socialist theory and socialist organizational practice. It was agrarian with a kibbutz orientation. In the state of Israel this socialism was only partially carried out within the Mapam and Achdut Haawoda parties and within the Kibbutz movement (Gilad and Meged 1954). Within the Palestinian organizations the Hawatmeh group seemed, in its theory at least, to reflect this kind of grouping. Its lack of strength within the Near East reflects the social conditions in the Arab area that militate against the successful development of truly socialist organizations (Schiller 1982).

The intertwining of social and ethnic confrontations makes analytical purity, however, a pious hope. This is especially true when dealing with the urban guerrilla. Urban guerrillas, from all shades of the political spectrum, cohabit significantly enough in the Near Eastern environments; their influence, however, has been negligible.

Let us look more carefully at the Zionist paramilitary organizations and, as a complete contrast, the Kurds. I will also refer to various Palestinian groups to strengthen points made about both.

PARAMILITARISM IN ZIONISM

THE HAGANAH

Even in the diaspora, but perhaps especially because organization first emerged there, Jewish paramilitary structure went hand in hand with party developments. By 1904/1905 in Vilna and in Odessa, defense organizations had sprung up in the Jewish community. These were primarily associated with Jewish socialist parties, within the Zionist movement, but also in the Bund (*Encyclopedia Judaica* (1971): 4: 1498–1507). In Palestine as well, the first paramilitary Zionist organization, the Haschomer (the guards), were founded by Israel Schochat. Schochat, a prominent member of the second Aliya (immigration to Israel) was a person with rather decided social revolutionary conceptions. The Haschomer had excellent contacts to the socialist Poale Zion party, which was founded in 1907 in Ramla. Prominent members were David Ben-Gurion and Izhak Ben Zwi. Both these groups were viewed with some suspicion by conservative Jews in and outside Palestine (Allon 1970:11–41; *Encyclopedia Judaica*, 14: 1440–1441).

But the Haschomer was a relatively small operation with about a hundred and fifty members. Major militarization of elements of the Jewish community in Palestine took place during World War I. Although it was the conservative Vladimir Jabotinski who conceived of the Jewish legion, most of its members, about five thousand soldiers, were decidedly left wing. When World War I ended, the Jewish community in Palestine was confronted with the beginnings of Arab nationalism and it is interesting that Jabotinski, who was then a member of the Zionist executive, opposed the creation of illegal paramilitary organizations. He feared, correctly, that they would come under the control of left-wing elements.

In 1919, however, the Histadrut (the trade union movement) and the Achdut Haawoda (Work Brotherhood political party) were founded. The Achdut Haawoda united all the socialist parties and elements of the Jewish community in Palestine and, in June of 1920, the Haganah (Defense League) was founded. The Haschomer had dissolved itself in April 1920 and Israel Schochat and his followers joined the Haganah. The important point is that the Achdut Haawoda was given the responsibility for the Haganah. Jewish paramilitarism in Palestine then was always tied to party structures and party ideology. It also could call on trained soldiers.

In the 1920s the Haganah was led by Josef Hecht. His attempt to dominate the Haganah led to his dismissal and disappearance from the political stage. The Haganah began to develop international contacts, and weapons were bought primarily in Austria. Ties sprang up between Austrian and German leftists and the Haganah. By 1924 the Haganah possessed 27 machine guns, 750 rifles, 1,050 pistols, and 750 hand grenades. There were 350 volunteers in the Haganah in Tel Aviv, and in Haifa, where the left-wing tradition was strong and a nascent Jewish working class was developing, the Haganah was even stronger.

Within the Haganah the so-called Hakibbutz movement formed around Schochat. This group was able to finance itself by open brigandage. In November 1923 the Hakibbutz ambushed and robbed a caravan of smugglers in Lebanon and was richer by £15,000 in gold. The funds were used to buy weapons, which were stored in a bunker in Khfar Giladi, five meters deep and thirty square meters in area. In addition, members of the Hakibbutz movement were trained abroad. Jerachmiel Lukazer got his training in a military academy in Berlin and came back to Palestine as a convinced communist. He led the so-called academy of the Haganah in Tel Josef. In the summer of 1925, Schochat had already visited Moscow. Apparently there was a steady coming and going of Jewish paramilitary people from Palestine to Austria and Germany and Russia where contacts were maintained with Austro-Marxists, left-wing German socialists, and communists. There is little or no research on this fascinating subject (Lev-Ami 1979:21–22).

Although the activities of Lukazer and Schochat caused conflict within its leadership, the Haganah was nevertheless able to maintain its national political integrity, and it did not become subject to Comintern control. Some of the members of the Hakibbutz movement in the Haganah went to Russia in 1927. Most of them, however, remained within the Haganah and in 1927 turned over to the Haganah the arms bunker in Khfar Giladi. By the thirties the Haganah had developed into a paramilitary organization with strong socialist ideals but with nationalist predilections. In addition, more and more an interlocking directorate was developing between the Haganah and the Histadrut, the Jewish trade union. The trade union, at this time, was also socialist in its ideals. What this meant was that Haganah members were either in the kibbutz movement or in the Histadrut. They had, then, a dual allegiance, which was really a unity. They belonged to economic organizations that were associated with their paramilitary organization. In addition, a political party watched over the entire complex. Of course, nothing like this was developing on the Arab side.

Arab nationalism, however, was blooming in Palestine, and the Arabs were forming paramilitary organizations as well. (I shall have more to say about this later.) The Haganah developed a conception of *havlaga*, which means self-restraint, as a reaction to Arab militancy.

Throughout the thirties the Haganah maintained this attitude. The theory behind it was that the Jewish community in Palestine should defend itself but not engage in any kind of direct offensive action against the British or the Arab community. This strategy continued into World War II. It reflected the close ties between the Haganah and the leadership of the Histadrut. The Haganah was able to extend its organizational net, which it had not overly exposed, throughout the Jewish community in Palestine. Many of the new immigrants in the thirties were more easily integrated into a paramilitary operation that practiced self-restraint than they would have been into a more volatile organization. The Haganah developed its own communications network, arms production, and international contacts throughout this period. Indeed it was able to function as an army in the field without much difficulty after the British left in 1948. Some of its prominent veterans were David Ben-Gurion, Moshe Dayan, Moshe Scharet, Levi Eschkol, Chaim Barlev, Pinchas Saphir, Teddy Kollek, and Izhak Navon. This is a roll call of prominent Israeli politicians of the fifties and sixties and indeed many are active still. Kollek is mayor of Jerusalem, Navon was the president of Israel and is active in the Labor party, Barlev is a prominent Labor party member of the Knesset (Shimon Peres, the current head of the Labor party and, at this writing, prime minister, was a very minor luminary). It is interesting to note that all of these Haganah members were subsequently members of the Mapai, the Israeli Social Democracy. In other words, they maintained their relatively moderate trade union socialism and carried it into government. In 1948 the Haganah could command a membership of 65,000 people. Most of them were members of the Histadrut. The Haganah was strongest in the Haifa area where Jewish socialism was strongest. But the Haganah was not the only paramilitary organization in the Jewish community in Palestine before the establishment of the state of Israel.

THE PALMACH

To the left and to the right of the Haganah, organizations much smaller than it sprang up in the wake of the conflicts with the British and with the Palestinian Arab nationalists in Palestine. Within the Haganah itself the strongly socialist and strongly nationalist groups around Izhak Tabenkin and his Kibbutz Meuchad movement moved for more decided action against the Palestinian community. Izhak Sade became the leader of this group, within the Haganah, which eventually developed into the Palmach. Sade had come from Russia where he had been a commander of a unit within the Red Army. Most of the members of the Palmach came from the Kibbutz movement. But Sade himself was a stonecutter in the city of Petah Tiqwa who had led a worker's battalion in Palestine in the twenties.

The Palmach existed unofficially, then, in the thirties. Although the official policy of the Haganah was restrained, Sade organized the highly mobile units of the Haganah which attacked Arab villages in which weapons, or guerrillas who had attacked Jewish settlements, were suspected. Sade's and Tabenkin's concepts were offensive in character. The close contacts maintained through the Kibbutz movement allowed for fast action. As determined socialists as well as nationalists, the Palmach consisted of some of the most highly motivated of Israel's paramilitary people. The Palmach was officially founded on 15 May 1941 and its official purpose was to cover the retreat of the British should Rommel's army reach Palestine. After Rommel's defeat, the British wanted to dissolve the Palmach but it had of course by then developed its own dynamics. It had also certainly existed before 1941.

The kibbutz structure allowed for the maintenance of units without pay. The kibbutzes themselves were able to maintain the logistics of the operations, and the kibbutz movement financed the Palmach. The movement remained organizationally within the Haganah. An examination of its leaders and the role they played in the State of Israel after independence shows that they formed the left wing of the Labor party alliance. Igal Allon, Izhak Rabin (he was one of the few who was not a member of a kibbutz), and Israel Galili are some of its most prominent alumni. Izhak Hofi is not so prominent but he was, until recently, the head of Mosad, the Israeli equivalent of the CIA. The Palmach had approximately five thousand members. It was a hardhitting and eminently successful paramilitary organization of dedicated socialists and nationalists within the Haganah. Its policies were carefully planned and its membership constant over the entire period of conflict. Its alumni in Israeli politics were also socialists and nationalists, but not nearly so prominent as the more moderate Mapai personages. The Palmach was also successful in its operations against the more haphazardly organized right-wing Israeli paramilitary organization, the Irgun Zwai Leumi, or Etzel.

THE ETZEL

The Etzel was founded in 1937. It too had been in existence for a while before it was officially founded (Begin 1951; Katz 1968). By 1931 the conflict between left-wingers and right-wingers within the Haganah caused Abraham Thomi, the commander of the Haganah in Jerusalem, to form his own organization within the Haganah. This so-called organization of the right, Irgun Jemini, was able to muster at the height of its strength in the forties at the most three thousand members. The Etzel by and large was an organization of the lower-middle-class Jewish urban community. There is only one analysis of Etzel membership and it is not complete, with only 143 members of the 1,442 asked answering the questions put to them. The largest group came from Poland, 31 of 143. The next largest group, 24 out of 143, came from Yemen. Similar questions put to the Haganah or the Palmach would certainly have resulted in a higher percentage of Russians (Avivi 1967).

Etzel leadership was European. Its members came mostly from oriental or Near Eastern countries. Most of them were self-employed workers or traders with a grammar school education. It was an organization based largely in the cities and associated with the right-wing Herut party. The Herut is a typical nationalist conservative party similar to the kind found in Eastern Europe in the twenties or thirties. It has strong ethnocentric predilections and represents the lower middle class. The Etzel was not a well-organized paramilitary organization and remained a small organization even for the tiny new Jewish community in Palestine. In 1939 there were probably no more than five hundred active members of the Etzel. Its propaganda was dramatic and extremely nationalist: It demanded both sides of the Jordan for the Jewish state. It viciously attacked Haganah's policy of restraint and indulged in individual terror against Arabs and British and against "leftist" Jews as well. It robbed Jewish trade-union banks and stole dynamite from the trade-union building company, Solel Boneh. Contrary to the policy of most of the Jewish community, it declared war on the British in 1944 while the Haganah continued its cooperation with the Allies.

The Etzel was responsible for the attack on the Arab town of Dir Yaseen and it was Etzel people that blew up the King David Hotel. The Haganah and the Palmach kept their eye on the Etzel throughout this period, that is, the period until the establishment of the Jewish state in 1948. After the Etzel declared war on Britain in February 1944, Palmach members kidnapped prominent members of the Etzel and interned them in a kibbutz to keep the Etzel under control (Schavit 1976). In the famous *Altalena* affair, it was the Palmach that sank the Etzel's boat, *Altalena*, filled with weapons from France. After Israeli independence, the Etzel by and large merged into the nationalist Herut (freedom) party. It is typical of this paramilitary organization that they could not construct the sinews of government or accept responsibility for national compromise after their dissolution as a paramilitary organization. They continued their volatile and emotional nationalism and the Herut party drew much of its support from the same classes of Israeli society that had supported the Etzel.

The most prominent of the Etzel's members, of course, was Menachem Begin. It is interesting to note that very few of the Etzel
members became prominent Israeli politicians. Perhaps Herut came
to power too late. But perhaps it was simply not in the nature of this
kind of paramilitary organization to provide the men to establish a
modern government. They did, however, play an important role in
the Herut faction of parliament until 1965. Some exceptions to this
rule are Jakov Meridor and Chaim Landau, both of whom became
ministers in Begin's government (Orland 1982). It is also interesting
to note that the commander of the *Altalena,* Eliyahu Lankin, became
ambassador to South Africa. The Etzel's international ties were to
elements of the right in France and, again, to the Union of South
Africa. But they also maintained contacts with the political representatives of the Israeli bourgeois community (the liberal General Zionists) and through them with the United States.

THE LECHI

A fourth paramilitary organization in Jewish Palestine was the so-
called Lechi, also known as the Stern Gang (Mohr 1974). The Lechi
is a typical city guerrilla organization. It harbored within its ranks the
kind of extremists that one finds in big-city terrorist organizations
today. Indeed, it was only capable of individual terror. Ideologically,
it seems to have been extremely left wing and right wing. In other
words, it maintained within it all the elements of extremism and
extremist psychological types that were active within the Jewish community in Palestine in that period. It is difficult to analyze its organization. It was made up, as are similar groups today, of small
hyperactivist cells. It obviously could not develop into any political
party. Typically, its only parliamentary list was headed by a visionary
leftist. It was also not organized along clear social and economic lines
as was the Haganah, the Palmach, or even the Etzel. Its members
could not agree on anything but violent activism. Its activities, however, seem to have been largely directed against the British and,
indeed, the United Nations after the British departure. It was responsible for the assassination of the British high commissioner for
the Near East in Egypt, Lord Moyne, and for the murder of UN
mediator Folke Bernadotte (Gerold 1963). Its alumni seemed to be
more active in right-wing parties of Israel than on the left. Izhak
Shamir is certainly its most prominent alumnus. It is assumed widely
that he planned both assassinations mentioned above. He was probably
a pure activist at the time of his association with the Lechi. He was
Begin's foreign minister and successor, but from 1955 to 1965 he was
active in Mosad under Labor. Matyhu Schmuelevitz, the head of

Begin's secretariat, is another prominent alumnus of Lechi. Geula Cohen, a young girl courier at the time, was a member of Herut but now is a leader of the ultranationalist Renaissance party in Israel.

An analysis of these four paramilitary organizations, even one as superficial as this one, is interesting for many reasons. The four groups are distinctly different. They are, however, representative of various types of paramilitary organizations that have appeared in the twentieth century. The Haganah represented a broad spectrum of left-wing or socialist Jewish thinking and was able to establish parallel organizations within the trade union movement, within the left-wing political parties, and within the agricultural sector. It was able to integrate new followers and to train them in paramilitary tasks. Indeed, it became a state within the state. It is a prime example of a modern paramilitary organization. It harbored within it the Palmach, a striking arm of high mobility and motivation. But the Haganah was never subverted by the Palmach. Had the ties to the Soviet Union that had developed in the twenties been maintained within a Jewish society in Palestine, the Palmach could have been the typical operational tool for Comintern control of the Israeli left. This, however, did not occur. As in the Partisan movement in Yugoslavia, the Israeli socialist paramilitary organizations retained their national independence.

The Etzel developed along the lines of many middle-class, extreme nationalist paramilitary organizations. There were many of this type in Europe in the twenties and thirties. In the postwar period, the OAS in Algeria, elements of the IRA, and of the Basque ETA, are similar. The Etzel was by and large ineffective as a paramilitary organization. It caused plenty of haphazard damage, but it did not in any way develop the political, economic, and social sinews or policies of a new state. It remained strident and oppositional. This may very well be a hallmark of this kind of organization. Its volatile nationalism and activism can probably only function in cooperation with an established military; when alone, urban middle-class imperatives preclude the political, economic, and social programs necessary for nation-building.

The Lechi is interesting as an organization of activists operating in an urban setting without clear political goals. In this it is a mirror of the anarchist groups of the late nineteenth century as well as the urban guerrillas of our own period. It is interesting to note that Lechi alone among the Jewish paramilitary organizations could form no functioning political grouping after independence. The Reschimat Halochamim (fighters list) managed to elect but one man in the first Knesset, the Israeli parliament.

Another interesting aspect of the Israeli experience is that Jewish paramilitary organizations had no Jewish traditional society in Palestine on which to build or to combat. Traditional societies, of course, offer intact structures within which an oppositional movement can operate. But they can also work as a monumental hindrance to effective operations. This is probably what crippled the Palestinians from 1910 to 1948. The Kurdish experience provides us with an excellent insight into this kind of phenomenon.

TRADITION-BOUND PARAMILITARY ORGANIZATIONS: THE KURDS

AGAS AND SHEIKHS—PERSONAL LEADERSHIP

Nothing could contrast better with the Zionist paramilitary organizations than those of the Kurds. The Kurds have maintained a constant demographic presence in the area of northern Turkey, Iraq, and Iran for almost three thousand years. They have invariably played an important role in the history of the area. They have, however, never enjoyed national independence. They may be the largest disenfranchised national or ethnic group in the world.

Precise figures for the Kurdish population are impossible to ascertain because of infrequent and inadequate censuses and deliberate understatements by central governments. Approximate figures are:

	Kurds	Total population
Iran	4,500,000	38,146,000
Iraq	3,000,000	13,134,000
Turkey	8,700,000	45,182,000
Syria	600,000	8,534,000
Lebanon	100,000	2,981,000
USSR (Armenia, Georgia, Azerbaijan)	200,000	14,031,000
	17,200,000	

(Short and MacDermott 1977)

There have been major and minor uprisings in Kurdistan since the middle of the nineteenth century. With the exception of a few precious years in the 1920s, following World War I, and in the 1940s, following World War II, in Iraq and Iran, respectively, no Kurdish national state could be maintained. All uprisings were crushed in Kurdistan despite the martial renown of Kurdish fighters. Kurdish paramilitarism has been a history of constant failure. My basic thesis here will be that it has failed because of its attachment to traditional social structures and its inability to coordinate modern political organization with its paramilitary units. In this, I may add, it bears a striking similarity to the Palestinian operations of the 1946 to 1948 period (Schiller 1982).

Fragmentation and particularism are central phenomena in Kurdish political and social organization. The extended geographic area in which the Kurds live was never centralized. The Kurdish emir system, which functioned under the Ottoman Empire for 300 years, was destroyed after the Tanzimat reforms of the Ottoman Empire and the rebellion of the Kurdish emirs in the nineteenth century (Iwaideh, 1960:147–345). Kurdish society then disintegrated into large, very loosely organized clans whose basic social and political organization was quite decentralized. The role of the leader of the clan, the aga, is strong only in times of internal or external conflict. Basic social patterns are not centrally regulated (van Bruinessen 1978). But many agas gained considerable economic advantage. Parallel to the strength of the agas rose the power of the sheikhs. These Muslim religious leaders were able to build up a parallel sociopolitical power to that of the agas. Clan, tribal, and religious allegiances always placed more claim on the loyalty of the Kurdish paramilitary men than did any conception of nationalism or the nation state. The principle of nationalism was the dream of the middle-class intellectual Kurd. But he usually lived far from the centers of military power in the clan areas. This is a situation that continues to this very day. Typical were the two aforementioned short-lived Kurdish republics, both of which were led by religious leaders (Eagleton 1963). One of the obvious demographic aspects of Kurdistan is its lack of urban centers. Sulaimaniyah or Arbil in Iraq and Mahabad in Iran are really just large provincial towns. Such intellectuals as there were and such political parties as did develop were always quite separate sociologically from the Kurdish forces in the countryside. Policy decisions were invariably made by agas or sheikhs.

Basically this situation was reflected in the leadership of the so-called Pesch-Merga, the Kurdish paramilitary organization. Mullah Mustafa Barzani had been the military leader of the ill-fated Mahabad Kurdish Republic in Iran. He was the only member of the leadership able to flee. With 800 followers he escaped the Persian army across the river Aras and entered the Soviet Union where he remained until 1958. Barzani is the scion of a line of sheikhs and religious leaders, but his family was relatively new to the northern region of Iraq from which he operated. It came from Persia in the nineteenth century. He therefore could reckon with the opposition of the great sheikhs of northern Iraq, for example, from the Zibari or Lolan clans. Some clans in the north like the Zibari, Harki, and the Lolan used Barzani's opposition to the Iraqi government to increase their influence in the north by cooperating with the Sunnite Arab and Iraqi governments.

Barzani's move into northern Iraq in 1961, three years after his return to Iraq as the leader of the Democratic party of Kurdistan, which he founded in 1946, had advantages and disadvantages for him. He was able, as a prominent fighting man and religious leader, to count on the support of many of the northern tribesmen. But he also faced the bitter opposition of many competing sheikhs and agas in the conservative north. The more conservative the area, the more the Kurdish leaders seemed to be interested in their own particularist *takiyah* (literally translated, their corner, or their spoils). Members of the clan were loyal in the first instance to their own clan. The more conservative they were, the more particularist they seemed to be. The idea of the nation was one that could be found in Sulaimaniyah, but it was far more prevalent among the tribes of southern Iraqi Kurdistan than in the north where Barzani was compelled to maintain his operations.

Sulaimaniyah, Arbil, and Kirkuk were urban centers in the south. The sheikhs of the Ako and Peschder tribes did not have much to fear from a Barzani operating in the north. They were willing to send some of their men to the north. This proved to be of some use to Barzani since these southerners were permanently available to him, whereas tribesmen from the north would constantly be slipping away to their relatives or would be loath to fight far away from their villages. Here again we can compare the Kurds to the Palestinians whose *fa'zaa* system of fighting levies meant that men could only fight in the immediate area of their villages. Indeed many of these fighters were more loyal to their individual leaders, also often sheikhs or simply bosses of groups of fighters, than to the ideas of nationalism or social justice. This was true in Kurdistan as it had been true under the *za'im* system on the Mediterranean coast. The za'im is simply the chief of the fighting unit, to whom one owes allegiance. The difficulties inherent in such a system were evident in Palestine in the thirties and are today in Lebanon. It is almost impossible to mount a consistent campaign. Overall discipline is also almost unattainable. Barzani's southerners may also have been of limited value since they spoke the Sorani dialect, whereas the northerners spoke Kurmanji (Solomon 1967).

THE KURDISH DEMOCRATIC PARTY AND PESCH-MERGA

Barzani had an element of strength in the Kurdish Democratic party which he had founded in 1946 and which he led after his return from the Soviet Union to Baghdad in 1958. But Barzani and his loyal tribesmen and religiously oriented Pesch-Merga were never on the best terms with the intellectuals of the Democratic Peoples' party of Kurdistan. The military operations of the Pesch-Merga were always kept separate from the operations of the party. And Barzani insisted on strong traditional membership in the Democratic party of Kurdistan. Examples are the appointment of Ziyad Aga and Sheikh Berzenci as members of the central committee.

In 1961, at the beginning of the open rebellion against the Iraqi government of Kassim, Barzani took as his major ally Abbas Mamand, the aga of the Ako clan of the south. In 1964 Barzani went a step farther. He purged the Kurdistan Democratic party of many of its left-wing intellectuals: Ibrahim Ahmed, a Sulaimaniyah lawyer, who went on to become prominent in the Patriotic Union of Kurdistan (PUK), Jelal Talabani, a Sulaimaniyah lawyer, who became general secretary of PUK and now leads a paramilitary force in Kurdistan, Ali Askari, a prominent farmer who was murdered in 1978, and Ibrahim Azo, an engineer, who was also murdered. Barzani obviously did not like lawyers, especially intellectual, Marxist lawyers from Sulaimaniyah like Hamsa Abdullah who had previously suffered the fate of the other four purged in 1964. What this meant, however, was that Barzani could never really develop a functioning political party. Loyalists like Abbas Mamand Aga or Sami Abd-ar-Rahman (an engineer, who now leads a Kurdish political party in Syria) or the Shiite lawyer, Habib Karim (now a civil servant in Baghdad), or the American-trained political scientist, Mustafa Qaradaghi (now a wealthy aga), or the doctor, Mahmud Osman (now an ineffectual would-be politician in Syria), or the journalist Salih Jusufi (murdered in 1980), or the Jewish Kurd, Naman Isa (who died of cancer in the late sixties) were not men with the kind of political connections that would enable them to establish a supportive urban superstructure. It is interesting that two of them, the Shiite Karim and the Jew Isa were members of religious minorities; the Kurds are by and large Sunnite.

Barzani's Pesch-Merga was significant in size: about forty-five thousand regulars and sixty thousand auxiliary troops (Vanly 1970:223 ff.). But they were all tied in one way or another to the traditional social and religious structure of Kurdistan. Barzani's word was fiat. There was no real political structure in the cities that could carry out complementary paramilitary activities. The Iraqi government was able to mobilize Turkomans and antinational Kurds in Kirkuk and so neutralized the Kurdish community in that important oil town. In addition the Iraqis moved Arabs into the Kirkuk area in satellite towns called, interestingly enough, Jaffa, Haifa, and El Kuds (Jerusalem) (Ibrahim 1982:637). By 1974 Barzani was operating in an area with a population of 1,500,000 Kurds. He had, however, only 3,000 academicians in the whole area, 120 doctors, 30 professors, and about 120 engineers. His lieutenants were loyalists who had always been with him: Abdul Wahab Atruschi, Raschid Sindi, and Isa Sawar (Ibrahim 1982:602).

The military office of the Pesch-Merga was run by Barzani's son, Idris, and the secret police intelligence of the Kurdish paramilitary organization, the Parastin, by Barzani's second son, Masud. A third son, by the way, supported the Iraqi government. It is a tribute to the cruelty and stupidity of the Iraqi governments after 1968, especially the Ba'ath governments of Al Bakr and Saddam Hussein, that Barzani's movement was able to grow without any political or social program.

Barzani became the undisputed leader of a powerful tribal army and here his position differed greatly from the religious leader of the Palestinians in the thirties, Hadj Amin Husseini. Husseini had never been able to unify the Palestinians. Indeed nobody has been able to do so since. His own traditionalism worked against him. The 12,000-odd unionized Arabs in the Jaffa and Haifa area were probably more nationalistic than the rural *fellahim*. But the *madani* (city dwellers), and the rural particularist Palestinians simply could never cooperate. Indeed leaders and parties sprang up everywhere and no coordinated action was ever possible. Newcomers like the Haurani (from Syria) struggled with indigenous Palestinians, Christians with Muslims, Kassimites in the Galilee with other regional leaders and movements. The weakness lay in the particularism, segmentation, and fragmentation of traditional societies (Ashkenasi 1981). This weakness proved the eventual undoing of the Kurdish uprising in the 1970s as well.

Barzani's early success was due not only to the cruelty of the Iraqis but to the direct international support he received in the early seventies, primarily from Iran, but also from the United States and Israel. American weaponry was sent through Iran and members of the Pesch-Merga were able to rest, when under stress, in the Shah of Iran's territory. Special units of the Pesch-Merga, especially the intelligence units, the Parastin, were trained in Israel. Mosad seems to have had quite a hand in this operation. Sawak, the Iranian secret police, was also active in training the Kurds.

The moment of truth came in 1975 (Ibrahim 1982:711). The agreement between Iraq and Iran over the Shat el Arab waterway, which gave the shah everything he wanted, immediately precluded his further support of the Kurds in Iraq. Barzani, who was in Teheran at the time, would not continue the fight without Iran. The entire revolt collapsed because it was tied to the word, charisma, and leadership of one man. No social structure had been established in the north to parallel and buttress the military operations. The goal had simply been a national Kurdish state without any concern for its eventual nature. Without a substructure the entire revolt disintegrated almost overnight, with the Pesch-Merga fleeing into Iran. All the weaknesses of this kind of paramilitary organization became evident. The loyalty of men to one man and not to ideas meant that operations would not continue.

Particularism meant that most of the tribal fighters would try to return to their homes instead of maintaining their organizations. The fragmentation of the society meant that no effective communication grids existed between those who wished to continue the armed struggle and the bulk of the Kurdish population. The lack of a political superstructure meant that the entire national movement imploded when the tribal and religious leaders gave up the battle. This is essentially what happened to the Palestinians in 1948. It took them twenty years to recover, if indeed they ever did. For the Kurds, Talabani has attempted to create a modern paramilitary organization operating from Syria and Iraq while the Barzani group has resumed functioning in Iran under his sons. It is questionable whether either group will be successful. Paramilitary organizations based on traditional social structures and without modern organizational techniques are not likely to succeed.

CONCLUSION

In this paper I have tried to sketch some of the paramilitary organizations that have been active in the pre– and post–World War II era in the Near East and make some broad generalizations about the forms and types of organizations, conflicts, and results. I have made no attempt to establish a theory of paramilitarism or guerrilla activity for, as Walter Laqueur pointed out, "such a theory would be either exceedingly vague or exceedingly wrong" (Laqueur 1977:5). But some generalizations for the Near East seem in order.

First, it seems that without a broad organizational structure in the countryside a successful paramilitary organization in the urban centers is impossible. The so-called urban, or city, guerrilla is doomed to be ineffectual without access to, and support from, an organized countryside. Mao's dictum that the city corrupts and the countryside must be organized for revolution seems to be valid. Jewish city-based guerrillas like the Lechi and the Palestinian groups in Jaffa and Haifa in the 1930s, had negligible significance in the political struggles of the 1930s and 1940s. Although the city guerrilla has the organizational ability to commit separate, and sensational, acts of violence and terror, his broad appeal is limited. His isolation from the society he purports to serve is apparent. His influence in the Near East has been minimal.

Second, the countryside must be organized by a well-coordinated group of educated cadres who may well be recruited from an urban setting. A paramilitary organization functions successfully when the political leadership maintains ethnosocial affinity in the broadest possible geographic area with significant and potentially militant parts of the population. This goal seems attainable only when ethnic paramilitary organizations have a strong social case to make as well. This case has been made under the banner of socialism in the examples looked at in this chapter in some of the Jewish groups in Palestine. Other examples in this century seem to verify this pattern.

Third, the success of some socialist groups does not exclude the ability of conservative forces to carry out a successful paramilitary operation—especially when this conservatism is, as it usually is, blended with the diffuse ideologies of ethnocentrism or nationalism. Our examples in this chapter, however, show that ethnic pride and unity is rarely enough. The Kurdish particularism within its ethnic structure and the weaknesses of its conservative leadership illustrate this very well. Weaknesses in Palestinian structure corroborate the judgment that one makes about the Kurds. Indeed, the ineffectuality of the Etzel in Israel is a further example of the weakness of national paramilitary groups when they are based exclusively on the more conservative elements in society. Although they were hardly traditionalists, Etzel's members shared the traditionalists' distrust of social reform and intellectual reformers. Apparently the middle class or bourgeois groups in society that gravitate to paramilitarism need an established army with which to cooperate.

Fourth, in societies that are still semifeudal, cooperation between the nationalist bourgeoisie and the more conservative feudal elements seems to be prohibitively difficult. The agrarian society would seem to be more susceptible to the blandishments of social revolutionaries. Paramilitary success in the Near East appears possible when ethnic attachment combines with the mobilization power and the appeal of a new and viable socioeconomic structure. The articulation and military prosecution of these goals depends on leaders and a leadership structure that provides for organizational efficiency and consistency. Only then can necessary but often unreliable international and/or regional support be transformed into political success. Our Israeli example, of course, is unfair in this regard since no Jewish feudal elements had to be removed in Palestine. But the Israelis, like other successful social revolutionaries, were the uprooted. They were searching for a new social structure within an old ethnoreligious pattern. In the Near East the line between religion and nation is thin indeed.

The ethnic pattern does not have to be religious, of course, but it is always something historically established and immutable like language, culture, homeland, or race. Ethnic attachment is the psychological reassurance for those striking out in new social directions. The new directions carry the implication that there can be no retreat. Social dislocation provides for continuity as well as impetus. Paramilitarism is, then, one of the basic and varying forms of political expression.

BIBLIOGRAPHY

Adamson, David. *The Kurdish War*. London: Allen & Unwin, 1964.

Allon, I. *Shield of David: The Story of Israel's Armed Forces*. London: Nicolson, 1970.

Ashkenasi, Abraham. *The Structure of Ethnic Conflict and Palestinian Political Fragmentation*. Berlin. Occasional Paper FGS AP–O.P. 2/1981. Freie Universität Berlin, 1981.

Avivi, S. *Hatchunot Hademographiot shell Havrei Etzel V. Lechi*. Tel-Aviv. Unpublished manuscript. Jabotinski Archives, 1967.

Ballance, Edgar O. *The Kurdish Revolt 1961–1970*. London, 1973.

Bauer, Yehuda. *From Diplomacy to Resistance: A History of Jewish Palestine 1939–1944*. Philadelphia: The Jewish Publication Society of America, 1970.

Begin, Menachem. *The Revolt*. London: W. H. Allen, 1951.

Bell, J. Bowyer. *Terror out of Zion*. New York: St. Martin's Press, 1977.

Bethell, Nicholas. *The Palestine Triangle: The Struggle between the British Jews and the Arabs 1935–1948*. London: André Deutsch Limited, 1979.

Chaliand, Gerard. *People without a Country*. London: Zed Press, 1980.

Eagleton, William, Jr. *The Kurdish Republic of 1946*. Oxford: Oxford University Press, 1963.

Edmonds, C. J. *Kurds, Turks and Arabs*. Oxford: Oxford University Press, 1957.

Encyclopedia Judaica. Jerusalem: Keter Publishing House.

Gerold, Frank. *The Deed*. New York: Simon & Schuster, 1963.

Ghassemlou, A. *Kurdistan and the Kurds*. London: Collets Holdings Ltd., 1965.

Gilad, Zerubabel, and Mosche Meged, eds. *Sefer Hapalmach*. Tel-Aviv: Hakibuz Hameuchad, 1954.

Hottinger, Arnold. "Der Kampf der irakischen Kurden um die Autonomie." In *Europa-Archiv*, Folge 12, 1965.

Ibrahim, Ferhad. "Die kurdische Nationalbewegung in Irak. Eine Fallstudie zur Problematik der ethnischen Konflikte in der Dritten Welt." Thesis. Free University of Berlin, 1982.

Ilam, Igal. *The Hagana: The Zionist Path to Power*. Tel-Aviv: Zemova Bitan-Modan, 1979.

Iwaideh, Wadi. "The Kurdish Nationalist Movement." Thesis. Syracuse University, 1960.

Katz, Samuel. *Days of Fire*. London: W. H. Allen, 1968.

Kenane, Derek. *The Kurds and Kurdistan*. Oxford: Oxford University Press, 1964.

Laqueur, W. Z. *History of Zionism*. London: Nicolson, 1972.

————. *Guerrilla: A Historical and Critical Study*. London, 1977.

Lev-Ami, Schlomo. *Bemavak u Bamered. Opposition and Revolt*. Tel-Aviv: Marchot, 1979.

Mohr, Nathan Yalin. *Lechi, Anaschim Rayonot Alilot*. Ramat Gan: Sikmona, 1974.

Nikitine, Basile. *Les Kurdes, étude sociologique et historique*. Paris: Imprimerie Nationale, 1956.

Niv, David. *Marchot Hairgun Hazwai Haleumi. The History of the Irgun Zwai Leumi*. 6 vols. Tel-Aviv: Hadar, 1975–1982.

Orland, Nachum. *Die Cherut Partei 1948–1965: Israels rechte Opposition*. Berlin: Freie Universität, 1982.

Schavit, Jakov. *Haseson*. Tel-Aviv: Hadar, 1976.

Schiller, David Thomas, *Palästinenser zwischen Terrorismus und Diplomatie.* München: Bernhard u. Graefe-Verlag, 1982.

Schmidt, Dana Adams. *Journey among brave men.* Boston, Toronto: Little, Brown, 1964.

Short, Martin, and Anthony MacDermott. *The Kurds.* London: Minority Rights Group no. 23, 1977.

Sim, Richard. *Kurdistan: The Search for Recognition.* Conflict Studies, no. 124. November 1980.

Slutzki, Jehuda. *Sefer Toldot Hagana.* 8 vols. Tel-Aviv: Am Oved, 1954–1972.

Solomon, G. "Some Aspects of the Kurdish Revolt," *New Outlook,* no. 4, May 1967.

van Bruinessen, M. M. "Agha, Sheikh and State." Thesis. Utrecht, 1978.

Vanly, Ismet Sherif. *Le Kurdistan Iraquien. Entité nationale.* Neuchâtel: La Baconniere. 1970.

12

Conclusion: Collective Purposes and Individual Motives

PETER H. MERKL

The time has come to look back along the winding road we have traveled reviewing examples of contemporary political violence and terror. This was not intended to be a travelogue of countries convulsed by violence nor a freak show of violent movements around the world. Our goal has been to clarify relationships, especially between ideology and violent action, rather than to catalog the extraordinary variety of political violence in a systematic fashion. In the second part of this book, in particular, we have attempted to relate a variety of highly subjective, individual motives for personal violence to the lofty ideologies that are frequently presented by violent movements and their sympathetic observers as the rationale for individual participation. The first part was more preoccupied with the range of different approaches to the study of political violence. In this concluding essay I shall try mainly to draw together the various threads of the second part, but with appropriate references also to the essays by Richard Drake, Adrian Guelke, and Robert P. Clark of the first part.

In so doing, moreover, I will not follow the example of some editors who are content merely to summarize and edit the collection of papers contributed by the other specialists present at the scholarly conferences in question. This editor intends to bring to bear as well the results of his own extensive research on the violence of the early Nazi party and on interwar fascist movements in other European countries. I also hope to blend in the insights gained at the extensive discussions of the papers presented at the 1982 International Political Science Association at Rio de Janeiro and the 1982 Council of European Studies conference in Washington and thereafter, which may reflect other current trends in the literature and at conferences on political violence. If this pluralistic approach to knowledge and insight should produce contradictions among the essays and papers or raise questions that have not been answered in them, we ask the reader's understanding for the infinite complexity of this subject. After all, no essay could possibly cover, say, the whole story of Basque political violence or the German neo-Nazis in a few dozen pages. No researcher, moreover, including this editor, is infallible on subjects that are often ambiguous or carefully hidden from view. It is in the nature of a true symposium that there may be unresolved conflicts of opinion or that it be left to the listeners or readers to make up their own minds on some questions.

After setting the stage with samples of various methods of studying political violence—the ideological approach (Drake), mutually reinforcing friend-enemy perceptions (Guelke), and the patterns of violent events (Clark's chapter 4)—we began the second part of our discussion with Leonard Weinberg's description of the "violent life" of Italian left-wing and right-wing terrorists. Weinberg is careful to describe the settings, "preconditions," and political situations behind the turn to violence of both the left and the right. But his chief focus is on what motivates the "red" and the "black" terrorists of Italy: the myth of the antifascist Resistance of 1943/1944, the "fallen rifle" of Renato Curcio's dead uncle on the left, and the last stand of Mussolini's Republic of Salò on the right against the left-wing partisans. As they terrorized Italy for a decade and a half, both sides made themselves believe that they were still fighting the noble fight of an earlier generation, but this time not only against each other but also against the Italian state, which they saw as subtly taken over, alternatively, by fascism or communism. The quasi-religious way in which some Italians still interpret the world, furthermore, determines the Messianic fervor with which the extreme right reacts to the secularization of modern society, to speak with Julius Evola, as well as the extreme left reaction to the loss of authority of its "church," the Italian Communist party (PCI). Here undoubtedly are the "totalitarian obsessions" of left and right which the historian Karl Dietrich Bracher noted in the German case, the absolutist claims of each of the opposing "churches" on the hearts and minds of their adherents. The Communist change of direction of the 1970s, moreover, left its radicalized young followers and friends in organized labor and the student movement in rage and despair, thus driving them to violence in the "fire sale" of the revolutionary drive. The student radicals, in particular, sought to attach themselves to "carrier populations" with long-standing grievances, such as the working classes, "the masses," or the Vietnamese, without necessarily asking for their agreement. The "borrowed misery" of the downtrodden[1] is then used to rationalize, depending on the personality of the terrorist, all kinds of extreme, aggressive actions.

Weinberg also relates the story of Italian neofascism and its turn to increased violence—there had been smaller skirmishes and raids on the communists and trade unions before—at about the same time that the left and the students went through the upheaval of 1968/1969. It is interesting here to compare Italian to West German neofascism: The mighty Italian Social movement with its 400,000 members (1975) and 2,000,000 voters forms a contrast to the pathetic Nazi revivals of the German Right party (DRP), Socialist Reich party (SRP), and NPD described in my chapter on neo-Nazi violence. The NPD had 28,000 members and 1,400,000 voters in 1967–1969, but can count on less than a fourth of that today. The violent Italian neofascists of Ordine Nuovo (now renamed Ordine Nero) were probably the perpetrators of the 1969 bank bombing in Milan that killed sixteen and injured eighty-eight bystanders, of a bomb at an antifascist rally in Brescia (1974) that killed eight and wounded eighty-five, and of the bombings of the Florence-Bologna train which a month later killed twelve and injured forty-eight.[2] Bombings such as these and others seem to be their specialty[3] and, again, the violent neo-Nazis of such groups as ANS/NA or the Hoffmann Group seem at best a pale copy both in size and virulence.

Finally, Weinberg follows a number of radical careers among the terrorist left and right, which permits more incisive insights into the process of radicalization among students and workers, such as the case of left-wing terrorist Romeo Giuseppe whose revolt began in elementary school and prominently included an anarchist "education" while he was in jail. These life histories are comparable to, though they lack the psychological depth of, Klaus Wasmund's account of the individual, step-by-step development of West German left-wing terrorists. Wasmund not only describes the development of German left-wing terrorist organizations in their first, second, and third generations and sketches their collective profile—social backgrounds, education, tensions between the terrorists and their parents—but also supplies insights into the "tracking" of the violent careers of the individuals of the Red Army Faction (RAF), a subject to which I shall return.

The second and third generations, the 2d of June movement, the Revolutionary Cells, and the *Guerrilla Diffusa*—and perhaps the more recent RAF recruits as well—require a rather different explanation from that used for the evolution and turn to violence of the first RAF generation. For the initiators, there was a tortuous path leading from student and political demonstrations of relatively low levels of violence to terrorist acts of increasing severity, beginning with the department store fires of 1969. Equally tortured interpretations by fellow terrorists of that generation found their path from the Marxist class struggle led by the vanguard of the proletariat to the "armed campaign" led by a "revolutionary intelligentsia," composed of the "revolutionary sections of the student movement," or a "faction" of an international Red underground army. The following generations of German left-wing terrorists could skip this painful transition and proceed directly to the new mode of violent assault on selected targets. In fact, the new recruits were obviously self-selected by visions of violent, "heroic" action rather than by ideology alone. At the same time, the RAF had arrived at the point where it no longer recoiled from killing or felt any need to justify the deaths of bystanders, chauffeurs, or guards at an assassination. The movement had taken a decidedly sociopathic turn toward killing without inhibitions or remorse.

INTERPRETING VIOLENT MOTIVES

As we did with the radical right, we can now contrast the German left-wing terrorists with those of Italy. There were 52 German terrorists in jail in 1982—29 of the RAF, 20 of the 2d of June movement, and 3 of the Revolutionary Cells[4]—and an estimated 200 still "legal" helpers at large, as compared with 1,357 Italian left-wing terrorists in prison and another 274 at large in 1983. The proportions between the sheer size of the Italian phenomenon and that of the Federal Republic are quite comparable to those on the radical right where there were 480 Italian terrorists in jail (versus 13 in Germany) and 79 believed to be still at large. Of course, it may be far more difficult to compare the cultural settings and preconditions in the two countries since there is no agreement in either case on what "causes" left-wing terrorism to flourish.

At this point, the discussion of various interpretations of Italian left-wing terrorism by Gianfranco Pasquino and Donatella della Porta comes in with several perspectives and scenarios that may highlight both the collective purposes and individual motives of the groups in question. Even though the authors reject the possible links between foreign conspiracies or secret services and domestic political terror as a *complete explanation* of Italian terrorism, foreign intrigue has always been a plausible scenario that has also been noted in other periods and parts of the world.[5] If it can ever be proven that the attempts on the lives of Pope John Paul II and of Lech Wałęsa by Mehmet Ali Aqca were instigated by the Bulgarian secret service, or the Soviet KGB, this would be only the most recent example of a long line of similar violent foreign plots. It is usually quite clear whether the collective purposes in a violent action instigated from abroad are limited to the foreign power or organization alone or are shared by domestic conspiracies. The individual motives of paid assassins, other materially or politically interested parties, or fanatic partisans can also usually be determined without great difficulty. Those who claim that terrorism is a result of foreign plots, in fact, frequently seem almost too transparent in their goals and motives, too obvious not to make us suspicious of the possible hidden motives and implications of a preference for this line of interpretation. Caution may be particularly in order before accepting sweeping theories of international networks of terrorist organizations, unless specific evidence for such international cooperation can in fact be produced.[6]

Professors Pasquino and della Porta go on to paint a telling picture of the themes of the "culture of 1968" in Italy, which contained the "germs of the terrorist culture[s]" to follow in the 1970s: the myth of the imminent revolution, the "democratic mask" of capitalist exploitation, and the emphasis on ideology and on putting "the movement" above the individual. The student movement, of course, died down in 1969 even though Lotta Continua tried to keep the flame burning. The syndicalist agitation of the "hot autumn" of 1969 also cooled off, in spite of the similar efforts of Potere Operaio. The third parent group of the Red Brigades, the communist offshoot Manifesto, became something of a gathering point of communist revolutionary fervor. The two authors are at pains to exonerate the Italian Communists—who had long indulged in this kind of rhetoric even though they have since become a mortal enemy of the left-wing terrorists—from responsibility for this unintended outgrowth. Many terrorists, indeed, are ex-Communists and the heady atmosphere of the communist subculture during the years from 1968, or 1967, to the alleged "betrayal" of the mid-1970s (the Communist eagerness for a "historical compromise"[7] with the ruling Christian Democrats) in many cases provided an important launching phase of their political socialization. They left the "traitor party," which in their eyes had indeed compromised itself, to pursue what they understood to be its authentic message with the only means open to a determined small minority in a democracy: terrorist violence. The alleged betrayal of revolutionary principles, however, has to be contrasted with twenty years of very unrevolutionary Communist party practice, especially at the local level. The young revolutionary blowhards, in other words, had mistaken words, or advocacy, for actions. They had misunderstood the message because *they preferred to hear only* the ritual clarion call to revolutionary violence, and not to understand the natural turn of the broadened mass movement toward political responsibility. The history of modern socialist movements supplies other examples of the revulsion of activists steeped in opposition at the seeming *embourgeoisement* of socialist leaders. In the confrontation of an "ethics of responsibility" to the "ethics of conviction," to speak with Max Weber, the latter wins out.

Since the vast majority of the party members and camp followers in the Italian communist subculture evidently followed the party leadership in hoping for a historical compromise and a public sharing of power with the establishment, this makes the violence-prone minority the children of a revolution that never transpired, a "left-wing deviation" in the sense of Lenin with whom they have claimed a curious kinship.[8] The political socialization and the attitudes of this particular generation grew out of the "fire-sale situation" of three burned-out reformist movements. The secession from the parent movement and the turn to violence, still, can only be explained with an analysis of the group dynamics of the small, fraternal groups of militants and their leaders.

How do individual motivations and collective purpose interact in this case? Perhaps we first have to relate the collective purposes of the terrorists of disillusioned Communist party backgrounds beyond their own conspiratorial group to the various "social bases" they claim. They seemingly intended both to create and to use their own most recent terrorist groups in order to propel the parent Potere Operaio and Lotta Continua into radicalizing action. This in turn might rekindle the revolutionary fervor in the giant Communist party, which ultimately would revolutionize the entire Italian state and society, conceivably flanked by similar developments in other European countries. The concentric circles of referents alone show that this is not collective action as the word is usually employed, as in strikes or other organized endeavors. In fact, the terrorist group itself is not its own collective reference group, but instead claims to represent the will of a larger group that has neither authorized the terrorists as its agents nor is lacking in organization itself through which its will as a group can be articulated.

We have tabulated the same variables for the movements discussed in part 2 as for the sampling of political violence in chapter 1 (table 1.1). Table 12.1 shows the extent to which the left-wing and right-wing violent movements of Italy and Germany, and even the urban guerrillas of Latin America, have operated along parallel lines. The left and the right, respectively, have on the one hand created recognizable patterns of method, victims, claimed social base, and ideology. On the other hand, there are some striking differences in their actual social bases, stemming from the presence of a large communist subculture in Italy for which neither Germany nor Uruguay nor Colombia offer equivalents. Instead, Uruguay and Colombia make up for it with a radicalized, intellectual fringe of students and professional people. A third pattern emerges in the rural guerrilla movements of

Guatemala and Nicaragua, which combine the student and professional elements with a substantial peasant and, possibly, Indian or
mestizo base. We have already encountered variants of this in the
rural guerrilla armies of Colombia and Peru (*Sendero Luminoso*).[9] A
fourth set of patterns shows up in the considerable variety of nationalist
movements of the Middle East, the left-wing ETA and the Corsicans,
the IRA, and the Tamil and Sikh separatists tabulated in chapter 1.
The fifth pattern comprises the religious zealots, perhaps including the
Sikhs, of the table in the first chapter.

VICTIMS AND SOCIAL BASES

As for the motivations of individuals in this context, it is probably
impossible to generalize. The several overarching collective referents
as well as the frequently arbitrary choice of victims of violent assault
cast some doubt on the logic of the motives. At their worst, the
motivation may simply be the archetypical one—the terrorists believe
they are the mysterious avengers of wrongs and the saviors of the
ideological equivalent of damsels in distress. The extraordinary amount
of romanticizing of left-wing terrorist actions in the literature and press
makes it difficult to separate left-wing heroes from villains, except
perhaps by reference to right-wing terrorists who are less likely to be
seen as heroes outside of their small groups. To clarify matters, I have
tabulated both the choice of victims and the claimed social bases, or
collective referents, in table 12.2 in order to shed some light on the
individual motives of Italian and German left-wing and right-wing
terrorists. For good measure I have also added ETA, which turns out
to be close to the left-wing mold.

The thought underlying the victim categories of table 12.2 is simply
that a terrorist movement, such as the Red Brigades, aiming at combating the "fascist state" and the capitalist system would select its
targets accordingly: High on its functional "hit list" must be government and party leaders of the established parties, such as Aldo Moro,
the Christian Democratic (DC) general secretary and the moving spirit
behind a number of cabinets, and DC strategies, such as the plan to
secure Communist (PCI) support for a DC government without the
"historical compromise" of taking the PCI into the coalition cabinet.
Government and party leaders at regional, provincial, and local levels
also may be logical choices, if in declining order. Since the terrorists
are acutely aware that their first line of conflict is with the judiciary
and law enforcement, furthermore, their selection of highly placed
judges and police chiefs makes sense, especially if it does not trail off
too much into settling personal grudges or into blind attacks on the
lowliest of *carabinieri*. Armed Proletarian Nuclei (NAP) and, less so,

TABLE 12.1

SELECTED VARIABLES OF LEFT- AND RIGHT-WING TERRORIST AND GUERRILLA MOVEMENTS

Who	What (mo)	To whom (actual victim)	Symbolic addressee	Claimed social bases	Actual social bases	Organization		Why (goals, ideology)
						Small	Large	
Italian left-wing terrorists	Assassinations, kidnappings, extortion	Judiciary, police, corporate and party leaders	"Fascist" state, capitalism, NATO	Communist revolution, proletarian masses	Students, PCI, syndicalists	Underground cells	Red Brigades, NAP	Total ("antifascist") revolution, communism, righting of injustices, liberation of Third World
Italian right-wing terrorists	Bombings, assassinations	Bystanders, communists, judiciary	"Communist" state, foreign influence	Occidental culture, Italian elite	Sons of old fascists, MSI	Underground cells	MSI, *Ordine Nuovo,* NAR	Destruction of modern society, defense against Soviet communism, and U.S. capitalism
German left-wing terrorists	Assassinations kidnappings, extortion, bombings	Corporate leaders, judiciary, party figures, U.S. officers	Capitalist state, US/NATO, imperialism	World revolution masses, Third World	Militant women, anarchists	Underground cells	RAF, June 2nd, Revolutionary Cells	Total revolution, communism, "coercion-free" society
German right-wing terrorists	Bombings, brawls	Foreigners, bystanders, police	Democratic, state, Soviet and U.S. dominators	German nation, certain national liberation movements	Sons of old Nazi	Squads of paramilitary groups	NPD, JN, and other groups	Germany for the Germans, Pan-German state, "ethnopluralism," some national revolutions, environmental defense

Who	What (mo)	To whom (actual victim)	Symbolic addressee	Claimed social bases	Actual social bases	Organization		Why (goals, ideology)
						Small	Large	
Latin American urban guerrillas	Kidnappings, assassinations, extortions, bombings	Foreign corporate figures, government leaders, foreign diplomats	"Fascist" state, foreign imperialism, capitalism	Proletarian masses, Third World	Students, professional class	Under- ground cells	*Tupáma-ros*, etc.	Total (anti-imperialist) revolu- tion, righting of injustices, Third World liberation
Latin American rural guerrillas	Guerrilla warfare, assassinations, bombings	Landlords, army and police, village officers	State, elected or not, imperialism	Rural masses, *campesinos*, Indi- ans, villagers	Students, professionals, peasants, priests	Guerrilla army units	Guerrilla army	Agrarian reform, redistribution of land, Maoism or communism
ETA	Assassinations, kidnappings, bombings	Spanish government leaders, police and army, *Guardia Civil*, corporate executives	Spanish state, capitalism	All Basques	Students, lower middle class, workers	Under- ground cells	ETA, EE, HB, PNV	Basque independence and unifi- cation, Destruction of Spanish state and capitalism, integral nationalism
Traditional Mideast nation- alists (Kurds, Palestinians)	Guerrilla war- fare, bombings	Ethnic oppressors, bystanders	Dominant ethnic state, dominant ethnicity	All Kurds, Pales- tinians, Arabs	Youth of same groups	Guerrilla commandos	Kurdish Demo- cratic Party, PLO, etc.	Independent Kurdish (Palestin- ian) state, driving out non- ethnics, restoration of property
Zionist nationalists	Bombings, guerrilla raids	British, UN officers, Arab officials	British power in Palestine, Arab resistance	All Jews everywhere	Urban lower middle class	Under- ground cells	Zionist groups	Jewish homeland, safety from re- ligious and racial persecution in a Jewish nation-state

TABLE 12.2

VICTIMS AND SOCIAL BASES (EXPANDED VERSION OF COLUMNS 3–6 OF TABLE 12.1) OF LEFT-WING AND RIGHT-WING TERRORISM AND THE ETA

ID	Government and party — hi	Government and party — med	Government and party — low	Judiciary and police, military	Economic-social system (banks) — hi	Economic-social system (banks) — med	Economic-social system (banks) — low	Minorities	U.S. Nato	General public — accidental	General public — deliberate	Symbolic addressee	International	National	Majority	Minority	Organization/group	Actual social basis
Italian left-wing	X	X	X	X	X	X	X		X	X		"fascist state," capitalism, U.S.	Communist world revolution		Proletarian masses	Communist subculture	Students, PCI, and syndicalists	Militant women and fringe [a]
Italian right-wing			X	X			X	X		X	X	"communist state," Soviet & U.S. influence	Occidental culture	Italian nation		Autonomia Cultural and ethnic elite	Old fascists	Sons of MSI, PNF, fringe
German left-wing		X	X	X	X	X	X		X	X		Capitalism, US-Nato, "fascist state"	Communist world revolution Third World revolution		Masses	Revolutionary intelligentsia Alternative scene	Revolutionary student movement	Militant women and fringe [b]
German right-wing			X	X			X	X	X		X	Democratic state, U.S. & Soviet domination	Certain nationalistic revolutions	German nation		Refugee ethnics, German unemployed youth	Persecuted old Nazis	Sons of old Nazis and fringe
Basque ETA	X	X	X	X	X	X	X			X		Spanish state, capitalism	French Basques, National liberation movements	Basque nation	Basque, in some areas	Basque minority in Spain	Basque nationalists	Young male Basque fringe

[a] Pertains to those in student, PCI, and syndicalist organizations/groups.

[b] Pertains to those in revolutionary student movements.

Red Brigade actions also have singled out correctional officials known to have personally "oppressed" them and their imprisoned friends. All functionaries, including the military, make plausible targets for left-wing terrorists. By comparison, the West German RAF or its successor groups, the 2d of June movement or the Revolutionary Cells, have not seriously attempted a political target higher than such regional figures as the Hessian minister of finance, Hans-Herbert Karry, or the Berlin CDU chairman, Peter Lorenz. The assassination of Federal Attorney General Buback, however, and other attacks on highly placed members of the judiciary fit the pattern more closely. ETA's spectacular assassination of Franco's prime minister, Carrero Blanco, and campaigns against Spanish law enforcement and the military again represent a version with as strong an emphasis on the state's apparatus of violence as we can find among the rural guerrilla armies of Peru, Colombia, and Central America.

The right-wing terrorists of Italy and especially of West Germany, by comparison, have not mounted anything like an "armed struggle" against the allegedly "communist state" or its democratic leaders regardless of their rhetoric. The Italian neofascists, to be sure, once attempted to blow up a train carrying the prime minister, Giulio Andreotti, and have bombed some Christian Democratic and Communist party (PCI) offices and meetings, such as the one in Brescia where eight people died and eighty-five were wounded. German neo-Nazi groups only had plans to bomb the offices of the diminutive Communist party (the DKP) and other communist groups and engaged in street battles with them on occasion. The Italians also have been known to assassinate judges and prosecutors on their trail or those investigating their connections with highly placed people in government, the judiciary, the secret service, and the police.[10] Clashes of the German neo-Nazis with "the system," by way of contrast, seem to be limited to brawls with police such as the melee described in chapter 8.

Next to the assault on the state and its leaders, as shown in table 12.2, the anticapitalist and antielitist thrust of left-wing terrorists can be expected to single out leaders of society and its business organizations. Here the West German terrorists seem to have been more systematic, with the murders of Hanns Martin Schleyer and Jürgen Ponto, two figures at the very top, while the Italians have for the most part been content with kidnappings (of less prominent figures), bank robberies, and extortion. There is a considerable range of actions from punitive assassinations or "knee-cappings of prominent managers," to kidnapping and extortion. The frequently violent clashes of nonterrorist German left-wingers with police over such "capitalist" phenomena as the construction of the west runway of Frankfurt Airport

(140 policemen injured) or of the nuclear plant at Gorleben (81 police wounded) also belong in the category of battling the socioeconomic system. Interventions into bitter industrial disputes also afford violent left-wingers opportunities for revenge with punitive violence as well as extortion relevant to the strike or lockout. In this connection also, we are reminded of the isolated cases, as with the Patty Hearst kidnappers, where left-wing terrorists insisted on a grand giveaway of food to the poor. This is the socioeconomic equivalent of the political demands made to publicize terrorist propaganda, or to release prisoners other than captive members of the terrorist group. Such altruistic actions are more than anything designed to enhance the romantic self-image and public Robin Hood image of the terrorists which usually suffers from bank robberies and extortions, not to mention killings and maimings.

Of the other victim categories in table 12.2—minorities, American and NATO military, and the general public—left-wing terrorists have particularly singled out the military. The RAF, and its successor groups in particular, soon graduated from minor attacks on American troops in the early seventies to the stepped-up activity of the years 1979 to 1981 when in rapid succession attempts were made on the lives of the American NATO commander, General Alexander Haig (1979), and General Kroesen, not to mention bombing attacks on U.S. soldiers and on the Air Force base at Ramstein.[11] Beginning in 1981, the massive West German peace movement and public uneasiness about the deployment of new Pershing II and cruise missiles offered the "carrier movement" and the public atmosphere in which terrorists of both the left and the right felt encouraged to attack U.S. officers and to sabotage NATO equipment. The considerable if nonterrorist street violence erupting on the occasion of President Reagan's visit to Berlin on 11 June 1982 (86 policemen injured) is another example of violence addressed, at least symbolically, to the United States and the North Atlantic Alliance. By comparison, the Italian left-wing terrorists were only marginally involved in violent actions against U.S. and NATO personnel and installations before the kidnapping of General James Dozier. This is all the more remarkable considering their strident anti-NATO and anti-imperialist propaganda. In fact, the abandonment in the mid-1970s of the long-standing PCI plank to get Italy out of the Atlantic Pact for the sake of the never-consummated historic compromise must have given particular offense to the ex-Communists and other militant left-wingers among the terrorists.

The remaining entries in the victim categories of the extreme right (shown in table 12.2) evidently constitute the hallmark of neofascist violence today. Both Italian and, especially, West German right-wing terrorists, however their official propaganda may soft-pedal the topic, have concentrated their selection of actual victims on ethnic minorities and Jews within their boundaries. Attacks on synagogues and Jewish shops in France, England, Belgium, Austria, Portugal, and Spain, as well as physical attacks on Algerians in France and colored Commonwealth immigrants in Britain, underline the ubiquitous nature of the menace of neofascist violence. The Italian and Spanish neofascist parties deny that they are anti-Semitic, to be sure, but there can be little doubt about the presence of a virulent, and violent, anti-Semitic minority in their midst, nor about the anti-Semitic graffiti on Mediterranean walls. In the case of the West German radical right there are the numerous incidents described in chapter 8 and the murder of Shlomo Levine. Much of the neo-Nazi violence is directed at Southeast Asian refugees and Turkish or other foreign guest workers and they may be subjected both to individual, unorganized attacks or, as in the case of the firebombing of Southeast Asians in a Hamburg hostel, to organized group action.

The case of the bomb exploding outside a Paris synagogue in 1980, killing and wounding twelve, is particularly illuminating. Even though the synagogue bombing was eventually traced to a Palestinian assailant, there has been no end to the string of bombings and attempted bombings of Jewish shops throughout France. There had already been five bombings in the years before the synagogue bombing outrage. A survey of the French weekly *L'Express* disclosed that one out of eight Frenchmen thinks that there are too many Jews in the country and one out of ten rejected the 1980 statement of President Giscard d'Estaing that the Jews were Frenchmen like everybody else. Polls have shown that French hostility to North Africans is shared by about half the native population, which says that there are too many of them in France. Indeed, since 1978 there have been radical right-wing squads, with names such as the Charles Martell Club or the French National Liberation Front that have attacked North Africans with bombs and guns, and others with names hinting at the German wartime SS, such as the "new right," national-revolutionary movements, or the National Front, the neofascist party that garnered 2,000,000 votes in the European elections of 1984. In 1980, prior to the synagogue bombing, a Fédération Nationale Européene (FANE) sent out a rash of death threats and was banned, following over one hundred violent anti-Semitic incidents in that year alone. The group soon reconstituted itself under the name Faisceaux Nationalistes Européens (FNE), a tribute to the old French *Faisceaux* of the 1920s which, in turn, had been named after Mussolini's old *fasci di combattimento* of 1919.[12] FNE was promptly accused of the synagogue bombing since some members had actually claimed credit for it. In addition, a frequent contributor to FNE's newsletter, *Notre Europe*, a former police inspector in Nice, came under investigation in connection with the bombing of the Bologna railroad station. Unfortunately, few of these links could ever be proven although neofascist violence has been real in France.

It should be noted also that some of these neofascist organizations, especially those of France, Germany, and Belgium, frequently collaborate. In Belgium, where there is a substantial level of prejudice against foreign workers, a Vlaamse Militanten Orde (Flemish Militant Order, or VMO), maintains an armed storm-trooperlike formation in black uniforms, and there are contacts and joint youth encampments that often bring together French, German, and Flemish neofascists. This fascist international also includes the Italian Ordine Nero and the Spanish Fuerza Joven and their imagery includes swastikas and other mementos of the Third Reich. Spanish neofascists have also been involved in plenty of street violence and attacks on Communist and Socialist party offices, and on trade unions and university buildings. There are two extreme-right parties in Spain, the Falange and Fuerza Nueva, and, of course, there is the forty-year tradition of Franco's dictatorship. The leader of the Francoist Fuerza Nueva, Blas Pinar, gave the neofascist international network a formal organization, the Eurodestra, with headquarters in Madrid. Pinar's group reportedly also maintains close relations with the Spanish secret service, the police, and the right-wing military whose sons probably constitute the bulk of Fuerza Joven and similar young neofascist militant groups. Although the wearing of paramilitary uniforms by civilians is prohibited in Spain, the Fuerza Joven gathers annually on the occasion of Hitler's birthday in SS-type uniforms with swastika armbands. Old Francoist and former SS officers trained an estimated three thousand members (in 1980) of this group in aggressive violence. Their gratuitous attacks on political foes and bystanders with knives, iron bars, chains, baseball bats, and pistols often seem to resemble more the soccer rowdies' violence than a well-considered political action. To sustain the enthusiasm of these young fascists, it is more important to get each of them into a physically aggressive mood than to give them a well-understood collective purpose.

The last entries in the victim columns concern the general public, or rather the extent to which actual victims are chosen from among innocent bystanders. Violent groups, by now, seem to feel, or express, little remorse about the accidental killing or maiming of members of the general public in the pursuit of their terrorist aims. Only a handful of Italian neofascists, and the perpetrator of the Oktoberfest bombing, however, have gone out of their way to cause massacres among bystanders, among passengers on a train, or at a train station. Unless we assign great importance to the fact that Bologna had a Communist mayor at the time or assume that the purpose was to blame the "red"

terrorists—and this would require excessive naïveté among the perpetrators—it is still difficult to deduce a plausible purpose from such
outrages. But then, the utter absorption of some neofascists in military
games and exercises is not easy to understand for a civilian mind either.
Perhaps committing a horrible massacre or multiple killing supplies
indescribable thrills of sadism and destructive power to sick minds—
thrills most people cannot even conceive of.[13] Maybe the thrill lies
in the inflicting of fear and horror upon the public, although the most
effective, attention-getting maneuver is the threat rather than the
execution of a sanguinary outrage. Bologna and the Oktoberfest bombing certainly contradict the adage that terrorists want "a lot of people
watching and a lot of people listening, and not a lot of people dead."[14]

Let us take one more look at table 12.2 for the "claimed social
bases" of the terrorist groups. Here we tried to distinguish the claims
of international, national, and majority support, as well as the more
modest claims of support from a minority, or a particular organization.
Rather strikingly, the Italian and German left-wing terrorists claim to
represent every collective reference group but the national. Even the
name, Red Army Faction, is meant to denote a part of a vast international Red revolutionary army. The neofascists, for their part, insist
that they represent, for example, the German nation even beyond its
present borders, but they also have international referents in styling
themselves as the defenders of "occidental culture," of the "European
nation," and, in the German case, also of certain national liberation
movements, such as of Ireland and Eastern Europe. The ETA also
professes to represent the struggle of some other national liberation
movements as well as of the French Basques. At the same time, the
Basque majority status in certain provinces and its status as a minority
in Spain cuts across our categories.

All the movements shown on our table claim to represent minorities
in their respective countries, and profess to represent the more truc-
ulent elements of organized groups such as the student movements of
the left or the allegedly persecuted old fascists of the right, respectively.
The ETA claims to speak for all the Basque nationalists who, of course,
have their own moderate party. A juxtaposition of the known social
bases (composition) of each violent movement with these claimed
minorities and organizations is very interesting. Most of the Red Brigade and NAP members indeed came from the communist subculture
or from a syndicalist or student movement background, except that
they, in actual fact, represent a very young and often female fringe of
these social groups rather than their mainstream. The West German
left-wing terrorists, lacking a comparable communist subculture in
their country, are largely the young and often female fringe of a student
and skilled or white-collar worker background.[15] Earlier generations

of the violent German left may well be more heavily related to the student movement of 1967/1969 than their present following. The violent neofascists of Italy and Germany come mostly from among the sons of the old Nazi or Italian fascist party (PNF) members, but again represent a fringe of these groups augmented by marginal people from all layers of society, from the working classes to upper-class professionals and university students. There are many ethnic German refugees among them, but hardly any members of the cultural elite of either Germany or, respectively, Italy.

There is one more minority, a more or less organized group, which left-wing terrorists in both countries claim to represent and from which they often draw recruits: the antiauthoritarian anarchistic subculture of Berlin, Hamburg, and Frankfurt[16] and its Italian equivalent, Autonomia. We could add to this the considerable numbers of intellectual sympathizers in the media, professions, and universities of either country who feel a sense of solidarity with at least some of the avowed goals of the terrorists although they are themselves not very likely to engage in any violent action. Some German terrorist sympathizers have even sheltered fugitive terrorists after drawing a mistaken analogy between themselves and Germans of an earlier generation who should have sheltered Jews from the murderous Nazi state. The anarchistic subculture and its intellectual spokesmen welcome the destruction of present authority structures in the hope that a better, "noncoercive" society may arise in their place. Viewed simplistically, their approximation of the ideological stance of left-wing terrorists makes them quasi terrorists themselves. But on closer examination, such a snap judgment more likely calls into question the uncritical acceptance— that is, without consideration of the complex interactions of individual motive and collective purpose—of ideology as the main cause of political violence. Even the lengthy discussion among the German student protestors of 1968, and among other anarchistic spokesmen since then, about when or under what circumstances the resort to political violence might be justified was far from a rationalization after the decision had already been made; many members of the first generation of West German terrorists hesitated and agonized over it. But once they had crossed the Rubicon of violence, the fine philosophical discussions and distinctions among thoughtful and often rather nonviolent people were pushed aside by rough, action-oriented people who brought their strong emotions and badly needed skills in handling weapons to the group. The second and third generations of German terrorists (after 1971), moreover, were clearly not "sicklied o'er by the pale cast of thought" of their predecessors. They were attracted more by the opportunities for violent, "heroic action" than by reasoned justifications of it.

CRITICAL IDEOLOGY AND TERROR

One need not be a certified left-wing critic, say of the Frankfurt School, to sympathize with the dismay of adherents of Karl Marx, Herbert Marcuse, or Jürgen Habermas at being blamed for the emergence of left-wing terrorists who on occasion like to quote one or several of these authorities. Radical critics are more likely to say with Autonomia Operaia spokesman Antonio Negri, "neither terrorism nor this state." There is indeed a broad area between social reformist movements (such as the Italian PCI of the 1970s or left-wing socialists in Germany and France) that by their very commitment to reforming the system support it, and the terrorists who have sworn to destroy it root and branch. Within this area can be found, for example, not only critical theory but the counterculture of urban communes and alternative life-styles in big cities like West Berlin or Amsterdam, or Hamburg, or the anarchocommunist "area of autonomy" posited by Autonomia Operaia before Negri's arrest in 1979.[17]

Autonomia became a home for masses of alienated Italian youth, especially at the universities, and for some of the socially marginalized poor of the cities and their environs. It is dedicated to "destructuring the capitalist system" but by such means as the formation of autonomous collectives, the repudiation of the work ethic, "proletarian expropriation," social agitation, and rather nonviolent, nonexploitative ways of self-actualization. In its aims, it is really rather self-contained and does not derive its *raison d'être* from making war on the larger society. Nevertheless, and in spite of Negri's attacks on the mindless "militarists" of the *brigatisti*, who have no mass base, it is not all that easy to draw a hard and fast line between Autonomia and the terrorists. They evolved together, and at times intermingled, during the years of crisis in Italy, which makes it difficult to see the autonomi as entirely nonviolent in their struggle to abolish all power by industrial sabotage, rioting, and diffuse acts of destruction.[18] The Alternativler and Greens of West Germany and their antinuclear friends in other countries also have found it difficult to banish violent people from their ranks and frequently lose control over what are supposed to be peaceful, pacifist demonstrations.

Still there can be no doubt that the hard-core, full-grown terrorism of the RAF or Red Brigade variety is a fundamentally different phenomenon which owes very little to critical theory or philosophical reflection, except perhaps in the earliest phases of a terrorist career.[19] Typical social (i.e., nonethnic) terrorists, as far as one can generalize at all, seem to get drawn into and swept away by certain emotional compulsions that at first may be associated with radical, critical, or anarchist ideas, but soon become the compelling and self-destructive fixations of their lives. The best example of this is the idea that the capitalist, "pseudodemocratic" state must be "forced" to declare its latent fascism openly. Although it shows little comprehension of what historic Italian and German fascism was all about, the basic idea that the capitalist state is inherently repressive and growing more "fascist" at an alarming rate is widely accepted among radical and anarchist circles. But the obsession with "forcing fascism out of the closet," whatever its rationalizations may be,[20] aims to be a self-fulfilling prophecy and clearly shows the overwhelming, romantic desire of the terrorists to be persecuted. Given the presence of a German or Italian fascist past, and of some (not normally dominant) repressive elements in law enforcement, moreover, this obsession reveals a kind of collusion and mutual attraction between these repressive elements and left-wing terrorists. It is this which has earned the terrorists the epithet the "red fascists" and generated the suspicion that they can hardly wait to bring back upon all what they claim to abhor.

The other idea-emotions are easily enumerated. One is the romantic illusion of taking action against imperialism, or against the universal "conspiracy of oppression" in the interest of "the masses," which are variously defined as the proletariat, the marginalized subproletariat of the cities, the Third World masses, or all of the above. But in actual fact, known terrorists have very rarely been the product of, or belonged to, any of these "masses." They are rather extreme elitists who have little respect for the common people and rarely maintain any contact that could reasonably apprise them of the needs of these masses. Instead of an idea, there only remains a gallant emotional posture against oppression. In the isolation of life in the underground or in jail, moreover, all human contacts of the hunted terrorist with the masses are likely to atrophy to the point where he or she cannot even relax and commune with ordinary people. They become reclusive prisoners of their own outlaw life, far from the sense of community they talk about. The idea that Third World misery might in any way be relieved by a random act of aggression in one of the Western metropolises is another emotional shorthand substitute for a sense of the complex outside reality.

Finally, there is the moral aspect: From high-minded universalistic goals, terrorist groups have almost inevitably lapsed step by step into the most limited quasi-military strategies of criminal groups, such as freeing prisoners or blackmailing innocents or, worse, their initial idealism soon turns into a grotesque caricature of itself under the pressure of "the struggle." As soon as they use violence to combat the alleged "structural violence" of administrative or technical rationalization they have jeopardized their own "critical" stance. To quote a former RAF militant mourning the passing of the innocence of serious *engagé* discussions among friends, "a man who runs around with a gun

transposes the center of his being to the gun."[21] He or she—for there have been many gun-toting female terrorists—becomes a gun instead of a critical thinker agonizing over the "crisis of legitimacy" in advanced capitalistic societies.

THE MYTH OF THE RIFLE

At this point, in fact, all terrorist movements, even the ethnic ones, seem to have in common the heroic myth of "taking up the rifle" of earlier struggles. Leonard Weinberg cites Renato Curcio who claims to have picked up the rifle that sank from his fallen uncle's hand during the days of the Resistance. Militant Italian or German neofascists frequently have a similar image dating back to the last days of the Republic of Salò or even the Kampfzeit of pre-Hitler Germany when in fact many a young Nazi storm trooper in turn fancied he was taking up the heroic battle of his fallen father or older brother for the fatherland in World War I. Basque, IRA, Palestinian, and Kurdish terrorists, at least after the armed struggle was started by others, a of taking up that rifle! The rifle or gun fetish is, of course, a phenomenon in many cultures including our own. Bu of ghetto dwellers anywhere who feel oppressed by especially if they are living amid a certain co crime or have police records themselves, the on a new meaning: For young men who f implicitly denies them their manhood ultimate equality. For militant, man or, in multiplication, the subma on Freudian theories of "peni on the origins of Italian simile for fighting back

In contrast to the
of defense, the u
priations" (ban
of brutal a
cappings
walking
of inflict
learned to
express an ar
cannot own or
matic end scene o
Zabriskie Point in wh
up in a blaze of fire aga
identify with the rebels a

In this connection, it becomes a matter of crucial importance to the interpretation of terrorist motives whether they are careful to restrict their attacks to what we called "functional victims" (in table 12.2), or their bombings to the destruction of physical objects only (for example, by choosing a time when a premise is not occupied), or whether they are completely reckless with regard to the maiming and killing of human beings, including innocent janitors and passersby, as with many of the neofascist outrages, ethnic terrorist bombings, and the like. There is a point at which the political motive is clearly overwhelmed by individual criminal impulses of the lowest pathological sort. The organization or government that would employ such monsters for its collective purposes (in police or army) also deserves skepticism instead of the respect otherwise granted to bona fide political motives.

At this point, the likely objection must be met that the "moral outrage" claimed as a motive by the terrorist organization[23] may be so extraordinary, the social injustice so overwhelming, or the "structural violence" or "institutional racism" so systemic that only a correspondingly great outrage could dramatize the righteous anger of the oppressed. This argument, at first glance, appears rather plausible, since it proceeds along the same lines as a plea of mitigating circumstances in a criminal case, say of manslaughter or murder, whose perpetrator can claim that he was justifiably enraged by an outrage committed first by the victim against him. But, on closer examination, transferring is individual reaction to collective motives poses some major prac- l and ethical problems. First of all, there is the difficulty of con- ng claims of moral outrage, especially in cases of continuing t ethnic or cultural confrontations where every new outrage is nd sincerely justified by the preceding assaults by the opposing t only is this an insane escalation of outrageous injustices on s but we have to assume that, to give a concrete example, bombing of the Provisional IRA (or the Ulster Defense) will kill or maim mostly innocents and not the perpe- preceding enemy outrage. In fact, the killers on both hosen executioners who have rarely suffered the other s on either their own bodies or on those of close kin from this perspective, then, the analogy of the out- ll not hold up and, instead, ethnic cultural terrorists g: "If you slay our innocents, we will slay your hardly a moral justification for injuring or taking

ral outrage" thesis becomes even more dubious lationships between the ethnic-cultural ter- y claim to defend or avenge. The terrorists elite, who usually find themselves at odds

with the larger ethnic associations or parties that could reasonably claim to have a mass basis and to represent their flock by an open process of gathering consent and legitimacy. The terrorists' sole claim to legitimacy, curiously, is that they are prepared to commit murders for the flock, and to suffer the consequences if they are caught, though the latter not willingly and sometimes with the fervent hope of being sprung from jail by their confreres outside. In some cases, as in the Basque country or among the Palestinians, the terror commandos may be able to count on food and shelter from friendly co-ethnics. In other cases, as in rural Vietnam[24] or Central America, the violent rebels use a system of systematic coercion and tribute to extract support from the peasants, which in itself casts doubt on their claims of consent and legitimacy. Most revealing, in any case, are conflicts between the terrorists and moderate organizations or individuals representing the interests of their community in peace and compromise. Whether it is the reaction of the Northern Irish terrorists on both sides to peace demonstrations or the assassination of Palestinian moderates by the PLO, it is impossible to escape the impression that the interests of the terrorists and that of their community are not quite the same, to say the least.

The simplistic rhetoric of moral outrage leaves other worrisome questions unanswered as well, in particular about reliance on the intensity of feeling. How, for example, can we account for the depths of despair that many militant environmentalists, and especially the foes of nuclear energy, are feeling today about the industrial degradation of the environment, the collusion of private entrepreneurs and governments, and the immediate dangers to our health and that of our children threatened by toxic wastes and the Three Mile Islands of this world? Fortunately, most environmental activists are deeply committed to nonviolent protest. But there are a few whose "moral outrage" may induce them to sabotage or blow up nuclear power installations. Others may be moved to spectacular acts of terror by a similar fixation on the evils of capitalism, or of our relations to the Third World. If any sense of great injustice, or of moral outrage, is enough justification, who is to say how outrageous an act of terror is proportionate to the cause? And who is to restrain unstable minds or minds lacking the judgment for gauging proportionality (as long as the terrorists are self-chosen volunteers) from gross misjudgments and overreactions on the basis of "moral outrage?"

RIGHT-WING TERROR AS A TEST

Explanations of left-wing terror that link it to outrage about certain modern problems or symptoms of modern social disorganization caused by urbanization and secularization (see Pasquino and della Porta, chap.

6) usually are not as readily applied to the terrorism of the radical right.[25] For one thing, and especially among most continental European intellectuals, the dream of the *one and only revolution* worthy of the name, the advancement of the organized working classes to power, still casts its spell. Even though advanced industrial societies today defy such simplistic explanations and Karl Marx himself has been dead for a full century, the motives of true proletarian revolution and moral outrage at capitalist injustice still have a convincing ring, whereas claims for a fascist or neofascist revolution, or even of "moral outrage" on the part of right-wing shopkeepers, farmers, or businessmen, are considered of doubtful validity or worse. Even with the claims of ethnic nationalisms (see chap. 8), the mind strains to find signs of the colonial or quasi-colonial domination and exploitation of one ethnicity by another, so we can declare one side an example of what Arnold Toynbee called the "external proletariat." A clear designation of an ethnic or cultural underdog, whether Basque, Irish Catholic, Northern Irish Protestant, Palestinian, or Kurdish, visibly relieves the mind, for the underdog is "entitled" to his revolution and perhaps even a little terror—as long as it is not too gory. Where there is a simple confrontation of rival ethnic nationalisms, however (Israeli and Palestinian, or American Black and Chicano), even the myth of the justified revolution, or of moral outrage, breaks down, perhaps to be replaced by a more analytic attitude toward political violence.

But let us return to the radical right, and leave aside for the moment the questions raised by ethnic terrorism all over the world. It is not difficult to find analogues on the right to most of the express motives of the ultra left. A hundred years ago and up into the 1930s, there was among several generations of French ultras a profound sense of alienation from the republican *pays légal* whose petty politicians were said to keep the real historic France, the *pays réal*, from shining forth in all its glory. There is a strong element of this in the alienated far right of Italy, Spain, and West Germany today which mourns the passing of their fascist times of glory and obviously regards those days— and mythical antecedents from earlier ages—quite differently from the rest of the public in their respective countries and the outside world. In this alienated world of theirs, for example, denazification in postwar Germany,[26] the violent overthrow of Mussolini's last regime by the Resistance, and the cold post-Franco revolution of Spain were perceived as great moral outrages and injustices. In France, and in many other European countries, the far right also likes to think of itself as defenders of an ancient faith and culture variously described as "the Occident," Christianity, or the West, all terms that are easily misunderstood by well-meaning Americans. This culture of the "Occident," presumably, is under siege by such insidious forces as modernism in many forms, in art and culture, city life and materialistic capitalism, democratic politics, parliamentary government, secularism and, with different overtones from the American right, communism. Belief in this ideology, and various hierarchical, elitist, and authoritarian variations of it,[27] is the equivalent of popular Marxism on the left. It is again a necessary, but not a sufficient, ingredient of becoming a violent right-wing terrorist.

To become a violent right-winger requires above all youth and a violent disposition. Neofascist parties, such as the Movimento Sociale Italiano or the National Democratic Party of West Germany are not very original in their programs which advocate essentially the corporatist Führerstaat of prewar fascism with little or no mention of war, imperialism, or racism. The terrorist Ordine Nero, the Nuclei of Armed Revolution, and Terza Posizione, just like France's FNE and MNR, Spain's Fuerza Nueva, or the West German groups[28] would probably have a great deal of difficulty struggling through a book as philosophical as Evola's or De Benoist's. For them, it is the violent action itself and, perhaps, serious personal maladjustments that galvanize them into most of the activities for which they are notorious. It does not take much to trigger a young male's motor instincts and to send him crashing into the horns of another rowdy young male on a Saturday night, or any time.

Considering, then, the evident inapplicability of many of the fashionable rationalizations of left-wing violence to the violent right, why do we insist on seeing left-wing violence in such a generically different light? Are left-wing terrorists—as distinguished from the similarly alienated but rather gentle ideological left-wing critics—really likely to be so much more intelligent and erudite than the violent young neofascists? Analyzing the Nazi storm troopers of the Weimar Republic from their own autobiographical descriptions of how and why they engaged in street violence, mostly against young communists, this writer arrived at several descriptive categories that may well serve both the terrorist right and left today. One was a common type of storm trooper characterized by an extraordinary amount of hostility toward all of Weimar society, including his own parents, teachers, and all other figures of authority in his life. We called him a "hostile militant" and found that his sociopathic attitude eventually led him and others of his type in disproportionate numbers into enforcer careers of the Third Reich, such as concentration camp guards or members of the secret police. Another even more common type was the "politically militarized" youth[29] who was characterized by (a) a great urge to march and fight, (b) an astonishing unconcern about the ideological goals and programs of the Nazi movement, and (c) his youth, generally having started a career as a storm trooper by the time he was eighteen years old. This type of young storm trooper was the perfect instrument of street violence, none too bright but prompt in following orders that might make a more mature person blanch.

From all that we know now about terrorists, it would appear that an ample majority of them, both right and left, and many ethnic ones as well, would fit into these two categories. In fact, along with a small element of ideologically committed communists or anarchists, these categories will hold a broad spectrum of left-wing militants from which left-wing terrorists, at least in Italy, have been recruited: a violent fringe of young trade unionists such as emerged from the "hot autumn" of 1969, the irreconcilable remainder of the student movement of those days—the bulk of the rebellious students simply "graduated" to jobs and families—and the revolutionary communists of Manifesto. Ethnic terrorists such as the IRA and Protestant militants show similar patterns only to the extent that their recruitment is fed from a carrier stream of massive demonstrations or from a broadly based, quasi-military popular culture of ethnic resistance, like the young Palestinians in the refugee camps.

DEMOGRAPHIC DIMENSIONS

The relative youth of the Weimar storm troopers, and the generational aspects of the Nazi revolt against the established parties of the day were important dimensions of our findings about political violence fifty years ago. Indeed, as Peter Waldmann writes (in chap. 9), "guerrilla movements are youth movements" and this explains much of their expectations, their idealistic attitudes, and their romantic inclination toward one-sided interpretations of historical events and of their own violent political role. All violent movements are youth movements with the bulk of their membership under twenty-five years of age, and many under twenty, or even under eighteen. This is not to deny that they may have their veterans of long-standing commitment and their older leaders. But the importance of their youthfulness lies in the explosive mixture of radical politics with the pains and sudden surprises of growing up, with the youthful ups and downs of their emotions, their gullibility in skillful hands, and their capacity for boundless enthusiasm for irresponsible, exploitative leaders and dubious causes. Since the problems of growing up particularly center around reaching sexual maturity and the establishment of stable relationships with the other sex, as we have mentioned above, the youth angle may also explain the large number of sexually disturbed young women and men among these groups. Last but not least, youth often means being at school or university, and relatively free from economic attachments and responsibilities. The young students are often concentrated together with their peers, making for rapid recruitment, in other words, and they have less to lose in the way of property or career employment than older people have. Given their physical exuberance and agility and their restless motor instincts, moreover, they can rise to external challenges or respond with alacrity to the beckoning of sinister propensities in their own hearts.

But this is not the only demographic dimension relevant to the subject of political violence. For one thing, there have always been important relationships between economic downturns and the outbreak of violent rebellion. The beginnings of the German student movement, of the extraparliamentary opposition (APO), and the NPD all coincided with the recession of 1966/1967. The earlier neo-Nazi wave of the early fifties, for that matter, might have been milder had it not been for the massive German unemployment of the early fifties which gave especially the displaced refugees little hope of being absorbed into West German social and economic life. In Italy and in other European countries, too, unemployment and general recession are more conducive to violent departures, even if the connection is never as simple as unemployment driving people to the barricades.

There are also proportions worth investigating between the incidence of violent crime and that of political violence in the countries under consideration. As compared with the vast but unknown amount of domestic violence—or serious violence between people who know each other—and the smaller but still horrifying amount of violence among human strangers (violent street crime), what is the magnitude of political violence in the countries most afflicted by it? Measured by the extraordinary public concern lavished on it, we would expect it to be very considerable. Of course, there are no statistics about domestic violence in Italy, but homicides, bodily injury, and other serious crimes against persons—robberies, extortion, and detaining persons against their will—are a matter of the official crime statistics. In the years 1977 to 1979, Italian courts prosecuted between 950 and 1,100 homicides, between 30,000 and 36,000 cases of bodily injury, and from 19,000 to 24,000 cases of robbery, extortion, or detainment a year. In 1978 there were also 11,000 acts of violence or "outrage" against public officials or "attacks upon the state," which suggests that rebellion against established authority is not the monopoly of terrorist groups. The statistics on Italian terrorist violence vary according to the source (see table 12.3). One anonymous but highly placed source in Italian law enforcement indicated in 1979 that the Brigate Rosse, Nuclei Armati Proletari, and Prima Linea had so far committed thirty-seven homicides, ninety-one injuries, and ten kidnappings by the start of that year, but emphasized also the far larger number of left-wing terrorist dynamitings, robberies, and other attacks, and especially de-

TABLE 12.3

TERRORIST ATTACKS IN ITALY, 1975–1981

Year	Number of attacks on record
1975	702
1976	1,198
1977	2,128
1978	2,395
1979	2,366
1980	1,264
1981	924

SOURCE: Istat

monstrative acts of destruction attributable to these three organizations.[30] The Red Brigades, in particular, preferred attacks on prominent persons while the other two groups seem to have more often chosen dynamite and other methods of destruction of things. Newspaper sources have updated some of these figures: between 1970 and 1982, the Italian Red Brigades alone were believed responsible for sixty-eight murders and eighty-five attempted murders, as well as for thirteen kidnappings. Over a dozen years,[31] in other words, less than six terrorist murders, seven murder attempts, and one kidnapping a year could be attributed to this large and very active terrorist group.

The size of these Italian groups and, at the same time, the magnitude of their decline in the early 1980s, can be gathered from the estimated three thousand terrorist suspects arrested over the years and the numbers arrested in the roundups of 1982 alone. In that year, following the kidnapping and eventual freeing of U.S. Brigadier General James L. Dozier, over nine hundred left-wing terrorists were jailed and about two hundred and fifty of them were persuaded by the Italian "repentants' law" to give evidence and denounce their erstwhile colleagues in the underground. The evidence surrendered by the repentants cleared up a number of earlier terrorist actions, led to additional arrests, and prevented several planned undertakings. Press reports claim that most left-wing terrorist groups, such as Front Line, the Communist Fighting Units and Communist Fighting Groups, and the Armed Proletarian Nuclei, though not the Red Brigades themselves, have practically disappeared. The trial of the kidnapping and murder of Aldo Moro, the Christian Democratic leader, alone resulted in thirty-two lifetime sentences and another twenty-seven prison sentences of six to thirty years for this and other killings. A second Red Brigades trial involving 300 suspects was still under way at the time of this writing.

On the extreme right, 275 suspected terrorists were imprisoned in 1982 and 30 of those took advantage of the repentants' law. Needless to say, such defectors, and the West Germans who have broken rank and begun to tell their stories, are sure signs of the breakdown of the morale and solidarity of the terrorist groups involved. They have broken the hypnotic spell their small groups had over them and worked their way toward an appreciation of the real world, both for themselves and with regard to the would-be victims and self-appointed executioners of European terrorism.

If the death and destruction perpetrated by Italian left- and right-wing terrorist groups at their height seem to make up but a modest share of the violence normal to that society, the share attributed to West German terrorism is even smaller as compared with the everyday mayhem occurring in this presumably peaceful society. The West German homicide rate for 1978, for example, was about 25 percent higher than Italy's, although there were proportionately fewer injuries reported to the police.[32] The number of killed, injured, and kidnapped by West German terrorists (see Wasmund, chap. 7) is far smaller over the years than the number produced by Italian terrorists. The situation in Northern Ireland, by way of contrast, is very different from Italy and West Germany. Here the "normal" homicide rate is rather low compared with the murderous violence meted out by the two sides in the civil disturbances: in the years 1975 to 1981, the annual number of homicides fluctuated between forty and seventy cases, a per capita rate quite similar to those of West Germany and Italy. The deaths resulting from the civil disturbance, however, rose from a low point of 13 in 1969 to a peak of 467 in 1972, and declined slowly to an annual toll of 80 to 100 in the years 1978 to 1981. Cases of people injured by terrorist bombs and raids have been more than ten times as numerous each year as the fatalities.[33] We can attribute the difference to several causes. One is the ethnic and religious nature of the conflict in Northern Ireland as compared with the social terrorism of Italy and Germany. Another reason may well lie in the presence of massive police and military forces in Northern Ireland, which both take and deal out a considerable share of the violence. And a third reason appears to lie in the reckless and murderous brutality of both sides toward noncombatant "civilians," who get maimed and massacred at a rate comparable only to that produced by the mad neofascist bombers of the Bologna railroad station or the terrorist at the Munich Oktoberfest. Religious fanaticism and ethnic prejudice apparently can make the more selective *brigatisti* and Baader-Meinhof terrorists look relatively humane.

TRACKING CAREERS OF POLITICAL VIOLENCE

Let us come back to summarizing the second part of this book, in which the authors attempted to lay bare the individual motives of political violence as contrasted with the collective motives claimed by violent movements. At the same time, of course, we have never denied the importance of the collective motives whether they are enshrined in programs, ideologies, or manifestos, or merely understood to be present by the public outside the movement in question. These collective goals play a major role in recruiting and maintaining membership, sustaining planned activities, designating friends and enemies (i.e., potential victims), and justifying slayings and destruction. If it were not for the organizations and their stated collective purpose of armed struggle, the violent individuals and their deeds would seem insane to the public and, perhaps, to their perpetrators as well.

Still, the collective motive does not exhaust the reasons why individuals join a violent group nor why they are willing to commit violent acts on its behalf. We have already tried to peer at the human face behind the ski mask of Italian terrorists as described by Leonard Weinberg and by Gianfranco Pasquino and Donatella della Porta. According to Weinberg, generational conflicts played a major role as elements of both left-wing and right-wing militant youth strove to overcome the more moderate, traditional patterns of collective action in both the Catholic and the socialist-communist subcultures of the country—and perhaps also in the smaller fascist subculture although less is known about the careers of many individual neofascist terrorists than about those of the left. Of particular interest here is the cross-cultural migration of terrorists from the Catholic subculture to the extremes of the socialist-communist subculture as in the cases of Renato Curcio and Margherita Cagol, which stand for many other brigatisti and members of Front Line or Autonomia. Is there an element in devout Catholicism that lends itself to this kind of violent secular zealotry or are we merely confronted with the statistical likelihood that, in a nation with such a large Catholic subculture, some individuals of devout background will show up among the terrorists as well as among most other groups? Catholic radicalism has plenty of historical precedents in Europe and convincing contemporary variants in Latin America where, even aside from the "theology of liberation," young priests and seminary students have often joined or sympathized with left-wing guerrilla bands and revolutionaries (see Waldmann, chap. 9).

Other terrorist careers described by Weinberg seem less surprising. The Armed Proletarian Nuclei (NAP) and its ex-convict and subproletarian clientele have many parallels, and so have the brigatisti from the left. Pasquino and della Porta, however, cast some doubt on the prevalence of marginal and subproletarian backgrounds among the terrorists. Weinberg's neofascist cases show less of a common denominator except for the universal line that pits the would-be terrorist against his elders—women seem much rarer on the violent right than on the left—who are berated for their compromises with moderate conservatives and liberals. Almost by definition, all extremists begin by rejecting reformist groups in their political vicinity and, more ominously, proceeding to calls for action in place of the mere advocacy of their elders. Even that is shared with a wide variety of activists who have no intention of hurting anyone. Terrorists, then, clearly stand out by attaching a murderous meaning to "action," whereas other activists are more interested in mobilizing and influencing people by means not involving horrifying deeds.[34]

Neither Weinberg nor Pasquino and della Porta find much of a social class basis at the root of the terrorist movements they discuss, with the possible exception of "marginals . . . of a different kind," namely, "members of displaced middle strata fighting for their social survival, of petit-bourgeois intellectuals affected by a status panic, involved in a process of proletarianization they hate and reject by resorting to violence." This description of the "red fascists" of the brigatisti, of course, is the same as that of the Italian and German (and many other) fascist movements of the interwar period and probably of some of the neofascists of today. Otherwise, most violent movements recruit members from a fairly broad mixture of social bases: university and secondary school students, including many dropouts, white-collar employees and clerks, skilled workers, unskilled laborers, independents and, again, many who failed or dropped out of one career or another. The West German left-wing terrorists, according to Klaus Wasmund (chap. 9) tend to be from a middle- and upper-middle-class background and are rather well educated. But, aside from their efforts to shake off these bourgeois eggshells, this class background tells us little or nothing about their motives. They can hardly be accused of representing or defending their social class. German right-wing terrorists come from a socially varied background ranging from unskilled laborers to medical doctors.

The Latin American guerrillas discussed by Peter Waldmann are generally Caucasian (not Indian) and said to come predominantly from the "radicalized petite bourgeoisie." But, as Waldmann points out, the bulk tend to be composed of secondary school and university students and, in the cities, of people from the professions and those public service positions toward which student careers would normally aspire. Priests and seminary students are also well represented. In rural guerrilla movements, a strong element of tenant farmers, small peasants, and laborers supplies perhaps the most cohesive social base and one to which one could attribute a motive of social reform or revolution. Urban workers otherwise are rare, especially among the guerrilleras. The social marginality of university students in most Latin American societies, of course, may give these terrorists something to escape from but it hardly explains their championship of the revolt of the lower classes, who generally show little interest in their "champions." The description of the social background of the etarras, to the extent that a consensus can be reached on their composition, again includes mention of university students and professionals, but also the legendary lower middle class, including small businessmen, white-collar workers, technicians, and, according to some sources, workers. Robert P. Clark concludes from his admittedly limited sample that, at least since the early 1970s, typical etarras have come from a working-class or lower-middle-class background. The beginnings of ETA, in contrast, are ascribed to students and intellectuals from lower-middle-class origins. In either case, it would appear that it is not social class as such but rather the youth and peculiar intellectual role of students that may spearhead a violent ethnic movement. Once established, such a movement may attract additional, and especially peasant or worker, support on a large scale because, among other things, it triggers government repression of these social strata. So expressed, this explanation may also suffice for some of the Middle Eastern examples of militant Zionists, Kurds, and Palestinians (see Ashkenasi, chap. 11).

While social class analysis turns out to be not much help in explaining individual motivation, this is not true of psychological analysis, such as analytical models of political socialization. In his essay on West German left-wing terrorists, Klaus Wasmund tellingly describes the stages by which many of these men and women became active participants. There is a preliminary phase of social disassociation from family members and friends, often in the form of "breaking with bourgeois society" or to escape into small groups deeply involved with drugs. This stage of dissociation in a person's primary relationships can be observed in a variety of similar movements of the left, the right, and even in ethnic movements, though perhaps to a lesser degree. Robert P. Clark, for example, at first emphasizes that the "etarras have relationships with loved ones that are normal to the point of being mundane." Later in chapter 10, however, he relates profound changes in the primary relations of ETA members after they have joined ETA and acknowledges the fact that the families of etarras do not support their violent acts even though they may share a sense of ethnic embattlement. There is a great temptation for sympathetic outsiders to overlook the obvious generational tensions and the explosive problems of young men growing up, which are also "normal to the point of being mundane" in many societies, including that of the Spanish Basques. Since the time when the youth section (Eusko Gaztedi) of the Basque Nationalist Party (PVN) first wanted to push the party into "armed struggle" against the Franco regime in 1957, there have been fierce generational confrontations with elders who still remembered the bloody Spanish civil war firsthand. Most of the older generation, like loyalist republican Spaniards elsewhere, were not at all anxious to see their offspring "pick up the fallen rifles" of their time of troubles, and the womenfolk—mothers, sisters, and sweethearts of the terrorists—felt a normal sense of horror about assassins and assassinations not easily compensated for by ethnic prejudice. There is also considerable dissension on the question of terrorism between the two branches of ETA, ETA militar and ETA politico militar. The latter has the backing of Euskadiko Ezkerra, the Basque left party, and considers ETA militar elitists and its terrorism "nonrevolutionary" posturing. ETA militar, in 1976, murdered the young ETA ideologue, Eduardo Moreno Bergareche, who had prepared the position papers for the ETA Assembly of 1973. The two groups also parted ways in 1980 when ETA politico militar made its peace with the new Basque regional government, while ETA militar and its political arm, Herri Batasuna, did not. Behind their split were obviously rather different conceptions—and emotional attitudes—of how violence and political purposes should mesh.[35] As Clark showed in chapter 4 (table 4.2), ETA militar has been responsible for the lion's share of the killings while ETA politico militar was more prominent in kidnappings.

In the case of right-wing terrorists, we still know too little about the average member except that many are exceedingly alienated loners before they find their identity in the violent deed. There is the added difficulty, perhaps shared by other terrorists to a degree, that many of the recruits of the right wing are very young and their period of recruitment very short. The explosive problems of growing up, in other words, and the prepolitical alienation of a future terrorist both unfold rather quickly and often without leaving much of a track to notice and record. A 1980 interviewing study of high school age students in the Frankfurt area and their perceptions of neofascism in West Germany involved also a few interviews with young neo-Nazis which are quite revealing:[36] while the sampling may be rather limited, all the neo-Nazi respondents told rather similar stories of early and rapid politicization at age fourteen to sixteen, with little or no parental or school influences—generally they were already in rebellion against their parents' views.

Young neo-Nazis, to judge by these cases and some others, do not grow gradually into militancy; they jump into it with both feet, after showing an obsessive curiosity about the history of the Third Reich and making at least a selective effort to read literature about it. In fact, they read left-wing periodicals, too, but seem to have firmly made up their minds on all political questions from the beginning, and manage to ignore, or disbelieve, anything about the Nazi record that is not to their liking.[37] They were already or are presently in such groups as the NPD, the Young National Democrats (JN), the People's Socialist movement (Party of Labor), or the Military Sports Group Hoffmann, and are very familiar with the other neo-Nazi groups and figures. They expressed themselves rather guardedly on the subject of violence, as might be expected, but were emphatic about their readiness to "strike back" violently if attacked or whenever one of theirs was "touched" by the "reds." They seemed to view themselves mostly as propagandists rather than as the strong-arm squads of their respective groups. In this respect they—at least the small numbers interviewed— again resemble the Weimar storm troopers whose proselytizing and missionary urge I examined in an earlier investigation.[38] It would have been too much to expect a real neo-Nazi terrorist to speak candidly and reflectively about serious violence, and so we can only guess at what goes on in the mind of a Gundolf Köhler as he prepares to blow up scores of innocent bystanders.

THE POLITICS OF HEROIC ECSTASY

The first dissociative phase is soon overcome by the initiative of a recruiter who often works in a group context such as a commune or other part of the alternative culture. In this setting, the actual recruitment takes place even though the organization may expect novices to first prove themselves by performing courier or logistics services at ever more incriminating levels. By the time they have committed their first bank robbery, assassination, or grand theft, the new terrorists are usually unable to return to living inside the law. The recruitment activities of the organization also tend to coincide with the "searching behavior" (see chap. 10) of the individual who, after consideration of possible alternatives, homes in on this politically violent career. The search also involves immediate and increasing politicization, although a terrorist's idea of politicization may deviate widely from the conventional perception of politics as partisan electoral competition. The young storm troopers of 1929 and 1932, according to this writer's research, often claimed that their elders were an unpolitical lot. On closer examination, however, it soon became clear they were speaking not of electoral or partisan politics but of their own brand of chiliastic, utopian crusade. Before the existentialist heroics of assassination—"I kill, therefore I am"—and of other terrorist coups, conventional political behavior seems pale and insignificant. The heightened thrills of the cloak-and-dagger life make a mere election seem boring.[39]

Once a recruit has gone this far and discovered the politics of heroic ecstasy for himself or herself, political ideology too may take on a new meaning. For some, the mysteries of Karl Marx or Antonio Gramsci reveal themselves and the exaltations of a Hitler or an Evola suddenly take on the joyous overtones of a faith of salvation. Perhaps the transformed minds of the high priests or priestesses of gun or bomb reinterpret relatively pragmatic prescriptions through the prism of violence into a cult of power and death. Perhaps it is mostly abnormal personalities of either sex in whom violent action triggers the first great excitement of their lives. To many terrorists, in fact, ideology continues to be a rather irrelevant and unnecessary preoccupation of some of their comrades and leaders.[40] Terrorism, after all, is a politics of action, not words, and not even of words of justification. For the "heroic" deed speaks for itself, at least to minds attuned chiefly to this language and to no other.

SMALL-GROUP DYNAMICS

The intense involvement in terrorist activity is also invariably mediated by a supporting small-group environment, which is at once the enveloping, loving family setting lost during the dissociative stage and a totalitarian monster that devours the rest of the recruit's soul. According to the descriptions given by ex-terrorists, the recruits totally surrender their sense of identity, their judgment, and their perception of the outside social reality to the group, which becomes their ego and superego writ large.[41] Sometimes, but not always, the ideological self-indoctrination and friend-foe demonology in the group play a major role in the socialization of new members as they find themselves drawn into total war against society. More often it is chiefly through intense relations with group leaders and fellow group members, as intense as any transference between patient and psychiatrist, that the dependence of the individual on the group is cemented. (See Wasmund, chap. 7.) Imperceptibly, the "loving family" of the group becomes a totalitarian world in which even facial expressions and innermost thoughts are not immune from the penetrating glance of Big Brother. An oppressive authoritarianism precludes any true search for consent and consensus. The combined impact of intense group pressures and utter psychological dependence of the individual on the group makes it well-nigh impossible to withdraw from the original commitment. To add to the burden, the organization ruthlessly threatens apostates and "traitors" with execution, a threat that is sometimes carried out.[42]

It is this sense of community, nevertheless, that the walking wounded from the broken homes, suffering the generational tensions described by Wasmund, long for. The left-wing terrorist groups offered

the psychological pseudosecurity needed by the weak egos of the Socialist Patients Collective (SPK) of Heidelberg. The Red Brigade "columns" or NAP cells undoubtedly have done as much for their
members. For the neofascists of Ordine Nero, the Hoffmann Group,
or Fuerza Joven, a warm sense of community is supplied by a quasi-
military or youth group camaraderie that similarly manipulates the
loyalty and enthusiasm of the individual members through their personal relationships with small-group leaders and comrades. In rural
guerrilla movements in Latin America and, perhaps less so, among
the Kurds and Palestinian movements of the Middle East, the sense
of community is also prized—and manipulated. The small-group dynamics in all of these movements seems to feed mostly on what Jürgen
Habermas once called the "politicization of private conflicts," conflicts
such as those inherent in generational tensions or heterosexual maladjustments. It is indeed a strange and explosive mixture of very private
and political motives, worthy of inspired psychological fiction, in
which the political medium of terrorist violence sometimes helps dis-
charge, so to speak, the explosive frustrations accumulated in the
private realm.

There has been little fictional or dramatic interpretation so far of
terrorists and their social milieu.[43] The late German moviemaker Rai-
ner Werner Fassbinder, whose sharp eye chronicled and dissected much
of the soft underbelly of West German society, also made a motion
picture about the "terrorist scene" in his country, called The Third
Generation. "I am convinced," he wrote about the terrorists, "that they
don't know what they're doing, and that the meaning of their actions
must be in the actions themselves, in the make-believe excitement
of danger—the mini-adventure in this frighteningly well and ever-
better administered system. Acting in danger, but lacking all perspective, . . . and seeking adventures for their own sake, living as if
intoxicated . . . those are the motives of the 'third generation.'"[44]
The sarcastic caricature of the make-believe politics of the terrorists
and their sympathizers in The Third Generation so provoked Hamburg
leftists that they disrupted and shut down its premiere, at the Hamburg
Film Festival of 1979 with stink bombs. Something of an anarchist
himself, who in many other films paraded his dreams of a happy life
free from coercion,[45] Fassbinder evidently rejected the pseudopolitical
overtones of the terrorist life and, instead, caricatured it as a violence-
prone Punch and Judy show.

By way of contrast to this "collectivization of loneliness," however,
there are also cases of complete loners among terrorists, especially of
the extreme right-wing variety, who seem to work themselves up to
grisly massacres of innocent people much in the way an unstable,
depressed person may drift toward the ultimate act of self-destruction.

Even when there seems to be a group context such as the quasi-military youth encampments of the radical right, it is quite possible that, for some of the youngsters, their fundamental loneliness is only superficially overcome by the rituals of camaraderie and there results a community without real communication. It may be a mistake not to acknowledge here the degrees of isolation that might distinguish the clinically insane maniac from the manic depressive with a "hell-of-a-fellow" complex, or any gradations in between. In either case, it might even be argued that the extremely public, attention-getting nature of a terrorist attack in itself, along with the strongly held belief that it is justified by a universalized cause—such as the struggle against capitalism, communism, or U.S. imperialism—makes it a kind of collectivization of the loneliness of the perpetrators, a pseudosocial identification of their deed with the good of the community.

Klaus Wasmund again tellingly describes the turn from the pseudocommunity to violent action (see chap. 7). He describes the fascination of sympathizers with the spectacular "liberating deed" of the terrorists and shows how the personal feelings of powerlessness can be compensated for by the model of violence. Members' very dependence on the group, and their isolation and loss of identity in the group, generate a sense of omnipotent, collective strength. And it is at this point that the group-held ideology is capable of fingering an "enemy" and of commanding a terrorist to kill without hesitation. Owing to the small-group dynamics, the ideology now plays a different role. It removes inhibitions against killing and maiming and provides glib rationalizations to the violent mind: A terrorist is born—often out of a rather diffident and seriously flawed personality—and will function to deadly effect, at least until he or she is removed from the supportive group environment.

NOTES

1. See also the interpretation of student and intellectual discontents by the sociologist Helmut Schelsky, *Die Arbeit tun die anderen.*
2. Three Ordine Nero leaders were indicted by the prosecutor for the bombing of the railroad station in Bologna, but the individual bomber(s) has never been identified. Hans-Josef Horchem, "European Terrorism: A German Perspective," *Terrorism* 6, 1 (1982), 40.
3. There were several other attempted train bombings as well as explosions at a Palermo police station and a Roman theatre. See also Bruce Hoffman, *Rightwing*

Terrorism in Europe (Santa Monica, Calif.: Rand Corp., 1982), pp. 3–6 for an account of the violent actions of the *Nuclei Armati Rivoluzionari* (NAR) since 1977 and of the collusion of the judiciary with the radical right.

4. See Hans-Josef Horchem, *Extremisten in einer selbstbewussten Demokratie* (Freiburg: Herder, 1975), pp. 28–33. *Guerrilla Diffusa* is known more for its involvement in demonstrations against nuclear plant construction, occupying houses, and for the ecological movement. The Revolutionary Cells began with the preparations for the Olympic massacre of 1972, later attacked the Chilean consulate and the El Al airlines office (1974), and continued bombing attacks through the second half of the 1970s, including targets like the Federal Constitutional Court.

5. See, for example, Dimitrije Djordjevic, and Stephen Fischer-Galati, *The Balkan Revolutionary Tradition* (New York: Columbia University Press, 1981), chap. 2 and conclusion, and Djordjevic, *Revolutions nationales des peuples balkaniques, 1804–1914* (Belgrade, 1965) or the copious literature on revolutions in the Middle East where foreign intrigues also played a major role.

6. In the German case, there is no evidence of direction from abroad even though many left-wing and right-wing terrorists have been trained in Lebanon, South Yemen, and Algeria side by side with Basque, Corsican, Breton, and IRA terrorists. The RAF has long maintained "diplomatic relations" with Al Fatah and the Popular Front for the Liberation of Palestine (PFLP), and Hoffmann and Roeder long had contacts with the PLO and with the American KKK, respectively.

7. The slogan of the "historical compromise" has always been pregnant with multiple and often unintended double entendres: Who was likely to be "compromised," the Christian Democrats (DC) by the Communists, or the latter by association with the long record of affairs and corruption of the DC? This never-consummated marriage of convenience, ironically, would merely have given public sanction to long-standing patterns of cooperation between Communist mayors and city councils and the DC central government.

8. Lenin, who denounced left-wing deviation as "an infantile disorder" in a famous essay, had little sympathy for terrorist actions though he may have associated them more with nineteenth-century anarchism than with the urban guerrillas of this age.

9. The Maoist Shining Path (Sendero Luminoso) is really in a class by itself because of its strong and rather doctrinaire intellectual leadership, which often gives it rather quixotic features, such as when it first announced its campaign by hanging dead dogs from the lampposts of the provincial capital, Ayacucho. Unlike other Marxist movements, Sendero has exhibited a curiously puritanical attitude toward village ways and an insensitivity toward the material needs of its very poor and illiterate campesinos, which reportedly caused some local uprisings in areas it controls. Its quasi-religious dogmatism has been similarly insensitive toward the urban poor in the provincial towns to which its violence is now spreading. In some ways, it resembles Pol Pot's Khmer Rouge more than the early Chinese Communist party.

10. For details, see also Hoffman, *Rightwing Terrorism in Europe*, pp. 3–6, and the sources cited there. Much of the more recent violence can be attributed to the Armed Revolutionary Nuclei (NAR), the terrorist arm of the semilegal right-wing group, Terza Posizione. For some time now, there have been charges of excessive judicial leniency if not collusion with regard to the trials of neofascist terrorists and the disclosures about the ultraright masonic lodge, P-2.

11. See especially the chronology in J. F. Pilat, "Research Note: European Terrorism and the Euromissiles," *Terrorism* 6, 7 (1984): 63–70, and, on both the left-wing and the neo-Nazis, the *Verfassungsschutzbericht* (1982), which speaks mostly of

neo-Nazi propaganda against U.S. soldiers and installations. But the reader will also recall a botched bombing attempt against American Forces Network station in Munich by a member of the Hoffman Group (see chap. 8).

12. See Hoffman, pp. 8–11. On the history of French fascism, see especially Zeev Sternhell, *La Droite Revolutionnaire*, and his chapter in *Who Were the Fascists? Social Roots of European Fascist Movements*, Stein Larsen et al., eds. (Oslo: Norwegian University Presses, 1980).

13. Bruce Hoffman points out (pp. 12–14) that the seeming preference of neo-fascists for bombs suggests a more primitive capability than the organization required for a kidnapping or an assassination. But there are other aspects involved here too, such as the primitive thrill of seeing something or someone blown up. Besides, left-wingers as well as neofascists have been known to use bombs on occasion, and have resorted to assassination attempts.

14. See Thomas Sheehan, "Italy: Terror on the Right," *New York Review of Books* (22 January 1981), p. 23. The argument that any massive act of terrorist violence is likely to wear down a society's will to resist would appear to ignore the evidence: Time and again, terrorism has more often rallied and consolidated public support for the beleaguered government rather than the opposite. Cf. Hoffman, *Rightwing Terrorism in Europe*, pp. 13, 25–26.

15. The defendants convicted in 1,678 German cases involving left-wing extremist lawbreakers have been characterized as between 21 and 30 years of age (78.5%), high school or university students (¿3.5%), 13.7% skilled workers, 12.5% employees, 9.3% unskilled, and 21% of other occupations. Politically, 75.8% belonged to the "doctrinaire New Left," 16.1% to the "non-doctrinaire New Left," and 8.1% to Soviet-lining communist groups such as the DKP. *Verfassungsschutzbericht* (1982).

16. The numerical proportions among West German New Leftists in 1982 were: about 3,700 members in 55 groups of the "undogmatic," or anarchist, New Left, whereas the "dogmatic" New Left or Marxist-Leninist K-groups and parties numbered 9,300 members in 52 organizations, not counting the Moscow-oriented communist groups. Ibid., p. 3.

17. Autonomia evolved from Potere Operaio in 1972. Arresting Padua political scientist Negri and charging him with directing the Red Brigades, as Thomas Sheehan put it well, was like "jailing Herbert Marcuse a decade ago on suspicion of being the brains behind the Weathermen." See his "Italy: Behind the Ski Mask," *New York Review of Books* (16 August 1979), p. 20, and Rossana Rossanda's interview in *L'Espresso* (12 June 1983), pp. 16–18.

18. Negri has also supported on occasion the idea of cooperation between Autonomia and the terrorist Front Line. See also Alberto Ronchey, *Il Libro bianco sull ultima generazione* (Milan: Garzanti, 1978). A Padua sociologist, Sabino S. Acquaviva, traces much of the strength of Autonomia from its religious roots and the crisis of Italian communism in the 1970s. See his *Il seme religioso della rivolta* (Milan: Rusconi, 1978) and *Guerriglia e guerra rivoluzionaria in Italia: Ideologia, fatti, prospettive* (Milan: Rizzoli, 1979).

19. The evolution of the Red Brigades from the student revolt of 1967/1968, the labor military of the "hot autumn" of 1969, and the Manifesto dissidents of the PCI initially resembles other ultraleft departures but the violent temper soon took command and drowned out the theoretical elements, as the bombers and gunmen and gunwomen seemed to take over from the gentler, more thoughtful radicals. Neofascist conspiracies and terrorism also did their share to hasten the process.

20. Their rationalizations range from the urge to proceed from words to action to the improbable assumption that the degree of general repression generated by

terrorist attacks would prompt the masses to rise against the oppressive state. See especially *Texte der RAF?* (Lund: Rote Armee Fraktion), p. 260. See also *Terrorismo e Violenza Politica*, Pasquino and della Porta, eds. (Bologna: Il Mulino, 1983), p. 241.

21. Bommi Baumann, *Wie Alles anfing* (Frankfurt: Sozialistische Verlagsauslieferung, 1977), p. 126.

22. Alessandro Silj, *Never Again Without a Rifle* (New York: Karz, 1979). A similar image has been popular among militant young blacks in American big-city ghettos, but it is directed almost exclusively at the intrusive white policemen who "hassles" them, rarely at the broader power structure.

23. See, for example, Barrington Moore, Jr., *Injustice: The Social Basis of Obedience and Revolt* (New York: M. E. Sharpe, 1979) whose argument makes a blank check of that "moral outrage"; or the essays in *The Rationalization of Terrorism*, David C. Rapaport and Yonah Alexander, eds. (Frederick, Md.: University Press of America, 1973).

24. See, for example, the account by Douglas Pike, *Viet Cong* (Cambridge, Mass.: MIT Press, 1966), pp. 110–118, 157–172, and chap. 13. Once the rebels have won by force of arms, of course, they have won their legitimate authority too, if only after the fact, and can say that the previous government authority had been based merely on coercion and not on legitimacy.

25. See esp. Franco Ferrarotti, "Social Marginality and Violence in Neo-Urban Societies," *Social Research* 48 (Spring 1981):183–222, where, among other signs of Italian urban decay, there is also an account of rising urban crime. Ferrarotti also offers a polemical refutation of Acquaviva's argument that social change in the 1960s brought a profound loss of faith and values to Italian society which may explain the rise of terrorism. Ferrarotti has written two more books on violence since, *Alle radici della violenza* and *L'ipnosi della violenza* (Milan: Rizzoli, 1979 and 1980, respectively).

26. In one of his earliest publications, Jürgen Habermas examined political attitudes among students at the University of Frankfurt in the early 1950s and uncovered the patterns of alienation among students from denazified families. Among other things, they were hostile to the new constitutional order of the Federal Republic, tended to abstain from political involvement with the constitutional parties, and preferred academic subjects such as ancient history and languages, which were likely to shield them from the "ugly" present. See his *Student and Politik* (Frankfurt, 1951).

27. See Thomas Sheehan, "Myth and Violence: The Fascism of Julius Evola and Alain de Benoist," *Social Research* 48 (Spring 1981):45–73, and the original sources cited there.

28. There is now a global directory of guerrillas and terrorist organizations with descriptions of each group, *Guerrilla and Terrorist Organizations: A World Directory and Bibliography*, ed. by Peter Janke (New York: Macmillan, 1983).

29. The young Weimar storm troopers, according to this not very representative count, consisted of about two-fifths "politically militarized" and one-eighth "hostile militants." Only about one-tenth appeared to be "fully politicized" and aware of their own ideology. See my *The Making of a Stormtrooper*, pp. 221, 257–282, and *Political Violence Under the Swastika: 581 Early Nazis* (Princeton, N.J.: Princeton University Press, 1975), pp. 639–647, 655–658.

30. The categories of the Italian law enforcement statistics may present problems for comparison with those of other countries. The figures that follow were defined as the numbers of persons accused of the crime in question against whom the courts have initiated prosecution. *Annuario Statistico Italiano 1981*, pp. 97–98.

31. It might be better to assume a shorter time span since it took the organization six to seven years to "graduate" to the frequency and intensity of violence reflected in these events, data. Even half the time span and the consequent doubling of the

number of victims per year would not change our conclusion very much. Compare also the events data on ETA attacks in chapter 4, above.

32. All of these figures are exclusive of traffic fatalities and injuries which, however, in a certain percentage of cases are part of the picture of the violence of modern society, as are other (also excluded) accidental deaths and injuries caused by human recklessness or negligence. For the West German figures, see *Statistisches Jahrbuch für die Bundesrepublik, 1980*, pp. 319–324.

33. See Great Britain, Central Statistical Office, *Social Trends*, no. 13 (1983):161 and 176. In 1972, the number of injured rose to 4,876, an appreciable portion of the total population of 1.5 million. By 1981, 2,165 persons had died as a result of the disturbances. Compare the ETA data reported by Clark in chapter 4, above: 287 killings, 385 woundings, and 24 kidnappings up to 1980, and we can probably add another 50% to killings by the end of 1983. The population of the four Basque provinces is 2.1 million but only a third of this number actually speak Euskera.

34. Political "action" can of course mean electoral or propaganda campaigns, organizing efforts among the rank and file, or attempts to influence or lobby with established leaders or officeholders. The word need not connote violent action at all.

35. ETA politico militar, on the one hand, strongly represents the leftist trend that has come to the fore since 1967 and especially since the spectacular Burgos trial of 1969. ETA militar, on the other hand, has more of a spirit of ethnic rebellion suffused with feelings of ethnicity so intense that they seem racial.

36. See Sochatzy, *Parole rechts*, pp. 243–268.

37. Thus they readily mark most German literature on the Third Reich as written "from the point of view of the Bonn government," which they berate as very inadequate and subservient to capitalism and to the "occupying powers." They also deny the facts of the Nazi holocaust.

38. See my *Political Violence Under the Swastika: 581 Early Nazis* (1975), pp. 391–409, and *The Making of a Stormtrooper* (1980), pp. 231–244.

39. Such disdain for conventional politics or electoral triumphs or defeats is not unknown, of course, among the more reformist Western communist or neofascist parties of today, when even the late Secretary Enrico Berlinguer of the Italian Communist party felt a reluctance to take the electoral reverses of his party in 1979 and 1983 quite seriously.

40. See, for example, the story of RAF defector Volker Speitel, "Wir wollten alles und zugleich nichts," *Der Spiegel* (1980), no. 31, pp. 36–49, and no. 32, pp. 30–39, where he describes, among other things, the replacement of ideological preoccupation of the former members of the student movement in his living commune by a kind of "pop" anarchism laced with drug abuse and contacts with the dropouts from more political underground movements of the left. The eventual emergence of a terrorist group, according to his account, was motivated by hero worship of, and personal loyalty to, prominent imprisoned terrorists, and not by a coherent ideology.

41. The psychological dependency of West German terrorists of the Red Army Faction on their group has been tellingly described by Volker Speitel who contrasted the "insanity of the group" with his own awakening and defection. See "Wir wollten alles und zugleich nichts (III)" *Der Spiegel* (1980), no. 33, pp. 34–35."One's whole existence was tied up in the group and one could not see the individual gun nut in it as a monster, only the whole group." Leaving the group meant a painful loss of direction and identity and intense guilt feelings over one's "betrayal" of the fellow members who for so long had determined one's whole life.

42. The 1974 murder of an alleged turncoat, Ulrich Schmücker, in Berlin by one of the self-styled commandos of the 2d of June movement (itself named after the day the student martyr of 1968, Bemo Ohnesorg, died from a policeman's bullet) proved

a watershed in the brief history of the New Left. It alienated many sympathizers and split the activitsts' opinions in several camps.

43. Nineteenth-century Russian novels aside, most of the literature appears to be about ethnic terrorism, as in Sean O'Casey's play, *Shadow of a Gunman*.

44. Quoted in *Der Spiegel* 34 (13 Oct. 1980), pp. 238–239.

45. In another film, *Germany in Autumn*, Fassbinder dramatized his profound fear of the repressiveness of the law once it is provoked by terrorist violence and unleashed on a hitherto open society. It is easy to relate one theme to the other. As the sociologist Jürgen Habermas has never tired of pointing out, the provocation of repressive measures by the state by "infantile," "left fascists" only serves to satisfy the short-term narcissistic longings of a few activists.

CONTRIBUTORS

ABRAHAM ASHKENASI is Professor of Political Science at the Free University of Berlin and has worked on problems of ethnicity, ethnic conflict, and nationalism. Two recent publications are "The Structure of Ethnic Conflict and Palestinian Political Fragmentation," *Fachbereich Politische Wissenschaft. Free University of Berlin* (1981), and *Modern German Nationalism* (Cambridge, Mass.: Schenkman, 1976), which is being revised. He is at present researching problems of ethnic conflict and urban management in several cities in the Near East, with emphasis on Jerusalem.

ROBERT F. CLARK is Professor of Government and Politics at George Mason University in Fairfax, Virginia. His major publications on Basque politics include *The Basques: The Franco Years and Beyond* (Reno: University of Nevada Press, 1979) and *The Basque Insurgents: ETA, 1952–1980* (Madison: University of Wisconsin Press, 1983). He is currently working on a study of the new Basque autonomous regional government.

RICHARD DRAKE is an Associate Professor of History at the University of Montana. Among his publications are *Byzantium for Rome: the Politics of Nostalgia in Umbertian Italy (1878–1900)* (Chapel Hill: The University of North Carolina Press, 1980, and Milan: Rizzoli, forthcoming); "The Red Brigades and the Italian Political Tradition" in *Terrorism in Europe*, ed. by Yonah Alexander and Kenneth Myers (London: Croom Helm, and New York: St. Martin's Press, 1982), and "The Red and the Black: Terrorism in Contemporary Italy," *International Political Science Review*, 5, 3 (July 1984): 279–298.

ADRIAN BLANCHARD GUELKE is a Lecturer of Political Science at the Queen's University of Belfast. He recently published "International legitimacy, self-determination, and Northern Ireland," *Review of International Studies*, 11, 1 (January 1985), and is currently researching Northern Ireland in an international perspective.

GIANFRANCO PASQUINO is Professor of Political Science at the University of Bologna and Visiting Professor of Political Science at the Bologna Center of Johns Hopkins University. He has written *Crisi dei partiti e governabilità* (1980) and edited *Le società complesse* (1983) and *Il sistema politico italiano* (1985). He coordinates a research program on Italian terrorisms. In June 1983 he was elected to the Italian Parliament as a senator for the Independent Left.

DONATELLA DELLA PORTA is a Research Fellow at the European University Institute in Florence and also affiliated with the Program of Study and Research on Political Violence and Terrorism at the Istituto Carlo Cattaneo in Bologna. She is co-editor (with Gianfranco Pasquino) of *Terrorismo e Violenza Politica. Tre Casi a Confronto: Stati Uniti, Germania e Giappone* (1983); editor of *Terrorismi in Italia* (1984), and co-author (with Maurizio Rossi) of *Cifre Crudeli: Bilancio dei Terrorismi Italiani* (1984).

PETER KLAUS WALDMANN is Professor of Sociology/Social Science at the Philosophical Faculty of the University of Augsburg. Recent publications are his "Gewalt in Lateinamerika," *Jahrbuch für Geschichte von Staat, Wirtschaft und Gesellschaft Lateinamerikas* 15 (Köln/Wien, 1978); "Alte und neue Guerilla in Lateinamerika— Folgen und Folgerungen aus der Revolution in Nicaragua," in *Verfassung und Recht in Übersee* 16, 4 (1983): 407–433; and "Sozio-ökonomischer Wandel, zentralistische

Unterdrückung und Protestgewalt im Baskenland," in Peter Waldmann et al., *Die geheime Dynamik autoritärer Diktaturen. Vier Studien über sozialen Wandel in der Franco Ära* (München, 1982), pp. 199–286. He is currently working on a comparative study of the origins and processes of violent separatist movements in Northern Ireland, the Basque country, and Quebec.

KLAUS WASMUND is a Lecturer in Political Science and Political Sociology at the Technical University of Braunschweig (Germany). His publications include: K. Wasmund and B. Claussen, eds., *Handbuch der politischen Sozialisation* (Braunschweig: Pedersen, 1982); K. Wasmund, ed., *Jugendliche—Neue Bewusstseinsformen und politische Verhaltensweisen* (Stuttgart: Klett, 1982); and K. Wasmund, *Politische Plakate aus dem Nachkriegsdeutschland* (Frankfurt: Fischer, 1985).

LEONARD BURTON WEINBERG is Professor in the Department of Political Science at the University of Nevada, Reno. He is the co-author of *Comparing Public Policies* (1977) and author of *After Mussolini: Italian Neo-Fascism and the Nature of Fascism* (1979). His articles have appeared in various professional journals, including *Terrorism*. In 1984 he was a senior Fulbright fellow at the University of Florence and conducted research on political terrorism in Italy.

INDEX

Acquaviva, Sabino, 151, 180–181
Almirante, Giorgio, 61, 148, 164; on
  Evola, 72, 78; strategy of, 154–155,
  160
Amendola, Giorgio, 180
Anarchism, 7, 39, 191;
  anarchocommunism, 61, 351; Berlin
  groups, 196–197, 206; Spontis, 206,
  248
Arendt, Hannah, 91, 119
Aristotle, 36
Aron, Raymond, 151–152
Autonomia Operaia, 61, 161. See also
  Counterculture

Baader, Andreas, 217, 221; and
  department store fire, 198–199,
  211–212; on RAF philosophy, 222
Basque terrorists (ETA), 26, 123–141,
  283–309, 342–345, 353; and Basque
  nationalism, 44–46, 349; and
  communism, 35–36; compared with
  other terrorists, 342–345; escalating
  violence of, 3; internal dissension
  among, 365; social background of,
  5–6; and Spanish democracy, 7–8, 47
Bell, J. Bowyer, 27, 98, 101–102
Benoist, Alain de, 3, 357
Bewegung 2. Juni. See West German
  terrorists
Botz, Gerhard, 38
Bracher, Karl-Dietrich, 248–249, 336

Castro, Fidel, 260. See also Cuba
Casualty rates, 126–129, 192, 359–361
Colombian terrorists, 23, 30
Communists, 171, 346; and dissident
  groups, 152–154, 158, 187, 340;
  Italian (PCI) and "armed party,"
  162–163, 177; moderation of, 4, 62,
  164, 183, 336, 341, 351; and
  terrorism, 61, 175–177, 339; West
  German, 43–44, 194, 220, 239–240,
  345

Corsican separatists, 26, 34, 48, 341
Counterculture, 7, 204–206, 248,
  350; of Berlin, 5, 196–198; in Italy,
  152–154, 161–164, 350–354; and
  terrorism, 42–43, 205–209
Crenshaw, Martha, 14
Criminal violence, 230; and political
  violence, 49–52, 245–246, 359–361;
  rising rate of, 230
Critical theory, 7, 248, 351–353, 357
Cuba, 5, 260, 262, 269, 311
Curcio, Renato, 11, 148–149, 159–160,
  362

Democracy and terrorism, 7–8, 52–53,
  145, 219–220; alienation of youth in,
  246–249, 267–268; vunerability of,
  146; weak and corrupt government
  of, 149–150, 181–184, 187–188,
  259, 271–272
Dictatorship and terrorism, 7, 146,
  294–297; action-repression cycle in,
  52–53, 261–262, 267, 275; effects of
  repression in 294–297; impossibility
  of reform in, 271; revolt against,
  274–275
Dutschke, Rudi, 195–196

Ensslin, Gudrun, 198–199, 211–212
Events data approach, 2, 3, 38,
  123–141
Evola, Julius, 3, 9, 61–89, 155, 357

Farinacci, Roberto, 66–67
Feltrinelli, Giacomo, 148
Female terrorists, 52, 151, 264–265,
  286, 353
Ferracuti, Franco, 50–53
Feuer, Lewis, 156–157
Fire sale theory, 4, 336, 340; and
  counterculture, 152–154; and decline
  of social movements, 183, 186, 194,
  235–236
French terrorists, 347–348

Freud, Sigmund, 70, 215, 353
Front Line (Prima Linea). *See* Red
  Brigades

Generational aspects, 362; of German
  RAF, 199, 337–338, 350; of guerrilla
  movements, 264, 358; interval of
  from cause to movement, 270; and
  terrorism, 156–159; of youth
  rebellion, 246–247, 364–365
Gramsci, Antonio, 8, 62, 73, 367
Guénon, René, 64, 66
Guerrilla movements, 5, 8, 23, 156,
  257–281, 317, 368
Guest workers (in Germany), 232, 236,
  243, 247, 347

Habermas, Jürgen, 195, 205, 351, 368
Hegel, G. W. F., 36, 64
Hitler, Adolf, 9, 67, 241, 247, 351
Hoffmann, Military Sports Group,
  240–245, 250, 366
Hoffmann, Stanley, 146
Honderich, Ted, 20

Ideology, 2, 147, 162, 194, 259–260,
  342–344, 350, 362; and collective
  action, 7–8, 42–45; critical,
  351–352; of ethnic nationalism,
  44–48, 91–121, 283–309,
  311–333; group, 218–221, 339,
  367–368; ideologues of, 21; left-wing
  origins of, 3–4, 42–43; popularized,
  28, 195; and prejudice, 41–42, 232,
  240, 249–251; and revolutionary
  success, 5, 222, 260; right-wing
  origins of, 35, 39–45, 145, 176; and
  socialization, 42–44, 53, 158–159,
  207–210, 362; and violent action, 2,
  8, 32–33, 35, 39–45, 145, 176
Ireland (Northern), 37, 46–48,
  91–121, 355
Islamic terrorists, 21, 24, 29, 32–33,
  341
Israeli terrorists, 25, 29, 31–33

Jenkins, Brian, 28, 30, 349

Kenniston, Kenneth, 158
Kühnen, Michael, 241, 250
Kurds, 6, 44–46, 315–318, 326–332,
  353, 356, 368

Land reforms, 30. *See also* Guerrilla
  movements
Laqueur, Walter, 100, 331
Larsen, Stein U., 14
Leadership and terrorism, 209–210,
  327–329, 332, 367
Lenin, 8, 176, 340
Lotta Continua. *See* Counterculture

Mao Zedong, 48, 150, 269, 331
Marcuse, Herbert, 351
Marx, Karl, 351, 356, 367; on
  economic motives, 70; Evola's
  rejection of, 155; and Marxists, 62,
  194–195; on terrorism, 79; on
  violent action, 8, 37
Marxist-Leninist groups, 145, 249, 260;
  Italian, 152, 162; West German, 196,
  209–210, 238, 241
Meinhof, Ulrike, 197–198, 215, 217,
  220–221
Melucci, Alberto, 183, 185
Modus operandi of terrorists, 245,
  302–303, 353–354, 360; of ETA,
  128–141; explained and tabulated,
  22–35, 340–350
Mommsen, Wolfgang, J., 14
Moral justification of terror; 10, 20,
  354–357; in counterculture, 350; by
  fantasy war, 53, 197–198, 219; by
  presence of threat, 28; psychological
  need for, 37–38, 219–221, 248; by
  religion, 24, 29; of totalitarians,
  248–249. *See also* Ideology
Morris-Jones, W. M., 14
Mussolini, Benito, 66–69, 147–148,
  336, 347

National Democrats (NDP) 5,
  231–239, 246–247, 249–250. *See
  also* Neo-fascism
Nationalism, 91–121, 123–141,
  283–309, 311–333, 342–344, 349;
  and antiforeign prejudice, 231–232,
  236–238, 243, 249, 347; Evola on,
  76; of German New Right, 235–239,
  240, 249–251, 347; and language,
  45–46; moderate and terrorist
  versions of, 29–30, 45–46, 48,
  354–355; of Third World nations,
  76, 108, 356; in West Germany, 234;
  after World War I, 40

Negri, Antonio, 61, 351
Neo-fascism, 4–5, 39, 41, 61–89,
    145–167, 229–255, 342–344;
    compared to left-wing terrorism, 345,
    358; conspiracies of, 41; early
    politicization of, 365; Italy and West
    Germany compared, 337, 349–350,
    359–361; moral justification of,
    356–357; in other European
    countries, 347–348; and prejudice
    346–348; psychology of, 50–53; and
    terror acts, 41, 48–49, 366, 368
Nietzsche, Friedrich, 65, 74
Nuclei Armati Proletari (NAP). *See*
    Red Brigades
Ordine Nuovo. *See* Neo-fascism

Palestinians, 25; attitudes toward
    terrorists, 10, 48, 355; Italian
    attitudes toward, 170–171; moderates
    versus terrorists, 355; nationalism of,
    29, 44, 330–356; paramilitary groups
    among, 317–318; PLO, 6, 10, 192,
    216, 368; reaction to violence of, 37,
    353; social structure of, 316–317,
    330–332; training of RAF terrorists
    among, 221; Zionist attitudes toward,
    321
Police violence, 51–52, 354
Potere Operaio. *See* Counterculture
Provisional IRA, 108, 119, 355;
    attitudes toward Britain of, 95,
    100–101; attitudes toward British
    army, 97–98, 104; Catholic church,
    108; and peace movement, 111; Irish
    Catholic attitudes toward, 10, 46,
    48, 108, 110–111, 119; and Irish
    republic, 96; New Ireland proposal
    of, 102; origins of, 91–121;
    radicalization of, 107–108; and
    sectarian violence, 107; and
    socialism, 95–96; and Stormont,
    98–99, 101–103; terror acts of, 22,
    32–33, 46–47, 115; units of, 34, 104
Psychology and political violence,
    191–228, 335–374; and idea-
    emotions, 7; and individual motives,
    3, 5, 9, 21, 200–201; and leadership,
    209–210; parent-child relations,
    202–205, 283–284, 289–292,
    304–306; political socialization, 4,
    11, 38, 49, 207–214, 294–300;

psychopathology, 4, 10–12, 49–51,
    172–173; reactive terrorism, 3,
    15–27, 91–121; in small groups, 5,
    50, 199–200, 206–209,
    214–225
Public opinion and terror, 21, 31, 47,
    349

Rauti, Pino, 72, 148, 155
Red Army Faction (RAF). *See* West
    German terrorists
Red Brigades, 4, 338, 342–345, 368;
    ideology of, 39, 53; Negri on, 351;
    origins of, 147–148, 187, 336; and
    PCI, 62, 162–163, 175–176, 183,
    339; socialization of, 11, 50,
    159–160, 162–163, 368; terror acts
    of, 8, 342–345, 359–361
"Red fascism," 30, 47–48, 195, 249,
    352
Religion and terrorism, 4, 10, 151–153,
    159–160, 265, 362–363. *See also*
    Acquaviva; Secularization
Resistance (Italian), 4, 147–149, 175,
    336, 356
Revolutionary Cells. *See* West German
    terrorists
Rosenhaft, Eve, 43

Sartori, Giovanni, 147
Schelsky, Helmut, 7
Secularization and terrorism, 151, 336.
    See also Acquaviva; Religion and
    terrorism
Separatism. *See* Nationalism
Shining Path (Sendero Luminoso),
    22–23, 30–33, 341
Sikh separatists, 25–26, 29, 31–34, 341
Sinn Fein, 92, 94–95, 108–110, 116,
    119
Small group dynamics, 5, 8–11, 37,
    200, 367–369; and authoritarianism,
    53, 216–224, 250, 367; and
    counterculture, 204–209; in different
    group settings, 21; and fantasy war,
    215–217, 220–221; and friend-enemy
    relations, 28–29, 53, 214–217, 250,
    367; and key experiences, 210–212;
    and larger organization, 34–35,
    212–214, 250–251; and leadership,
    209–210, 217, 367; and parent-child
    bonding, 53, 202–204, 367; sense of

Small Group Dynamics (*continued*)
   belonging in, 203–207, 212–220,
   367–369
Soccer rowdies, 5, 229–233, 249–250,
   348
Social background, 4, 9; and
   counterculture, 5; of ETA terrorists,
   5–6, 285–293, 364; of interwar
   European right, 39–41; of Italian
   terrorists, 178–180, 185, 362–363; of
   Latin American guerrillas, 5,
   264–267, 362–364; of Middle
   Eastern nationalists, 6, 317–318,
   326–332; of RAF terrorists, 5,
   191–228, 363; and social
   marginalization, 4, 185, 355
Socialization of terrorists, 4, 9; and
   aggression, 38; in family 38, 48–49,
   51, 173, 231, 246, 283–284,
   289–292, 303–306; and generational
   conflict, 156–159, 233, 246,
   265–266, 270, 364; and native
   tongue, 294–295; neo-Nazis,
   230–232, 235–236, 243–247; or
   resocialization, 11, 173, 306–307;
   and searching phase, 296–300; in
   student movements, 153–154,
   243–244, 267–268; in subcultures,
   151–152, 180–181
Sontheimer, Kurt, 248
Sorel, Georges, 78, 80
SS (Nazi Saalschutz), 76, 236, 247,
   347–348
State-sponsored terror, 20, 186
Stormtroopers (SA), 13, 49, 235,
   245–246, 250–251, 353, 357–358,
   366
Student movements, 157, 358–359;
   and ETA terrorists, 287, 297; in
   Italy, 153–154, 174–175, 183–184,
   336, 342–343, 349; and Latin
   American guerrillas, 30, 265–266,

274; and RAF terrorists, 5; in West
   Germany, 193–196, 243–244,
   342–343, 349–350; after World
   War I, 40

Tamil (Sri Lanka) separatists, 22, 29,
   30–33, 341
Tilly, Charles, 38
Tolkien, J. R., 41
Trotskyism, 260

Ulster Defense Association (UDA), 97,
   99–107, 112–116; attitudes toward
   Britain of, 113; attitude toward
   Catholics of, 99–100; origins of,
   91–93; and sectarian violence,
   106–107, 116; terrorist acts of,
   115–116; and Ulster constabulary, 97;
   Ulster independence proposal of,
   113–114; Unionist party and, 97
United States, 247, 258, 342–343,
   369; Evola on, 75; German youth
   and, 195; Nazi party of, 242;
   political violence in, 27–28, 32–33,
   312–313; power of in Central
   America, 269–270, 272–275; RAF
   attacks on forces of, 192, 346;
   support of for Kurds, 330; as symbolic
   addressee, 32–33

Value crisis and terrorism, 180–181

Weapons fetish, 13, 51, 53, 148, 231,
   245–246, 250–251, 352–353
Weber, Max, 200, 224–225, 339
Weimar Republic, 5, 13, 20–21, 28,
   38–41, 43, 243, 250, 257
West German terrorists, 5, 11, 42–43,
   45, 52, 239–246, 250–251
Wilkinson, Paul, 27, 117

Zionism, 6, 46, 314–326

Designer:	U.C. Press Staff
Compositor:	Publisher's Typography
Printer:	Edwards Bros., Inc.
Binder:	Edwards Bros., Inc.
Text:	11/12 Goudy
Display:	Goudy